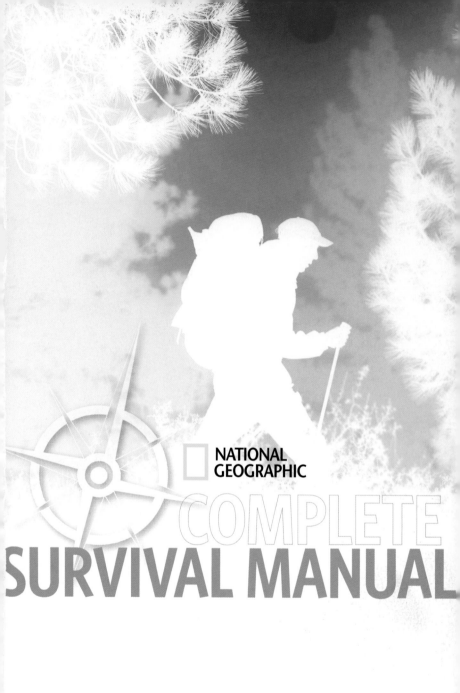

NATIONAL
GEOGRAPHIC

COMPLETE

SURVIVAL MANUAL

NATIONAL GEOGRAPHIC
COMPLETE
SURVIVAL MANUAL

BY MICHAEL S. SWEENEY
FOREWORD BY MIREYA MAYOR

NATIONAL GEOGRAPHIC
WASHINGTON, D.C.

AUTHORS
Michael S. Sweeney Chapters One through Eight and Appendix
Michele Kayal Chapter Nine
Elizabeth Towner Chapter Ten

CONSULTANTS
Mireya Mayor National Geographic emerging explorer, TV wildlife correspondent, and primatologist
Larry Stanier Internationally certified mountain guide and snow avalanche consultant

SURVIVAL ESSAYISTS
Maria Fadiman NATIONAL GEOGRAPHIC EMERGING EXPLORER
Jesús Rivas NATIONAL GEOGRAPHIC GRANTEE AND SUBJECT OF NGTV AND *NATIONAL GEOGRAPHIC* ARTICLES
D. Bruce Means NATIONAL GEOGRAPHIC GRANTEE, AUTHOR, AND SUBJECT OF NGTV SHOWS
Mireya Mayor NATIONAL GEOGRAPHIC EMERGING EXPLORER AND NGTV CORRESPONDENT
Tommy Heinrich PHOTOGRAPHER AND NATIONAL GEOGRAPHIC FUNDED EXPEDITION TEAM MEMBER
John Hare NATIONAL GEOGRAPHIC GRANTEE AND CONTRIBUTOR TO *NATIONAL GEOGRAPHIC* MAGAZINE
Mike Horn ADVENTURER FEATURED IN NATIONAL GEOGRAPHIC'S *ADVENTURE* MAGAZINE
Kenneth Broad NATIONAL GEOGRAPHIC EMERGING EXPLORER
Pat C. Wright NATIONAL GEOGRAPHIC GRANTEE
Ken Garrett PHOTOGRAPHER FOR *NATIONAL GEOGRAPHIC* MAGAZINE AND NATIONAL GEOGRAPHIC BOOKS

HOW TO USE THIS BOOK

LEARNING SURVIVAL SKILLS IS AN EXCITING but complex endeavor. National Geographic Explorers spend years learning how to survive in the wild. Preparation plays a significant role in surviving an unforeseen emergency. Even the experts occasionally find themselves in risky situations, and having a comprehensive survival manual to study and consult can help save lives. The book is divided into ten chapters, plus an appendix. The first two chapters provide basic skills. The next six chapters (Chapter 3 through Chapter 8) provide skills by temperate zone: temperate forests, swamps and rain forests, high mountains, desert, polar and subpolar regions and open water. The final two chapters cover survival in and around your home (Chapter 9) and storms and disasters (Chapter 10). The appendix provides additional detailed information—including National Geographic maps of each temperate zone—and the index helps you quickly locate information.

1. CHAPTER OPENER
Gives overview of environment and historic accounts of travelers there.

2. ICONS
Represent the topics covered in each chapter: Preparation, Fire, Water, Shelter, Food, First Aid, Hazards, Signaling, Navigation, and National Geographic survival story.

3. SUBHEADS

Each chapter is organized into ten subheads represented by a corresponding icon, featured in the chapter opener. This makes it easy to identify each section.

4. ARTICLES

Short, informative text explains survival subjects.

5. EXPERT TIP BOXES

Survival tips from the American Red Cross, Boy Scouts of America, Girl Scouts of the USA and the U.S. Army are easily identified by their logos.

6. HOW TOS

Step-by-step instructions with illustrations.

7. ESSENTIALS

Bulleted lists of must-have information and gear.

8. LISTS

Easy-to-read items highlight important elements relating to the articles.

9. CHAPTER AND PAGE INDICATORS

Navigation elements give chapter and page number.

10. SURVIVAL STORY

First-person story corresponds to the terrain covered in the chapter.

'**ve** been chased by elephants, bitten by snakes, charged by gorillas, attacked by sharks, stranded in monsoons. On countless occasions, I've run out of food in the middle of some remote rain forest without even a small village in sight. I've dangled from a 14,000-foot cliff, helpless at the end of a fraying rope. I'm an explorer who has survived all of these encounters through training, a little luck, and a lot of experience.

Doing the right thing in an emergency is the key to making it through potentially dangerous, if not fatal, situations. Keeping a cool head, being prepared, and knowing what to do when one of these situations arises requires training and practice. That is why a survival guide is such an important piece of equipment. Read it cover to cover, by chapter or in sections. Learn the information and practice the skills. Don't wait until your car slides off the road in a sudden snowstorm on a remote mountain road to learn about cold-weather survival. Know how to decide whether to stay put or hike toward rescue; what materials you should burn to make visible signal fires in different environments; how to use any watch as a compass; how to signal a rescue plane; how to feed yourself when you're stranded in remote wilderness with no supplies; how to make rope from plants; where not to pitch a tent; the opposite techniques for defending yourself against grizzly versus black bear attacks; how to make a flotation device from your pants; and how to tie knots that won't fail.

For those who venture into the wilderness with the luxury of preparation (rather than being thrust into an unexpected survival situation), this book provides guidance on choosing, packing and using the right equipment as well as how to respond to unforeseen annoyances, obstacles and disasters. While the outdoors can provide beautiful, inspiring, memorable and mesmerizing experiences where you can let go, relax, and literally stop to smell the flowers, it can just as easily turn on you. And in that instance, the Boy Scout and Girl Scout motto "be prepared" can make all the difference.

I wasn't always so prepared. Until I began my primatology career in earnest, I had very little experience in any place wilder than city streets. As a child, I wasn't even allowed to join the Girl Scouts because my mother thought camping was "too dangerous." But my academic aspirations, coupled with the opportunity to study primates in the rain forests and jungles of South America, changed all of that. In order to collect the essential data for my work, I needed to be in the field. With hope and trepidation, I applied for a small grant, and was happily rewarded. I would make the leap from the ivory tower to the jungle floor.

On the fateful day I accepted the grant—trading a relatively safe and civilized lifestyle for a pair of hiking boots and a backpack—I rushed to the local bookstore in search of an all-encompassing book on survival. I was going on a five-month expedition in Guyana and Suriname to study rare, small monkeys, and this would be the first time I would encounter such fearsome critters as tarantulas, fer-de-lance snakes, vampire bats, and piranhas. I needed a survival guide I could trust; one that included stories from recognized experts in their fields—world-renowned explorers, scientists, and adventurers—not extreme risk takers or thrill seekers.

To my surprise, there were none. Sure, there were lots of books on the subject, but none that covered all the different environments and potential situations I would eventually face. And, even if I bought them all, carrying them in addition to my gear was not an option. After hacking through impenetrable forest for hours, weeks, or sometimes months, I learned to loathe carrying anything more than the essentials on my back. That is why, when I began working with National Geographic on this manual, I insisted on two priorities: it had to be comprehensive—everything you'd need in the wilderness—and it had to be portable.

Finding a lightweight and thorough emergency manual that also covers survival in home environments is an even greater challenge, as there are many guides for different man-made disasters and terrorism-survival scenarios. But none come close to being a "complete" survival manual. Until now.

The *National Geographic Complete Survival Manual* was designed and composed by experts and real-life explorers—the very people who, on a daily basis, come face-to-face with the harshest environments, most dangerous animals and most extreme conditions. Emerging Explorer Maria Fadiman spends much of her time avoiding poisonous snakes, frogs, and scorpions in South American rain forests in pursuit of new uses for plants by native populations. She tells of her experiences in Chapter 1. Emerging Explorer Kenneth Broad's work as an ecological anthropologist takes him into very narrow underseas caves, hundreds of feet deep. He shares his near-death experience in Chapter 8.

This book is divided into ten chapters. The first two chapters are designed to familiarize you with survival basics: fire, water, shelter, food and first aid.

Chapters 3 through 8 focus thoroughly on a specific environment: temperate forests (Chapter 3), swamps and rain forests (Chapter 4), mountains (Chapter 5), deserts (Chapter 6), polar and subpolar regions (Chapter 7), and water (Chapter 8). Each describes solutions to challenges and risks particular to those habitats. At the end of each chapter is a first-person survival story from a National Geographic expert in that particular environment. These personal stories combine culture, environment, and survival, giving you a global perspective. How-to diagrams, essential lists, pictures and expert tips—from the American Red Cross, U.S. Army, Girl Scouts and Boy Scouts—are spread throughout the chapters.

At the end, a complete appendix gives you packing checklists, a guide to edible plants (with full-color images), step-by-step instructions for tying essential knots, semaphore signals, world maps of each environment, and critical first aid information. A detailed index makes it simple to look up tips on the precise survival skills, regardless of temperate zone.

Perhaps you're an avid hiker or a camping enthusiast. I know I am. Whenever I get a break from being in the field on assignment, I'm ready for an outdoor adventure. Though I'm now experienced in rain forest terrain, I like to check out techniques for surviving in different environments. And reading about my colleagues' near-death experiences, such as that of my advisor, National Geographic grantee and internationally renowned primatologist and biologist Pat C. Wright, reminds me of how fragile even the most seasoned of experts are when confronted with the indifference of Mother Nature.

This book is useful even if you never intend to leave your city or town. Chapters 9 and 10 cover natural disasters such as hurricanes, fires, tornadoes, floods and volcanoes. Having grown up in South Florida and survived Hurricane Andrew (my house didn't), I can personally attest to the importance of being prepared for such emergencies at home. A few days after Hurricane Andrew, when I was allowed to return to my neighborhood and I found my television in my neighbor's front yard, I began to formulate a more streamlined household evacuation plan that I rely on to this day.

After spending more than ten years conducting scientific research in the field, filming dozens of wildlife documentaries for National Geographic, and earning the recent title of a National Geographic Emerging Explorer, I can finally hold my own in the great outdoors. In my early research, when I first ventured into some of the most remote regions in the world, I had never even been camping and didn't know how to set up a tent, let alone how to build a shelter. One of the first things I learned is that, in the field, you can't prepare for everything and you never know what to expect. Getting lost, spraining an ankle, and getting your last pack of matches wet are all distinct (and in my case, inevitable) possibilities. Looking back, it's a miracle I am still around to write this. I've had a GPS run out of batteries, my satellite phone lose signal and my entire food supply devoured by wild animals... all on the same trip!

But I am still here to tell you about it, and that's what experience and practice will do. And that is also why I cannot encourage you enough to practice the survival skills covered in this manual, while *not* in the midst of a crisis. This book helps you to deal with these and other situations so that you can ap-preciate the aesthetic beauty of nature while recognizing potential sources of fire, shelter, and food. After becoming familiar with the book, you might even be able to look at a plant and know whether you can eat it or use it to relieve pain, even if you don't know its proper scientific name.

Get familiar with the different techniques and scenarios, and ask yourself the ever-popular "what if" questions (e.g., What if I get lost? What if I run out of food? What if I run into a 400-pound silverback gorilla that's eating my food?). Before you know it, you will be a more skilled camper, hiker, or explorer— and most important, a living one!

Becoming survival-savvy enables you to do more than just survive. In addition to coming out alive, I have brought the wild to others in the form of pictures, films, and discoveries. I've lived among villagers who had never seen a foreigner and I have witnessed never-before-documented cultural practices. I've seen previously unexplored parts of the world. I have taken my daughters into the field with me to see beauty that most people only read about. Being survival-savvy enables anyone with curiosity and a love of nature to overcome the fear and awkwardness that keep most people from attaining an intimate knowledge of the natural world. This book can help you and your loved ones appreciate, respect, and safely enjoy the wild in distant countries or in your own backyard.

Whether you're an outdoor amateur or an accomplished explorer, the *National Geographic Complete Survival Manual* should always have a place in your backpack. Now go explore with confidence!

Scientifically speaking, history's greatest survival story ended in failure. / Ernest Shackleton and his crew of 27 hoped to be the first explorers across Antarctica. Instead, ice floes crushed their ship offshore. The men gathered on the floating ice and watched the *Endurance* sink on November 21, 1915. As nobody else knew of their plight, they had to find their own way out across 800 miles of ice and ocean in lifeboats. / Yet all lived, inscribing an astonishing page in the annals of survival. Like the 1970 Apollo 13 moon mission that returned safely after a devastating explosion in space, Shackleton and his men achieved a "successful failure." They had the basics of survival: proper clothing, means to obtain food and water, shelter (in tents and overturned boats), and a good plan. In Shackleton, they also had the most crucial element: a cool mind. / "An ordered mind and a clear program were essential if we were to come through without loss of life," Shackleton wrote. / Surviving isn't about luck, although luck can play a role. In forests, in deserts, on water, or even in disasters near home, the difference between life and death is often a matter of mental and physical preparation.

MIND&BODY
BASICS

WITHIN THIS CHAPTER

14   24   28   34   38

PREPARATION

Preparation begins with knowing, and accepting, what lies ahead. "Genuine wilderness exploration is as dangerous as warfare," wrote Theodore Roosevelt after nearly dying on an Amazon River tributary in 1914. "The conquest of wild nature demands the utmost vigor, hardihood and daring, and takes from the conquerors a heavy toll of life and health." / With all respect to TR, vigor, hardihood, and daring are not enough. Surviving far from civilization is more than conquering nature. Experts in survival techniques say that people who try to be heroes quickly die. They have stamina, but they lack the proper attitude. Nature is a powerful adversary, and survivors humble themselves before it. / Those who forget that lesson do so at great price. Jon Krakauer noted in his book about climbing Mount Everest that a professional guide exhibited overconfidence. "We've got the Big E figured out," the guide said. "These days, I'm telling you, we've built a yellow brick road to summit." That guide died on the high slopes. Similarly, the protagonist in "To Build a Fire," Jack London's story about a man walking in the Yukon when the air registered -75°F, had the right equipment, deep knowledge of his environment, and a crippling supply of hubris. He died because he was "without imagination. He was quick and alert in the things of life, but only in the things, and not in the significances." He froze because he had only one chance to build a fire, and he made one mistake. / Life-and-death situations rarely forgive errors. Though there are always exceptions, reports of people who die in the wilderness often read alike. They didn't expect danger. They got lost. They panicked. They died of thirst, injury, or too much heat or cold. They failed to take simple precautions. / By planning and by keeping your wits about you, you can avoid making, or compounding, potentially fatal errors.

essentials

EMERGENCIES VS. ROUTINE TRIPS

Many techniques described in this book are for emergencies only. On routine trips, follow the "leave no trace" philosophy and minimize your impact on the natural environment.

PACK OUT all of your trash.

LEAVE ALL PLANTS intact; do not cut or pick anything.

LEAVE ALL ROCKS and natural formations as you found them.

STAY ON TRAILS to spare undergrowth; remember, alpine moss campion takes 25 years to grow about six inches.

MINIMIZE unnecessary noise to preserve tranquility for wildlife and for fellow campers and hikers.

USE RESTROOM FACILITIES provided; otherwise bury waste at least six inches deep.

USE ONLY DESIGNATED fire circles; in backcountry use camp stove.

ALWAYS USE biodegradable soaps.

WHEN WASHING DISHES, remove solid particles and pack out with trash; scatter dishwater far from site.

CAMP IN ESTABLISHED SITES or on surfaces least covered by vegetation.

LEAVE animals alone; view and photograph from a distance.

YOUR BEST CHANCE OF SURVIVAL

IF YOU ARE LOST, think "stay." Stay calm. Stay put. And stay cool—or warm, depending on the environment.

Ninety-five percent of rescues in survival situations take place within 72 hours of a missing-persons report reaching authorities. Rescuers probably are on their way, especially if you filed a travel plan with a friend before setting out. You'll simplify things if you stay. If you drove to a trailhead, your vehicle will attract attention, and you can advertise your location with mirrors, fires, and smoke. Resting comfortably while you await rescue reduces your need for food and water and keeps you safe from hazards of travel, such as mountains, deserts, rivers, and ice.

Leave only if you know rescue won't happen soon; your site doesn't meet your needs, such as medical help or sufficient water; and you know how to get out. Figure out where you must go, and whether you have enough water to finish each leg of the journey. Create a ground-to-air signal such as a large cloth arrow indicating your exit route.

STRENGTH IN NUMBERS

SOCIAL DYNAMICS ARE never so obvious as when a group is under stress. Conflict arises over decisions that affect the group's welfare. Weaknesses of character become magnified. "Under such conditions whatever is evil in men's nature comes to the front," Teddy Roosevelt noted on his exhausting, demoralizing trip through the uncharted Amazon jungle in 1914. One of his companions turned to stealing food and murdering a pack bearer. While Roosevelt's scenario was among the most extreme, being lost even for a day or two can cause discord in a group and affect the chances of rescue.

Everyone in a wilderness scenario should know the strengths and weaknesses of those in their party. People with disabilities or medical conditions may need more time to rest. Very young children can withstand surprising hardships, and the elderly often have mental toughness that comes from life experience and having survived previous difficulties. Neither, however, can walk as far or as fast as able-bodied adults, and the pace of the trip should be timed to those of the slowest participants. Conversely, it is good to know who has a talent for organization or a skill in food collection. If one member of the group is adept at building a fire and another has skills in first aid, that knowledge is useful in assigning tasks in a way that will boost the chances of rescue.

IDENTIFY SKILLS OF FELLOW SURVIVORS

>>> **Medical knowledge**
>>> **Plant identification**
>>> **Navigational ability**
>>> **Fire-building skills**
>>> **Shelter identification or construction**
>>> **Familiarity with local terrain**
>>> **Knowledge of local weather patterns**
>>> **Signaling**
>>> **Cardiovascular fitness**
>>> **Physical strength**

In a survival situation, waste no time in assessing key strengths of your fellow survivors.

CHOOSING A LEADER

"PEOPLE SURVIVE better in numbers," says survival expert Laurence Gonzales. They organize to help one another, to carry out necessary tasks, and to keep each other alive.

Some groups choose a leader, though often one simply emerges. Sometimes the leader is a guide or officer of the ship or plane whose crash precipitated the survival situation. While the leader should consult with the group, he or she must make decisions for the good of all. Leadership includes bolstering the emotional health of the group. Cast into a survival situation, individuals may suffer guilt, depression, resignation, anger, and a host of other negative emotions. A leader should work to minimize panic and fear while contributing to a positive

mental atitude. Strong leaders reduce stress by keeping group members busy and by fostering teamwork. Focusing on necessary tasks, such as building a fire, helps morale. Leaders should work to raise group members' confidence in each other.

Some scenarios involve people who were friends long before their survival test. Group members who know and trust each other are likely to work well together—at least at first. Increasing stress will likely cause problems, as the group becomes hungry, wet, cold, tired, or emotionally frayed from living in close quarters for days at a time. Knowing how members of a group react to adversity will help a leader make wise decisions.

In some cases, no leader may arise, or a minority of individuals may feel the group is being poorly led. If you find yourself in such a situation, opting to heed your own counsel may be the hardest decision you will ever make. Sometimes going it alone is the right choice. Laurence Gonzales wrote in his book *Deep Survival* of a girl who walked out of the Peruvian jungle to safety while all of her companions from an airplane accident waited for rescue—and died. The girl knew the thick jungle canopy would prevent planes from seeing the survivors on the ground. She followed her own counsel and lived.

A LEADER'S TASKS

>>> **Consult with the group but take responsibility for decisions.**

>>> **Inspire, but do not feign confidence.**

>>> **Determine group members' expertise and utilize this knowledge for making decisions.**

>>> **Monitor the group members for signs of depression and negative emotions.**

>>> **Promote positive attitudes through teamwork, assignment of tasks to the most qualified individuals, and achievement of goals.**

SURVIVAL KITS

THERE IS NO such thing as the perfect survival kit. The right kit will vary with the nature of the trip and the experience of those on the journey. In general, it should be simple, small, affordable, functional, and waterproof. Most of all, in the hands of someone lost in the wild, it should be as familiar as a razor or a toothbrush. Any kit prepared for use in an emergency should be field-tested before it's needed. A wire saw for cutting limbs should be given a trial in the backyard. A magnesium rod should be sparked on a routine camping trip, even if there are plenty of matches to start a fire. Having a kit but never using it until "do-or-die" day is like jumping on skis for the very first time and heading for a black-diamond slope.

Items that can serve a multitude of uses are most desirable because they conserve space and weight. The Boy Scouts' red neckerchief is a good example. It can be drawn across surfaces to collect dew for drinking, soaked in a stream to cool the head, knotted to make an arm sling or ankle brace, or used as a signal flag. Elastic bandages can be used in splints and as part of the treatment for snakebite. A shiny space blanket can be used for creating an emergency shelter, signaling to a search-and-rescue team, or melting snow and ice to make drinking water.

Crucial items such as a stout knife, a compass, and a whistle to attract attention should be tied to cords and hung around the neck for easy access.

If you are in a survival situation, water and shelter likely will be your greatest needs. A kit that includes the means to purify water and provide for an emergency shelter is invaluable.

BASIC SURVIVAL KIT

>>> **First aid items**
>>> **Water purification tablets or drops**
>>> **Fire-starting equipment**
>>> **Signaling items**
>>> **Food procurement items**
>>> **Shelter items, such as tent, hammock**
>>> **Lighter, metal match, matches**
>>> **Knife**
>>> **Needle and thread**
>>> **Signaling mirror**
>>> **Wrist compass**
>>> **Fish and snare line**
>>> **Fishhooks**
>>> **Candle**
>>> **Small hand lens**
>>> **Solar blanket**
>>> **Surgical blades**
>>> **Water bladder**

EXPERT TIP In preparing your survival kit, select items you can use for more than one purpose. If you have two items that will serve the same function, pick the one you can use for another function. Do not duplicate items, as this increases your kit's size and weight.

U.S.ARMY

MAKE ROPE FROM NATURAL MATERIALS

1. Test possible materials (grass, vine, stringy bark, etc.) by knotting a piece. If it doesn't break, it's usable.

2. Lay strands—one slightly shorter than the other—parallel to each other and knot them together at one end. Divide in half.

3. Twist each half once clockwise.

4. Twist halves together counterclockwise.

5. Repeat steps three and four, splicing in a new strand as the shorter half runs out (make sure to overlap by at least three inches).

6. Make stronger rope by braiding three of these ropes together.

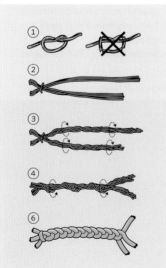

TRAVELING SOLO

LOST AND ALONE. Lost and alone. It sounds like a Hollywood cliché. But there is something inherently destabilizing about realizing you're on your own in a survival situation.

Surprisingly, children under six years old have one of the highest survival rates in desperate situations, such as being lost in the woods. Why isn't exactly clear. Scientists speculate they exhibit classic cause-and-effect responses. They seek to satisfy basic needs—warmth, food, water—as soon as they arise. In so doing, they act in their best interests until they are found.

If you're lost and alone, stay where you are. Think over what you know about shelter and fire. Conserve your energy. Stay warm. When you feel better, make your survival plan.

Empty your pockets and your backpack. Examine everything and see to what purpose you can put it. Pocket mirror? Good for signaling. Safety pin? Good for a fishhook. Your spirits will soar if you remembered to pack plenty of water and some high-calorie snacks, such as hard candies and granola bars.

With a little ingenuity, you can even make some of the most basic items you need, such as rope.

SOURCES FOR MAKING ROPE

>>> Fibers from trees, especially oak, mulberry, cedar, hickory
>>> Animals: tendons from large game, hides
>>> Grasses: dogbane, milkweed, stinging nettle
>>> Plants: yucca, agave

CONQUERING FEAR

"HE MUST HAVE LOST himself in the sand-haze and wandered till his camel broke down; and there died of thirst and heat," Col. T. E. Lawrence ("Lawrence of Arabia") wrote of an Arab who succumbed to panic. "Fear and panic...tore at the brain and reduced the bravest man to a stumbling babbling maniac in an hour or two; and then the sun killed him."

Fear kills. Panic takes many forms, often, as with "woods shock" (see bulleted text, below), unrecognized by victims. Get control before it's too late.

To do so, experts suggest you remember the word STOP. It stands for Stop, Think, Observe, and Plan.

Stop: Halt physical activity. Sit and try to slow your heartbeat and breathing. Inhale slowly through your nose, counting slowly to three, hold the breath for a count of three, then let out the air slowly through your nose or mouth, while counting to least three. This breathing technique gives you a structured way to focus and calm down and signals the brain to relax.

Think: Once your body has slowed a bit, think about your situation and what you can do about it. Cognitive functions improve as breathing slows.

Observe: Use your senses to take in the terrain around you, the state of your companions, and particularly any injuries. Assess what you have and don't have to face your situation.

Plan: Thinking and observing, start to fashion your strategy. How can you best respond to your situation? Don't be afraid to revise your plan, as needed.

Some experts add a fifth step: Act. No plan is useful if it is never executed.

WHAT IS WOODS SHOCK?

>>> Term dates from at least 1873
>>> Refers to confusion that can benumb even competent people in the wilderness
>>> Accompanies loss of spatial orientation
>>> Causes otherwise rational people to act irrationally
>>> Treat by following S.T.O.P. steps above

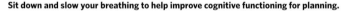

Sit down and slow your breathing to help improve cognitive functioning for planning.

ASSESS PRIORITIES

THERE IS NO PERFECTLY ordered checklist of what to do in a survival situation because the conditions of the environment and the health of those confronting it will vary. The first step, however, is always the same: Stop, Think, Observe, and Plan.

Depending on injuries, first aid may compete with the above for top priority. Finding adequate water typically is the next priority, especially in a desert, because without it the body and mind quickly stop functioning. However, locating or creating shelter may take precedence over finding water. In extreme cold, for example, getting into a proper shelter can fend off exhaustion and sustain the will to live. Or adequate water may already be at hand.

Food is lower on the list of priorities because the average person, burning the body's stores of fat, can survive for days or weeks without it.

The rule of threes (see Chapter Two) says the body cannot go without oxygen for longer than three minutes, so a person who has stopped breathing must receive immediate help. Within three hours, the body should be protected from rain and snow, as well as from blazing sun and temperature extremes, in order to avoid hypo- or hyperthermia. Within three days, the body must have water and sleep. Within three weeks, the body must have food; however,

though survival does not depend on finding food immediately, food and fire have strong psychological effects on a group stranded in the wilderness.

CONCRETE STEPS TO RAISE YOUR ODDS OF SURVIVING

>>> Cultivate a strong body and mind; a regimen of physical exercise before going on a planned wilderness adventure will provide needed stamina.
>>> Acknowledge your fear, then step back and observe it as if from a distance.
>>> Keep busy; performing tasks large and small takes the mind off the circumstances that promote fear.
>>> Think positively, and promote positive thoughts in others.
>>> Know how to use everything in your survival kit.
>>> Promote humor; Lancaster University psychology professor John Leach writes that humor is "a vital organ for survival."

EXPERT TIP Some people with survival training have died because they did not use their skills. A key ingredient in any survival situation is the mental attitude of the individual(s) involved. Having survival skills is important; having the will to survive is essential.

U.S.ARMY

CONQUERING PANIC

WHEN YOU REALIZE you're lost in the jungle or the desert, your adrenal glands pump out hormones in response to the "fight or flight" instinct. Pulse increases. Breathing becomes faster and shallower. Sugar revs the metabolism. Vision narrows and temporal perception seems to dilate. Fine muscle control evaporates.

Small wonder that survivors must master their internal environment before they attempt the external one.

You'll need to blunt the impact of your adrenal glands' chemical cocktail. Follow the advice of *The Hitchhiker's Guide to the Galaxy*, a fictional reference work that novelist Douglas Adams described as "the standard repository of all knowledge and wisdom." On its cover, in large and friendly letters, the guide says, "Don't panic."

Not panicking, as simple as it sounds, prepares the way for a survivor's rational mind to do its job. You will grow confident as you do simple tasks and see results. You will count your successes rather than your setbacks. You will fashion and execute a survival plan that makes sense. You will be in the moment, and you may find that on the edge of losing your life, you have never been so alive.

You'll need to use different parts of your brain. The part that figures out where you are (and if you're lost) gets confused in the wilderness with its lack of familiar visual cues, such as buildings and streets. The part that controls your seeking a goal, such as the desire to move out of a place of confusion and find a familiar location, is tied up with emotions. A strong emotional reaction tends to trump rational thought in a survival situation, which helps explain why so many people who get lost keep going forward, getting more and more disoriented, when reason favors turning back and retracing their steps. The survivor's trick is to respond to the urge to take action by harnessing that emotional energy and channeling it in constructive ways.

SURVIVOR ACTIONS

>>> Remain calm upon finding yourself in a survival scenario.
>>> Look for patterns in the environment and then define the situation.
>>> Exercise self-control.
>>> Forget the odds of survival—or fight them without pause.
>>> Make good decisions that account for plenty of variables; take calculated risks.
>>> Balance boldness and humility; be open to what the world can teach you and respect the power of nature.
>>> Enumerate any threats that must be faced.

NONSURVIVOR ACTIONS

>>> Losing mental clarity and control upon facing the survival scenario
>>> Defining the situation first, then gather information to fit that mental map
>>> Giving in to anxiety, running, hyperventilating, thrashing about, and generally wasting energy
>>> Dwelling on the odds of survival
>>> Staying rigid in decision making
>>> Assuming infallibility
>>> Giving up

THE WILL TO SURVIVE

EQUIPMENT, TRAINING, experience. Not bad to have. But not enough.

Survivors need something more.

The Army Survival Manual calls it "the will to survive." In explaining why some who have no survival training live while some who have plenty of survival skills die, the manual notes that a "key ingredient in any survival situation is the mental attitude of [those] involved. Having survival skills is important; having the will to survive is essential."

Survival expert Laurence Gonzales has a punchier name for what separates the saved from the sad-fated: heart. The right stuff is not what's in your pack, although it might help. It's not what's in your memory, although knowledge never hurts. No, it's the thing that burns in your soul.

In their darkest moments, all survivors faced the crucial question of whether they would live. All answered: Absolutely.

THE WILL TO SURVIVE—HOW IT WORKS

WHEN THEODORE Roosevelt cut his leg in the Amazon jungle in 1914, he knew he would suffer a life-threatening infection. He vowed to die rather than risk the lives of his companions trying to carry him, or his body, home. But Roosevelt's son Kermit refused to leave his father behind. When TR heard the news, he decided he must—and would—survive. "I saw that if I did end it, that would only make it more sure that Kermit would not get out," Roosevelt told a friend after the ordeal. "For I knew he would not abandon me, but would insist on bringing my body out, too. That, of course, would have been impossible. I knew his determination. So there was only one thing for me to do, and that was to come out myself."

The decision to live precedes the actual living. Some people give up while others push on. Some have been conditioned to conquer or surrender to challenges, ranging from the common, such as school, to the extraordinary, such as war. TR had a will of iron, forged in a life of physical and emotional challenges. Without it, he would have died, plagued by fear and doubt.

S.U.R.V.I.V.A.L.
ACCORDING TO THE ARMY
SURVIVAL MANUAL

>>> S. Size up the situation—your surroundings, physical conditions, and equipment.
>>> U. Use all your senses; undue haste makes waste.
>>> R. Remember where you are; pay close attention to where you are and where you are going, and don't rely on others to keep track of the route.
>>> V. Vanquish fear and panic.
>>> I. Improvise; see how to adapt tools to new purposes.
>>> V. Value living; don't give up.
>>> A. Act like the natives; discover how they survive.
>>> L. Live by your wits, but for now, learn basic skills.

WATER

It is an understatement to say water is crucial to life. Water is life. You will die if you don't drink water within two or three days. Even cutting back causes distress. / "Lack of water is always the most severe privation that men can be condemned to endure," wrote Ernest Shackleton. The need is greater in hot climates, where the body loses water more rapidly through perspiration. Physical activity, altitude, stress, and illness or injury also hasten the loss of water and its need for replacement. But even sitting quietly in a shelter in Arctic cold, you must drink at least 2.3 liters—more than half a gallon—each day to replace the water you lose and to function efficiently. / If you lack water, conserve your energy. Don't smoke or drink alcohol. In a hot climate, exert yourself only at night. Also try breathing through your nose and eating only a minimum. / Without water, the human body rapidly deteriorates. Blood becomes thicker, making the heart work harder to pump it. Impaired circulation reduces the ability to shed excess heat in hot climates or retain heat in cold ones. As dehydration increases, the body pulls water from cells to keep blood flowing, which damages cell membranes and increases cellular salt concentrations. / Your biggest challenge may be finding water that's clean enough to drink. Most of the Earth's surface is covered with undrinkable saltwater, and most of the rest—stored in ponds, lakes, streams, and rivers—is contaminated with microorganisms and chemicals. You will need to develop water-purification skills to survive in the wild. But what if you have no means to purify water you collect in the wilderness? You may have to weigh your options. Going without water threatens life. So too may the illnesses caused by drinking impure water. You may decide to drink, and survive, in the short run and deal with any life-threatening illnesses later.

WATER BASICS

THE STANDARD recommendation is to figure one gallon of water per person per day for wilderness consumption. That's also the amount recommended for storage for home emergencies. Desert conditions require more water.

Each person venturing in the wild should carry as much water as is comfortable, along with a purifying device if no fresh water is available.

Carrying as much water as you need for extended trips is impossible. Besides being bulky, each gallon weighs about eight pounds, making the aggregate unwieldy. Thus, long-distance hikers as well as people in survival situations must know how to find, store, and purify water.

For short trips, water can be carried in a variety of containers.

Metal vacuum flasks are almost unbreakable but can be heavy when filled.

Plastic bottles are lightweight and tough but may melt if left too close to a fire.

Pouches clipped to the belt or worn on the back allow water to be easily accessed while keeping hands free.

Large plastic water bags can be hung from trees for use in a large camp.

Water bladders such as polypropylene Platypus containers or CamelBaks (place in backpack, drink through tube) are nearly weightless and collapse flat when empty.

EXPERT TIP Water is the safest liquid to drink. Avoid drinks with alcohol or caffeine in them as they dehydrate the body. They can make you feel good briefly, but make the heat's effects on the body worse. Do not smoke cigarettes. American Red Cross

No matter the appearance of water, always purify it before drinking.

EFFECTS OF DEHYDRATION

LOSING UP TO five percent of body fluids causes thirst, weakness, nausea, and irritability. Pulse increases, and skin may become flushed. Judgment may be seriously impaired even if the body loses only two percent of its fluids.

Losing up to ten percent causes headaches, dizziness, and tingling in limbs. Sufferers may lose the ability to walk and speak clearly. Skin may turn blue, and vision may begin to blur.

Loss of 15 percent severely impairs vision and hearing, swells the tongue, and makes urination painful. Sufferers may be unable to swallow, or may exhibit signs of delirium.

Loss of more than 15 percent usually causes death.

Many signs of dehydration match common physical symptoms of fear and panic. When the two are combined, they strike the body doubly hard.

HOW AND WHEN TO DRINK

IT'S BEST TO take small drinks at regular intervals, such as every hour, to prevent dehydration.

Look for obvious signs of dehydration in yourself and your companions: dark, sunken eyes; dark, smelly urine; fatigue; and shriveled skin. Begin drinking immediately.

The optimal drink for someone who already is dehydrated is plain water. Salts and minerals in sports drinks can interfere with the body's absorption of water.

Don't wait to become thirsty before you start drinking or looking for water. A noticeable thirst begins when the body is two percent dehydrated. It's difficult to drink more than a quart of

water at one time without experiencing discomfort; therefore, once serious dehydration begins, it may take hours to return your body to a healthy state.

WATER PURIFIERS

⋙ **Pump purifiers.** Work a pump to push water through a filter and treat it chemically to kill microorganisms.

⋙ **Bottle purifiers.** Fill the bottle with untreated water, let it work its way through the filters, and start drinking.

⋙ **Chlorine solution.** Add specified amount to water in a sealed container, wait three minutes, shake, and then let the water sit for a half hour.

⋙ **Iodine tablets or drops.** Mix specified amount with water and then let it stand for a half hour.

⋙ **Pots for boiling.** Strain water through a sock and let boil for several minutes; kills microorganisms but does not remove chemical impurities.

essentials

GOOD SOURCES OF WATER

There are pure sources of water around you, as well as sources readily available that must be purified.

FRESH-FLOWING streams. Must be purified, regardless of appearance.

FRESHWATER lakes. Must be purified.

DEW. Pure when it condenses.

RAIN. Pure before it hits the ground.

SNOW AND ICE. Boil to make drinkable.

GROUNDWATER that fills a hole dug at the base of a dune. Must be purified.

WATER stored in vines, barrel cactus, banana trees, and other plants. Pure from plants.

WATER FOUND IN ANIMALS

IN GENERAL, don't suck animal flesh or drink animal blood if you're thirsty. The former is likely to be high in protein and require plenty of the body's water for digestion. The latter has the same problem and also is likely to have a high salt concentration. However, certain animal bodies contain drinkable fluid. Fish have a column of fresh water along thier spines as well as drinkable moisture in their eyes. Aborigines in Australia dig up burrowing desert frogs and squeeze life-giving water from their bodies. And camels can be slaughtered for the brackish water stored in their humps.

essentials

BAD SOURCES OF WATER

Your body will scream at you for liquids when you're dehydrated. Fight the urge to drink the following.

URINE. Contains harmful body wastes as well as salt, which increases dehydration.

BLOOD. May carry diseases, is burned like food in the stomach (which uses up a portion of the body's water), and contains salt.

SEAWATER. Drinking increases dehydration.

DRINKS containing alcohol. They contribute to dehydration and impair judgment.

WATER HOLES that have a chemical shine or smell. Likely contaminated.

WATER FROM LAKES that do not drain, as in desert basins. May contain alkali salts.

FOOD

A human body needs to take in about 2,000 calories a day to maintain itself. That's the norm for most situations. In a harsh climate such as the Antarctic interior or the thin air of a high mountain chain, the caloric minimum may rise to 4,500 to 5,000 calories a day. / Without food, the body starts to burn its own fat for energy. When that's depleted, the body cannibalizes its own tissues to stave off starvation. / Long before the descent toward death, which begins after around three weeks without food, a person experiences "food stress." Hunger preys on the mind, causing fixations and fantasies about food. / To the hungry person on the edge of survival, food fulfills not only a physical but also a psychological need. Shackleton noticed a marked improvement in his men's emotional health when he increased rations from 9.5 ounces per day to a bit more, even though nothing else about their dire situation on the Antarctic ice had changed. / "Regardless of what it is, eat it," Korean War prisoner of war Gene M. Lamm told John Leach in *Survival Psychology*. "If you miss one meal as a prisoner, it will take you weeks to regain your lost strength."

BASIC FOOD ELEMENTS

YOUR BODY NEEDS a variety of foods They help the body maintain itself.

Carbohydrates are easily digested and supply rapid energy—particularly good for doing hard work under stress. They include grains, pasta, fruits, and vegetables. For a lightweight food full of energy, carry trail mix or hard candy.

Proteins build muscle and tissue. They come from meat, fish, and fowl. Don't eat protein when dehydrated, as its digestion requires lots of water.

Fats burn slowly, giving energy over long periods. They include cheese, animal fat, butter, nuts, and eggs. Fatty foods provide warmth in cold climates.

Vitamins occur naturally in most foods, but you can also pack a vitamin-mineral supplement. Minerals also occur naturally in foods and in water.

FOODS YOU SHOULD CARRY

FOR ALL TRIPS: Granola bars and small hard or chewable candies. Keep them in your survival kit for the bursts of energy they provide.

For day hikes: Trail mix, dried fruits, and other roughage. These contain fiber, nutrients, and carbohydrates. Snack on them as you go.

For longer trips: Plan for more elaborate meals that include a variety of foods. Consider the weather, distance traveled, available cooking gear and water, and dietary needs when choosing among canned, dried, freeze-dried, and preserved foods.

Canned foods are ready to eat and do not need fire or water, but add a lot of weight to a backpack.

Dried foods are much lighter but require plenty of water to reconstitute them—water that must be carried in or purified on-site. (Eating dried foods before they soak long enough will steal water from a person's intestinal tract and possibly cause a dangerous blockage.)

Freeze-dried foods retain their texture. These foods are lightweight and satisfying but must be soaked before cooking.

Small cans or bags of preserved fish or meat provide necessary protein without adding a lot of weight to a backpack, but digestion requires extra water.

Rice and beans, and other legumes are satisfying and rich in carbohydrates. They may require a little experimentation to cook properly on a camp stove.

Beverage powders have relatively little nutrition, yet drinks such as tea, cocoa, and coffee give warmth and comfort. Starting your day with a hot cup of coffee or tea can provide a psychological boost, suggesting your situation isn't as bad as it seems. Powdered drink mixes also are handy if you are forced to collect water from pulverized vegetable matter or a brackish stream, or if you treat it with iodine. Purifying your water will kill germs but may not do anything for an unpleasnt taste. Sprinkling a powdered flavoring on the water may help you keep it down. That's an important consideration, as vomiting causes severe water loss.

End your day by eating protein or fat before going to bed. Digestion will help keep you warm throughout the night.

EDIBLE PLANTS AND ANIMALS

FOODS FOUND in the wild are either plants or animals. Both provide necessary nutrients in varying amounts. Though an ounce of meat has more nourishment than an ounce of vegetable matter, it usually is harder to obtain. Plants don't run away as you try to collect them.

Plants are good sources of carbohydrates, which the body burns for energy. Nuts and seeds help balance the diet by providing proteins and fats, while plant foods containing sugars have calories for supplemental energy. Many plants can be kept from spoilage by drying through exposure to sunlight, fire, or air.

Young plant shoots are softer and more nourishing than old ones, as are young leaves. Leaves should not be boiled too long or they will lose their vitamins.

Obtaining meat requires skills to capture animals. An immediate need for protein can be satisfied by gathering easy-to-capture, abundant animals such as insects, crustaceans, snakes, and fish, whereas snares or weapons are needed to bring in larger animals. Beware the relatively high-energy expenditure of hunting.

Animal flesh should be cooked to kill microorganisms. However, in an emergency situation where fire for water purification is unavailable, the survivalist may choose to deal with an immediate hunger and thirst, and get treatment later for any resulting diseases.

The Army Survival Manual notes, "You can, with relatively few exceptions, eat anything that crawls, swims, walks, or flies." A crucial step is overcoming the aversion to unusual foods.

GENERAL FOODS TO EAT

>>> Aggregate berries, such as raspberries and blackberries.
>>> Nuts; among the most satisfying plant foods, high in fat.
>>> Insects; found everywhere, easily caught, high in protein and fat.
>>> Freshwater fish.
>>> Crustaceans.
>>> Birds and their eggs.
>>> Mammal flesh.
>>> Soft, new-growth spruce and fir needles.
>>> Seaweed.

GENERAL FOODS TO AVOID

>>> Saltwater fish that have sharp spines or parrotlike beaks.
>>> Mushrooms and fungi (too much risk of misidentifying a poisonous species).
>>> Ticks, flies, and other potentially disease-carrying insects.
>>> Toads.
>>> Insects that bite, sting, or have hairy or brightly colored exteriors.
>>> Liver from polar animals; likely to contain toxic levels of vitamin A.
>>> Any unfamiliar plant until you subject it to the edibility test (see Chapter 3).

COOKING FOR SURVIVAL

COOKING FOOD KILLS parasites that could cause disease. In addition, gathering at day's end around a roaring fire promotes a sense of well-being and maintenance of body heat, which are essential in survival situations.

You must be scrupulously clean in preparing and disposing of food in order to prevent attracting pests. Cook only enough food for one meal at a time, although you may choose to keep a pot of water simmering in order to have clean water handy. Burn any leftover food scraps. If your clothes take on the smell of smoke or food odors, remove them before you go to bed and place them at least 100 yards downwind from where you camp.

If you wish to carry food that will spoil, such as meat, consider smoking it or drying it by cutting it in strips and laying it in the sun (see Chapter 6). Keep meats separate from foods you intend to eat raw, such as apples and oranges. Store all food in containers (as airtight as possible), placed out of reach of animals.

Do not build a fire if you cannot control it. Fires released by high winds or sparks in thick brush may cause widespread blazes that threaten your survival. Learn how to shelter or isolate your cooking fire. Common methods include cooking in a pit, isolating fire in a ring of bare earth, and building a screen of rocks to shelter fire from wind.

EXPERT TIP , Boiling water for at least one minute should kill any microorganisms present and make it safe to drink. The water will taste better after boiling if air is added to it. This can be done by pouring it between two clean containers several times to aerate it.

American Red Cross

A portable stove allows you to cook without having to use an area's natural resources.

FRESHWATER FISH

FISH ARE RELATIVELY easy to catch and high in protein. They are best when fresh, going straight from the stream to the skillet.

To prepare, immediately gut and clean your catch, as follows:

Slit the fish from vent to throat. Take out the viscera. Also remove the dark blood vessels and kidneys, which appear as dark lines near the backbone. Remove scales by holding the fish near the tail and scraping with the back of your knife. Leave the head, fins, and tail intact if the fish is small, to avoid disturbing small bones. If you must wait before cooking the fish, put it in a clear, watertight plastic bag in a container of ice.

Use the viscera as bait to catch other fish. Bury any extra guts; otherwise their odor will attract scavengers and insects.

In survival situations, look for fatty fish such as salmon. Some fish, such as rainbow trout, are so lean they may cost more calories to catch than they return as you eat them. (One pound of rainbow trout may contain only 200 calories, and thus a steady trout diet must be supplemented with other, fattier foods.)

how to

MAKE A LINE AND HOOK

1 Find a small, thin piece of bone, turtle shell, or wood, sharp enough to use as a hook. Tie a piece of string, dental floss, or twine to the middle of it.

2 Turn the hook parallel to the string and bait with worm or grub. Make sure bait covers hook entirely.

3 Tie the other end of the twine to a long stick to use as a fishing pole. Toss baited hook into water; when bait sinks to bottom, pull twine back in and recast.

4 The fish will swallow the bait, lodging the sharp object inside.

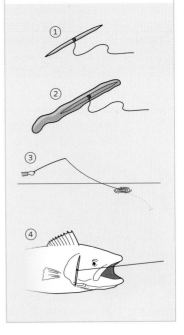

Hunt only for survival and then kill only what you need. Otherwise, harm no animals.

LURES AND TRAPS

THE ADVANTAGE OF lures, nets, and traps to someone in a survival situation is simple: Many can be made in a short time and then left alone to do their work. You can make a net to catch fish from string, rope, or cords, or from pieces of clothing. Traps can as simple as a death pit, or elaborately fashioned from sticks, cords, or scrounged materials. Fishing lures can be baited and set on a running line to be checked at regular intervals. If you don't have fishhooks in your survival kit, you can improvise them from safety pins, slivers of bone, thorns, barbs, or zipper tabs.

An intelligently designed set of traps and lures has the potential to gather more food than can be brought down with a rifle. However, under the wilderness philosophy of "leave no trace," don't catch any game unless you must consume it to survive.

There is no such thing as a trap that's good for all game. Figure out what species of animals live nearby, and then design traps and lures for them. Using the right bait can attract animals like a magnet. The bait should be familiar to the animal, but not so common that the animal can get it easily elsewhere. Small game are attracted to peanut butter.

SURVIVAL LURES/TRAPS DOS AND DON'TS

>>> Do: study the habits of the animal you wish to catch.
>>> Don't: try to steal game from a predator animal, even if the predator has left the kill.
>>> Do: net or catch fish with your bare hands, if you must do so to survive.
>>> Don't: rely on lures and traps as your only source of food.
>>> Do: set and regularly check multiple traps and lures.
>>> Don't: accidentally get caught in one of your own traps.
>>> Do: trap on game runs.
>>> Don't: trap too close to an animal's lair, as it will become suspicious.

FIRST AID

To stay alive, stay well. / While some degree of risk-taking is required in virtually all survival situations, avoid risky actions that are unnecessary and likely to cause injury. / Some health risks are unavoidable. Hypothermia is a constant threat in the Arctic, as are dehydration and hyperthermia in the desert. Hiking over uneven terrain may cause a sprained or broken ankle; sharp sticks and rocks cause cuts; and bites and stings can lead to shock. / Everyone venturing into the wilderness should have a basic knowledge of first aid. It's not enough to have just one expert in the group, particularly if that person is the one who needs medical attention. You must know how to recognize and treat injuries because there's not likely to be an ambulance coming to your rescue. / You always should carry an emergency first aid kit when you leave civilization behind. It'll help with treatment of basic injuries. However, as with all survival scenarios, you'll need to figure out how to make do when unforeseen health problems arise. Your calm response to a medical problem is the best first step to recovery.

HOW TO USE THE FIRST AID INFORMATION IN THIS BOOK

FIRST AID INFORMATION appears throughout this book. Each chapter contains a section on potential medical situations common to that chapter's particular terrain and climate. Look for the first aid heading and cross-references to other chapters.

Take the first aid advice in this book for what it is: an introduction to a large and complicated subject. This advice is not meant to substitute for certified first aid or CPR training, emergency medical services training, or a formal medical education. None of the information in this book qualifies you to diagnose or prescribe treatments. Leave real medicine to the experts.

Instead, this book aims to give you enough basic information to make informed decisions about preventing and treating injuries—and doing a good enough job so that you and your companions survive until you get professional medical care.

FIRST AID BASICS

TAKE A COURSE in first aid and cardio-pulmonary resuscitation from a qualified instructor, such as the American Red Cross, and read more detailed reference books. In particular, look for books and classes on dealing with typical backcountry injuries. Sprains, broken bones, and stings and bites are not unusual, but neither are severe allergic reactions, shock, hypothermia, dehydration, and other health hazards that may demand immediate attention when you are far from professional health care. Everyone in a group venturing into the wilderness should have a basic understanding of first aid. You never know—the group member whom everyone counts on to treat illness and injury may be the one incapacitated by a fall or anaphylactic shock.

First aid also is what the term suggests: first. If you have a medical emergency in the wilderness, your choices may be to do what you can or watch as someone suffers and perhaps dies. Basic care requires follow-up, which should be done by a physician as soon as possible. Only a doctor can make the best assessment of the extent of an injury and its best treatment.

First aid also means taking care of yourself first, so you can take care of others. Treat seemingly minor problems such as blisters and stings to keep them from becoming incapacitating.

GENERAL FIRST AID KIT

>>> **Adhesive bandages to prevent infection to cuts and to cover blisters.**
>>> **Roll bandages—gauze, crepe, etc.—for keeping wounds clean and closed, for securing dressings, and for immobilizing limbs.**
>>> **Triangular bandages for binding large areas or fashioning a sling.**
>>> **Tape for affixing and holding dressings and bandages in place.**
>>> **Painkillers, especially for moving somebody who is injured.**
>>> **Antiseptic for cleaning wounds.**
>>> **Soap for cleansing and handling wounds and basic hygiene.**
>>> **Needles, thread.**
>>> **Prescription medication, if any, for yourself and dependent group members.**
>>> **Scissors for trimming bandages, snipping thread, etc.**
>>> **Foot-care products, such as corn pads, for preventing blisters and limiting the impact of foot injuries.**
>>> **Safety pins for securing bandages and making temporary sutures.**

essentials

PRIORITIES FOR ASSESSING AND TREATING INJURIES

Look for the worst, first, as you assess how to treat an injury.

PERFORM these steps in this order:

REMOVE the injured person from the scene if further injury is likely to be caused by staying.

HOWEVER, do not move a victim who may have a spinal injury.

IF BREATHING or heartbeat has stopped, immediately attempt restoration.

THEN HALT any bleeding.

THEN TREAT wounds and burns.

THEN PUT fractures in splints.

THEN TREAT for shock.

FIRST AID FOR CHILDREN

CHILDREN AREN'T little adults. They react differently to external stimuli. That's important when making decisions regarding first aid for them.

Children have smaller body masses than grown-ups and are likely to get dehydrated and suffer from heat exhaustion much more quickly.

Monitor any children in a survival scenario for signs of dehydration or heat injury, and make sure they drink plenty of liquids. If they do not want to drink as much as they should to stave off dehydration, try adding fruit flavoring to their water bottles. Oral rehydration salts added to a child's drink will speed recovery.

Diarrhea hastens dehydration among adults and children, and again, it works much more quickly on children's smaller bodies. Get all victims to drink plenty of water. Feed infants bananas, applesauce, and rice cereal. Feed older children bland foods such as dry toast and crackers, and consider providing a safe, child-sized dose of antidiarrhea medicine.

Beware if a child complains of headache or flulike symptoms, as they may signal dehydration.

Children are likely to physically tire more quickly than adults. However, many have a surprising psychological toughness that will help them survive.

EXPERT TIP Make no assumptions about the nature of an emergency until you have gathered as much information as possible. If a victim is conscious, ask what happened and where he or she is hurt. If the person is unconscious, look around for clues as to what might have happened.

American Red Cross

SPRAINS AND FRACTURES

YOU CAN'T ALWAYS tell right away if an injury is a break or a sprain.

If pain and swelling do not subside, keep the injury immobilized with a splint and don't let the victim aggravate it. If the limb is merely stiff, the victim should try to work out the injury. Sprains should be bandaged, but minor ones don't have to be rested.

Some breaks are easy to spot: the bone pokes through flesh or a limb hangs unnaturally. Swelling and inability to move a limb may point to a fracture.

Broken bones should be immobilized. This helps control pain, keeps sharp edges of bone from slicing flesh and possibly causing infection, and reduces risk of shock.

Breaks should be immobilized prior to moving the injured person. Splints support fractures, immobilize injuries, and minimize further complications. A broken leg can be bound to its uninjured companion; a broken arm can be bound to the torso or splinted in an L shape and suspended in a sling.

EXPERT TIP Splint/sling the injury in the position you found it. Immobilize the area both above and below the injured joint and check the circulation of the injured area after immobilizing. Splint only when you have to move or transport someone to seek medical attention.

American
Red Cross

how to

SPLINT A BROKEN BONE

1 If you cannot put pressure on or move a limb and suspect it is broken—and you cannot reach medical help—you may need to make a splint. Choose two rigid objects long enough to immobilize the joints above and below the injury. Place them on either side.

2 Insert padding between injury and splints.

3 Secure splint by tying in place. Bind tight enough to support the injury and prevent the splint from moving, but loose enough to permit circulation. Consult the appendix or a full first aid guide for more information on fractures, sprains, and dislocations.

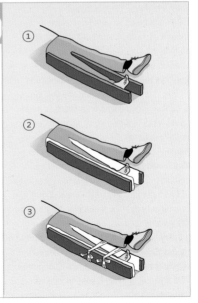

HOW I SURVIVED: JUNGLE SHOCK by MARIA FADIMAN

Which way do my tracks go? I am standing deep in a jungle in Ecuador, not far from the field station where I have been studying sustainable and nonsustainable methods of collecting fiber plants and palms. As an ethnobotanist and National Geographic emerging explorer, I work with indigenous peoples, documenting their uses of plants—

for everything from building materials to medicinal remedies. I have been through these forests around the station hundreds of times. I have never been lost here. Usually, if I find myself slightly off course, I retrace my tracks in the soft earth of the rain forest floor—as good as throwing down bread crumbs.

But I have made a mistake this time, a serious one. I was less focused than usual since I was taking a morning off to hike and explore the dense, green, heavily canopied forest teeming with life. I walked slightly off the trail to investigate something and when I started to head back to the trail, I walked first in one direction, then thought I'd gotten it backwards and walked the other, compounding the problem. Now, peering at my boot marks in the mud, I realize I've obliterated the outline of my boot print. The canopy of the forest hundreds of feet overhead is dense and thick, filter-

Geoscience professor Dr. Maria Fadiman studies the relationship between people and plants in Ecuador, Galápagos, Tanzania, and Zimbabwe.

ing the sun to a twilight at the forest floor. I have no landmarks but the leafy greenness that is starting to look the same in every direction. I am lost.

At the research station, we'd often joked about getting lost in the rain forest, thinking it wouldn't really happen, not to us, anyway—seasoned professionals, biologists, rain forest researchers. I try to remain calm, remember my training, but though I logically know the risk of striking out into the growing twilight, I feel compelled to move—fast. I start barging across the rain forest, thinking I will end up hitting the trail.

Scrambling up hills, trying not to think about snakes and scorpions, only focused on beating the sun. How many hills are there? Where am I? Sweat drips down my face, my water bottle is half empty, and the sun is going down.

I knew I'd hiked downhill from the station, so when I find a creek, I head uphill. Scrambling, falling, and splashing, I am frantically filling my rubber boots with water, soaking my feet. Thoroughly wet, I scramble up the bank, sweating and panting, and flail my way onto what seems like a trail.

The sun is now gone, but the moon gives light. I put my flashlight in my pocket, saving the batteries for later. Eyes peeled for nocturnal snakes, I reach a steep hill, slick from rain. I lose my grip and fall, hard, sliding all the way to the bottom. Bruised, but not seriously injured, I pick myself up and head to the trail, which should be just to the right.

I reach into my pocket to take out my flashlight, but feel slackness where it should have been. I pat my pockets, crestfallen, looking in the darkness toward the slope. The moon has now disappeared and it's nearly pitch-dark, so I start moving very slowly. I am aware that I am on the edge of a sharp dropoff. If I go the wrong way I'll slip off the eroded part, and shoot down the cliff. I still feel like I know this area, can't imagine I'm now operating out of a panicked

false sense of knowing. I feel my way forward, touching nothing familiar, yet thinking every minute that if I just get a few feet further, just at the top of this rise, just beyond the next tree trunk, I will suddenly find myself in familiar territory. Suddenly the ground beneath me gives way and with tremendous velocity, I shoot down a steep slope. On the way down, I manage to grab hold of a tree branch, cutting my hands and arms, then slipping again as the branch cracks free. This time, I'm sprawling down the hill, out of control. I smash hard into something blessedly, but painfully, solid. A fallen tree has broken my fall. Dizzy, I reach down and feel my legs, afraid of what I will find. I find that I can move them, though they are painfully bruised.

All I can think of is getting back up the hill to the trail. I feel with my hands until there is a break in the vegetation, pulling myself up and hopelessly sliding back. The reality of poisonous critters and my bare hands feeling through the mud begins to dawn on me once I stop floundering and finally sit, resigned to a night on the rain forest floor, alone, no flashlight, mosquito net, or hammock.

I lie back, prop my feet against a tree so that I don't topple down the mountain, feel for a palm frond, kick it, in case something already lives in it and get under the leaf. If there is no rain, and nothing eats me, I will be all right. The nightly downpour that I knew would come soaks the ground and I lie in the mud for a few hours.

"Fadiman!"

I rouse from my exhausted slumber to hear familiar voices shouting my name. Scrambling to my feet, I see flashlights bob past me. "Here I am!" I shout back.

How terribly and beautifully empty the Libyan desert appeared when Antoine de Saint-Exupéry soared above it in December 1935. Not a tree, not a blade of grass broke the monotony of sand and stone. / Then his Caudron C-630 Simoun mail plane crashed. Saint-Exupéry and his navigator emerged unhurt, yet faced long odds. They had some grapes, one orange, and a bit of coffee and wine. Their best guess put them hundreds of miles from civilization. / What to do? / They did not panic. Instead, they mastered their environment to stretch their chances of survival. / Saint-Exupéry made a plan: Explore during daylight. Light nighttime bonfires from the wreckage to act as beacons and provide heat. Collect dew with a rag and a parachute. / On the fourth day, after draining the last bit of moisture, "a clock...started up in me," Saint-Exupéry recalled. They knew their only hope was to walk out. They used a compass to keep a steady course. They rested when exhausted and burrowed into sand to stay warm. Finally, they stumbled upon a Bedouin...and salvation. / Fire, shelter, navigation, and signaling: along with finding water—these forge the chain of survival.

ENVIRONMENT:
BASICS

PREPARATION

Humans are masters of survival in their day-to-day environments. The trick is to stay alive when thrown into unfamiliar environments. / True survivors immerse their senses in their surroundings and adapt to what's new. They open their eyes and ears, seeking clues about patterns defining the forest, glacier, ocean, or desert into which they have been cast. They take stock of resources and hazards, use natural objects to their advantage, find or make shelter, create fire. / Survivors also know how to add up the score when they play against Mother Nature. They assess what they need to survive and whether their environment can provide it. If they decide that their resources allow them to stay put, they devise ways to live until help arrives. If they've been dealt a poor hand, they figure out how to navigate toward civilization. / Saint-Exupéry began his ordeal believing that desert life "evaporates like a vapor." How could anything live in the desert, he asked himself. But as he examined the ground, he found burrows made by a fennec, a sand-dwelling fox. "My curiosity was aroused. What was there in the desert for these animals to live on?" he wondered. He followed tracks that led to more fennec holes, surrounded by shrubs and shells of snails. "And there I stayed a bit," he wrote, "ruminating and telling myself that a man was able to adapt himself to anything." He found joy in the fennecs' survival, and pushed on to find his own. Saint-Exupéry thought of his wife's grief and suffering should he die, and decided he must figure out a way to return to her. The odds were stacked against him, but he discovered the first rule of survival: Anything is possible.

RULE OF THREES

REMEMBER THE RULE of threes as you analyze your environment.

You'll die in three minutes without oxygen. If a member of your party has stopped breathing, he or she must receive immediate assistance. Emergency first aid takes precedence in a survival situation.

You'll need protection from wind, snow, desert sun, and other severe weather conditions within three hours, or face the consequences of exposure. Finding adequate shelter thus becomes the highest priority after assessing medical needs in many, but not all, survival situations. In a favorable, temperate climate, a warm fire and shelter from the elements may not be essential for maintaining life, but they boost the sense of well-being so necessary for survival.

You'll need water in three days to replace moisture you lose through sweat, respiration, urination, and defecation. You'll also need to sleep within three days to avoid the physically debilitating effects of exhaustion.

Although you'll be hungry soon after starting a survival situation, your body probably won't need food, strictly speaking, for three weeks. Most humans have reserves of fat that can keep them alive for weeks if they have enough water to drink. In addition, your body soon will stop sending "hunger" signals to the

brain after you stop eating. However, there is no denying that food, like shelter and fire, has potentially enormous psychological and physiological benefits for a group that finds itself stranded in the wilderness.

essentials

YOUR ENVIRONMENT

When you find yourself in a survival situation, answer these questions to make the best decisions.

IS THERE a water source? Is it adequate? Can you purify it?

IS THERE ENOUGH fuel for fire?

WILL YOU be able to stay warm and dry inside a shelter?

IS THERE ENOUGH TO EAT? Can you find additional food sources?

CAN YOU USE RESOURCES at hand to signal a rescue team?

ARE YOU SAFE from hazardous weather? From dangerous animals?

ARE THERE POTENTIAL health hazards if you stay? If you go?

WILL YOU be able to get a good night's rest?

EXPERT TIP Stop and try not to panic. Sit down and evaluate the circumstances. Try to determine the last location where you knew where you were. Orient yourself to the landscape by using a map (if you have one) or try to recognize familiar landmarks.

Girl Scouts.

FIRE

Fire is central to survival. First and foremost, its heat helps maintain body temperature. Failure to regulate the warmth of the body's core ranks as one of the most common causes of death in the wild. Knowing how to make fire can spell the difference between life and death. / In assessing the need for fire, it is best to follow the Boy Scout and Girl Scout motto: Be prepared. As Saint-Exupéry discovered, even the Sahara can become dangerously cold. / Fire has a variety of uses that are key to survival. Heat provides physical and mental comfort. Light and smoke attract attention over great distances, calling to search and rescue teams. A bright blaze drives away potential predators and pests. Heat dries clothes. Heat kills parasites in food and makes most animal and vegetable matter easier to chew and digest. Hot food also helps warm the body, stretching the calories that must be burned to maintain core temperature. Smoke and heat from a fire dry food to preserve it for later consumption. Fire can bake handmade clay cooking pots and harden or shape wood for tools or weapons. Fire boils water, sterilizing it for drinking and medical uses. / Fire also poses potential hazards. Untended, it can set a forest or grassland ablaze, threatening the lives it had been created to save. And the gaseous byproducts of combustion, left unvented in an enclosed space such as a tightly sealed tent, can cause suffocation.

FIRE'S THREE VARIABLES

FIRE HAS THREE COMPONENTS: fuel, air, and heat. Adjust the three variables to fit your purpose. More air makes a brighter signal fire. Less air tamps the flames, producing hot coals and extending the fire's duration. Different fuels produce different forms of smoke. Dark smoke is good for signaling during daytime, especially against a background of snow or sand. Light smoke stands out against dark trees, such as those in a coniferous forest.

BUILD AN A-FRAME FIRE

1. Make an "A" out of three pieces of fuel.

2. Lean kindling perpendicular against the crossbar of the "A" with an air space underneath it.

3. Pile dry tinder on top of the kindling.

4. Light tinder from bottom, through kindling. After tinder catches, slowly add kindling.

5. Gradually add fuel, leaving space for air. Add wood at regular intervals.

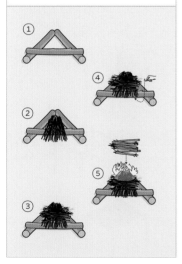

TYPES OF FIREWOOD

TINDER AND KINDLING start a blaze. Tinder is anything that glows upon accepting a spark. Natural sources include anything that is bone dry and has a high ratio of surface area to volume. Woody sources include birch bark and tiny sticks whose surface has been feathered with a knife. Other sources are burdock and cattail heads, moss, and dry leaves and grass.

Kindling—sticks the thickness of a pencil—will start to catch as tinder burns. As the fire grows, introduce increasingly larger kindling to expand the flames. Building the fire gradually ensures it will stay lit and get hot enough to ignite larger fuel.

Softwoods, like pine, burn quickly. Hardwoods, like maple, burn the longest and the hottest.

ADVERSE FIRE CONDITIONS

>>> Wind: Light fire in a trench or in a hollow dug into the side of an earthen bank, with exit hole for ventilation.

>>> Damp ground or shallow snow: Light fire atop a layer of rocks or earth laid on a floor of green logs.

>>> Deep snow and swampland: Elevate fire off the ground, using a "temple" fire platform.

>>> Rain: Build fire under a slanted tarp.

EXPERT TIP Hardwoods, such as oak, hickory, birch, ash, eucalyptus, and mesquite, produce a long-burning fire with lasting coals. Softwoods, such as pine, spruce, cedar, and aspen produce a quick, hot fire and provide excellent fuel for starting a long-burning fire with harder wood.

Girl Scouts.

BUILDING A FIRE IN RAIN

DON'T LET A LITTLE RAIN stop you. Use sticks and rope to set up a tarp at an angle over your fire site, close to the ground, but high enough that flames won't burn it once your fire is lit.

Split a thick pine log to build a fire from the dry interior side. Once lit, the resin will burn even in direct rain. Holding the log under the tarp, dig into the dry inner part to shave off dry tinder. Unless the log has been long submerged, the inside will be dry. Collect kindling from areas sheltered from rain such as under dense brush.

OTHER TYPES OF FUEL

ALTERNATIVE SOURCES of fuel include dried animal dung, peat, and coal. Also, engine oil, antifreeze, and tires burn and give off heavy black smoke. If natural tinder is scarce, try rubbing petroleum jelly into cotton balls or pocket lint.

In the Libyan desert, Saint-Exupéry burned the splintered wing of his airplane using gas drained from the engine. He added bits of magnesium from the other wing to create a bright, white flame visible over immense distances.

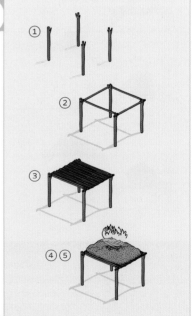

how to

MAKE A TEMPLE FIRE

1. Drive four green sticks—each three to four inches in diameter, two to three feet long, and with forked ends—into wet or snow-covered ground.

2. Lash green crosspieces between the tops of the four sticks, using the forks to help hold the crosspieces in place.

3. Place layer of closely packed green logs (so as not to burn) atop the crosspieces.

4. Cover green logs with several inches of earth.

5. Light fire atop the elevated earthen base and suspend cooking pot over fire with a pole supported by two Y-shaped branches.

MAKE A TEPEE FIRE

1. Dig a shallow square into dry earth.

2. Cover the bottom of the hole with a layer of green sticks.

3. Create a cone-shaped "tepee" of small, dry kindling by standing sticks on end and balancing tops against each other.

4. Add a protective rock wall on one side of tepee if necessary to shelter it from wind.

5. Leave a hollow space at the bottom of the tepee for tinder, and an opening where you can add more.

6. Slowly build the thickness of the tepee adding more sticks.

7. Place plenty of dry tinder inside the tepee.

8. If you have a candle, light it with a match to extend initial burn; use candle to light tinder.

9. Add more tinder as needed to increase the flames, creating oppotunity for the larger sticks to catch fire. Once fully lit, the tepee will create a large fire, evenutally burning with great heat. The longer and larger it burns, the hotter the fire will become. The green wood platform will eventually burn, so monitor the fire carefully.

STAR FIRE

A STAR-SHAPED FIRE of hardwood logs will burn for hours. To make a star fire, arrange four logs in the shape of a "plus" or cross sign, and set fire in the center. As the ends of the logs burn away, push the logs closer together to maintain the flames, or leave them apart to create coals for cooking.

Fires should never be left unattended. Make sure to put out the fire by sprinkling with water and stirring with a stick until the coals are not hot.

essentials

MAKING FIRE WITHOUT MATCHES OR A LIGHTER

You never know when these skills will come in handy.

FOCUS SUNLIGHT on tinder with a magnifying glass.

USE BOW AND DRILL to create heat from friction.

USE HAND DRILL with softwood spindle and hardwood fireboard to create sparks.

USE FLINT and steel, metal match, or magnesium rod and striker.

USE SPARKS from car battery.

SHELTER

Shelter helps regulate the body's core temperature. It is essential for staying warm in cold climates, cool in hot ones, and dry in rainy ones. A good shelter is large enough for a comfortable night's sleep, but small enough to be snug and warm. / A substantial shelter protects against animals, mosquitoes, and other pests; shields against wind and rain; and promotes a deep sleep, which is crucial for maintaining energy and a positive attitude. / Deciding on the proper type of shelter requires an assessment of terrain, climate, season of the year, and available resources. Victims of a plane or car crash may find the wrecked vehicle, if it is in no danger of catching fire, better than anything they can find or make. Those cast into a survival situation after dark may have to use any available space and await daylight to search for better shelter. Caves, walls of piled rocks, and hollows in the ground reduce the bite of wind. Beware low and high ground. Cold air and frost tend to collect in depressions, which may make for an uncomfortable night's sleep. The highest ridges or hilltops, on the other hand, are likely to be raked by winds.

SHELTER REQUIREMENTS

WINTER SHELTERS should be designed to retain heat while being open to ventilation. Summer shelters should protect against rain and insects.

In general, entrances should face east to catch the rising sun, but shelters in a northern temperate zone should have a clear exposure to the south to catch maximum light and heat.

Shapes and materials can vary widely as conditions and resources change.

Consider the spectrum of Native American shelters: They ranged from igloos to thatched huts, from earth lodges to skin-covered tepees.

Unless you are thrown into a survival situation with no chance to prepare or pack gear, tents generally are the best portable shelter option. Tents deflect rain and wind, trap body heat, provide a bit of privacy, and protect you and your gear from insects and other small pests.

SHELTER DECISIONS

CHOOSING THE BEST shelter requires you to evaluate the likelihood of rescue and how much time you have to work before it gets dark. Constructing a shelter, requiring a significant investment of time, makes sense if you plan to wait for help to arrive or need to heal from injury before moving on. Assembling a series of temporary shelters is a better alternative for those attempting to walk more than one day to safety.

Some shelters, such as tents, fit into either situation—good for long- or short-term living. If only an hour or two of daylight remains and no tent is available, a simple shelter made from a pile of forest debris, overhanging branches, or a stretched poncho may have to suffice for one night.

If you're not carrying shelter materials, evaluate your surroundings to decide on the best materials at hand. These may include branches, snow, sand, and leaves.

NATURAL SHELTERS

>>> Caves and crevices in rock walls (beware of making fires in small caves as the flame will quickly use up available oxygen)
>>> Bed of dry needles beneath closely spaced evergreen boughs
>>> Tree roots and fallen tree trunks, augmented with roof of sticks and grass
>>> Trench scooped out of sand and covered with brush or tarp
>>> Snow trenches and tree pits—snow-free areas around base of tree

EXPERT TIP When selecting a natural formation, stay away from low ground such as ravines, narrow valleys, and creekbeds. Low areas collect the heavy cold air at night and are therefore colder than the surrounding high ground. Thick, bushy, low ground also harbors more insects.

U.S.ARMY

UNDERSTANDING TYPES OF TENTS

TUBE TENTS ARE LIGHT, easy to rig, and deflect wind. One-person versions are ideal for backpackers but are not as warm as two-person versions, which double the amount of trapped body heat.

Wedge-shaped, two-person ridge tents have space for storage and cooking under the flysheet. They can be erected in a wide variety of conditions.

Domed tents rely on tri-pole construction for strength in high wind. Their sides can be strengthened by packing exterior walls with snow.

Geodesic dome tents are sturdy but must be lashed down in high winds.

SAPLING OR BRANCH SHELTER

THIS SHELTER OPTION won't work in desert or polar regions. However, for hikers who get lost in the woods, it's a practical way to take advantage of readily available building materials: young trees, sticks, leaves, and grass. Start by choosing two roughly parallel lines of saplings. If there are no trees small enough, drive pliable branches into the ground.

Clear the ground between the lines. Tie the tops of saplings or branches together to form a frame for a curved roof, like that of a quonset hut.

Place a waterproof barrier such as a tarp over the frame. It could be as simple as a plastic sheet. Weigh down the edges of the sheet with rocks to keep it in place.

If no artificial roofing material exists, you can weave a roof to protect you from rain by forming a lattice of sticks. Fill in the lattice with leaves, grass, and turf.

EXPERT TIP Look for tracks, scat, scratches in the soil, or other signs that an animal has used the shelter recently. If not, and you decide that the shelter is suitable, you should leave some sort of sign, such as a piece of clothing, outside the shelter to alert searchers.

Girl Scouts.

how to

MAKE A CIRCULAR STONE SHELTER

1. Find a natural, dry hollow in the ground.

2. Build up a low wall of stones around the hollow to make enough room to sit inside. Don't make it too big; large shelter spaces do not retain heat well, especially if the ground is already cold.

3. Cover the circular space with a lattice of branches, interwoven with leaves and other light, organic material that will deflect rain.

4. Caulk the stone walls with a mixture of mud and leaves.

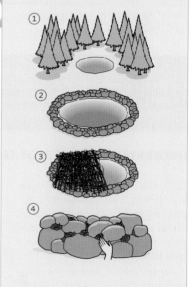

essentials

SHELTER DOS AND DON'TS

Remember these simple concepts to make the most effective shelter.

DO: ALLOW yourself plenty of time before sunset to begin making your shelter.

DO: SITE your shelter on flat ground with a water source nearby.

DO: BUILD near fuel source for fire.

DO: MAKE your shelter a comfortable size—not too big or small.

DO: BUILD near open spaces where you can set up signals for rescuers.

DO: REMEMBER to provide ventilation, even in cold weather.

DON'T: SITE your shelter in a relatively low or high spot.

DON'T: ERECT shelter near a lone tree; it will attract lightning.

DON'T: SITE your shelter in the center of a forest, where you cannot be seen from the air.

DON'T: BUILD shelter in an avalanche or flash flood zone.

DON'T: BUILD shelter on a game trail; you are inviting predators to visit.

DON'T: LIGHT a fire inside your shelter unless you are certain free air circulation will prevent buildup of toxic fumes.

LONG-TERM SHELTER

MOST OF THE SHELTERS described in this book are intended for short-term occupation. However, if you decide that any immediate search for you is likely to have been abandoned and you consider it unwise to move, you should build a comfortable, sturdy shelter—and wait.

Long-term shelters include caves and huts of wood, rushes, and/or sod.

Caves are permanent homes to many people worldwide. Caves above a valley floor are likely to be dry and cool. Some even have interior water. Partially seal the entrance with rocks or wood to keep out the wind.

Logs can be placed atop one another in interlocking patterns to form the frame of a hut. Use mud, leaves, and sod to chink the gaps.

Rushes make a strong building material when bundled together. When tied with a clove hitch knot, they can support a roof.

Sod is an excellent building material. Cut it into rectangles and use them like bricks. Pioneers built sod homes in the Midwest that are still warm and sturdy after more than a century.

NAVIGATION

Waiting to be rescued is usually the smart thing to do, but sometimes you must move on. Perhaps nobody knows you're in trouble, you're stuck in a harsh environment that doesn't supply you with water and food, or you know that what lies over that next chain of mountains is better than where you are now. / You'll need navigation skills. You may have to read a map and compass. You may need to interpret a readout from a global positioning system. You may need to follow natural or artificial signs that mark trails through difficult terrain. / Smart travelers examine their intended routes before setting out. They note the direction of rivers, the location of high ground, and other significant features of the terrain. However, you may be thrust into a survival situation without any knowledge of the landscape and its challenges. If that happens, you'll need to read the terrain. Can you walk along a high ridgeline and see the land in all directions? Can you follow a river as it seeks the lowest route through rocky terrain? Can you interpret the sun and stars to figure out the four points of the compass? Can you physically trek through snow and ice, or powdery desert sand, or along scree-covered mountain slopes? / Even if you stay put, you may need navigation skills. Your own personal navigational aids—whether drawn on paper, marked with blazes or cairns, or simply committed to memory—may take you through dense forests or confusing canyons and allow you to return to reliable sources of food and water. / Modern navigation devices are nice, but as with all equipment carried into the wilderness, it's good to have a backup. Compasses may become difficult to read in high latitudes through magnetic deviation and occasional geomagnetic disturbances. Electronic position-indicating tools may lose battery power. Stars, however, always point the way on a clear night.

NAVIGATIONAL AIDS AND DEVICES

MAPS, COMPASSES, and global positioning systems are common tools for planning and following a route.

Topographic maps are particularly useful for hikers. Such maps represent the height of terrain by connecting points of equal altitude with lines. Choosing the right scale is important; maps that cover hundreds of miles may not show important geographic features. A useful scale for people on foot is 1:50,000, meaning that every foot on the map represents 50,000 feet on Earth's surface.

Compasses point toward magnetic north, which varies from true north. They are powerful navigational tools, especially when accounting for their magnetic variance.

Global positioning systems have revolutionized navigation on land and sea. Handheld units receive microwave signals from orbiting satellites and interpret them to locate the receiver's location by latitude and longitude, which can be plotted on a map. Unless the satellite signals are blocked by terrain such as canyon walls, the precision attained by multiple signals on civilian GPS systems generally provides a reading accurate to within 50 horizontal feet.

KNOW YOUR MAP'S GRID LINES

HORIZONTAL AND VERTICAL lines on maps indicate latitude and longitude, which are useful for orienting yourself to north, south, east, and west as well as figuring distances and tracking linear progress. Vertical lines are called "eastings," and horizontal ones are "northings."

Grid references always provide the easting before the northing. A common grid reference is a six-digit number. The first three digits contain two digits for the vertical line reference plus the nearest tenth of an easting. The final three are the same information for the northing. Thus a grid reference of "123456" is a sort of shorthand for an easting of 12.3 and a northing of 45.6.

A topographic map produced by the U.S. Geological Survey most often has a line for true north (the pole), magnetic north, and grid north. You may choose any one of these three lines as navigational reference, as long as you're consistent with map, GPS, and compass.

TYPES OF MAPS

>>> **Mercator:** Projects Earth's spherical surface onto a cylinder wrapped around the Equator; scale correct only at Equator, longitude lines very distorted near poles.
>>> **Lambert conformal conic projection:** Projects Earth's surface onto a cone with apex over one of the geographic poles.
>>> **Universal Transverse Mercator (UTM) grid:** Places grid lines on a projected map to form a series of identical squares; easy to understand and use.
>>> **Globe:** The most accurate way to map the surface of a sphere.

BE COMPASS COMPETENT

THERE'S TRUE NORTH, which is the pole. There's "grid north," which is indicated by the eastings of grid maps. And then there's magnetic north. That's what a compass needle indicates.

The difference between true north and magnetic north usually is inconsequential near the Equator but significant close to the poles. Magnetic variation often is indicated at the foot of a map. The difference must be added or subtracted from a compass bearing to give a proper directional reading. If a map lacks an indication of magnetic variation, point your compass at Polaris. The angle between the needle and the compass's "N" is local magnetic variation.

Plot your course on a map, taking note of significant terrain features. Note your bearing, and follow it with your compass. As you hike, compare the terrain you encounter with your map and compass bearing to verify your course.

If you are lost, take a "back bearing" on an unusual feature such as a saddle, which appears as a figure eight on a contour map. Rotate the compass dial until its north arrow lines up with north as indicated by the needle. Place the compass on the contour lines indicating the saddle on the map, and then rotate it so the north arrow points toward grid north. Draw the back bearing line along that bearing. Take another back bearing on a second topographic feature roughly 90 degrees from the first. When that feature's back bearing is drawn on the map, your position will be indicated where the lines cross.

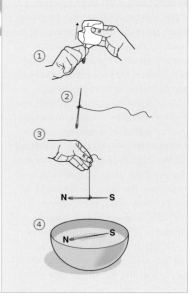

how to

MAKE A COMPASS

❶ Smoothly stroke a needle or razor blade in one direction 50 to 100 times with a piece of silk or a magnet.

❷ Tie a piece of thread around the middle of the needle.

❸ Dangle the needle so it swings to point toward magnetic north.

❹ Alternative: Float a magnetized needle in a bowl of water. Place the needle on top of a bit of light organic matter and let it move freely.

FOLLOW A "HANDRAIL"

BEARINGS ARE UNLIKELY to be precise on most compasses, and following them may put you up to ten degrees off your intended course. Over great distances, this could cause you to miss a particular point, such as a fork in a road or a campsite established on the edge of a river. In order to not miss your destination, aim deliberately to the left or right, and then walk in the direction of that bearing. This is particularly useful if your destination is distant and hidden by trees or hills. Take a bearing toward a linear feature such as a road, ridge, or river that runs along or near where you want to go. When you reach that line, turn left or right and follow it like a handrail. This "deliberate offset" is actually a programmed error in your bearings that you turn to your advantage. When you reach the river or other linear feature, you know you must turn left or right to find your destination. Note: The farther you are from the point you wish to reach, the more you must aim to left or right to avoid missing it.

EXPERT TIP Somewhere north of Canada's Hudson Bay lies the center of a natural magnetic field strong enough to pull the top of a compass needle toward itself. This area is called magnetic north and is more than 1,000 miles away from the North Pole, or true north.

WALK IN A STRAIGHT LINE

TAKE CONTINUAL BEARINGS with your compass to maintain a straight line as you walk long distances. Humans tend to veer slightly to the left or right as they walk as a result of imbalance, the difference in the length of their legs, and their favoring a dominant eye. The deviation is not noticeable over short distances but may cause a person to walk in a circle after a few hours.

Whenever possible, follow established paths and hike in single file to minimize impact.

USE YOUR WATCH
AS A COMPASS

ANALOG WATCHES—the old-fashioned kind that have hands—function as compasses when combined with the movement of the sun.

In the Northern Hemisphere: Point the hour hand toward the sun. Find 12 o'clock. Bisect the angle formed by 12 o'clock and the hour hand with an imaginary line. That line points south.

In the Southern Hemisphere: Point the 12 on the watch face toward the sun. Bisect the angle formed by the 12 and the hour hand with an imaginary line. That line points north.

Don't feel bad if you wear a digital watch: You can make it work as a compass, too. First, figure what the hands of an analog watch would look like if it represented the current time. Sketch that watch face on the ground, pointing the hour hand for the current time toward the sun (Northern Hemisphere only; see rules for Southern Hemisphere, above). Fill in the rest of the hours. Bisect the angle between the current hour and the 12. That line points south.

GPS NAVIGATION

A HANDHELD GPS simplifies navigation when its longitude and latitude readouts are plotted on a topographic map. (Some GPS models contain an electronic map, but it may not provide enough detail to be useful in a survival situation.) Each reading should be marked on a map to indicate progress along the line of travel.

essentials

GPS BASICS

A handheld global positioning system is an invaluable navigation tool.

GPS READOUT does not indicate changes in terrain; cliff or ravine in line of movement does not show up on-screen.

GPS CAN HELP you follow a straight route; it will not indicate the easiest one.

STUDY YOUR MAP to look for good places to change direction, and enter GPS coordinates.

IF GPS FAILS, use compass bearings and dead reckoning.

AVOID ERROR common to GPS navigation by aligning map and GPS to common reference system, such as World Geodetic System (WGS) 1984.

USE YOUR GPS in conjunction with a compass. Some compasses now on the market are designed to work with GPS receivers.

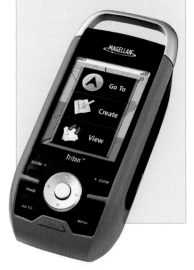

NAVIGATE BY SUN AND PLANT SHADOWS

NO COMPASS? No problem. The well-ordered universe contains its own compass rose.

The sun moves up and down the horizon as the seasons change, but it rises due east and sets due west on the vernal and autumnal equinoxes, in late March and late September. At midday in the Northern Hemisphere, sunlight comes from the south and casts shadows pointing north. Heat and light from the south also affect plant growth, which can be examined for clues on cloudy days. Thicker leaf and needle growth is likely on the south side of trees, particularly in high latitudes. In the mountains, some species of trees favor southern exposure, and others favor the shade on the north side of a ridge. Plants may also lean toward the sun. Be aware that strong winds also may bend plants.

Use your judgment to figure if sun or wind has pushed or pulled plants in one direction.

how to

MAKE A SHADOW STICK

1 Use a pebble to mark the tip of a vertical stick's morning shadow.

2 Draw a circle on the ground around the stick, using the pebble as a point on the arc and the stick as center. Pivot a string to draw the circle.

3 As the sun ascends, the stick's shadow shrinks. After midday, the shadow lengthens. Mark the spot where the growing shadow touches the arc in the afternoon. Now, two pebbles, widely spaced, form an east-west line. West is marked by the first pebble.

NATURE'S DIRECTIONAL CUES

>>> Shadows cast at noontime point north in Northern Hemisphere, south in Southern Hemisphere.
>>> Moss and lichen favor shady sides of objects—generally north and northeast.
>>> On hills in Northern Hemisphere, look for deciduous trees on south slope, evergreens on north slope.
>>> In Rocky Mountains, look for limber pines on south slope, Englemann spruce on north.
>>> In deserts, the barrel cactus leans south.
>>> If you know dominant wind direction, check for how trees lean.
>>> On slopes facing sun, greatest snowmelt occurs on trunks' south side.

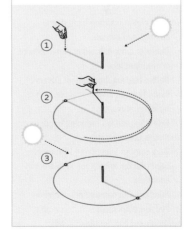

USING TOPOGRAPHIC MAPS

TOPOGRAPHIC MAPS, which reveal features of the terrain, are extremely useful in the wilderness. If you can match the landscape features you see with their symbols on a map, you can locate yourself, check your progress toward a desired goal, and navigate around cliffs, canyons, and other potential obstacles.

Elevation above sea level is represented by contour lines that connect points of equal height. Contour lines usually are printed in brown. The map indicates the vertical distance between two contours. Analyzing the contour lines between your point of origin and where you want to go will reveal how much you must climb or descend, as well as the presence of obstacles such as steep cliffs or deep canyons. Figure the distance between two points by measuring with a ruler and comparing with map scale indicators.

Take good care of your topographic maps. Help them last a long time by properly folding them and carrying them in waterproof packets. You can buy waterproof maps or pay to have paper maps covered with water-resistant, transparent coatings.

TERRAIN MARKINGS ON TOPOGRAPHIC MAPS

>>> **Blue.** Water, including lakes, rivers, streams, and swamps
>>> **Blue with cross-hatched or dotted interior.** Intermittent lake
>>> **Dotted blue line.** Intermittent stream
>>> **Black.** Features made by people, such as buildings, dams, etc.
>>> **Green.** Vegetation, including woods
>>> **Brown.** Contour lines
>>> **Dark contour lines.** Every fifth contour line is darker to help you keep track of elevation
>>> **Numbers with contour lines.** Elevation
>>> **Red line.** Main roads
>>> **Broken red line.** Secondary roads

READING CONTOURS

>>> **Valleys.** Lines form a V or U shape
>>> **Hill.** Represented on map as series of concentric circles or ovals
>>> **Summit.** Represented by the smallest loop inside concentric circles or ovals
>>> **Depression.** Represented as the smallest loop inside other circles or ovals, with tick marks indicating low elevation
>>> **Gentle slopes.** Represented by lines roughly parallel and far apart
>>> **Steep slopes.** Represented by lines roughly parallel and close together
>>> **Cliff.** Contour lines merge; tick marks may indicate fall-off side
>>> **Ridge.** Look for long, thin ovals; sloping ridge bisects the ovals longitudinally

BASIC MAP DISTANCE MEASUREMENT

THE SCALE OF A MAP compares the distance on the map surface to the corresponding horizontal distance on the ground. This ratio is expressed as a "representative fraction," such as 1/62,500 or 1:62,500, which would indicate one unit on the map is the same as 62,500 units on the ground.

To figure distance on a map, measure between two points on the map with a ruler and multiply by the denominator of the representative fraction. If the map has a graphic scale, line up an edge of paper between the points you want to measure and make tick marks next to the points with a pencil. Move the paper next to the scale for a reading.

To measure distance along a winding river, put a tick mark on a piece of paper, place it over the start of the river's curve, and put a corresponding tick on map and paper. Align the paper with a relatively straight portion of the curve and make another set of ticks. Keep this up until you've covered the entire curve, then move the paper alongside the scale for a reading.

how to

MEASURE DISTANCE TRAVELED

1 Determine your pace by estimating the length of your stride and dividing into 63,360 (number of inches in a mile). For example, at an average pace length of 30 inches, a hiker would average 2,112 paces per mile on flat ground.

2 Count paces as you go; for the example above, transfer a pebble from one pocket to another every 100 paces.

3 Once you've got 21 pebbles in the previously empty pocket (for the example pace length of 30 inches), put one pebble in a third pocket to keep track of miles.

4 After several hours, determine your average miles walked per hour. Calculate future travel over the same type of terrain by multiplying hours walked by average miles per hour (allowing for stops, difficult terrain).

CARRY AN EXTRA MAP

IF YOU HAVE A CRUCIAL MAP, make a photocopy or buy a spare in case the original gets lost or damaged. Depending on the area, you may be able to print a sufficient supplemental map off the Internet. A second map, in smaller scale, is useful if you wander beyond the edge of your main map.

EXPERT TIP Determine how many normal strides it takes you to cover a certain distance. For example, 30 meters and 100 feet are used. Determine the paces in both feet and meters because some maps are given in feet (USGS Topographical Maps) while orienteering maps are drawn in meters.

Girl Scouts.

EXPERT TIP The main constellations to learn are the Ursa Major, also known as the Big Dipper or the Plow, and Cassiopeia. Neither of these constellations ever sets. They are always visible on a clear night. Use them to locate Polaris, also know as the polestar or the North Star.

U.S.ARMY

NAVIGATING BY THE STARS

IN THE NIGHT SKY, the constellation of Orion the Hunter is easy to find. The three stars that make up Orion's belt rise almost exactly due east and set almost exactly due west no matter what time of year and no matter where on Earth you observe them. How high Orion's belt ascends in the night sky depends on your latitude—at the Equator, it passes straight overhead, while at the poles it lies near the horizon.

The North Star, Polaris, points due north. In the Southern Hemisphere, the constellation of the Southern Cross points the way toward due south. (There is no southern counterpart to the North Star, so navigators use the long arm of the Southern Cross to find true south.)

Common stars also indicate direction. Except for Polaris, they wheel in a great arc across the sky as our planet rotates beneath them. Rough estimates of direction can be obtained by watching how the stars move overhead on a clear night. If they appear to rise, you are facing east. If they appear to fall, you are facing west. In the Northern Hemisphere, if they appear to move in a flat arc from left to right, you are facing south. Flat arcs from right to left indicate north. The last two directions are reversed in the Southern Hemisphere.

USING THE MOON

>>> A waxing or waning moon's illuminated side faces the sun; use that to find east or west.
>>> Draw a line from the top horn of a crescent moon to the bottom horn and extend it down to the horizon to find due south.
>>> When moon is full, it rises close to due east near vernal and autumnal equinoxes.
>>> The light and dark sides of the moon are separated by a line aligned north/south.

FINDING THE NORTH STAR

>>> Locate the Big Dipper.
>>> Draw a line between the two stars on the front edge of the Dipper, from bottom to lip.
>>> Extend the line four times the length of the original line segment.
>>> At the end of the line is Polaris.

SIGNALING

While awaiting rescue, try to attract attention. After rescuers know your location, you can pass along more detailed information, such as injuries and the need for food or water. The letters SOS have been a standard distress signal since the *R.M.S. Titanic* sank in 1912. They can be spelled out on the ground with logs, rocks, or cloth; transmitted by radio; or sent as Morse code (dot-dot-dot, dash-dash-dash, dot-dot-dot) by sound or light waves. Radio communicators aboard ships and planes typically use "Mayday," a phonetic spelling of the French "m'aidez" (help me), to indicate distress. / Survivors of plane and car crashes have access to a variety of signaling devices. Mirrors can be removed to reflect sunlight and direct it toward passing planes. Mirrors also can be improvised from any glass objects or polished metal. Sunlight bounced off mirrors can be seen up to 30 to 40 miles away under good atmospheric conditions, and a reach of 100 miles has occasionally been reported. / Fires make an excellent signal. They can be seen over extended distances during the night, and their pillars of smoke stand out in the daytime. Groups of three fires in a straight line indicate distress. Use your ingenuity to find fuel for signal fires. A wrecked vehicle contains materials that burn brightly and create smoke. Gasoline added to woodpiles will make them suddenly flare. Flares and flashlights from car trunks and glove compartments also can be used for signaling. Familiarize yourself with handheld flares to avoid firing them accidentally—they give out a bright, hot flame that can cause serious injury. Flares that can be fired into the air are visible over great distances. Some types of flares come with parachutes that extend their descent time, leaving them more time to burn in the sky and attract the attention of possible search-and-rescue teams.

Don't forget a portable cell phone charger—powered by the sun, hand-crank, or batteries.

COMMUNICATION DEVICES

DON'T OVERLOOK obvious communication devices. A cell phone or band radio in a car or truck is the easiest way to call for help, assuming signals are not blocked and receivers are within range.

Shortwave radios tend to get optimal reception outside urban areas because of less interference from electrical devices.

Satellite phones make telephone connections via orbiting geostationary communications satellites from virtually any spot on the planet's surface. They're an invaluable survival tool. Although their initial price and cost per minute make them too expensive for most people, satellite phones are likely to follow the cost curves of personal computers and other high-technology devices as they are refined and mass-produced.

Use your car radio to gather weather information that may affect survival plans, especially in desert terrain where rainstorms can cause flash flooding on the spot or dozens of miles away.

TOOLS FOR SIGNALING

>>> Whistles (see "How to Make a Whistle out of an Acorn Cap" on the opposite page)
>>> Metal objects, banged together or by a stick or rock
>>> Fires: Light can be seen during night, smoke during day
>>> Reflectors: mirrors, shiny metal
>>> Cloth laid out in shapes or letters
>>> Snow, branches, logs, or earth mounded and shaped into letters
>>> Flashlights, strobe lights
>>> Radios, cell phones, satellite phones
>>> Emergency satelite beacons

EXPERT TIP An emergency signal can be blowing a whistle, flashing a mirror, lighting a fire, or making a pile of rocks with a message attached. At night, send up a flare or use a flashlight as a beacon. The color royal blue, which is unusual in nature, is good for attracting attention.

American Red Cross

LEAVING CAMP? LEAVE A SIGNAL

IF YOU ABANDON your camp to walk toward civilization or if you leave the scene of a plane or car crash, leave information (see specifics below) for potential rescuers to find.

Think about making your messages easy to see from the air, and make supplemental messages that are easy to find by people on the ground. Make a large arrow of cloth or any material that contrasts with the dominant ground color and point it in the direction you took as you left camp. Put more arrows or other signs on the ground as you travel. They will help lead rescuers to you and also help you find your way back if you become lost or must return.

In your abandoned camp, leave messages in weatherproof, conspicuous places. The messages should give details about your group and its plans. Who is traveling with you? Where are you going? Is anyone hurt? Do you have enough food and water? Place these messages in trees, hang them from tripods, or put under a rock atop a cairn. Use markers to point to the messages; it's important they don't get overlooked.

how to

USE A SIGHTABLE MIRROR TO SIGNAL AIRPLANES

1. Point mirror toward sun. Look through sighting hole on back side; find circle of reflective mesh.

2. Gently jiggle mirror back and forth until you see a glowing ball on mesh.

3. Locate airplane inside sighting hole, without losing track of glowing ball.

4. Gently tilt the mirror to align the glowing ball atop the plane.

5. Rock the light back and forth across plane to avoid blinding pilot.

how to

MAKE A WHISTLE OUT OF AN ACORN CAP

1. Find a hollowed-out acorn cap with smooth interior and no holes or breaks.

2. Hold it between both thumbs and forefingers, with thumbs forming a V shape on top.

3. Blow into the V space between your thumbs. Adjust slightly until you are able to make a sharp, shrill sound.

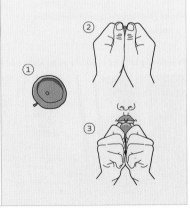

VISUAL SIGNALS

FIRE AND SMOKE can attract attention over great distances, particularly in regions where spotters are on the lookout for forest fires. Smoke signals have been seen as far away as 50 miles, and fires bloom like giant sunflowers at night. Fire, smoke, and light signals are enhanced when placed atop a ridge or hill.

If you believe rescuers are looking for you, have a pile of combustible material ready to ignite at a moment's notice. Start the fire when you hear an engine. Green branches produce smoke. A wet blanket can be used to contain the smoke and release it in puffs of three as an emergency signal. Burning a lone, dead tree in a clearing makes a particularly effective beacon.

Try to visualize how the Earth's surface appears from the air. Consider building mounds to cast shadows.

Arrange rocks, brush, snow, and earth to form shadow patterns in a commonly recognized distress signal, such as groups of three. Use space blankets or tarpaulins to spell out SOS or one of the symbols of the international ground-to-air code.

SIGNALING WITH FIRE

>>> Groups of three is a distress signal.
>>> Isolated tree fire also means distress.
>>> Put green boughs or oil on fire to make smoke.

essentials

INTERNATIONAL GROUND-TO-AIR CODE

Form the following letters on the highest and least-tree-covered point you can reach, using rocks, branches, colored material or clothing, lines drawn in dirt, sand, or snow, etc.

F: Need food and water

I: Serious injury; need medical attention or evacuation

X: Unable to move

ARROW: We are traveling in this direction

II: Need medical supplies

LL: All is well

To make signal fires as smoky as possible, pile high with green wood, leaves, and grasses.

PRECISION IN GROUND-TO-AIR SIGNALS

YOU CAN USE YOUR BODY to send simple messages to a pilot. The most important message—"Pick me up!"—is communicated by standing straight up with both arms extended vertically over the head. Memorize the basic ground-to-air codes or carry a guidebook containing the signals, such as this one, to remind yourself how to convey the correct message to a pilot in an emergency. It could save your life.

Be aware, too, that the wrong movement or body shape could have fatal consequences.

Carl McCunn, a Texas photographer, died in Alaska in 1981 because he gave the wrong signal at the wrong time. McCunn arranged for a bush pilot to drop him in the wilderness with 500 rolls of film and and enough provisions to last him for months, but forgot to arrange to be picked up before winter. A plane spotted him as his ammunition was running out, and he tried to signal that he needed help.

Unfortunately, as he recorded in his diary, he raised only one arm and pumped his fist—which the pilot interpreted as the universal signal for "I'm OK and don't need help." McCunn learned the correct signals later by examining a printed square of paper on the back of his Alaska hunting license. It had stick figures illustrating the most common ground-to-air body codes. "That's probably why after they flew somewhat away they returned for one more pass and on that one I gave no signal at all. (In fact I may have even turned my back to the plane as it passed.) They probably blew me off as a weirdo," he wrote.

essentials

BODY SIGNALS TO PILOTS

These codes supplement simple messages you can create with letters or arrows on the ground.

STAND STRAIGHT with arms extended straight up: Fly toward me or pick me up.

STAND STRAIGHT with arms parallel to ground: Hover, or we need medical help.

STAND STRAIGHT and flap arms: Descend.

STAND STRAIGHT with arms parallel to ground, then bent at elbow to bring hands toward head: Fly toward me.

SQUAT AND POINT with arms extended: Land in direction to which I'm pointing.

STAND STRAIGHT with arms overhead, rocking them from side to side: Do not attempt to land here.

LIE DOWN and extend arms over head: Need medical help.

STAND STRAIGHT with one arm overhead and the other pointing down: All is well.

AUDIBLE SIGNALS AND CODES

SOUNDS ARE GOOD for signaling over shorter distances. Sounds carry far over water, but trees, terrain, and weather conditions absorb and distort sounds over land. In the wilderness, most rescuers who responded to shouts or whistles made first contact only within 200 yards. In deserts, open sea, or polar regions, sounds are more effective.

The honking of a car horn or the report of a gun can attract attention over far greater distances. Striking two metal objects together or hitting a pole against a hollow log or tree spreads a distress call much farther than a human voice.

Whistles are good audio signaling devices over short distances because high-pitched sounds are easier to pinpoint than low ones; in addition, they do not tire the vocal cords.

Like light signals obscured by canyon walls or banks of trees, audio signals work best when they are not blocked. Send out audio signals in groups of three to indicate distress, or give the signal for SOS in Morse code—dot-dot-dot, dash-dash-dash, dot-dot-dot. Although Morse code has virtually disappeared from use, this combination of signals spelling out three letters is still widely recognized.

If you attempt to send an audio signal by radio, phone, or emergency beacon, don't waste the battery. If your message does not result in an immediate reply, switch off the device, wait an hour or two, and try again. Or signal when you hear a plane engine.

USE A SHORTWAVE RADIO

>>> Choose a shortwave radio that easily stays tuned to a specific frequency.

>>> Also look for models that tune in weak signals and reject unwanted ones.

>>> If you have one, use an exterior wire antenna to get the best reception.

>>> Disconnect external antenna during electrical storms.

>>> Tune in 31-meter and 41-meter bands; they are most popular and most likely to have listeners. Also try 19- and 25-meter bands.

>>> Avoid 13- and 16-meter bands if you find atmospheric disturbance.

>>> Broadcast emergencies at 15 minutes before and after the hour—an international silent period when you are most likely to be heard.

essentials

CELL PHONE AND RADIO DOS AND DON'TS

Proper use of a cell phone or radio can aid discovery and rescue.

DO: USE phones, radios on high ground.

DO: HIKE to ridge tops if signals are blocked in valleys.

DO: TUNE to channel 16 of VHF radio, the recognized emergency channel.

DO: TURN the VHF antenna perpendicular to an airplane flight line to maximize the signal.

DO: GIVE Mayday signal or SOS in groups of three.

DO: EMPLOY an external antenna, if you have one, to boost signals.

DO: CARRY extra batteries for your radio and signaling devices.

DON'T: WASTE battery power of electronic communication devices.

DON'T: TRY to send radio or phone signals in narrow canyons.

DON'T: EXPOSE radio or phone to moisture, wind, or sand.

DON'T: BROADCAST nonstop if you do not get a response.

DON'T: GIVE UP signaling; try varying times, channels, etc.

PERSONAL LOCATOR BEACON

PERSONAL LOCATOR beacons (PLBs) have recently become available to American citizens. Although they are expensive, they are powerful and accurate signaling devices.

When you buy a PLB, your personal frequency code is registered.

Carry it with you into the wild, even on routine trips, since emergencies are unpredictable. Take extra batteries, too. Some versions are smaller than a brick and weigh slightly more than a pound.

When you activate the beacon, it sends out two signals. The first, at 406 MHz, goes to a satellite alerting rescuers to your emergency. The second, at 121.5 MHz, attracts searchers on the ground. When coupled with a GPS program, the PLB can lead rescuers to within several dozen yards of your location.

TIPS FOR USING PLBS

>>> Sending out a false-alarm signal is punishable by hefty fines. Activate the beacon only in a real emergency.

>>> Store your PLB in its water-resistant cover.

>>> Register your emergency medical information when you buy a PLB; it will be available to the rescue team.

HOW I SURVIVED: KILLER BEES by JESÚS RIVAS

As a National Geographic explorer and an anaconda expert, I travel the flooded plains of Venezuela searching for, and studying, these deadly creatures. But the 20-foot serpents are not the only daily hazards I encounter. One day, at the height of the wet season in Venezuela, my friend

Alejandro was assisting me in searching for anacondas from a boat while I searched the riverbank on foot. Intent on my work, I lost sight of Alejandro on the boat. After a while, when I sought Alejandro, I was surprised to see the boat, empty, spinning in circles in the middle of the river around a dead tree. I called for Alejandro but received no answer. Finally I heard him yelling weakly from over 500 yards downstream of the abandoned boat. He shouted across the river that he had been attacked by killer bees and barely managed to escape by jumping into the water after "fighting" with them.

National Geographic grantee and biologist Jesús Rivas has been the subject of numerous National Geographic Television shows and *National Geographic* magazine articles.

In almost all confrontations between killer bees and people, the serious attacks are invariably a result of people accidentally doing exactly the wrong thing. Bees attack to defend the established nest from a potential enemy. When they sense a threat, the bees will make their presence known by buzzing and flying around you, as if to say, "Get

out of here." Leaving immediately tells them that you are not a threat. However, many people panic and instinctively begin to frantically swat and slap at the bees. This tells the bees you are indeed a threat. A hive may contain as many as 60,000 bees, so you have no hope of killing them all. Once you kill one, it will be very difficult to convince its sisters (all the workers are females) that you are not a threat. When a bee stings, it dies anyway; the ones that do not sting you but are only warning you do not deserve to die.

I knew that Alejandro needed to be taken to a hospital ASAP. However, the boat that was spinning by the nest of angry bees was our only means of transportation. I also knew the noise of the engine and the heat of the day anger the bees and made for a very inconvenient scenario for rescuing the boat. Loud noise angers bees that are already on the defensive. An instinctive response when bees attack is to make noise and start yelling and swearing from the pain of the stings. What you should do when bees attack is to yell "Bees!" once, loudly, to warn your companions. Then move away quickly— preferably by land rather than water, in order to avoid aquatic inhabitants, such as crocodiles, freshwater stingrays, and electric eels.

Alejandro had an undetermined number of stings, and he had no other hope than my rescuing the boat. I knew that in wet season the piranhas, although always present, would be at low density and unlikely to be a threat. I was not so confident, however, regarding the 3.5-yard-long Orinoco crocodile that I had just seen 100 yards away, not to mention the many other crocs that I had helped reintroduce to the area and were commonly seen in that stretch of river. Still, my major concern was the bees still buzzing over the boat. I yanked my straw hat down over my ears, secured my sunglasses, and swam to the boat; I made sure that the visor of my hat was too close to the

water for the bees to fly in, but open enough to let me breath and see where I was going. I approached the spinning boat and made a quick lunge over the back side and hit the off button of the engine. I ducked down again to my safe position in the water and heard an endless number of bees hitting my hat and buzzing threateningly around my head. I controlled the fear and resisted the temptation to fight them and thus expose my body over the water, hoping desperately that they didn't find the opening that I was using to breathe. Eventually I grabbed the keel of the boat and slowly dragged it down the river, away from the hive. After a few hundred yards, I was finally free of bees. When I found Alejandro I removed over 90 stingers from his face alone, and I could see a similar density of stings scattered over the rest of his head. His hands and arms were also covered with stings as a result of his trying to fight them off. I was certain that he had received no fewer than 300 stings. As we headed back his conditioned worsened—he was regurgitating, repeatedly and his pale face indicated that he was about to faint. Two hours later we were in the hospital, where the doctors, accustomed to this kind of emergency, treated him immediately. Fortunately, Alejandro was not allergic to bees and no further complications occurred. I wasn't sure if it was his hardy condition or pure stubbornness that kept him alive, but much later he told me that he had prayed to God that if he survived this attack, he would give up his bachelor days, return home, and marry his high school sweetheart.

He kept his word.

When naturalist Henry David Thoreau ventured into the Maine woods in the mid-1800s, he went forth with confidence. / He packed a tent, insect repellent, map, compass, plant books, ax, knife, provisions, and utensils. He paddled streams and lakes in a birch bark canoe, pitched camp near water's edge, and ate like a sylvan king. He and his companions supplemented their provisions with moose meat, fish, lily bulbs, "tree cranberries" (*Viburnum opulus*), hemlock tea, blueberries, and raspberries happily plucked along the portaging trails. "Another name for making portage would have been going a berrying," he wrote. / Thoreau knew others feared the forest. For many outsiders, the woods, while lovely, were also dark and deep. "I have made a satisfactory dinner off a dish of purslane which I gathered and boiled, yet men have come to such a pass that they frequently starve, not from want of necessaries but for want of luxuries," he said. He tellingly observed the word "savage" derives from *sylva*, Latin for "forest." / The woods can indeed be wild and dangerous. Yet of all Earth's climate zones, temperate forests are among the most hospitable for those who seek merely to survive—and who know what to do.

TEMPERATE FOREST

PREPARATION

Thousands of people get lost in the woods each year. Some die. Yet the means of obtaining food, water, fire, and shelter are all around them. In the 19th century, Lewis and Clark's expedition survived on pawpaw fruits and bitter snowberries, and eked out a year-round existence in the northern Plains and Rockies. Pioneers gathered chokecherries and serviceberries. Mountain men trapped and skinned beavers and then ate the fatty meat of their round bodies and flat tails. / Since then, much of North America's temperate zone, which extends from the Tropic of Cancer to just below the Arctic Circle, has been filled in with cities. Adventurers who get lost in the woods today know they probably are not far from civilization and are unlikely to face an extended ordeal, especially since deciduous and coniferous forests have plenty of water, plant life, and game. / Still, it makes sense to be prepared. Take a compass, maps, fire-making tools, water, and the other items recommended here. Finally, expect the unexpected: temperate forests can be cold, hot, wet, windy—all in one day.

ENVIRONMENTAL EXTREMES

CHALLENGES ARISE from weather that ranges from blistering summer heat to frigid winter cold, and from dry to wet. Weather extremes tend to be greatest far from the ameliorating effects of the world's oceans.

A specific location's mood can vary greatly, as outdoorsman Chris McCand-less discovered on an Alaskan sojourn. As chronicled in Jon Krakauer's book *Into the Wild*, the splashing brook McCandless crossed to enter the out-back in spring 1992 morphed into a dangerous torrent in late summer, stranding McCandless and contribut-ing to his eventual starvation.

PACKING TIPS

TEMPERATE FORESTS RANGE greatly in conditions, depending on season and location, so make sure to check weather averages and forecasts for your dates of travel. The body loses more than a quarter of its heat through an exposed head, so headgear is perhaps the most important layer. A wool covering is essential in for colder temperatures, while wide-brimmed hats shelter eyes from sun and rain. Cotton bandannas soaked in water provide quick cooling.

Footwear—shoes and socks—should be chosen for terrain, temperature, and durability. Heavier boots are necessary for high mileage but are unnecessary weight for shorter day hiking. Footwear should be well insulated and support the ankles and arches. Waterproof versions are important for most trips. Wear a thin layer of socks next to the foot to wick sweat away and decrease friction, and layer with a thicker wool or synthetic sock to provide cushioning and protection from the cold.

Layering clothes is as important in the temperate forest as in other environments. Start with silk or other breathable synthetic long underwear, followed by a second layer worn loose to trap insulating air, covering arms, wrists, and neck. The third layer, which absorbs moisture from the second layer, should be easy to remove to avoid overheating. A final, outer layer faces the elements and acts as a shell against rain, cold, or sun. It should breathe or have vents. Pants with zip-off legs in water-resistant fabrics are ideal for all temperatures. A hat shelters the eyes and helps regulate body temperature.

essentials

WHAT TO PACK

When packing, consider the weather forecast, site conditions, planned activities and personal comfort.

SHOES: Select appropriate boots for temperature, terrain; waterproof versions are best

SOCKS: Double layer (thin and thick)

UNDERWEAR: Consider climate; synthetic materials dry fastest

OUTER CLOTHING LAYERS: Should cover arms, wrists, and neck, be easily removable and breathable and act as a shell against rain, cold, or sun

PANTS: Convertible pants with legs that zip off/roll up to make shorts/capris in synthetic materials are a good all-purpose choice

HAT: Wool cap, brimmed hat, bandanna

HAND GEAR: Mittens, waterproof gloves

BACKPACK: Internal frame pack with chest and hip straps

SLEEPING BAG: Hooded, with temperature rating appropriate for conditions

BIVY SACK: Provides space to sit comfortably

TENT: Consider size, terrain, weight, ease of use

ADDITIONAL: Water purification system, knife, fire-making materials, cooking implements, survival kit, signaling mirror, whistle, map, compass, GPS, tarp, solar blanket

FIRE

Crack! That's the sound of dry branches breaking, a good indicator of wood that's ready for a fire. / You can't start a fire with damp, wet, or green wood. Branches and logs on the forest floor tend to absorb water from the ground, so gather firewood from dead, gray branches still attached to standing trees. Even in wet weather, wind desiccates branches surrounded by air, and the inside of a branch stays dry even if the exterior is wet. / As with all fires, you'll need to start with tinder and kindling. (See Chapter 2 for basic fire-making techniques.) You'll need a grapefruit-size ball of tinder, which you can gather from a variety of plants. Dry grass, cattail down, and the outer bark of red cedar trees make good tinder, as does the inner bark of the maple. Henry David Thoreau's Indian companion in Maine swore by the bark of white pine, hemlock, and canoe birch trees when collecting the best tinder and kindling. Dead logs on the ground may contain dusty inner bark; dry, rotten wood. Dry leaves and sticks can be crumbled or chopped. All make good tinder, which should be fine as a "matchstick" to accept a spark.

LIGHTING A FIRE

MAKING A SPARK requires friction. A match will do. So will the wheel and flint of an old cigarette lighter, which will shed sparks even if all the liquid fuel is gone. Striking a flint with steel also creates sparks, and using a magnesium alloy as a flint ensures large flashes. Magnesium-block fire starters are sold commercially. The silver-colored bars come with a black, rough striking tool embedded in one side. While a block of magnesium won't easily burn, the shavings scraped off its surface with an old knife can be placed in a depression in the middle of a dry pile of tinder to catch fire. Magnesium burns at an astonishing 5,400°F, pouring a tremendous amount of heat in a hurry into your tinder.

Build your fire a safe distance from your tent and keep the flap zipped against smoke.

EXPERT TIP Leave an air space under the top bar of a triangle of kindling. Lay a handful of tinder upright against the top stick. Hold a match beneath the tinder until the flame burns up through the tinder, then place additional tinder and kindling onto the fire.

Girl Scouts.

THOREAU'S MATCHES

MATCHES WON'T BURN when wet. When Thoreau asked his Indian companion how he made fire in the Maine woods, in response, the Indian brought out a box of friction matches, flint, steel, and tinder from a yellow birch tree. "But suppose you upset [your canoe], and all these and your powder get wet," Thoreau asked. "Then," the Indian said, "we wait till we get to where there is some fire." Thoreau responded by triumphantly holding out his own vial of matches, "stoppled water-tight," and announcing that even if the canoe capsized and they and all of their gear were thrown into the water, they would have dry matches. The Indian, Thoreau reported, "stared without saying a word."

how to
CUT WOOD

1. Snap off dead branches.

2. Use a wire saw or ax to cut dry tree limbs.

3. A big, solid knife can function as an ax. Put the knife against the wood and hit it with a rock.

4. Place your feet squarely in nonskid shoes on level ground. Swinging an ax safely requires good footing.

5. Hold ax with both hands and swing with smooth, brief strokes to stay on target.

FIRE SAFETY

DON'T BUILD a fire where the flames could easily catch on surrounding vegetation, such as drought-stricken grasses and other vegetation, and directly beneath tree branches. Keep the fire small enough that you can easily control it.

Winds can make it difficult to light a campfire, but once ablaze the flames can easily spread. A foot-deep trench will shelter fire from wind yet provide enough air for combustion. Rock walls made of large rocks and mud also can shelter a fire from wind. Don't use shale or other porous rocks that might explode when heated.

Wet all campfire ashes to be sure they don't smolder and reignite; however, do not drown them so as to make it difficult to light your next fire in the same place.

If a campfire jumps to surrounding brush, immediately smother it. Forest fires move quickly, especially in wind. If wind pushes fire away from you, run into the wind. If wind pushes fire toward you, seek a fire break, such as a river, large clearing, or ravine.

WATERPROOFING MATCHES

MATCHES BURN LONGER and repel water if covered with paraffin wax. You can prepare matches at home, before your trip. To coat wooden matches, melt candle wax in a double boiler. The inner pot should be old and no longer used for cooking, or well lined with aluminum foil. Drop the matches into the wax and leave them for a few seconds. Remove with tweezers and let them dry, heads up, by sticking their bottoms into a piece of foam plastic.

When the wax dries, put the matches in a match safe—a small, watertight container with a lid. For safety matches, glue a piece of striking material to the inside top of the lid. The match safe will keep contents safe from water. Put enough matches in the safe to fill it without cramming them tightly. Ideally, a match should not stick, and should shake free into the palm of your hand. Scratch the wax off match head with your fingernail before striking.

DEALING WITH DAMP MATCHES

>>> Roll damp match in your hair; static electricity can help dry it.
>>> Strike damp match at a sharp angle instead of dragging it perpendicularly.
>>> When damp match ignites, light a candle or other longer-burning object, to buy time to catch your tinder on fire.

how to

BUILD A HEAT REFLECTOR

1 Next to your campfire, but outside flammable range, pound two pairs of stakes into the ground, about three feet apart.

2 Stack branches tightly on top of one another between the stakes and pack tightly to create a solid wall.

3 Secure each pair of stakes at the top by tying them together with twine, or rope made from grasses or plants (see "How to Make Rope from Natural Materials" in Chapter 1)

4 If possible—space and materials permitting—build another identical reflector on the opposite side of the fire. Sit with your back to one reflector, facing the fire.

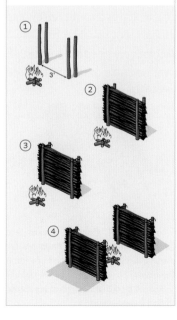

USE A HEAT REFLECTOR

REFLECTORS CONCENTRATE the heat of a fire. Sit on one side of a fire and fashion a reflector on the other side. The reflector not only will increase the heat you feel but also channel smoke upward. For even greater heat, have a boulder or tree stump at your back to act as a second reflector.

You can make your own reflector, or pair of reflectors, out of wood, as shown at left, or create a natural reflector out of a rock wall or large tree stump. Another method creates a high wall of logs slightly angled above the fire. Start by pounding two short stakes a few feet from the fire site. Then pound a second, longer set of stakes much closer to the fire site so they line up with the short stakes. Angle two green logs so they are braced against the short stakes, lean into the long stakes for support, and extend above the fire site. Stack green logs horizontally against the tilted beams to make an angled reflector. Such a device will not only increase the heat felt on the opposite side of the fire but also increase the fire's burn time.

So-called space blankets, used in medical emergencies to conserve body heat, also make good reflectors. These sheets of Mylar plastic coated with aluminum are lightweight, easily folded and carried, and astonishingly efficient at reflecting heat. Note that if the metallic coating has worn away, the blanket has lost its heat-reflecting properties. Hang the space blanket on the opposite side of your campfire in whatever shape best reflects the heat toward you. Tie it using a knot as is shown in the appendix of this book rather than by making a hole. Other things to use as reflectors are pieces of wreckage, especially large metal parts.

WATER

Gravity draws rainwater toward the sea. Look for water in low places in the forest, such as in valley bottoms, at the bottom of cliffs, and in rocky pools and crevices. If you are fortunate enough to be near a stream, draw water upstream from camp. Wash clothes and use the latrine downstream. / In winter, snow and ice can be collected and heated for water. They should not be melted in the mouth, however, as they may contain impurities that cause disease. In addition, the heat required to melt frozen water may seriously reduce the body's core temperature, causing physical stress. / In other seasons, green vegetation is a sign of water. In grasslands, a line of willow trees indicates a water channel. / Water in the wild is almost certain to be contaminated with microorganisms. Water can be purified in many ways. Commercial filters strain out microbes or treat raw water with chemicals. Bottled iodine in a 2 percent solution or chlorine tablets can be added to water to kill harmful bacteria. / Boiling water to purify it eliminates iodine's distinctive taste. Microbes are killed at about 180°F. As the boiling point of water varies with altitude, it is safest to boil water for ten minutes and let it cool before drinking.

FOLLOW ANIMALS TO WATER

ANIMALS NEED WATER just as you do, so keep eyes peeled for wildlife that may lead you to moisture.

Bees and flies normally stay within a couple of miles of their nests and must have access to water.

Listen for frogs when darkness falls; they, too, stick close to water.

Grazing animals drink at dawn and dusk. Watch for convergence of tracks in mud or dirt. Caution: Snakes and large carnivores know that finding water means finding food. Don't become their prey.

Follow a trail of ants climbing a tree to find a water deposit.

Mountain springs and glacial streams are relatively pure, but beware ground contaminants.

EXPERT TIP The American Red Cross recommends having a gallon of pure water a day per person for drinking and sanitary use. If you plan to store water for a while, use a food-grade–quality container, such as a 2-liter bottle with a screw-cap lid.

American Red Cross

KNOW THESE DRINKABLE WATER SOURCES

DON'T ASSUME that even the most sparkling of streams is pure unless you have recent evidence to the contrary. Purify water you collect in the wild by straining and boiling it, or by using a filter and chemical treatment.

Water is common on mountains in the form of melting snow or glacier ice. Through ice and snow are pure as they fall, they pick up contaminants when they hit the ground and, upon melting, flow over it.

Water collects at the bottom of hills, ravines, and canyons. Lines of green vegetation signal its presence. On flat land, look for the crooked lines of brush and willow to signal creeks and rivers. Rain also collects in stone basins, large leaves, and hollow trunks.

Do not attempt to use water that has a chemical sheen or smell.

WATER YOU CAN DRINK

>>> Rainwater from recent showers
>>> Snow or ice, bright white, not gray or tinted
>>> Dew on plants
>>> Plants with cavities carrying moisture
>>> Beware lakes and streams, as their raw water is likely to be contaminated with microbes

GET WATER FROM LEAVES, VINES, AND DEW

IN CLIMATES with hot days and cool nights, water vapor in the atmosphere condenses as the temperature drops. It can be licked or wiped off a metal object, such as a car hood.

Trees draw water from beneath the surface of the earth. This water can be collected by tying a plastic bag around a limb containing healthy leaves. The leaves' respiration will condense on the inside of the bag and collect at the bottom. Even leaves cut or plucked from trees and shrubs will produce moisture inside a bag. Don't let the leaves touch the bag; instead, elevate them with some rocks and raise the top edge of the bag with a stick.

Some plants are natural water collectors. The appropriately named pitcher plant collects water in a reservoir. The water must be strained to remove insects. Vines contain moisture that drips when cut. Make the cut as high as you can, as capillary action will pump water upward. Angle the cut end of the vine over a container to collect the water that drips out. Beware, as some varieties of vine are poisonous. Don't drink any milky fluid from a vine, or any liquid that causes skin irritation. If unsure whether the liquid is safe, use the U.S. Army's "Universal Edibility Test," described later in this chapter on page 89.

how to

COLLECT WATER FROM DEW

① Wrap legs with clean clothes or towels and tie them in place. If you have no clean clothes, choose the least dirty ones, likely shirts since they are less in contact with the ground than pants or socks.

② Walk through shrubs and tall grass around sunrise, when dew forms, until clothes or towels are saturated. Squeeze out water into a container, or if you have no container, suck it out of the fabric. Dew, a pure form of water as it condenses out of the atmosphere, is drinkable unless it formed on a contaminated surface. As an alternative, mop up dew using a towel and wring it out; be sure to collect dew in early morning before it evaporates.

EXTRACT WATER FROM FISH

FISH CONTAIN LIQUID you can drink. Cut through the backbone near the tail while holding the fish head down. Then tilt the fish head up to allow the drinkable spinal fluid to drain. Suck the fluid out of the eyes. Although a fish doesn't hold a lot of water, survivors reported feeling strong psychological benefits from drinking.

Don't drink animal blood as a substitute for water. It's salty and is digested like food, which uses up part of your body's water. It also may carry pathogens.

FINDING DRINKABLE WATER

Water is everywhere in the temperate forest, not just in rivers and lakes. Look for ways to get it out of air, soil, and living tissue.

COLLECT rain on tarp.

GATHER snow below its surface.

WIPE up dew with a rag.

WORK a knife into a maple tree to collect sap from the hole.

DIG into soil for groundwater.

EXTRACT drinkable liquid from fish.

CUT a vine as high as you can and wait for the pumping action to push water out.

DIG FOR WATER

WATER CAN BE FOUND by digging in boggy ground. Scoop a hole about one foot deep and wait for water to seep into it. It will be silty at first, but remove it a few times until a clear pool forms. This water can be purified for drinking. Avoid collecting water near dead animals, foul-smelling mud, or mud covered by green slime, as it is likely to be contaminated. Look for water in places where it may lie hidden just below the surface; groundwater creeps toward lower elevations. Good places to dig for water are amid patches of green plants; in the gravel or mud of a dry streambed; and in the dunes along a sea coast. Above the coastal water line, fresh water often will pool in the bottom of a hole dug between sand dunes, or float atop a layer of salty water. If the hole contains only saltwater, it can be distilled for drinking.

HAZARDS OF DRINKING UNTREATED WATER

>>> Giardia: intense abdominal cramps and diarrhea—note that dogs may not show these ill effects
>>> Hookworms: lethargy in animals and people
>>> Cryptosporidiosis: nausea, stomach cramps, dehydration, vomiting, fever

SHELTER

As you choose a place for shelter in the temperate forest, remember that air is heated by day and cooled by night. Air becomes denser as it chills; cool air sinks and flows in channels toward low ground. On cool nights, make your shelter partway down a lee slope to avoid the coldest air in valleys and depressions. In the heat of summer, seek shelter that catches cool air yet is out of the way of any potential flooding. Use common sense in choosing a site for shelter. You want to be near sources of water and fuel. If you await rescue, site your shelter in a conspicuous place that can be seen from the air or, if this is not possible, tie a brightly colored piece of clothing outside your shelter that will be visible to potential rescuers. / Set up your shelter before doing any other chores at your campsite, such as cooking. Pack your tent the same way every time so that you know where each part of it is, and how to put it up quickly and systematically. / Shelters should be an appropriate size; resist the temptation to build or buy one too big. The right size is large enough for protection but small enough to contain body heat.

Trench shelters require a lot of work but provide emergency warmth in snowy woods.

WHERE TO PITCH A TENT

THE BEST TENT site is in the shelter of trees, away from any dead trunks or branches that might fall. It should be close to water, but not so close that sudden floods might wash over the site or that the roar of rushing water drowns out potential noise from approaching animals or other humans. The site should be level and protected from winds.

In winter, you might camp on frozen ground that would be unusable in summer.

Find your site and have your tent erected and dinner cooking before twilight. Begin looking about two to three hours before dusk for an appropriate site to bed down.

WHERE TO PITCH . . .

>>> **On flat, dry, level ground**
>>> **Near water but not dangerously close**
>>> **Near natural windbreaks such as trees**
>>> **Near artificial windbreaks such as walls of snow**
>>> **With entrance facing sun for light and warmth, or facing downwind in cold weather**
>>> **In clearings or amid low brush**

EXPERT TIP Cold climates require an enclosed, insultated shelter....As a general rule, unless you can see your breath, your snow shelter is too warm and should be cooled down to preclude melting and dripping.

U.S.ARMY

WHERE NOT TO PITCH A TENT

AVOID LOW GROUND, as it tends to collect cold air at night and may be home to thick clouds of insects. Do not pitch a tent over an animal burrow or next to an animal path, as you may invite unwelcome visitors and predators that may also frequent the area.

Try not to pitch your tent on very slanted ground, as you will likely slide to the downhill side during the night. Avoid ground covered in sticks and rocks, as they can tear your tent.

Avoid wet ground or ground that may get soaked in a storm—riverbeds, ravines, floodplains, etc. Do not court disaster by pitching a tent near a natural lightning attractor, such as a lone tree or the top of a ridge.

Stay clear of anything that may fall, especially in high wind. Avoid dead branches of any species, as well as healthy cottonwoods and poplars, which shed branches in wind.

AVOID PITCHING . . .

>>> **In the inside bend of a river (possible floods)**
>>> **Downstream from a latrine**
>>> **In the path of a potential avalanche, mud slide, or rockfall**
>>> **Under dead trees, which could topple**
>>> **On wet ground**
>>> **Under dead limbs, which may fall in storms**

MAKE A MILD-WEATHER SHELTER

MAKE A DEBRIS hut for quick shelter.

Begin construction with a ridge pole. Set one end on the ground and elevate the other on something sturdy, such as a stump. Angle large sticks along both sides in an inverted "V." Make the sides flat enough to shelter your body, yet steep enough to shed rain and snow.

Cover the ribbing with small sticks and brush. Top with light, dry, insulating debris—grass, leaves, pine needles—to a depth of three feet. Add a final layer of branches to keep the debris from blowing away. Insulate the floor with more debris. Finally, create a door plug by piling more debris that you can pull shut once you are inside.

TARPAULIN-AND-POLE SHELTER

>>> A variation on the lean-to uses a large tarpaulin and three poles.

>>> Start by securing a long pole to a tree at about waist height.

>>> Lay the other two poles on the ground on either side of the long pole.

>>> Drape the tarp over the long pole and wrap it around and under the two companion poles on the ground.

>>> The two poles on the ground secure the tarp, which forms a floor when stretched beneath the long pole.

>>> Put small stakes inside the edges of the small poles to keep them from moving.

how to

BUILD A SIMPLE LEAN-TO

1 Locate a good, safe camp area, away from ditches and lowlands that may flood. Find a long, strong branch and lean it on a low branch of a tree. The lower the branch on the tree, the less heat will escape from your shelter.

2 If you have any kind of tarp material, clear the leaning branch of twigs and throw it over, staking it down on either side.

3 If you do not have a tarp, find leafy branches and prop them against the leaning branch.

4 Fill in any still-exposed parts of the lean-to with moss, rocks, leaves, and whatever else you can find to block wind, rain, or snow.

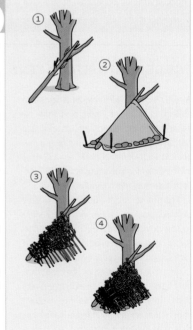

MAKE A SHELTER FOR SEVERE WEATHER

IN WINTER, it's usually easy to find shelter in a forest. Big evergreen trees, such as spruce and fir, form natural canopies of green boughs that shield the soil near their trunks. Snap or hack off boughs from nearby evergreens and layer them at an angle to form a lean-to, closing off the sides of the space beneath the limbs. A tarp can be stretched across the limbs to keep out dripping rain or drifting snow. Soft evergreen limbs—avoid the sticky needles of the spruce—can be spread on the ground to make a bed.

As any child who has built a snow fort knows, snow is an excellent insulator. The simplest snow shelter is a snow cave. It can be built by digging into a large, deep snowbank or drift. These usually form away from the wind near a riverbank or ridge, but the chosen site should not be under a potential avalanche. New, loose, or powdery snow also should be avoided. The entrance ought to be angled 45 degrees away from the wind to keep new snow from piling up outside the entrance. The living space should not be too big, in order to conserve heat, and one large snow cave for a group is more efficient than a series of small ones for each individual. The entrance should be partially blocked with more snow or backpacks once the cave is occupied, with a small ventilation space at the floor for fresh air and a small escape hole at the top, punched open with a stick, for release of carbon monoxide. Simple candles may be sufficient for heat. Body heat also will warm the interior. A sleeping platform can be made with a tarp or a pile of evergreen branches.

essentials

BUILDING A TRENCH SHELTER

Stopped in woods on a snowy evening? It may not be as poetic as it sounds. Get into a trench to stay warm—and alive.

ALIGN IT CORRECTLY: Wind should blow from the foot to the head to minimize erosion.

CUT THE TRENCH: Cut out blocks of snow to form an oblong hole a bit larger than a sleeping bag. The blocks of snow should be about 8 to 12 inches thick.

MAKE THE ROOF: Cut a triangular block to prop upright at the foot. It serves as a support for the roof. Angle the snow blocks over the trench to form a peaked roof. The lower edges of the blocks can be fitted into a thin groove cut along the lip of the trench.

BEDDING: Bed down on a tarp, tree branches, piles of soft evergreen needles, or other insulators. Don't sleep directly atop snow.

CLOSE IT: Block the doorway with more snow or a backpack, but leave a ventilation hole.

ALTERNATE ROOF: A trench roof can be made by weaving branches and covering them with snow.

ALTERNATE SNOW DOME: Pack a deep mound of snow atop pile of evergreen boughs. Snow should be at least one foot thick at top of dome, and two feet deep at base. Toss water on snow to harden it, or let it harden naturally over two to three hours. Dig dome entrance at a 90-degree angle to wind. Tunnel in to remove evergreen core, leaving a few branches for bedding.

If caught in a tent in a summer thunderstorm, move belongings away from the sides.

MILD WEATHER SHELTER HAZARDS

TENT CAMPING in warm weather seems idyllic. Mild spring, summer, and early-fall nights have ideal temperatures for sleeping, and forests are lively with songs of birds and insects. However, potential dangers lurk in and around summer shelters.

Open flames should be kept away from tents and never allowed inside. Aside from the danger of spreading a fire, gases from the fires contain asphyxiating chemicals. Fires should be kept downwind from shelter to minimize the chance of embers blowing inside. Tents are treated to retard fire, but these chemicals gradually lose their effectiveness.

To create ventilation, zip open the flaps on the tent to expose the mesh windows and vents, but take care to keep the mesh part tightly zipped against bugs and pests. It's difficult to rid a tent of mosquitoes once they're inside. If the tent gets a hole in it, patch it as soon as possible.

Make sure the rain fly is correctly attached. If the tent and fly touch, condensation may collect on the inside surface of the inner tent, run down the walls, and soak the bedding.

Tents should not be pitched under dead limbs, which may fall in storms, nor under trees that easily shed their branches. Nor should a tent pole be the highest object in a field during an electrical storm.

Do not make shelter along a game trail. Don't invite noctural animal visitors such as bears—keep food and its odors away from shelter and do not sleep in clothes you wore while cooking.

WATCH OUT FOR:

>>> Snakes and other pests entering shelter
>>> Buildup of carbon monoxide (do not use stove or any open fire in tent)
>>> Lightning strikes
>>> Collapse of tree limbs in high winds
>>> Food odors attracting bears and other large animals
>>> Flooding

SEVERE WEATHER SHELTER HAZARDS

WINTER SHELTERS TEND to be well insulated. When they're totally enclosed, carbon monoxide accumulation inside the shelter poses a greater danger than during warmer months. The gas, formed by incomplete combustion, is absorbed into the bloodstream, where it interferes with hemoglobin's ability to absorb oxygen. Carbon monoxide can build up in the blood over a number of days, or a lethal concentration can rapidly overwhelm an unknowing victim. The gas is odorless and colorless, and victims tend not to know they are suffering its effects until they begin to pass out, collapse, or suffer headaches or extreme nausea. Victims must be moved immediately to a fresh-air environment. They may need mouth-to-mouth resuscitation. A snow shelter must have at least two ventilation holes. One low lets air in, and one high lets air and other gases out.

Snow shelters are temporary and should be inspected regularly. Abrasive, blowing snow can erode the exterior. A snow wall can deflect the wind, and extra snow can be packed on to replace any blown away. The interior should not be warmed too much, as overheating may weaken the roof, causing its collapse. Ventilation holes must be kept open. It is wise to mark the entrance and orient it to the immediate surroundings, so it can be found during a snowstorm.

Clothing is likely to be damp or wet after you have built a shelter in the snow and then entered it to warm up. Remove damp clothes before going to bed. You can warm and dry your clothes by placing them behind your knees, where they absorb radiant body heat.

Take special pains to keep your feet warm and dry. Warm frozen boots by stuffing them inside a cloth and placing it behind your knees.

Caves, rocky crevices, and large trees with low-lying branches can all serve as shelter from wind and snow. Beware of rockfall; noxious, trapped air; and any animals that call caves their home.

WATCH OUT FOR:

>>> Excessively cramped shelter construction, limiting or halting air circulation
>>> Buildup of poisonous gases
>>> Too much heat, weakening snow walls and roof
>>> Clothing and boots staying cold and damp, inviting illness and foot trouble
>>> Avalanches
>>> Condensation freezing inside tent due to improper fixing of tent layers, followed by loss of thermal insulation

EXPERT TIP Lightning often strikes the tallest object in the area. At the first sign of an impending storm—towering thunderheads, darkening skies, lightning and thunder, and increased wind—seek shelter. If caught outside during a lightning storm: Stay way from tall, solitary objects such as trees.

Girl Scouts.

FOOD

There are plenty of things to eat in the woods. The trick is knowing what's good for you. / In August 1992, a young couple found a shocking note on the door of a city bus rusting in the Alaskan wilderness. / "S.O.S.," it said. "I need your help. I am injured, near death, and too weak to hike out of here. I am all alone, this is no joke. In the name of God, please remain to save me. Thank you, Chris McCandless. August?" / McCandless, age 24, had gone into the wild that spring like his hero, Jack London. He had hoped to explore his own soul, to find himself, far from anyone else. He took a bag of rice, a rifle, and a stash of books, including one that identified edible plants. He had planned to live by his wits for the summer, then hike out. / Three moose hunters arrived at the bus, joining the young couple, and one of the new arrivals summoned the courage to step inside and shake a blue sleeping bag. Inside was the lifeless body of McCandless. It weighed 67 pounds and contained almost no subcutaneous fat. / Aside from the conclusion that McCandless had gotten in over his head, author Jon Krakauer investigated the death and attributed it to vegetable poisoning. Krakauer initially concluded that McCandless had mistaken a toxic plant for an edible one. On further review, Krakauer decided he probably had made a different kind of bad assumption. He had eaten the supple, benign roots of the wild potato, and, after the roots became tough late in the season, ate the plant's seeds. They contained a toxic alkaloid. / McCandless had natural foods around him, but his death underscores an important lesson: Unless you are absolutely certain a potential food is safe to eat, don't consume it without first testing it for poison (see test steps on the opposite page).

POISON TEST

IT IS ESSENTIAL TO EAT only plants that you can positively identify as food. Accidental poisoning is a likely outcome of confusing one plant for another, such as the edible and poisonous varieties of fungi. As many people thrust into a survival situation will not have developed the expertise to tell one plant from another, the Army's *Survival Field Manual* recommends a "Universal Edibility Test" to determine whether a plant can be eaten. The test requires 24 hours to complete and has 13 steps, so it should be done only on plants that exist in abundance.

UNIVERSAL EDIBILITY TEST STEPS:

>>> Separate plant into parts such as leaves, stems, roots, flowers, etc. Test only one part of plant at a time.
>>> Sniff for strong or acid odors. Smell alone does not guarantee a plant is edible or inedible.
>>> Do not eat for 8 hours before test. While waiting, test plant for contact poisoning by touching part to be tested against wrist or inside of elbow. Any reaction normally occurs within 15 minutes.
>>> During the test, put nothing in your mouth except purified water and the plant.
>>> Prepare a small part of the plant you are testing; touch the prepared plant to your lip.
>>> If there is no burning or itching after three minutes, hold a bit of plant on your tongue for 15 minutes.

essentials

MAKING TEA FROM PINE NEEDLES

SPRUCE NEEDLES have high levels of vitamins C and A.

GATHER FRESH PINE and spruce needles— the latter are sharp and square, completely surround their twigs, and prick your fingers like little knives.

BRUISE THE NEEDLES with a stone and drop into boiling water.

REMOVE WATER/NEEDLE MIXURE from the fire and steep for five to ten minutes.

>>> If there is no reaction, chew the plant and hold it in your mouth for another 15 minutes. Do not swallow.
>>> If you feel no irritation, swallow the bit of plant.
>>> Wait 8 hours. If you feel ill, induce vomiting and drink a lot of water.
>>> If you feel no ill effects, eat a quarter cup of the same plant, prepared the same way as in the test. Wait another 8 hours. If you're still OK, the plant part you tested is safe for eating, at least in the way you prepared it.

EXPERT TIP Do not assume that because one part of a plant is edible, other parts are, too. Likewise, do not assume that if cooked plant matter is edible, the raw matter must be, or vice versa. Finally, note that different people may have different reactions to the same plant.

EDIBLE PLANTS

THE LIST BELOW enumerates a few of the most common types of plant and animal food found in temperate forests that can be enjoyed once their identities have been verified. For a more complete list, see the appendix.

Acorns. They're abundant in hardwood forests. Tannic acid makes them too bitter to eat straight from the oak tree, but the bitterness can be removed by boiling shelled acorns until the water turns yellow. Repeated boilings in fresh water may be necessary. Once the tannin is gone, acorns can be dried in a skillet. They can be eaten raw or grown into flour. Prepared acorns also can be roasted and ground into a coffee substitute.

Black walnut. The green husks stain hands dark brown. Inside are nuts rich in vitamins, fatty oils, and protein.

Burdock. This plant has burs that stick tightly to clothes and helped inspire Velcro. Don't eat them, though. The plant's edible parts are the leaf stems, which can be peeled and cooked.

Clover. The leaves are good raw or cooked. Flowers and roots also are edible.

Daisy. Young leaves can be eaten raw.

Dandelion. In an hour of need, this plant rapidly shifts from weed to welcome food source. Flowers, buds, stems, and young leaves are edible raw. Roots should be boiled in salted water.

Juniper. The berries, which give gin its distinctive flavor, are too bitter to be eaten raw unless they are mature and purple. Dried and ground into powder, they can be added to flour.

BEST BETS: PLANTS

>>> Acorns are abundant and easily gathered.
>>> Dandelion leaves are tasty and nutritious, and the plants are ubiquitous.
>>> Maple trees offer many edible parts, including sweet sap.
>>> Raspberries, blackberries, and mulberries are easily identified.

PLANTS TO AVOID

>>> White berries, mushrooms, and any red plants unless you know they are safe.
>>> Highly toxic flowers include foxglove, lupines (such as the Texas bluebonnet), monkshood, buttercup, and the appropriately named death camas.
>>> Wild castor bean seeds.
>>> Horse chestnuts, also known as buckeyes
>>> Anything growing in contaminated water, unless the plants are boiled first. They may contain giardia or other parasites.
>>> Any plants marked by mildew or fungus.
>>> Any plants with milky or discolored sap.
>>> Any plants with beans, bulbs, or seeds inside pods.
>>> Any plants with a bitter or soapy taste.
>>> Any plants that smell like almonds in their woody parts or leaves—could indicate the presence of cyanide.

EDIBLE ANIMALS

NEARLY ALL ANIMALS can provide nourishment. Their own will to survive makes them a tougher meal to collect than vegetation.

Mammals tend to move at dawn and dusk. Some graze all day, while others, such as rabbits, eat mainly at night. Look for animal signs such as tracks, scat, and teeth marks on fruits, nuts, and vegetables.

Rabbits are among the easiest animals to catch with a snare or kill with a thrown stick or stone. Unfortunately, their meat is so low in calories and essential nutrients that some 19th-century trappers starved to death eating nothing but rabbit.

Grouse and ptarmigan also can be brought down with a stone. If you miss, the birds fly only a short distance, allowing a second and third chance to stun them.

Beetle grubs can be found under rotten bark. Termites and ants can be collected by pushing a peeled stick into a mound and then withdrawing it. Grasshoppers can be roasted and eaten once their legs and wings have been removed.

Survival author Bradford Angier recommends the sluggish porcupine as an animal "even the greenest tenderfoots, even weak with hunger, can kill with a weapon no more formidable than a stick." Pound it on the head, then turn it over and slice into its belly. The large liver is "surprisingly toothsome," Angier wrote.

Many small animals are relatively easily trapped. Setting traps lets you spend time gathering other kinds of food.

Traps can be simple or quite elabo-rate, with the latter variety taking some time and difficulty to construct. Survival author Cody Lundin questions whether it makes sense for a novice to expend energy constructing traps and snares. Unless they are extremely successful, he suggests the calories ingested may not equal the calories burned, including the energy required to prepare the meat.

If you build a trap or snare, put it near where the animal eats or drinks. Animals are suspicious about traps placed near their homes. Traps should be made strong to subdue a struggling animal and, if possible, well camouflaged.

BEST BETS: ANIMALS

>>> Adult females often make the best game animals, as they have good flavor and an abundance of meat.
>>> Young animals are lean.
>>> Old animals are more likely to be tough.
>>> Insects are relatively easy to catch and have a high protein content.
>>> Porcupines are easily killed, and their meat is tasty.
>>> Birds, their eggs, and freshwater fish can be gathered with a little ingenuity.
>>> Grubs, except those on the underside of leaves, are good to eat.

ANIMALS TO AVOID

>>> Wasps: aggressive, inflict painful stings
>>> Brightly colored insects: likely toxic
>>> Toads
>>> Box turtle: flesh likely poisonous

how to

MAKE A DEADFALL TRAP

1 Find three sticks, roughly the same size. One will be the upright, one the diagonal, and one the horizontal.

2 Upright stick: Make a notch in the center and sharpen top end.

3 Horizontal stick: Carve slot at center, notch top near one end.

4 Diagonal: Carve notch near one end, sharpen other end.

5 Assemble: Drive upright stick into ground. Insert horizontal stick into notch on upright and diagonal stick onto top of upright. Insert the diagonal stick's pointed end into the notch on the horizontal stick. Place bait on free end of horizontal stick and balance weight on top of the diagonal stick, which is poised over bait.

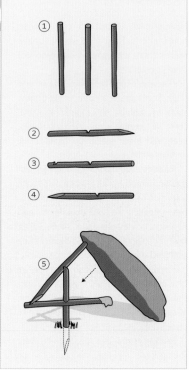

CATCH FISH

FISH LIKE TO FEED where they feel safe, so think like a fish to locate them. Overhanging banks, fallen logs, and rocks offer shelter. In swift water, fish may be found on the lee side of a boulder, where the water moves less quickly.

All freshwater fish are edible. They can be speared, caught on a hook, or netted. Fish can be trapped by channeling them through a narrow, funnellike opening in a wall fashioned of sticks or stones. Once inside the small enclosure on the other side, the fish can be captured. Be careful handling catfish. Spikes in their fins and

whiskerlike barbels can cause painful puncture wounds.

To make a landing net for fish out of a T-shirt, cut two small holes in the seam at the hem and thread the forks of a small sapling into the openings. Push the two forks all the way around to the far side from the original openings. Cut a small hole where the tips of the forks meet. Push both tips through the hole and tie them together. Then push them back inside the hem. Knot armholes and neck opening to close the shirt. Cut off excess fabric so it does not drag in the water.

Keep campfires as small as possible to conserve fuel and minimize environmental impact.

EXPERT TIP Do not store food inside tents, duffel bags, or packs. Mice and other animals will chew through clothing and packs to get to the food. Careful cleanup will help to keep away unwanted ants and other insects.

Girl Scouts.

how to

MAKE A TRIPOD TO COOK OVER AN OPEN FIRE

1 Lean three sturdy sticks together into a tripod formation.

2 Lash the sticks together at top.

3 Tie a fourth stick to the lashing (find stick with series of forks pointing upward or create with knife or ax).

4 Suspend a cooking pot by its handle, hung on one of the upward-pointing forks of the fourth stick.

5 Relocate pot to higher or lower fork to change cooking temperature.

COOK OVER AN OPEN FIRE

MANY FOODS CAN be eaten raw, but most animal flesh and many plants should be cooked to kill microorganisms. The simplest cooking utensils are a pot, a fire, and a spoon. The pot should have a lid to keep the contents from being contaminated by falling or blowing debris. Pot and fire also should be sheltered from wind. Combine freeze-dried foods such as fruit and main meals all in one water-filled pot in order to conserve fuel and simplify cleanup. All utensils should be thoroughly cleaned, and hands washed, before cooking. A variety of camping stoves and fuels can be carried into the wilderness. Food also can be cooked over a natural heat source. Common cooking methods include a spit and fire and cooking on hot rocks.

FIRST AID

First aid for the temperate forest follows many of the principles for basic first aid that you would use in a suburban or rural home environment. The added challenges of the temperate forest include awareness of specific poisonous plants and animals, as well as the climate challenges of your location. Temperate forest first aid kits should include all of the basics found in Chapter 1, plus mosquito repellents and additional treatments for snakebites, bee stings, and tick bites. / While it is wise to prepare for anything from hypothermia to sunburn, the most common outdoor injuries naturally should draw the most attention. These are, in descending order of likelihood, cuts, sprains, bruises, and broken bones. Fingers and hands suffer the most, often as a result of an unfortunate meeting with an ax or knife. Next most common are injuries to feet, toes, and legs. / Halt profuse bleeding as soon as possible. Elastic bandages and sterile dressings applied directly to the wound usually will stop blood loss. Pressing on the inner side of the armpit or between the two major tendons that can be felt on the underside of a flexed knee may close the blood vessels to the arm or leg.

Your feet are an important asset in survival. Keep them dry and treat blisters early.

BRING THE RIGHT STUFF

PACK A FIRST AID kit on all trips into the forest. It should include painkillers, laxatives, and stimulants, as well as medications you normally take. Antiseptics, gauze, and elastic bandages can help treat wounds and sprains. Baking soda and salt from your cooking gear have medicinal uses. Scissors and tweezers can help make cuts and remove splinters. A printed guide to first aid will help you identify and treat injuries.

TREAT BLISTERS

>>> Clean with soap and water.
>>> Puncture with sterilized tool.
>>> Gently press to expel liquid.
>>> Cover with gauze pad and plastic tape.
>>> Do not apply tape directly to blister; wound must breathe to heal.

EXPERT TIP If you suspect a victim has a broken bone, do not move unless the injured area is totally immobilized. If the skin is pierced by a broken bone or you suspect a broken bone under an open wound, take steps to prevent infection. Cover it with sterile dressings before immobilizing the injury.

American Red Cross

BUG BITES

TREAT INSECT BITES by soaking in water. Apply a paste of baking soda and water to relieve swelling and discomfort. A bit of mud also may ease symptoms. If stung by a bee or wasp, scrape the stinger out of the skin. Wash the wound and apply ice, aspirin, calamine lotion, baking soda, or meat tenderizer with a sterile pad.

TREAT BITES AND SMALL WOUNDS

>>> Drain and clean around bite or wound.
>>> If the bite or wound becomes infected, soak in hot brine or apply hot compress.
>>> Use lining inside a raw egg shell as a poultice, especially on a boil.
>>> Cover with sterile pad.

AFTER A FALL

IF THE VICTIM is unconscious, check for pulse and respiration. CPR may be necessary in an emergency. Check for bleeding, not just in the limbs but also in the hair and scalp, mouth and nose, and pelvis and abdomen. Halt bleeding with elastic bandages, gauze, and direct pressure. Relieve the pain of sprains and fractures with padding and bandages, slings, and splints. Apply ice to swelling.

TREAT LARGE WOUNDS

>>> Do not wash an open wound.
>>> Prevent prolonged exposure to the air; close the wound with sterile bandages and adhesives as soon as possible.
>>> Do not touch the wound with your fingers.
>>> Remove foreign objects only if they can be easily grabbed with sterile tools.

HAZARDS

Be ready to change a survival plan in the temperate forest to accommodate severe weather. A storm may limit visibility, contribute to hypothermia, and turn a trail from an easily traversed walkway to a sea of mud. Adverse conditions are likely to add to the time required for a journey, requiring you to gather more food and build more fires. / Rivers present a common hazard. They cannot usually be bypassed, and rivers with lots of S-curves in a forest don't allow a wide view to judge the best site for crossing safely. Seek out natural bridges, wide places where the river slows, and stepping-stones in the riverbed. / Be aware of dangerous animals in the woods. You aren't likely to have a close encounter with a bear or cougar, but you should know how to respond to a potential attack. Moose, though not as fierce-looking as predators with sharp teeth and claws, are aggressive and dangerous. / Snakes, insects, and other small animals pose some of the most common hazards in the wild.

BIG ANIMALS

BEARS, COUGARS, AND moose are among the most dangerous large mammals in the wilderness. Grizzlies generally are secretive and act aggressive only when provoked or threatened, while black bears are inquisitive and are unlikely to break off an assault once they commit to attack.

As bears can outrun and outfight any human, it's wise to recognize and respond to an aggressive act. Grizzlies flatten their ears like dogs and sometimes growl to indicate an attack. If a grizzly attacks, respond by playing dead—lying flat on your stomach with legs spread and hands over the back of the neck with fingers interlaced. If a grizzly rolls you onto your back, keep rolling to be belly down. Do not fight unless the grizzly begins to lick any wounds. Black bears are different. They won't stop attacking if you play dead. You must fight back to persuade the bear to call off the attack. Try hitting the snout or eyes with a rock or stick.

Cougars normally avoid being seen. If you encounter a cougar, do not run. Pick up small children and try to make yourself look big by opening a coat or raising an arm. Talk in a confident tone and slowly back away.

Give moose plenty of room. They attack if threatened but will not try to eat you. If you encounter a moose while hiking and the moose doesn't notice you, do not draw attention to yourself; resist the urge to approach. Wait until the moose moves away before proceeding. If the moose notices you, speak in soothing tones and back away.

MOOSE

DON'T BE MISLED by the majestic moose. Moose are among the most aggressive animals in the temperate forest. Whereas bears and cougars have nasty teeth and claws, the vegetarian moose attack viciously with their antlers and front feet, kicking or stomping their victims—sometimes to death.

Moose cows aggressively defend their young, particularly in spring and early summer, and bulls get protective during the fall mating season. Do not hike with dogs in moose country, as moose react angrily to them. If you see a moose, give it plenty of room, and back away slowly. A moose is not interested in eating you, so if it charges you, run away, hide behind a tree, or climb high to avoid it. If a moose knocks you down, curl up in the fetal position, protect your head, and do not move.

BEAR-PROOF YOUR CAMP

>>> **Avoid carrying and spreading odors that may attract bears.**
>>> **Wash yourself and your clothes to remove natural and food scents whenever possible.**
>>> **Do not leave food scraps around after eating.**
>>> **Do not eat, cook, or keep food in tent.**
>>> **Do not go to bed wearing clothes tainted by food odors.**
>>> **Urinate in toilets or outhouses, or if there are none, on rocks or bare ground to minimize odors; urine attracts wildlife.**

BEAR SAFETY

MAKE NOISE—sing or talk—while walking in bear country in order to avoid surprising an adult bear. As an added precaution or if you are hiking alone, attach a bear bell by rope or clip to the outside of your back. Bears usually do not want to encounter you any more than you want to encounter them. However, if they are surprised or feel threatened, they may attack. Bears are particularly dangerous when protecting cubs or defending food they have killed. If you do accidentally encounter a bear, give it plenty of room; you cannot outrun or out-climb it. If you can move slowly away, do so; otherwise stick with your group, talk to the bear, wave your arms to let it know you are human and not prey. A can of pepper spray, shot into a bear's eyes, may deter an attack—or merely make the bear very angry. If you use pepper spray, carry a big can, keep it near you, and use it only when attacked. Fire it in short bursts, preferably with the wind at your back to keep it from stinging your own eyes.

BEAR FACTS

>>> Only about one person every three years is killed by a bear in the United States.
>>> You can reduce your chances of an unpleasant bear encounter by following a few simple rules.
>>> Never store food in your tent.
>>> Hang food in a bag tied to a rope that is tossed over a tree limb high above the campground.
>>> Store garbage properly.
>>> Store food so bears cannot smell it.
>>> Eliminate food odors. Change out of the clothes you cooked in before going to bed.
>>> Don't hike with dogs. Dogs may antagonize a bear and provoke an attack.

how to

MAKE A BEAR BAG

1. Secure food and dirty clothing in two tightly sealed plastic bags of roughly equal weight; tie one bag to one end of a rope and a rock to the other end of the rope.

2. Find a tree with a sturdy branch in sight of your shelter area and throw the stone affixed to the rope over the branch at least several feet from the trunk.

3. Hoist the bag up to the branch; remove the stone and secure the other bag to the rope.

4. Push the second bag up with stick until the two are at roughly equal height.

SNAKE WATCH

SNAKES AVOID PEOPLE when possible, and the danger of being bitten by a venomous one is far less than getting a life-threatening disease from food or water consumed in the wild. The most common North American venomous serpent, the rattlesnake, announces its presence around humans by buzzing the rattles on its tail, making it easy to avoid unless it is surprised.

To lessen your chance of snakebite, don't sleep next to tall grass or brush, where snakes may choose to hide. Don't thrust a hand or foot into a dark place, such as a hollow log or crevice, without first looking inside. Don't step over a fallen log; instead, step on top and look at the other side to see if a snake is resting there. Look where you are walking in the wild.

Rattlesnakes, copperheads, and cottonmouths are known as pit vipers, named for the pit between their eyes and nostrils. Pit vipers generally hunt at night, using the sense organs in their pits to locate prey.

EXPERT TIP Each year, a few people are bitten by sharks, mauled by alligators, and attacked by bears.... However, each year more victims die from bites by relatively small venomous snakes than by large, dangerous animals. Even more victims die from allergic reactions to bee stings.

U.S.ARMY

BEYOND SNAKES

STATISTICALLY SPEAKING, insects pose a far greater health risk than snakes. Far more people die each year of anaphylactic shock from bee stings than from snake venom. Insects and arachnids in temperate forests include:

Scorpions live in decaying organic matter and feed at night. To prevent them from hiding in boots, place your boots upside-down atop sticks thrust into the ground when you go to bed.

Brown recluse spiders live under debris and in dark places such as caves, hollow logs, and piles of rocks.

Black widow spiders live under logs and rocks, and in shade. They have a red hourglass on abdomen.

Ticks live mainly in woods and grasses. They can carry Rocky Mountain spotted fever and Lyme disease. Experts believe it takes a few hours for a tick to transmit the disease to its host, so inspect your body regularly, particularly after passing through thick brush. Insect repellent applied to the clothing will help ward off ticks, as will tucking pantlegs into the tops of socks.

SIGNALING

The universal message of distress is communication signals in groups of three. Using a wet blanket to briefly cut off a column of smoke, you can send up three puffs to alert a rescue team. Three gunshots, three separate fires spaced 100 feet apart, and so on convey the same message. / In winter, simple messages can be stomped into the snow. Orienting the message along a north-south axis will increase the shadows falling in each letter and provide contrast. Evergreen branches can be added to the letters to make them stand out. In rocky fields, piles of rocks, logs, or trampled grass can be used to form large letters, ideally 40 to 100 feet long. SOS is a simple and effective message. Forming a large arrow shape on the ground indicates to the pilot the direction you have gone or intend to go. / Your voice is quickly worn out by shouting, so use a whistle when trying to attract attention with sound. Whistle blasts carry farther than a human voice and are easier for listeners to pinpoint. Three blasts means distress. Condensation on a winter's day can freeze the pea in a police whistle, so carry a version without a pea. Give whistles to children in the backcountry and instruct them in their use.

BEST AREAS FOR SIGNALING

TRY AN OPEN FIELD, open land along a stream, snowy fields, or anywhere you can create contrast between light and dark, or against the green background of the forest. Signals also stand out atop a ridge. Lying on the ground will make your body surface appear larger from the air. In the middle of a forest, a fire attracts attention but should be contained to avoid spreading danger-ously. Tying down the top of a tree so it doesn't sway like its neighbors will also create visual contrast.

SIGNALING WITH FIRE

IN THE WOODS, the best way to attract the attention of rescuers also is the best way to stay warm: fire. Making fires as bright as possible at night, and as smoky as possible in daylight, enhances their visibility. Smoke or flames from a signal fire may be rapidly spotted by the watchers in towers or planes who scan the ground in summer for evidence of wildfires. Throwing oil on a fire creates thick, black flames, while adding damp, green foliage results in a thick blanket of white smoke. At night, a single tree in a clearing can be torched to make a distress sign. Signal fires have been seen as far as 50 miles away. If you are near a body of water, setting three fires on anchored or tethered rafts will make them stand out.

FIRE SIGNAL POINTERS

>>> **Bright fires: best at night**
>>> **Smoky fires: best during the day**
>>> **Three puffs: a signal for distress, using the universal rule of threes**
>>> **Three fires, 100 feet apart: an unambiguous distress signal.**

how to
SIGNAL WITH FIRE

1. Find a clearing large enough that flames or smoke can be seen by a rescue plane. Build a tepee fire, but don't light it. Stack plenty of additional fuel nearby.

2. Assemble smoke-generating materials in a pile next to the fire: For white smoke that will contrast with green surrounding forest in warm weather, add green grass, ferns, and moss to the fire. In winter, add oil or rubber for dark smoke that will stand out against snow and leafless trees.

3. Place boughs or tarp over fire; reserve fuel and smoke generators to keep them dry.

4. When rescue plane appears, light fire. If wind keeps smoke from rising, increase the fire's heat by adding fuel, to force smoke upward. Be careful not to smother fire.

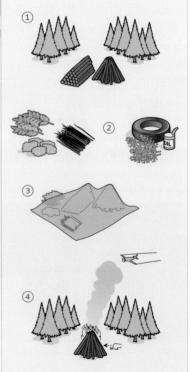

NAVIGATION

Wandering deep in a thick, temperate forest can lead to "woods shock." The term dates from an 1873 article in *Nature* magazine and refers to the spatial confusion that can confound people lost in wilderness. Particularly in a thick forest, where branches obscure the view of surrounding landmarks, woods shock can create emotional distress. / Woods shock can be dealt with like other fear and panic (see Chapter 1). A topographic map, detailing terrain features such as elevation, can alleviate fears, especially when combined with an altimeter, compass, or handheld global positioning system. Topographic maps reveal hills, depressions, ridges, and waterways, with contour lines marking terrain of equal elevation. The most widely used U.S. Geological Survey maps show detail at a scale of 1:24,000—in other words, one foot on the map is equal to 24,000 feet on the earth's surface. These are also referred to as "7.5 minute" maps. They're a good size because they allow examination of surrounding terrain in an appropriate level of detail—not so small to be useless for navigation, and not so large that hikers soon step off the grid.

Avoid woods shock by remaining aware of your surroundings with maps and compass.

essentials

PLAN YOUR ROUTE

Form a plan for your journey in the woods and leave an itinerary with trusted friends before you leave. The itinerary should include:

A DESTINATION and intended route, out and back. Photocopies of topographic maps with the route highlighted are ideal.

A TIME OF DEPARTURE and expected return. Trips often take longer than expected, and unexpected troubles can add time, so estimates should be padded by a few hours.

A DESCRIPTION of the vehicle taken to the jumping-off point, along with information about everyone on the trip. Names, ages, clothing, medical conditions, etc., will help rescuers in their search.

A REASON for taking the trip. Mountain bikers carry different equipment and seek different destinations than rock climbers. Knowing what the missing group set out to do and what resources it carried will help rescuers re-create the journey.

A SET OF FOOTPRINTS for each person in the party. Having group members preserve their prints will make it easier for rescuers to positively identify their tracks. An easy way to save footprints is to step onto a piece of aluminum foil just before starting the trip. Each sheet can be labeled with the person's name and left on the dashboard.

IF THE HIKE GOES AS PLANNED, the group leader must remember to call the two trusted contacts so they don't alert the authorities.

FIND AND FOLLOW WATER COURSES

MAJOR STREAMS and rivers are marked on topographic maps. If you encounter a small stream, following it will take you to lower ground and more significant waterways. Water provided the backbone for transportation before the invention of the railroad, and thus rivers usually lead to civilization. (This is not always the case. Rivers may end in a swamp. In the Great Basin of Utah and Nevada, rivers lead to the desolate Great Salt Lake or evaporate in the desert.)

On high ground, rivers may be difficult to follow as they cut through steep rocky walls. On low ground, rivers may meander and create marshes and swamps. In both cases, it may be easier to leave the banks and follow the waterway from a distance or cut across its loops. Or consider building a raft to float a wide, gentle river.

Seventeen-year-old Juliane Koepcke followed waterways to safety in a famous escape in 1971. She and a dozen other passengers survived a fall into the Peruvian jungle when a lightning strike destroyed their airplane in 1971. Koepcke examined her environment carefully and decided that rescuers would be unlikely to spot her through the jungle canopy. She chose to follow the rivers in hopes of finding civilization and staggered to safety 11 days later. The others waited behind, and died.

USE BLAZES, CAIRNS, AND OTHER TRAIL MARKERS

EXPERIENCED DEEP-WOODS hikers constantly take in their surroundings, mentally noting where they have been and where they are going. Such mental maps are useful in retracing steps. Another way is to mark trails with brightly colored ribbons or tape. A roll of surveying tape tucked in your backpack can be used to delineate a trail through trees and rocks. Arrows fashioned from rocks or sticks can point the way.

Other signs include cairns, which are rocks stacked one on top of the other, and blazes. Cairns are formed from available, loose rocks. They may be used as signals to other hikers or to symbolize achievement of a summit. Rocks placed by others should be respected. Hiking etiquette is for each hiker to add a single rock, taking care not to knock down or displace any of the others. Cairns should not block animal trails or holes, or damage plants by their placement.

Blazes are cut at chest height into the thin bark of a tree with the downward stroke of an ax or stout knife. Trees along a marked trail may have blazes on both sides, for hikers coming and going. In other places, blazed trees on the side of a trail may have a single chop facing the path. Turns along a trail are indicated with longer strokes being paired with the original blaze. A long stroke below and to the right of a blaze means "turn right." A long stroke below and to the left of a blaze means "turn left." Three vertical blaze marks indicates a warning.

Established routes have different types of trail-marking systems. Make sure you are familiar with the type of marks used along a route before venturing out.

MAP-MAKING ON THE GO

IF YOU DON'T HAVE A MAP, you may want to make your own. A map can be useful for finding your way back to camp if you wander to collect food or water, or are out seeking lost children. A good vantage point, such as the top of an isolated tree, will allow you to see more of the contours of the terrain than you can take in from ground level in the forest. Number and mark the direction of the ridges you see, and remember that the invisible low spots between the ridges are likely to contain water. Mark anything that is significant: strangely shaped rocks or trees, waterways, etc. If you spend much time in one place, you may continue to fill in your map with information about food sources, game trails, and rock quarries that can be used for fashioning crude tools.

If you have a compass, you can use it to pinpoint the directions leading to objects on your map. A compass works well with any map, but like other survival gear is best when used often enough for the bearer to feel comfortable using it in an emergency. Tie your compass to a cord and wear it around the neck, so it's always handy.

how to

MAKE YOUR OWN MAP

1. Make your own system of indicating contour lines, showing how land rises and falls around you. Fill in ridges as far as you can see.

2. Add trees and rocks with odd shapes that you instantly recognize.

3. If you have cached food or set up animal lures or traps, mark their locations. It's easy to forget in a forest, where so many trees look alike.

4. Leave blank spaces in your map, which you can fill in when you learn more about your surroundings. Update your map regularly.

EXPERT TIP Locate an intermediate landmark toward which the direction-of-travel arrow is pointing—a tree, a boulder, or other feature—and walk to it. Take another bearing, identify the next landmark in line with the arrow, and go to it. Continue until you reach your destination.

Cairns are formed from available, loose rocks and often signal achievement of a summit.

H ead down, walking and observing the ground closely, I halt abruptly, two feet short of the nose of an Eastern diamondback rattlesnake just as I am about to take my next step. I take a couple of photos, noticing through the lens the short tail that marks her as a female, a little over two years old, and probably still immature. She is not large, about three

feet long. She faces me, stretched out, stiff and still. I freeze. But my movements have already startled the snake into rattling and she coils up. I see a flash of movement. It all happens so suddenly. Without any time to recoil from her strike, I feel a slight pinprick on the top of my right forefinger. A small jewel of crimson blood and I am overwhelmed by the gravity of my situation. I am all alone in the outdoors with no one to help me. I suck the small puncture wound, from which some blood and clear serum are oozing. I take stock of my situation and try to calm myself. My predicament is grave. I have to walk back to the kayak, paddle across the bay, and drive myself to help. Immediately I feel a little pain at the puncture wound, but more alarming, the tops of my forearms and the backs of both hands began tingling within seconds of the bite. Recalling

Bruce Means, National Geographic grantee and biologist, is dedicated to conservation of the coastal plain of the southeastern U.S.

that paralysis caused me to collapse after just four minutes the first time I was bitten by an Eastern diamondback, I know this time that every second will be precious. I swing my pack onto my back and begin walking, grimly, in a straight line for my kayak.

I feel panicky because I know that I must go against all medical recommendations and exercise vigorously to reach help. I do not run, but move with determined purpose. I reach my kayak exactly ten minutes after the bite, and about half a mile from the snake.

My legs are shaky and both my legs and arms tingle strongly, with a sort of numbness coming over them. My forehead, mouth, and temples also have the tingling numbness. My finger is not swollen or in pain. In fact, the bite itself is no more distressing than any puncture wound.

I let myself down into the kayak and begin paddling. I make good, strong strokes, but do not thrash wildly at the water and lose efficiency. My hands, arms, legs, and feet are getting progressively more numb. The tingling increases to a buzzing feeling. I am dehydrated, so I stop paddling and locate a bottle of water and take a drink. The roots of my teeth are tingling. And now my tongue tingles.

Finally, 21 minutes after being bitten, my kayak noses onto the beach at the end of a sandy road. I try to move my legs—nothing but spastic jerks. I cannot lift myself using my arms on the gunwales. So I roll the kayak to my right and fall on my side in the water. I pull myself out of the kayak and drag myself to shore. I try to stand, but crash to the ground in a twisted jumble. My legs are definitely paralyzed. I have almost no control over them.

The crawl to the car is the scariest part of my whole ordeal. I am so uncoordinated that when I feel sandspurs in my palms, I do not try to remove them because I probably can't pick them from one hand using the other. I fight off

visions of dying in the sand and urges to lie facedown and grief-stricken. I clench my jaws and remember my determination. I use the car door handle to pull myself up, get the door open, and laboriously heave myself into the driver's seat. My arms are still functional, though numb and tingling.

Using my arms and hands, I can push and pull each leg to depress and release the clutch and brake pedals. I get the car started and am barely in control—I gun the engine and crash through roadside brush.

In about three minutes, the one-mile drive goes successfully to the parking lot of a building where I can find help. I turn off the ignition and jolt to a stop at the curb and then clumsily fall out of the driver's seat onto the pavement, bruising my hands and knees on the knobby granite asphalt. Struggling to all fours, shaking like a leaf, I am unable to move forward across the rough-surfaced parking lot. I lie down and discover that I am easily able to roll. I must have made a crazy sight, a grown man rolling across the hard asphalt surface of a parking lot. Later, I discover that I bashed my left shin badly and cut my right big toe somewhere along the way, but I never felt either injury.

The first part of my life-threatening ordeal is over when I reach up to the building's door handle, praying it isn't locked, and feel it release. I crack open the door, pull myself in past my shoulders, and, now prostrate on the floor, begin bellowing, "Help!" As the third "Help!" rolls down the hall, I look to see a man hurrying towards me. A great sense of relief sweeps over me when he calls 911 and I realize that my life is now in other people's hands.

If it had been fiction, the critics would have called it unbelievable. / Isabel Godin, a well-born Peruvian, walked into the Amazon rain forest in a heavy silk dress in 1769. She believed the 3,000-mile descent of the river system would be the best way to reunite with the husband who awaited her on the coast. / Her nine traveling companions died of starvation, thirst, disease, and violence by marauders. Porters abandoned her. She wandered nearly two months before rescue. In two centuries of Amazon exploration, no outsider had survived even a few days under such conditions. / Godin found water on plant leaves and ate eggs and fruit. Every morning, she awoke believing "the Almighty had preserved her," she recalled, and staggered onward. / The jungle tried to kill her in myriad ways, just as it attacks the unwary today. Heat and humidity tortured her with thirst. The dark, tangled forest floor confused her. Ants stung her. Mosquitoes and botflies consumed her living flesh, as she had neither shelter nor protective netting nor proper clothes. / Yet Godin reunited with her husband. Her miracle of survival, and the tragedy that befell her companions, speaks to the challenges the jungle prepares for naive intruders.

SWAMP &
TROPICAL RAIN FOREST

PREPARATION

Rain forest heat and humidity can severely tax anyone. Aspiring visitors should be in good health and used to regular exercise before a jungle trip. Even so, they will need up to a week to acclimatize. / Jungle gear should be as light as possible. The steamy climate, combined with carrying a heavy load, can bring on heat illness. / Adventurers planning to enter the jungle need vaccinations (see "First Aid" in this chapter), special gear, insecticide, and clothing to stay cool yet fend off pests. If planning a long trip, travelers should consult with the locals about weather, terrain, and hazards, or hire a native guide. Locals know which streams teem with leeches or piranha, which roads are washed out, and other essential news. / Still, rain forests are not the dark wilderness they once were. Agriculture, mining, highways, and communication systems have opened once-remote areas. Jungle adventurer John Walden said that when he joined a recent effort to retrace Teddy Roosevelt's River of Doubt trip, he saw networks of logging roads and miners' trails. In one village, he found the inhabitants watching *Star Trek* on a generator-powered satellite TV.

RAIN FORESTS VS. JUNGLES

RAIN FORESTS are temperate or tropical forests receiving at least 80 inches of rain per year, with a dense canopy that stifles ground plant growth. Jungles are any tropical land of dense and tangled vegetation. Jungles are found in rain forests where sun reaches the ground (e.g., along rivers).

Lowland rain forests have a dense, leafy canopy 100 feet above the forest floor. Rainfall can total as much as 450 inches per year.

Highland rain forests' constant mist adds layers of moss and ferns to the vegetation. Rocky surfaces and thick tangles of plant make the terrain extremely difficult to traverse.

Most tropical, coastal jungles are ringed by mangrove swamps—clusters of saline-loving trees and shrubs.

essentials

PACKING FOR THE RAIN FOREST AND SWAMP

Preparing for jungle travel reflects the challenges of a damp, warm environment teeming with microbes and insects.

HIKING SHOES that are well broken in, light and comfortable, dry quickly, fit above ankle, and have a deep tread

SPARE DRY SHOES for wearing in camp; sandals with hiking treads (such as those made by Chaco, Teva, or Keen)

SOCKS, quick-drying synthetic or wool

PANTS that are loose, lightweight, light-colored, and long-legged; tuck legs into socks to avoid contact with leeches, etc.

SHIRTS that are long-sleeved, loose, with mesh sides and back, made of polyester or nylon or a blend of the two

PONCHO or breathable lightweight rain jacket (polyamide, for example)

LIGHTWEIGHT HAT with a brim to protect against light, heat, and debris from canopy

LAMINATED MAPS for navigation

MOSQUITO NET and insecticides

HANDLING HUMIDITY AND THICK VEGETATION

TRAVELERS ARE BOUND to get wet during the day, but they must dry out at night. Wet feet are prone to infections and may shed sheets of skin. Clothes must be cleaned and properly dried to prevent skin diseases. Mold grows on clothes that stay damp, so avoid cotton, which tends to stay wet. Do not dry clothes on the ground in sub-Saharan Africa, as they will draw the tumbu fly's maggots.

Laminate maps to protect against dampness and mold. And remember, maps combined with compass or GPS give a location relative to topographical features, but may hold little practical information about how to move toward a destination through dense vegetation.

ACCLIMATE

>>> Expect heat and extreme humidity.
>>> Reach and maintain optimal weight to minimize impact of jungle climate.
>>> Before jungle trip, exercise for at least four days in a hot, humid environment.
>>> Allow minimum of four to six days in jungle for body to acclimate.
>>> Get used to being wet, from rain, brushing against plants, and sweating; it keeps your body cool.
>>> Keep body, particularly feet, dry at night.
>>> Beware of heat illness; make sure everyone in your group knows the signs.

EXPERT TIP There is less likelihood of your rescue from beneath a dense jungle canopy than in other survival situations. You will probably have to travel. You should take a machete, compass, first aid kit, and a parachute or other material for use as mosquito netting and shelter.

U.S. ARMY

SHELTER

Tents are not always recommended in the rain forest. In South America, for example, snakes and other ground dwellers find their way into tents through the tiniest of holes, and heat and humidity turn tents into sweatboxes. In addition, clearing space for a tent on the jungle floor is time-consuming, and rarely thorough enough to prevent spiky plants from perforating the floor. / Existing shelters built and left by previous travelers can provide the best sleeping arrangements. / When faced with constructing a shelter, a traveler should choose high ground. It should not be near swamps, riverbeds (which can flood suddenly in a downpour), or ant infestations. The bedding should be off the ground, away from dampness and potential invasion by insects and other pests. Shelter options include platforms, hammocks, tarps, and A-frames. Mosquito nets and insecticides—or a layer of mud smeared on the skin in an emergency—are essential for a good night's sleep. Make sure the netting is suspended away from your skin or mosquitos will bite you through it. / Rain forests didn't get their name by accident. Rainstorms arrive suddenly and often with great intensity. Don't assume a clear sky will last an entire night; prepare for a downpour.

Make use of cleared sites, structures, and platforms built by previous travelers.

how to

BUILD A PLATFORM BED WITH CANOPY

1 Push four stout limbs into the ground for bedposts tall enough to support a bed, you, and a canopy. Or look for some trees that may already be the proper distance apart.

2 Select four crosspieces strong enough to support your weight. Notch the vertical posts at least a foot up and lash two crosspieces to posts at notches (see "How to Make Rope from Natural Materials" in Chapter 1).

3 Select four shorter crosspieces for head and foot of bed and canopy, lashing two to vertical posts just above long crosspieces.

4 For the canopy, repeat the process, placing the notches several feet higher.

5 Lay many thin but sturdy branches perpendicularly across the two longest crosspieces to make a bed frame. Cover with leaves and grass for a soft sleeping surface.

6 Repeat Step Four for the canopy, covering with a tarp or large leaves to shed water. Drape a mosquito net from the underside of the canopy over the bed.

HANG YOUR HAMMOCK

HAMMOCKS PROVIDE a quick way to create a sleeping space off the ground.

Comfortably rigging a hammock takes practice. A hammock should be high enough that a sleeper's midsection doesn't touch the ground, but low enough to allow an occupant to fall safely. Sling a hammock's support ropes through the sleeves of a mosquito net.

Two knots are crucial: The half hitch secures to a horizontal support, such as a limb, while the camel hitch secures to a vertical support, such as a trunk (see Appendix).

WHAT YOU SHOULD KNOW ABOUT BAMBOO

BAMBOO, a variety of grass, grows in damp lowlands throughout the tropics and the southern United States. Height and diameter of the stems vary greatly among the hundreds of species, with some stands growing more than 100 feet tall.

Bamboo is the fastest-growing woody plant. Some species grow one foot per day.

Canes may look insubstantial, but they are surprisingly strong. Travel through bamboo often requires slashing a path with a machete, leaving sharp, dangerous spikes along the trail.

Bamboo canes can be a cooking utensil, a transportation or construction material, a source of water, a material, a fire saw (a source of friction to create heat), and, when sharpened, a spear or digging tool.

USE BAMBOO

>>> Use hollow section of thick cane as a trough to boil water or roast meat.
>>> Cut stout, ten-foot canes to make a raft.
>>> Use thick sections like two-by-fours to build a shelter.
>>> Bend green stalk, tie top near ground, and cut off tip to collect water overnight.
>>> Use thick blade as a digging tool.

A-FRAME BED WITH BAMBOO

A-FRAME CONSTRUCTION is similar to that of a platform bed, except the two pairs of corner posts lean toward each other until their tops cross, forming a tri-angle. Bamboo can be cut or bent to form the frame. The bedding surface is built as in the platform shelter, creating an "A" shape when seen from either end.

In the absence of manufactured materials for a roof and walls, thatching made of large leaves sheds water effec-tively. Palm fronds, elephant grass, and banana leaves are ideal. Leaves with long stems, such as palm, can be made to interlock by winding their stems around a thin branch and hooking them over or under the stems of leaves on either side.

Bamboo split lengthwise can be laid in combinations of up and down rows to collect and channel water to the sides of the roof.

RAIN FOREST INSECTS

RAIN FORESTS abound with a wide array of insects that bite and sting. They live amid the plants and animals, in the soil, and on nearly every conceivable surface. Get your bedding off the ground and prepare your insect defenses to avoid becoming a meal for mosquitoes, ants, and other pests.

Ants are by far the most prevalent. They so dominate the lowland rain forest that they out number all vertebrates combined. "No matter where you step, no matter where you lean, no matter where you sit, you will encounter ants," wrote the American biologist Adrian Forsyth. The sting of the giant conga ant (*Paraponera clavata*) is one of the most painful nonfatal experiences. The pest, which lives in the American tropics, is also known as the bullet ant because victims liken its bite to being shot.

Other insect pests include fire ants, chiggers, ticks, jigger fleas, botflies, wasps, bees, and scorpions.

REPEL INSECTS

SPRAY CONTAINING 15 to 30 percent DEET (aka "jungle juice") repels mosquitoes, ticks, flies, chiggers, fleas, and gnats. Higher concentrations may endanger your health. Also try Avon's Skin So Soft, especially effective on no-see-ums.

Spray the ankles, lower legs, and waist. Put on your socks and spray the tops. Put on your pants and spray a band from both cuffs to midcalf. Give your shirt a light dusting. Spray your hands and rub your hair. Dot your face, neck, and ears. Shower or wash off and reapply at least daily.

essentials
INSECT DOS AND DON'TS

Plentiful insects are a reality of the rain forest. Know what to do with—or without—preparation, to avoid bites and stings.

DO: USE insect repellents such as DEET or permethrin. Read instructions thoroughly.

DO: SMEAR your skin with mud or oil if you have no netting or repellent.

DO: APPLY repellent to ropes that suspend bedding.

DO: CHECK your body regularly for insect bites and attached ticks, especially on scalp and body crevices.

DO: USE mosquito netting over your bed and make sure you don't roll against it as you sleep; mosquitoes will bite you through the net.

DO: COVER your head at all times to prevent pests from dropping or crawling into hair.

DO: LIGHT a smoky fire to deter mosquitoes.

DON'T: WALK barefoot in jungle/rain forest.

DON'T: WEAR perfume or use fragrant soaps; the odor attracts bees and wasps.

DON'T: WEAR floral-patterned clothing; it also may attract pests.

DON'T: LET wet clothes dry on the ground. Insects will lay eggs inside them.

FOOD

Plants grow in abundance, with fruit available at any time. / Gathering food is complicated, however, by the layering of life. The biologically richest stratum is in the canopy; the poorest is on the dark forest floor. The most tempting fruit may be out of reach. Yossi Ghinsberg, a young Israeli who survived a three-week ordeal in the Amazon rain forest in 1981, found a novel way to harvest the fruits on high branches. He tied the end of a fishing line to a rock and tossed it over a branch laden with fruit. He grabbed both ends of the line and pulled, snapping the branch and making fruit rain down. / Among plants, bananas are plentiful and versatile. Eat the fruit raw or cooked. Cut down a tree near its base and scoop out the center of the stump, and it will fill with water. "Besides its cool agreeable shade," explorer Henry Morton Stanley wrote in 1878, "the banana-plant will supply a peasant of Uganda with bread, potatoes, dessert, wine, beer, medicine, house and fence, bed, cloth, cooking-pot, table-cloth, parcel-wrapper, thread, cord, rope, sponge, bath, shield, sun-hat, even a canoe. ... With the banana-plant, he is happy, fat, and thriving; without it, he is a famished, discontented, woe-begone wretch, hourly expecting death." / Among animals, insects are abundant—with palm grubs a delicacy—and fish from the rivers are a satisfying meal. Turtle flesh is a last resort; so many are now endangered. Nineteenth-century Amazon naturalist Henry Walter Bates described women making sarapatel soup from turtle entrails. Steaks cut from the turtle's chest can be cooked in their own fat or minced and cooked with farina.

FIND FOOD IN THE RAIN FOREST

LOOK FOR FRUITS in the canopy. National Geographic explorer Wade Davis survived on banana peels, lemons, and other finds while lost for a week in the Colombian rain forest. If birds and monkeys eat a particular fruit, chances are you can, too. However, some fruits contain toxins that are neutralized by a bird's or monkey's digestive tract. If you're not sure whether a fruit is good to eat, give it the Universal Edibility Test (see Chapter 3).

Young shoots from the coconut, sago, and sugar palms are edible. Sago palms have a pith inside their stems that can be boiled and eaten like rice. When a mature sago palm is cut just before it flowers, its interior yields enough starch to feed a person for a year. To get at the starch, cut away half of the trunk, scoop out the white pith, pound it as fine as you can, knead it, and strain it. Beware: Not all palms are edible. The growing tip of some palm trees is good raw or cooked and tastes like celery. Palm hearts—she called them palm cabbage—helped Isabel Godin survive the Amazon Basin.

Look for birds' eggs in nests near ground level. Remove the eggs and eat them raw, or catch the adults when they return to the nest.

Harvest young bamboo stems by swinging a machete into canes a few inches off the ground. Split the canes and scoop out the tender, white flesh inside. It can be boiled like asparagus.

Look for Brazil nuts on dry ground in South American rain forests. High in fat and nutrients, they have sustained many an Amazon explorer, including Teddy Roosevelt as he traveled through the Brazilian wilderness to explore the River of Doubt in 1913 and 1914.

Sugarcane also grows in the tropics. Peel the exterior and chew the insides raw.

BEST BETS: PLANTS

>>> Yams
>>> Palm hearts
>>> Coconuts
>>> Mango
>>> Sugarcane
>>> Wild figs
>>> Brazil nuts

BEST BETS: ANIMALS

>>> Bees—adults and grubs
>>> Birds and their eggs
>>> Capybara
>>> Catfish
>>> Hairy spiders (Theraphosa leblondi)—singe off hair and roast in embers

EXPERT TIP The best places to forage is on the banks and streams of rivers... There are almost an unlimited number of edible plants to choose. Unless you can positively identify these plants, it may be safer at first to begin with palms, bamboos, and common fruits.

U.S. ARMY

FOODS TO AVOID IN THE RAIN FOREST

IF SOMETHING looks fierce or attracts attention to itself with bright, toxic colors, it's probably not a safe food source.

Avoid eating, or even touching, any psychedelically colored frogs, toads, snakes, and salamanders. Their coloring indicates the presence of poison. Some secrete toxins powerful enough to kill large animals.

Don't hunt jaguars and peccaries. They may attack even when unprovoked.

Likewise, give piranha a wide berth. They attack anything that moves in the water and may snip off a piece of flesh.

Don't eat raw shellfish. Its flesh likely carries parasites.

Among vegetation, avoid the castor oil plant. Its prickly pods induce vomiting, sometimes fatally.

Nettle trees grow near water in the tropics. Their leaves are spear-shaped and sharply toothed. Seeds are poisonous.

Strychnine tree fruits are about the size and shape of oranges, ranging from white to yellow-red. The tree grows in India, but has related species in many rain forests. Seeds contain poison.

Don't pick any more than you need of anything. Picked fruit will quickly spoil, whereas fruit left on the vine will last much longer.

EXPERT TIP If you are weak, do not expend energy climbing or felling a tree for food. There are more easily obtained sources of food nearer the ground. Do not pick more food than you need. Food spoils rapidly in tropical conditions. Leave food on the growing plant until you need it, and can eat it fresh.

PREPARING FOOD IN THE RAIN FOREST

FOOD SHOULD BE COOKED and eaten as soon as possible in the rain forest and jungle. Raw food, such as fruit that falls from trees or flesh stripped from an animal, quickly spoils in the hot, moist, microbe-saturated environment.

Clean a fish by removing the digestive tract and organs. Wrap the flesh in banana leaves tied as tightly as possible with bark and roast it until it is thoroughly cooked. Or cook it on rocks heated by coals.

Cook animal meat, such as from a capybara or a tapir, inside a stout section of bamboo. Cut into the bamboo with a machete at a 45-degree angle until you

can pop out an oblong section to use as a lid. Scoop out the bamboo flesh inside. Place the meat in the bamboo pot and suspend it over a fire using Y-shaped sticks. Once the meat is cooked, eat what you like and leave the rest in the original pot, sealed with the lid. If kept inside the pot in this manner, the meat will stay good for three or four days.

To roast vegetables, make a fire on the ground, or on a raised bed of earth and green boughs if the ground is wet. Cook yams, taro, wild bananas, and yuca in the coals.

Enjoy fresh fruits after peeling and discarding the skins.

FIRST AID

Germs rapidly reproduce in the moist, hot climate. Many are carried by the huge number and variety of insects. Others are spread through impure water and through human contact, which becomes a health issue where sanitation systems are crude or nonexistent. / Intestinal infections can be treated with antibiotics. Diarrhea results from a variety of bacteria, viruses, or other parasites in food contaminated with human feces. Prevention begins with drinking only sterilized or carbonated water (carbonation kills germs); eating thoroughly cooked foods; and consuming fruit only if you have peeled it yourself. Treatment options include antidiarrheal medicine. Rehydration salts help restore the water a body loses through loose stool. If rehydration salts are not available, drink orange juice with salt and sugar added. / Most skin infections stem from failure to keep clothes and skin dry. Do not apply antibiotic ointments; these will trap moisture and attract dirt, which will stick to the wound. Allowing infected skin to dry in sunlight generally cures infections. Prevention is as simple as bathing often and allowing the skin to dry in the open air or sunlight; changing socks to keep feet dry and clean; dusting feet, socks, and boots with powder from time to time; and removing shoes while sleeping. Keeping hair short helps prevent insect infestations.

Rain forest insects often seek salt content in sweat, such as these stingless Trigona bees.

TREATING DISEASES OF HEAT AND WET SKIN

IMMERSION FOOT is a common disease among travelers who cross many streams with dry ground in between. The soles of the feet never get a chance to dry between submersions and as a result become tender, white, wrinkled, and highly susceptible to chafing, which makes walking painful.

Chafing occurs in other places on the body when hikers are forced to wade waist-deep and stay wet. The insides of the upper thighs, for example, can become red and inflamed. Use petroleum jelly or baby oil to protect against, and reduce, chafing. Denim is inappropriate because it holds water next to the skin; light-fabric trousers with minimal layers are best.

Fungi and bacteria grow in hot, moist skin. Ringworm and athlete's foot appear when skin doesn't dry thoroughly.

essentials

WHAT TO ADD TO A JUNGLE FIRST AID KIT

Clean wounds and allow them to dry. Bites and stings, large and small, must be treated.

ANTIBIOTIC for infections

ANTIDIARRHEAL medication (any over-the-counter treatment)

ANTIFUNGAL cream for foot diseases

ANTIHISTAMINE for simple allergic reactions

ELASTIC bandages for snakebites

EPINEPHRINE auto-injector pen; to counter severe allergic reactions

LIDOCAINE hydrocholide; relief for excruciating stings

ORAL rehydration salts

PERMETHRIN CREAM and shampoo to repel insects and treat head lice

PETROLEUM JELLY to prevent chafing, and also to spread on botfly maggots under skin

PREVENTING DISEASES OF HEAT AND WET SKIN

>>> Bathe often and dry yourself in air and sun.
>>> Wear clean, loose, dry clothing.
>>> Keep feet dry; dust with powder and change socks frequently.
>>> Consider not wearing underwear to avoid creating a humid layer of trapped air next to the skin.
>>> Dry feet at night, and whenever possible during the day.
>>> Remove shoes at night and do not store socks in shoes.
>>> Do not sleep in sweaty or wet clothing.
>>> Treat any skin sores and bites immediately with oral antibiotic.

TREATING BITES AND STINGS

IF AN INSECT BITES you, do not scratch the wound. It will disturb the skin and raise the risk of infection. To relieve pain, apply lidocaine to bites and stings, such as that of the banana spider.

Other ways to relieve or cool the pain of bites and stings include applying mud and ashes; coconut meat, a cold compress, and crushed garlic cloves.

Store clothes and boots off the ground and always shake them before putting them on. Scorpions and spiders sometimes hide in the damp darkness of clothes left outside. Scorpion stings are extremely painful. Clean and dress the sting area. Treat scorpion-bite victims as you would for shock.

Mosquitoes are not mere annoyances. Anopheles mosquitoes spread malaria parasites in the world's tropical regions. The parasites invade human red blood cells, resulting in 2 million to 2.5 million deaths each year. Prevent mosquito bites with repellents and appropriate clothing and netting. Take particular care at dawn and dusk, when insects are most aggressive.

CAUSES OF INFECTIONS

>>> **Typhoid and cholera:** fecal-oral infection caused by poor sanitation and hygiene
>>> **Malaria and yellow fever, dengue:** spread by mosquitoes
>>> **Dysentery and diarrhea:** intestinal infection caused by drinking tainted water
>>> **Blood fluke:** caused by exposure of open sore to bad water
>>> **Sleeping sickness:** spread by tsetse fly's bite
>>> **Hookworm:** contracted through bare feet on ground

PREVENTING AND TREATING MALARIA

>>> **Use netting and repellent.**
>>> **If traveling at dusk or dawn, wear long sleeves, pants, socks. Always wear a hat.**
>>> **Make a smoky fire at campsite.**
>>> **Look for the first symptoms—chills, fever, headache, sweating—one to three weeks after exposure.**
>>> **Treat symptoms as they arise—rehydration for diarrhea, warmth for chills, etc.**

EXPERT TIP Take shelter from tropical rain, sun, and insects. Malaria-carrying mosquitoes and other insects are dangers, so protect yourself against bites. In the tropics, even the smallest scratch can quickly become dangerously infected. Promptly treat any wound, no matter how minor.

U.S.ARMY

HAZARDS

Explorer Henry Morton Stanley likened the experience of journeying through the central African rain forest and jungle to the ten plagues of ancient Egypt. The undergrowth was so thick and thorny in the jungle that a tiger could not move through it, the air such a thick miasma that its concentrated form would act quicker than chloroform, he said. / "Horrors upon horrors" populate the jungle, Stanley wrote. "Boas above our heads, snakes and scorpions under our feet. ... Malaria in the air we breathe; the road is infested with 'hot-water' ants, which bite our legs until we dance and squirm like madmen." / Rain forest and jungle creatures may seem pestilent to modern-day travelers as well. Insects assault the skin. Snakes are rarely seen and inflict few bites, but the number of venomous species is high and their toxin quite painful and potent. Biting and stinging fish and reptiles roam the rivers and streams. / Stanley was wrong about malaria—it's carried by mosquitoes, not floating freely in the air. Microbes thrive in the rain forest environment and look for the chance to invade a host. Travelers must keep clean, drink only purified water, protect themselves from insect bites, and clean and dry their skin as often as they can.

Wear a tightly fastened mosquito net and take needles and thread to repair holes.

INSECT PESTS

THE VARIETY OF INSECT pests in rain forests and jungles is too large to explore here. Instead, here are some of the more common hazards.

Fire ants, now in the southern United States, originated in the tropics. Their stings cause pain, but not as much as those of conga ants. Ant bites can raise pustules that fill with clear liquid. Treat them with antibiotics when they rupture. Severe anaphylactic reactions may require an EpiPen injection.

Chiggers infest grassy areas. Tropical varieties cause inflammation and an itch more powerful than their temperate-climate cousins. Prevent bites by applying DEET to boots, socks, and lower pant legs.

Ticks live on jungle mammals just as they do in temperate forests. They spread diseases and must be removed. Trekkers should check their bodies regularly for ticks and other pests.

Jigger fleas burrow into human feet and lay eggs. The fleas must be completely removed under sterile conditions to prevent secondary infections. Guard against jigger fleas by never going barefoot in a jungle.

Botflies spread their eggs by attaching them to the bellies of mosquitoes. When the mosquito bites a human, the botfly larvae detach and penetrate the flesh. Maggots develop and grow under the skin. Botfly maggots can be encouraged to emerge by smearing their breathing pores with fingernail polish, moist tobacco, plant latex, or petroleum jelly.

Wasps and bees flourish in the jungle. So-called "killer bees" originated in arid regions in Africa. They escaped from a Brazilian research center in the 1950s and spread northward, reaching the southern United States in the 1990s. They are more aggressive than European bees, but their reputation as predatory killers is exaggerated. They sting only in defense. Nevertheless, multiple bee stings are painful and may cause a strong allergic reaction.

OTHER HAZARDS

>>> **Coral snakes: kill with neurotoxin**
>>> **Pit vipers (fer-de-lances, bushmasters): kill with toxin that attacks blood and flesh**
>>> **Peach palm and other spine-bearing plants: cause scratches, deep cuts**
>>> **Sawgrass: sharp blades slice skin**
>>> **Poison dart frogs: Skin toxin can kill if it touches an open wound**
>>> **Bats: carry rabies, inhaling powdered bat dung in caves can cause disease**
>>> **Piranhas: deliver painful bites, nip off fingers and toes, not enough to kill humans**
>>> **Stingray: excruciating stings with venomous, barbed tail**
>>> **Electric eels: charge with such force it can knock a person out and cause drowning**
>>> **Wasps and bees: deliver painful stings**
>>> **Scorpions and spiders: bite with painful and deadly force**

Beware snakes near water, like this rattlesnake on a mangrove branch in the Everglades.

AVOID HAZARDS IN THE WATER

THE WATER CREATURE most feared by natives of the Amazon Basin isn't the crocodile or the piranha. The former usually has known habitats, such as low rivers in the dry season, and can be avoided. Crocodiles and caimans rarely attack humans. And there are no confirmed human deaths from piranha, although they occasionally bite off fingers and other chunks of flesh.

No, the most feared water animals are the candiru and the stingray.

The candiru is a tiny parasitic catfish that swims into the urethra of a person urinating in water. The fish's spikes lodge its body firmly in the urethra, causing great pain. Native methods of getting the fish to let go include giving the victim fruit tea from the jugua tree.

The stingray lies invisible under the sand and silt of clear water. When disturbed, it jabs its barbed tail spike into its victim's leg. The painful wound becomes infected and festers. Natives walk cautiously in shallow, clear water, agitating the sand in front of them with a stick to dislodge any hidden rays.

Leeches are common in swamps and jungle streams. They are not poisonous, but their suckers penetrate the skin, providing pathways for germs to enter the body. Tuck pant legs inside wool or synthetic socks, or into tops of boots, or wrap them with elastic bands to prevent leeches from swimming up the inside of the trousers.

EXPERT TIP Swallowed or eaten, leeches can be a great hazard. Treat water from questionable sources by boiling or using chemical water treatments. Survivors have developed severe infections from wounds inside the throat or nose when sores from swallowed leeches became infected.

U.S.ARMY

WATCH OUT FOR WATER SNAKES

THE ANACONDA, or water boa, is the world's biggest snake. It grows up to 30 feet long in the Amazon Basin. It is non-venomous but crushes animals as large as adult deer by surrounding its prey with its coils and tightening its grip.

Naturally, folklore has fashioned stories about this creatures's power. The Spanish authors of a popular 18th-century travelogue about the Amazon rain forest gave a colorful description to the snake the natives called *jacumama* (anaconda): "It is a serpent of a frightful magnitude and most deleterious nature.... They generally lie coiled up and wait till their prey passes near enough to be seized. As they are not easily distinguished from the large rotten wood, which lies about in plenty in these parts,

they have opportunities to seize their prey and satiate their hunger."

Anacondas' fame has also inspired movies in which they move like lightning and swallow adult humans alive.

The truth is far less entertaining. Anacondas rarely attack humans, and when they do it is usually a defensive response to danger. Bites and constriction do, pose a threat. However, there are no documented accounts of anacondas eating people. Some folktales describe the snakes as having attacked and consumed people at water's edge, but this type of attack has never been officially documented.

Other water-loving snakes often can be found along the banks of rivers and streams in the rain forest. Watch for them as you hike along the river's edge or step into or out of a canoe or raft. Away from the water, don't step in places where snakes are likely to hide. If you must cross a log on a rain forest trail, always step on top of the log and then step down to the forest floor a full pace away from the log's base. Snakes like to hide in the dark, cool space where the log rests on the forest floor.

how to

REMOVE A LEECH

1. Do not burn off a leech as it will regurgitate into your skin, which will likely cause an infection. Instead, move your fingernail under the thin end of the leech to break the seal on its oral sucker. It will try to reattach, so move quickly to Step 2.

2. While continuing to hold the oral sucker free, use another fingernail to break the seal on its anterior suction device (the thicker end of the leech).

3. Flick leech away and treat skin with antibiotic. Due to the anticoagulant released by leeches, the bite will bleed profusely. Treat as any other bleeding wound.

NAVIGATION

Don't fight the jungle. Look for ways to take advantage of natural breaks in the vegetation. Ridgelines generally are easier to travel because they minimize the number of stream and river crossings and generally are not as thickly overgrown. They also catch breezes that sweep away many flying insects. / Avoid secondary rain forest and other thick vegetation, such as that lining a river, where possible. / Beware of how quickly jungle soil can change character. Rain churns red dirt into mud. Rice fields become soft and soggy in wet weather. Swamps are difficult to cross. / Rivers and streams form the highways of the rain forest. Riding a raft or a log floatation device will speed travel, but beware predators, rapids, and narrow canyon channels, which may flip or trap watercraft. Always scout ahead. The overturning of a raft nearly killed Isabel Godin and set her on her trek to walk out of the Amazon rain forest. Impassable sections of a river must be portaged to avoid risk of drowning. / Thick jungle growth may complicate the use of map and compass. You may not be able to see prominent landmarks through thick vegetation. Although a compass or GPS may help you figure out where you are, getting to your intended destination in a straight line may be impossible. Plan to move along easy routes and figure your progress with pace count, compass bearings, and dead reckoning. Or follow a stream marked on your map.

MOVE THROUGH THE JUNGLE EFFICIENTLY

MOVE GRACEFULLY and smoothly through tangled growth. Pushing through vines and branches invites cuts and puncture wounds from spikes and thorns, as well as bites from insects in the foliage. Clear a path with a machete only if you need to do so, as in a stand of bamboo. Try to look through the jungle, not at it. You will spot more natural breaks and game trails in the undergrowth.

TRAVERSING SWAMPS

SWAMPLAND IS among the most difficult terrain to traverse. Shallow water may be difficult or impossible to cross on foot, yet its lack of depth may prevent movement by most boats.

Navigation is further complicated by the lack of prominent terrain features—the monotony of brush, grass, and trees makes one channel look much like another.

A johnboat is well suited for swamp travel. It is long, shallow, flat-bottomed, and stable. The narrow design allows it to be backed out of dead ends. Canoes also work well in swamps. They are narrower and more maneuverable than johnboats and can be carried over obstructions. However, they lack the stability of a johnboat, which remains sturdy when an occupant stands up.

OBSTACLES

HIGH HEAT AND HUMIDITY, coupled with the work of walking through thick vegetation, quickly tire most travelers in rain forests and swamps.

The worst groundcover probably is bamboo, which usually must be cut with a machete. However, bamboo tends to grow in stands, and it may be possible to navigate around it.

Walking through swamps may slow the rate of progress to as little as 100 to 500 yards per hour. In the rainy season, flooding may simplify travel by allowing the use of boats.

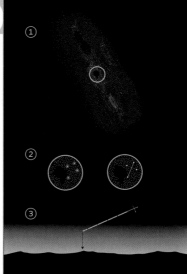

NAVIGATE BY THE SOUTHERN CROSS

1 Trace the Milky Way until you find the Coal Sack—a dust cloud like a black hole amid the stars. Locate Southern Cross just to one side, with its eastern and southern stars among the brightest in the sky.

2 Draw a line through the long axis, starting at the higher star.

3 Extend line 4.5 times its length, then drop your eye to horizon. The point at which your line of sight intersects the horizon is due south.

JUNGLE NAVIGATION TIPS

IF YOU DON'T HAVE A GPS, use a pace count to measure distance in the jungle. A rough estimate of paces per mile is 2,100. However, pace counts vary by length of stride and terrain being crossed. Practice measuring and counting your paces to figure the distance you cover over rough terrain.

Don't be reckless when following a jungle trail. Trails may quickly become overgrown with vegetation, or they may not conform to markings on a map.

If you become lost, try to figure your last known position. Use your pace count to figure if you may have walked past your destination. Compare the surroundings with a map and your GPS. Look for features that would appear on your map—rivers, mountains, etc. Don't hesitate to turn around and retrace your steps, following a trail or machete cuts in the vegetation.

If you plan a jungle trip, buy a new-model GPS. Old-style versions don't work well under a thick jungle canopy. If you have an old model, use it in open space near a river or in a clearing.

USE A MACHETE

>>> Swing easily.
>>> Chop downward and as low as you can so that stems and branches will fall away from the path.
>>> Don't leave bamboo spikes; they can puncture a foot.
>>> Slicing creeper and high growth may make it fall on your path; you can walk over it.
>>> To conserve energy, don't make any unnecessary cuts.
>>> Part vegetation with a stick to avoid bugs, snakes, and plant spikes.
>>> Check skin frequently for insects disturbed by the machete.

VISIBILITY IN RAIN FOREST FOGS AND RAIN

WEATHER PATTERNS in tropical rain forests have predictable humidity, heat, and rain, as well as inky darkness at night.

Tropical rainfall is usually intense and brief, and often occurs at the same time of day, in afternoon or early evening. The rain may be so intense that it severely reduces visibility and makes travel impossible. After a rain, heavy ground fogs may last for hours until the rising sun burns them off.

Fog and damp mist often shroud highland tropical rain forest. The combination of limited atmospheric visibility and steep, slick jungle terrain makes movement in mountainous jungles extremely difficult.

Underneath a thick jungle canopy, overhead vegetation may block the sun and most sunlight. Navigation by stars and moon, as well as cast by shadows, becomes difficult.

MANGROVE SWAMPS

Mangrove swamps create some of the most difficult travel conditions.

Visibility is blocked by curtains of roots, branches, and vines. Streams sometimes form channels that can be followed on a raft or boat, but the root systems usually preclude a clear path.

A compass or GPS provides useful information about bearings, but straight lines are impossible to travel in a mangrove swamp.

A U.S. Army manual urges avoidance of mangrove swamps, but acknowledges a survivor may need to walk out.

Mangrove swamps abound in wildlife that can be hunted and fished, including crabs and catfish. They may also teem with leeches, crocodiles, and snakes.

TYPES OF SWAMP FOREST

Mangrove swamps are identified by bark. Red mangrove thrives in well-flooded terrain. It combines aerial roots that grow down and ground roots that grow up, weaving a curtain of wood. Black mangrove is more open, with fewer root mazes. White mangrove is the most open. Other types of swamp forests include palm swamps, with large ferns and palm trees; catival swamps, with high, closed canopies; and coastal thicket swamps, which mix salt-tolerant shrubs and coconut palms.

how to
SURVIVE QUICKSAND

1. Don't struggle; grab hold of any solid branch lying on the quicksand and lie on top of it.

2. If you don't have access to a branch, increase your surface area by arching your back and slowly wriggling your feet apart.

3. Treat the quicksand like a fluid on which you must float. Don't try to walk out; lifting one leg adds weight to the other, sinking it deeper. Continue leaning back and increasing your surface area until your legs rise to the surface and your body floats on the sand.

4. Slowly work your way back to solid ground by moving snakelike, one limb at a time while keeping body weight distributed.

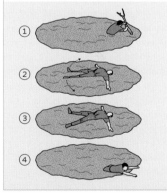

EXPERT TIP To move easily, you must develop "jungle eye." You must focus on the jungle farther out and find natural breaks in the foliage. Look through the jungle, not at it. Stop and stoop down occasionally to look along the jungle floor. This action may reveal game trails that you can follow.

U.S.ARMY

remember the moment it struck me that something was terribly wrong. It was about four days after I had cut my hands while hacking through a virtually unexplored and impenetrable rain forest in South America on my first trek studying Sakis—rare, sweet-faced, long-tailed South American monkeys.

I was so busy keeping an eye out for the "real dangers" of the Guyana rain forest, like deadly venomous snakes and jaguars, that I did not pay much attention to these little scrapes, other than to take precautions right away by slathering them in antibiotic ointment. But now my hands were blistered and swollen like balloons. And I had another apparently unrelated set of symptoms on my knees and thighs: red streaks and gaping raw surface wounds. I pondered, with some alarm, the cause, and appropriate treatment. I applied more antibiotic ointment.

Under different circumstances, I would have immediately seen a physician or at least called one, but in this case, I was in the middle of nowhere, with no satellite phone, no e-mail access, and no village in sight, let alone a medical facility.

I sat by the campfire trying to decide what to do, since leaving my own expedition was not an option. Too

National Geographic emerging explorer and wildlife correspondent Mireya Mayor is a primatologist working to protect rare and critically endangered primates in the wild.

much grant money was at stake, not to mention I also didn't want to let down my expedition co-leader, who had also worked so hard to get us here. My hands had continued swelling to the point that I was no longer able to brush my teeth or zip up my pants without a struggle. I finally realized I might have let things go too far when I saw the expressions of disgust in faces of the otherwise placid villagers, who asked me to cover up my hands, which they thought had been steam burned. "Ok, maybe my hands do look bad," I thought. More wounds were appearing and now the red streaks were up to my stomach. I decided that, at the shameful cost of being labeled a quitter, maybe it was time to go home.

Once I had made my decision to leave, it took me two more days to walk to a village and arrange for a boat to take me back. I became very aware of just how useful hands are when navigating though the forest, something I had previously taken for granted. Once in the capital, I went to the main (and only) "hospital," where there were more dogs and chickens in the waiting area than patients. The doctor brought me into a private room and asked how I had burned my hands. He didn't believe me when I told him I hadn't burned them, and he began applying a silver cream used to treat burn victims. He then walked over to a little table and picked up one of several open (and quite obviously used) syringes. When he said, "This shot of calcium will do the trick," I knew it was time to leave—not only the expedition, but the country. Despite his explanation that using a new needle on every patient that walked into the hospital would be too costly, I respectfully declined and starting making arrangements to head back to the States. The flights were all full, but even with a roomful of waiting passengers, the airline clerks found me a spot on the very next plane. Frankly, I think the clerks just couldn't bear to look at my hands. When the plane landed, attendants required me to wait until a wheelchair escort arrived to take me to the main terminal. I guess it really hit me then that I did not look good. At the hospital in Miami, my mom greeted me and immediately began to cry when she saw my hands, which were by now swollen to the size of volleyballs. Later, I overheard my doctor speaking to the nurse outside my room, saying it was the worst case of blood poisoning he had ever seen and that if I had been delayed by just one more day I probably would have died. I apologized to my mom.

I remained hospitalized for the next ten days, hooked up to IVs, taking strong antibiotics for the infection and steroids for the swelling, and slowly I tried to regain the use of my hands. I had a systemic (blood) infection. Had those red lines—which I now recognize as the visible signs of systemic infection—completed their journey up my legs and stomach to my heart, I would have died. Slathering on the antibiotic ointment hadn't helped because the moist paste had not allowed the wound to dry, and the dirt that stuck to the ointment only furthered the infection.

Having learned this, I would later go on to save two team members' lives on two different expeditions by recognizing the telltale signs of systemic infections. Neither of them could imagine that their tiny scrapes had poisoned their blood, even as the poison was shooting in red streaks toward their hearts. So remember two things: First, allow wounds to dry and if red streaks appear, seek medical attention immediately. Second, it's not only the deadly snakes or the malarial mosquitoes you need to watch out for in the rain forest—it's those pesky little cuts.

Life feels difficult in high mountains, Nando Parrado concluded after assessing his odds of survival. / In 1972, a plane carrying Parrado and his Uruguayan rugby teammates crashed 12,000 feet above sea level in a remote section of the Andes. Most passengers survived the impact, only to emerge into an icy lunar landscape. / They saw no animals or plants. The thin air tore their lungs and made their hearts pound during the slightest physical activity. Steep cliffs surrounded them, rising to 17,000 feet. At night temperatures plummeted far below zero. / "We were absurdly out of place here, like a seahorse in the desert," he thought. "Life is an anomaly here, and the mountains will tolerate that anomaly for only so long." / Yet Parrado and two companions, unskilled in rock climbing and unaccustomed to cold weather, walked out of the mountains and fetched help. They improvised insulation from seat cushions, water collectors from bottles and metal sheets, and snow gear from salvaged wreckage. Although they had begun their journey expecting a summer rugby game, Parrado and the other survivors lived 72 days on wits and courage.

HIGH MOUNTAINS

WITHIN THIS CHAPTER

PREPARATION

People disagree on what constitutes a "mountain." To America's colonists, the 3,000-foot Appalachians seemed formidable. However, settlers in the Andes would have called those mere hills. Differences make generalizations difficult. Travelers should learn conditions of mountains they intend to cross. / Mountains are classified low or high based on elevation and local relief, or ascent from surrounding terrain. Low mountains have local relief of 1,000 to 3,000 feet and summits that support trees. High mountains exceed 3,000 feet in local relief, and treeless peaks, glaciers, and year-round snow are common. / In any high mountain survival situation, prepare for thin air, extreme weather with sudden changes, rock and scree slopes, avalanches, and lack of food. Gravity adds a new risk. "Climbing a mountain is a struggle," Parrado said. "But descending is more like surrender. You are no longer fighting gravity, but trying to strike a bargain with it." Parrado tried sledding but quit after ramming a snowbank at 60 miles per hour. / If a rescue attempt is likely, stay put. If conditions demand movement, follow the safest route in daytime to lower ground.

THOROUGH PLANNING

PREPARING FOR TRAVEL in the mountains begins with physical conditioning. Assess your readiness by hiking uphill, making gradually higher climbs. Exercise to build strength in leg muscles and the cardiovascular system. Train yourself to use a compass, altimeter, map, and global positioning system. Plot routes in advance, but be ready to change them based on weather conditions. Carry layers of clothes for sudden shifts in temperature; prepare to prevent sunburn, windburn, and frostbite. As there is likely little to eat, carry high-energy foods.

ACCLIMATE TO ALTITUDE

>>> Take time to adjust to thin air above 8,000 feet.
>>> If ascending, stop for two nights at 9,000 feet.
>>> At higher altitudes, climb only 1,000 feet a day to reduce risk of altitude sickness.
>>> Once acclimated to a particular elevation, you remain so until you ascend or descend.
>>> Without acclimation, slow down. Consider taking the prescription drug Diamox above 8,000 feet.
>>> Be aware that people acclimate at varying rates, and a few never do.

SURVIVE A PLANE CRASH IN THE MOUNTAINS

A PLANE CRASH sets off an extensive search. Rescuers likely will have a rough idea of your location by following your flight plan and last recorded position. Most often, the risks of leaving a plane in high mountains exceed the risks of staying. However, you may need to move away from the wreckage because you are exposed to cold, wind, and snow; in danger from avalanches or falling rocks; or short on food. If you are in a group, dispatch scouts in pairs to survey the surrounding terrain. They should stay within visual range of one another and mark their route as they leave the wreckage so they can follow it back. The scouts should not move at night, nor should the crash survivors try to get through an unknown, potentially dangerous landscape in the dark. Try to light three signal fires. If you move, seek natural shelter, pile up rocks, or dig.

WHAT TO DO

>>> Move away from the plane until you're sure the fuel will not ignite.
>>> Return when it's safe because wreckage should be easy to spot from the air.
>>> Debris can be used for shelter and signaling, and may contain food.
>>> If you must leave, indicate your direction.
>>> Go downhill.

EXPERT TIP The challenges raised by mountain travel often are matters of distance and remoteness. You and your group will require appropriate gear and provisions, just as for any trek adventure, but you also might need to prepare to be more self-reliant than when you are close to or at trailhead.

BASIC CLOTHING

WEAR MULTIPLE LAYERS of clothing. The outermost layer should be waterproof, windproof, and hooded. Protect against heat loss through the head by wearing an insulated hat with earflaps or a woolen tube, sometimes called a "head-over," under the hood. Woolen, fingered gloves worn under mittens provide the best protection for hands, but spare pairs of socks can double as emergency gloves. Wear two pairs of socks under calf-length, watertight, broken-in boots. Pack sunglasses and sunscreen to protect against blinding sun caused by thin air, clear sky, and snow reflection. Sunglasses can be improvised by cutting eye slits in cardboard.

SPECIAL CLOTHING

IN SURVIVAL SITUATIONS, you won't always have gear with you, but if you do have the chance to prepare and pack, be sure to include items to protect you from the extreme cold. Lightweight but durable gear is best, especially at high altitudes where any movement is required. Clothing with waterproof but breathable shells, such as Gore-Tex, provides protection from the elements. Inner layers are important too; use them to trap body heat yet keep you dry.

GEAR UP FOR MOUNTAINS

>>> **ECW ("extreme cold weather") canteen.** Stainless-steel, double-walled, and highly insulated vacuum bottle with silicone mouthpiece to keep lips off icy metal.
>>> Gas heater for melting snow to make drinking water and cook food. Must keep fuel and stove clean.
>>> Dome tent. Bury it partway in a snow bank to stabilize it.
>>> Personal locator radio or satellite radio. They generally work on line of sight, so use them on high ground and don't waste batteries.

MULTI-PURPOSE POLYETHYLENE BAGS

CARRY BRIGHTLY COLORED, lightweight polyethylene sheet bags. You can use them for temporary shelter from wind and rain. You can spread them to collect water or signal a plane.

Climb into them fully clothed to stay warm, and pack in extra insulating material. If you must wade an icy stream, place your clothes inside the bag before you cross and hold it above the water.

TECHNICAL TRAINING FOR MOUNTAINS

STEEP MOUNTAIN terrain ranks with open ocean and the poles as the most potentially dangerous environment on earth. Besides the obvious hazards of falling on steep, loose rock or ice, there are the more difficult-to-assess hazards of falling rock, avalanches, and crevasses. If you are considering travel in steep mountain terrain, train with an IFMGA (International Federation of Mountain Guide Associations)-certified mountain guide or school. Learn how to climb up and down on rock, snow, and ice and how to use the tools of the craft safely. Practice on smaller snowfields, glaciers, and crags. Then work into larger mountains, never forgetting the most important pieces of equipment: your alert mind and sound judgment.

CLIMBING GEAR FOR STEEP ROCK AND ICE

>>> Climbing rope, helmet, harness, rock shoes
>>> Protection: camming devices, nuts, chocks, pitons, and bolts
>>> Carabiners and slings to connect the system
>>> Crampons
>>> Ice axe or axes
>>> Ice screws

EXPERT TIP Monitor weather forecasts in the days leading up to your departure. Use your best weather sense while you are in the field, too. If stormy conditions turn you back, remember that the mountains will still be there the next time you want to head for the high country.

MONITOR THE WEATHER

BROADCAST WEATHER FORECASTS should be compared with local conditions in assessing risk. A handheld, personal weather station can provide local data and sound an alert when it calculates a storm's approach. Cloud shapes point to weather changes. Puffy cumulus indicate unstable air, and storms if they grow into cumulonimbus. Flat stratus usually mean stability. High, horsetail cirrus often indicate a storm's arrival the next day. Wisps of snow on distant ridges indicate the approach of wind.

BEWARE BAD WEATHER

>>> Thunderstorms. Watch for afternoon buildup of cumulus clouds. Do not climb; seek shelter.
>>> Lightning. Count seconds between flash and thunder; divide by five to get distance in miles. Kneel on a dry pad and discard metal objects. Stay alert until 30 minutes after last thunder.
>>> Traveling storms. Look for low clouds rising and clouds at different heights, or thickening and lowering of cirrus clouds. Severe snowfall likely in winter.
>>> Fog, whiteout. Conditions prevent travel.
>>> Hail. Large stones cause serious injury.

FIRE

Fire is crucial at high altitudes. For every 1,000 feet of elevation you climb, the temperature drops about 5°F. Trouble is, thin air and cold temperatures first restrict and then eliminate trees, a potential source of fuel. The so-called "tree line" ranges from 2,000 feet in Scotland to 12,000 feet in southern Colorado, to 15,000 feet in Ecuador. Above that height, only alpine vegetation grows. Alternative fuel sources may include airplane wreckage, grasses, and low heath—or virtually no fuel at all, as Nando Parrado and his rugby teammates discovered in the Andes. High winds and rain or snow complicate lighting and maintaining fire. / To light a fire in wind, build it in a trench or natural hollow protected from gusts, or behind rocks stacked into a semicircular wall. Use the largest, most stable rocks available, and chink gaps with mud. If you're below the tree line, a good source of dry wood during a rainstorm is a thick pine log. Split it and build fire in the dry interior. Tarps can shelter small fires if the wind blows from a constant direction. In snow, build fire atop a base of rocks, plane wreckage, or dirt.

Use rocks or other natural formations as a barrier against wind and precipitation.

HIGH ALTITUDE COOKING

LOW PRESSURE AT high altitudes causes water to boil below the sea-level boiling point of 212°F. At one mile high, the boiling point is 201°F; at 10,000 feet, it is 194°F.

Increase cooking times and amount of water. Keep adding water to replace what boils away. Soak dehydrated foods longer before cooking.

CARRY STOVES AND FUELS

>>> Good for fires where fuel is scarce or non-existent. Stoves that are sturdy light easily at high altitude, and burn a variety of fuels are best. Keep stoves clean, and turn them off before you sleep.

>>> White gas: Works in all temperatures, resistant to blowing out in wind. Avoid using old fuel, which decomposes.

>>> Gasoline and kerosene: Require regular elimination of soot buildup.

>>> Alcohol: Relatively low-temperature flame adds cooking time to meals.

>>> Butane: Liquid will not vaporize in subfreezing cold. Use mix of butane and propane instead.

>>> Aviation oil: Congeals in cold; requires heating before it will ignite. Do not use in cooking. Mix at ratio of one part aviation fuel to four parts oil for emergency fire.

how to

CARRY A FIRE

1 To move embers from one spot to the next while traveling, or keep ember ready for starting signal fires, find a metal soft-drink or other can or nonburnable receptacle (Native Americans used animal horns). With a sharp object, poke holes in the sides.

2 Place a layer of slow-burning material such as moss on the bottom of the can. Place the embers on top of the moss.

3 Place another layer of slow-burning material on top of the embers. Don't pack too loosely or tightly. The former will cause the embers to flare; the latter will suffocate the fire.

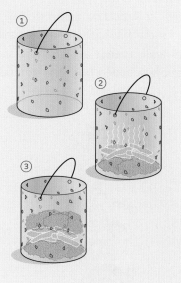

WATER

"The cold was always our greatest agony," wrote Nando Parrado of his 72 days in the Andes, "but in the earliest days of the ordeal, the greatest threat we faced was thirst." In thin air, the human body works harder to supply oxygen to the bloodstream. The body accelerates breathing to maintain a steady intake of oxygen from an air-starved environment. Each exhalation removes moisture from the body. Cold mountain air also is drier than warm, sea-level air, adding to the body's water losses. Dehydration swiftly overtakes the novice mountain traveler. Climbers must drink vast amounts of water just to maintain equilibrium. Carrying two quarts on a daylong mountain hike in moderate temperatures is recommended. / Rushing streams typically flow out of mountain ranges. They, like other water sources in the wild, should be purified before drinking. / Snow and ice should be melted to make drinking water. Sucking on a ball of snow may satisfy thirst for a while, but the cold robs the body of heat, speeds dehydration, and causes injuries to the mouth. Snow scooped from the ground may contain microorganisms.

GET WATER FROM THESE SOURCES

>>> Rocky ground. Look for springs. Porous limestone encourages seepage.
>>> Cliff bases.
>>> Clay bluffs. Clay holds water; green vegetation on a canyon wall may indicate its presence.
>>> Dry streambeds. Dig at the outside of stream elbows; water may be just below the surface.
>>> Beware of water near old mine shafts and ore dumps. It likely is contaminated.

essentials

MELTING SNOW

Do not eat snow or ice. They rob the body of heat and increase thirst. Melt with fire, sun, or body temperature.

COLLECT snow from close to the ground. It is more tightly packed, and will yield more water than snow near the surface.

MELT ice and snow over a stove or by placing it on a dark, reflective surface in direct sun. Make a depression in the center of dark material to collect the water. A dark piece of cloth or a flat rock is adequate.

BREAKING ice into chunks speeds melting with less expenditure of fuel.

MELT a small amount of snow in a pot. Let water get warm before adding more. Add new snow gradually. Melt only what you need, and drink the water when it is a pleasant temperature.

PACK snow into a bag of porous material, such as a sweater tied shut, and suspend it next to a fire. Collect the drips in a container beneath the bag. Be careful not to hang the material too close to the blaze.

SQUEEZE snow with hands to get moisture.

PUT snow in a clear bottle and let sunlight melt it.

IF YOU HAVE no external method of heating snow, place it in a waterproof bag between layers of clothing and let your body heat melt it.

WHEN IN DOUBT about water's purity, boil it. Do not add ice to cool the purified water.

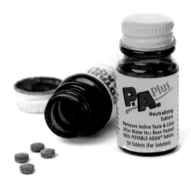

FIND WATER IN SNOW, ICE

CHOOSE ICE OVER snow for melting into drinking water. Ice lacks the insulating air pockets of snow. Thus, ice contains a greater volume of water, which will be released with less heat. Snow near the ground is better for melting than snow near the crust. Compaction increases water yield.

Glaciers are rivers of ice. They flow from the tops of high mountains toward lower elevations. Streams emerge from their leading edges; water collected there should be strained to remove grit and dirt. Glacier ice may look clean, but there is no guarantee it is free of microorganisms. When in doubt, purify drinking water.

PURIFY SNOW AND ICE

>>> Conserve fuel for survival. Clean-looking snow in a remote location is likely ok as is.
>>> If snow appears dirty, boil vigorously.
>>> Disinfect with iodine or chlorine tablets.
>>> Filtration. Bacteria are stopped by a membrane with openings 0.4 microns wide.

SHELTER

Even in the tropics, mountains can be icy. High, barren peaks provide little shelter from wind, ice, and snow. Air rising over mountains drops rain and snow, especially on the windward side, and gusts howl through passes and over ridges. Weather shifts quickly at high altitudes; sudden storms can be deadly. Jon Krakauer, writing about his 1996 ascent of Mount Everest in the book *Into Thin Air*, recalled noticing a few wispy clouds as he stood on the summit. He did not realize they evidenced a bone-rattling storm, which surprised and killed several of his climbing companions. / Shelter construction above the tree line is complicated by lack of building materials. Depressions in rocky walls may provide some relief from wind and snow. Rocks also can be piled into windbreaks and shelters. Chink any openings, and fashion a roof from any available sheeting or other materials. / In an icy environment above the tree line, tarps, snow trenches, and snow caves provide quick shelter. / If you travel in mountains, follow this military survival rule: estimate the time until a storm hits. If it's enough to build a shelter, do so. If not, return to your previous night's shelter.

MAKE A SNOW DOME

USE A TARP to fashion a snow dome in a half hour:

Make a mound with materials at hand. Cover with tarp or cloth.

Compress snow at least a foot deep atop the mound.

As roof hardens, dig in and remove tarp and other contents. Enlarge dome.

Poke ventilation hole in roof. Partially block entrance. Sleep on tarp.

how to

BUILD A SNOW TRENCH

1. Using a shovel, pot, stick, etc., dig trench in snow where snow is at least five feet deep—for example, a firmly packed snowdrift. Keep loose snow in pile next to trench.

2. Dig trench at least three feet deep to take full advantage of snow's insulating properties. Make trench long and wide enough to accomodate you while lying down. Lay tarp, branches, pine needles, etc., on bottom so you're not lying directly on top of snow.

3. Crisscross branches and pine boughs across top, leaving hole for entrance (downwind).

4. Using excavated snow, make foot-high snow mound on top of covered support. Pull branch over door. Allow ventilation.

MAKE A SNOW CAVE

>>> Dig into a large, deep snowbank or drift. Go one yard, then turn 90 degrees and enlarge.
>>> Angle the entrance 45 degrees away from the wind to minimize snow buildup.
>>> Keep roof at least 18 inches thick.
>>> Once you occupy the "cave," partially block its entrance with snow or a backpack.
>>> Allow air to vent at floor and through a small hole in the roof.

UNDERSTAND RISKS OF HYPOXIA

>>> Beginning around 8,000 feet, thin air may cause vomiting, headache, and accelerated heartbeat.
>>> Risks increase with elevation. Mild symptoms may go away in three days to a week if the victim does not go higher.
>>> Everyone is at risk around 12,000 feet.
>>> Extremely high elevations bring on pulmonary or cerebral edema, a dangerous fluid buildup in the lungs or brain. Symptoms may begin with coughing, wheezing, difficulty breathing, and confusion and increase to include swaying while walking, disorientation, hallucinations, and social withdrawal.
>>> Children, heavy drinkers, and the overweight are most vulnerable.
>>> The elderly generally are at lower risk.
>>> Acclimate at one altitude before sheltering at a higher one.
>>> Increase carbohydrates and proteins in diet as you go higher.

EXPERT TIP A few day's rest and drinking plenty of fluids may help the individual to acclimate. If the symptoms persist or the individual worsens, descend 2,000-3,000 feet to the elevation where the individual first began to feel badly. If she does not feel better, seek medical attention.

Girl Scouts.

FOOD

Extreme exertion at high altitude can burn as many as 15,000 calories a day. Yet at the tops of the world's tallest mountain ranges, almost no food grows. Even the air above three miles high is virtually sterile. / Travelers into the highest elevation pack in their own high-calorie foods. At lower elevations, fish and game, such as deer and elk, become plentiful. The roots of certain wildflowers such as balsam root provide necessary vitamins, and even lichens that grow on rocks provide nutrition. There are no poisonous lichens, but all varieties must be soaked overnight and then boiled to eliminate unpleasant acids. / Many varieties of trees have edible buds, shoots, sap, and/or inner bark. Needles can be boiled or steeped into a vitamin-rich tea. Berries and small twigs also provide nutrition, but you must be sure you know what kind you're eating. Juniper berries can be eaten raw or cooked. Cedar trees, however, are poisonous in all their parts.

MUSTS FOR THE MOUNTAINS

A PORTABLE GAS STOVE will come in handy in the mountains for melting snow and ice for water, and for warming and cooking food, especially if you are in rocky, icy, or snowy terrain with few fuel sources.

Other items to bring include freeze-dried meals, water in double-shell non-metallic canteens, high-carbohydrate trail snacks, mixes for hot drinks (they warm bodies as well as morale), and wrapped hard candies.

THE HUMBLE DANDELION

THE COMMON DANDELION grows in sunshine in low mountains. All parts of the plant are edible.

The leaves, flowers, and buds are good in salads, and the roots can be boiled and eaten as a vegetable.

Dandelion plants are members of the chicory family, so their roasted, pulverized roots yield a coffee substitute.

Dandelions contain high concentrations of vitamins A and C, as well as calcium. Their milky sap can be used

FOOD AT ALTITUDE

>>> **Deer. Plentiful in low-mountain woods across the United States.**
>>> **Elk. Larger than most deer and much less common; travel in herds called "gangs."**
>>> **Fish. Cool mountain streams of North America often teem with trout. Trout can be caught using a line and hook. See instructions for making your own on p. 32.**
>>> **Mountain goats. Inhabit impossibly steep alpine terrain but yield thick, warm coat. Pursue only with very accurate weapon.**
>>> **Rabbits. Can be snared or hunted; low in nutritional value, will not sustain you long.**

AVOID THESE PLANTS

All parts of cedar trees are poisonous.

Corn lily, aka false hellebore, resembles a corn plant. It's highly poisonous.

Death camas, aka death lily, flowers in six parts with heart-shaped petals.

Mountain laurel is a poisonous shrub growing eight to ten feet tall. Its clusters of white flowers contain pink dots.

Poison ivy is prevalent throughout North America. Its smooth, serrated, glossy leaflets grow in clusters of three.

USE TREE BARK, NEEDLES, PINECONES

>>> **Boil spruce needles—they're square and sharp—in water to make tea rich in vitamin C.**
>>> **Inner bark of birch trees can be eaten raw, or cut into strips and boiled like spaghetti. Sap also can be eaten straight from the tree.**
>>> **Piñon nuts are good roasted or raw. They also can be ground into flour.**
>>> **Pine tree seeds of all species are edible. Boil or bake young cones in spring, or peel and eat the bark off young twigs.**

Eat plants and animals only in survival situations. For planned travel, pack all food with you.

FIRST AID

High altitudes raise the risk of severe, unique injuries. Hypobaric hypoxia, the low-oxygen state of thin mountain air, can cause mental and physical illnesses. Both, in turn, can contribute to physical injuries caused by loss of coordination, lack of attention, and exhaustion. Falls, extreme winds, and injuries from falling or sliding rocks pose the danger of broken bones—no small thing in a harsh environment, where breaking an ankle can mean a death sentence for a lone traveler. / Travelers at high altitudes can lessen their risks by starting off in good physical condition and taking time to acclimate to their environment. / Take precautions against the cold, bright sun, thin air, dehydration, and injuries caused by ice and loose rock. / Be aware of infectious diseases even though you may be in a cleaner environment. Malaria-carrying mosquitoes fly as high as 6,000 feet at the Equator. Mountain streams may look sterile but teem with parasites such as giardia, whose victims require evacuation and medical treatment. Diseases caused by close human contact increase in frequency among groups at high altitudes because of the tendency to share small living quarters.

CARRY A PERSON DOWN A MOUNTAIN

GETTING AN INJURED person out of the mountains is exhausting work. Search-and-rescue teams with a helicopter offer the optimal alternative. If you do it yourself, consider using a sledge or litter on snow cover. Brake a sledge's descent by walking in front. Over short distances, one person can transport another with a fireman's carry or piggyback. Two people, one with hands under the victim's knees and the other with hands under the armpits, will go farther without tiring. Traverse broken ground pointing your downhill foot 45 degrees down from the direction you are walking for maximum stability. Over short distances, transport a conscious victim with a four-hand seat carry, formed by two rescuers holding each other's wrists to form a "seat."

KEEP CLOTHING CLEAN and dry. Avoid sweating. Change out of socks as soon as they become damp.

Protect your face and hands, especially in high winds.

Wear loose layers of clothes; avoid tight boots that pinch circulation.

If in a group, check your companions' exposed flesh for freezing. Warm frozen spots with bare hands.

essentials

TREATING ALTITUDE SICKNESS

The best treatment for high-altitude sickness is to move the victim to lower elevations. In some cases, failure to move results in death.

ACUTE mountain sickness (AMS). Brought on by too-rapid ascent that does not allow body to adjust to hypoxia (lowered availability of oxygen). Symptoms include headache, vomiting, fatigue, nausea, dizziness, difficulty sleeping, and weight loss. Eating carbohydrates may offer some relief. Return to last comfortable altitude, recover, and then resume ascent at slower pace. Acclimation in a few days also may end symptoms.

HIGH altitude pulmonary edema (HAPE). Generally appears after a rapid ascent above 8,000 feet. Onset may occur with second night's sleep. Symptoms include wheezing, gurgling, coughing, and other signs of respiratory distress, as well as confusion and hallucinations. Victims die without treatment. Give them bottled oxygen if available and move them downhill as soon as possible.

HIGH altitude cerebral edema. Onset usually after HAPE. Symptoms similar to other high-altitude illnesses but also include severe disorientation and a swaying upper body when walking. HACE can kill in as little as 12 hours.

how to

RECOGNIZE FROSTBITE

1 If exposed skin turns red or hurts, cover up or take shelter.

2 Flesh beginning to freeze becomes uncomfortably cold, and may go numb or tingle. Skin turns red, then pale.

3 Shallow frostbite: Place fingers under armpits, feet beneath clothing and against a companion's stomach. Avoid massage, fire, rubbing with snow.

4 Deep frostbite: Treat at a hospital. Thawing on-site invites pain and infection.

SKIN AND ALTITUDE

The sun's ultraviolet rays strike the Earth more intensely at high altitude because they pass through a thinner layer of atmosphere. Sunburn develops much more quickly, and more severely, in thin air, particularly when solar radiation bounces off ice, snow, and rocks. Skin injuries may occur even on overcast or partly cloudy days. Take precautions by applying a sunblock of at least 15 SPF to all exposed skin.

HAZARDS

Weather produces some of the most dangerous mountain hazards. It doesn't stay static. It moves and changes, sometimes quite suddenly. Weather plus exposed, steep terrain make a tough combination. / High mountain ridges and peaks are raked by strong winds caused by solar heating and the collision of air masses with barrier ranges. Snow gets deposited along inclines, building up in layers until instability causes it to break free in an avalanche. Fog and mist collect on the windward side of mountain ranges and in hollows and depressions, limiting travelers' visibility—particularly around 6,000 feet elevation, the zone of most common cloud cover and precipitation. Storms pummel exposed peaks with precipitation, setting off stream-channel floods and lightning strikes in summer and building deep winter snow fields that hide dangerous crevasses and depressions. / Low mountains aren't exempt from bad weather, although they typically lack the extreme cold found at high summits. Rainstorms make trails slick and can touch off floods. Flash floods can occur in low or high mountains, particularly if a storm seems to stall in one place. Rocky terrain, lacking a thick layer of soil to absorb rain, sends storm waters shooting downhill. Rapid water chutes in narrow canyons make crossing hazardous. Blizzards, especially in high mountains, prevent travel.

RECOGNIZE HAZARDS AT ALTITUDE

Above tree line: High winds, snow, rain, hail, and lightning. Snow builds up on cornices and in avalanche zones. Glaciers, or year-round rivers of ice, contain deep crevasses. Ice boulders calve off the end of hanging glaciers.

Below tree line: Greater precipitation creates threat from avalanches, floods, etc. Rain on grass and shrubs along trails may create a hiking hazard.

Travel becomes more difficult in mountains because of rugged terrain.

Blizzards' whiteout conditions disorient and erase tracks. Avoid travel; take shelter.

CHANGING WEATHER

WEATHER VARIES FROM day to day and place to place. A single location may have snow, sun, high winds, rain, and calm. Storms may bash against exposed windward peaks but do little on the leeward side, or in sheltered valleys. Varied terrain subtly alters storms:

Sun and wind strike mountains unevenly, generating local winds and weather patterns.

Storms are deflected and channeled by peaks. Summer thunderstorms may be localized by terrain.

Lines of storms moving in from the west may expose an entire mountain range to severe weather. In winter, blizzards—marked by winds of at least 35 miles per hour and visibility of less than a quarter mile—can smother a mountain like a cold, wet blanket.

Precipitation squeezed out of air as it cools and rises may settle halfway up a mountainside for days at a time.

Mountains near large bodies of water receive extra windward precipitation.

Winds and extreme cold, both common at high altitude, combine to create wind chill indexes that flash-freeze any exposed skin.

BAD WEATHER WARNING SIGNS

>>> Halo around sun or moon getting brighter.
>>> Decrease in air pressure. If you have not climbed higher, double check your altimeter, then prepare for bad weather.
>>> Horsetail cirrus clouds descend and thicken. A storm may be a day or two off.
>>> Lowering of clouds. Cumulonimbus thunderclouds may be forming.
>>> Change in wind direction along with rapid temperature increase.
>>> A variety of cloud levels, all moving and getting thicker.

EXPERT TIP If caught outside in a winter storm, try to find shelter. Pitch a tent, prepare a lean-to, seek a windbreak, or build a snow cave for protection from the wind. Try to stay dry and cover all exposed parts of the body.

Girl Scouts.

AVALANCHES POSE a significant threat to all travelers in high mountains. Most destructive slab avalanches occur on slopes between 30 and 45 degrees. At shallower inclines, snow buildup lacks the tension to trigger a large slab avalanche. At higher inclines, snow doesn't stick enough to create a hazard.

Rock walls at the top of a slope raise the danger of avalanches because falling objects may set the snow in motion. Likewise, trees and rocks caught up in an avalanche's path can kill you.

Convex slopes—where rock bulges outward—are at higher risk than concave slopes. Also dangerous are snow-filled gullies, snowy buildup on the lee side of a mountain (the windward side is compacted), and places where fresh, deep snow has dropped on steep ground.

Avalanches occur when stress is added to a slope such as more snow, rain, rising temperatures, falling rocks, or the weight of humans or animals. Avalanches are very difficult to forecast, but at least be aware of significant environmental changes and avoid crossing or venturing onto snow slopes without consulting local avalanche experts.

essentials

WHAT TO DO IF CAUGHT IN AN AVALACHE

Learn the reactions you must immediately take. It could save you or a companion.

SHOUT. People nearby will mark your spot before the snow hits you. This helps them calculate where you might end up.

BEGIN a backstroke swimming motion to stay on top of snow, breathe through nose.

THRUST an arm in the air. Exposed hands have led to rescue.

CURVE the other arm in front of the face and chest to make an air pocket.

STAY calm if buried. Struggle uses oxygen.

SHOUT when you hear rescuers. They begin their search immediately.

SEARCH for victims immediately. Odds of suffocation increase dramatically with time.

VICTIMS typically are deposited at the deepest snow at the end of the slide.

AVALANCHE probes thrust in snow in a systematic pattern will eventually, if possibly too slowly, help locate victims.

TRAVELING THROUGH AN AVALANCHE ZONE

>>> In general, avoid avalanche-prone areas. However, if you absolutely must cross, send one person across at a time.
>>> Travel in shade before noon. Sunlight raises the air temperature, and fresh heat can start an avalanche.
>>> Look for likely avalanche paths indicated by broken trees. Stay above them on ridges.
>>> Carry brightly colored avalanche tape, locator beacon, shovel, and probe. Make sure you know how to use them correctly.

HAZARDOUS ICE FORMATIONS

THE HAZARDS OF ICE formations at high elevations:

A glacier is a mass of ice originating on land, with an area larger than 100 square yards. It is either moving or has moved in the past.

Glacial streams are formed when runoff from melting ice creates deep, cold, well-scoured channels. Beware lack of solid footing if crossing.

Crevasses are deep fissures in ice caused by floes encountering cliffs and changes in slopes. They align themselves at right angles to the source of greatest tension. Crevasses are hard to see when covered with snow, and if you fall in, they cause injuries and are very difficult to escape.

Ice falls are the broken boulders of ice below a glacier flowing over a steep edge. Ice avalanches are common. Avoid at all costs—very dangerous.

Cornices form when blowing snow creates a crest extending beyond the edge of a rock ridge. Beware of breaking the cornice and falling.

DANGERS OF FAST-MOVING MOUNTAIN STREAMS

>>> Sudden rains can rapidly change water volume.
>>> Melting glaciers increase flow during heat of the day.
>>> Dangerous rapids and waterfalls are likely.
>>> Water speed can unbalance hikers.
>>> Soaked skin in cold environment is a severe threat to health.

EXPERT TIP Indicators of [avalanche] danger include the following: Signs of previous avalanches, steep terrain, accumulation of new snow, variations in the quality of snow layers, especially if one or more layers are airy, granular, or in slab, air temperature rising to near or above freezing.

Avalanche paths may be indicated by broken trees. Avoid hiking along such routes.

MOUNTAIN MICROCLIMATES

WEATHER CAN BE chaotic in the mountains. Breezes may blow only a short distance from gale force winds, while a summit may separate rain from sun.

Microclimate conditions are caused by sun and wind on some slopes but not others; the different altitudes of terrain; and the influence of mountain peaks and valleys on the movement of weather fronts. Travelers should prepare for a variety of microclimates.

FOG AND MIST

>>> Fog and mist occur frequently in mountains because of the interaction of terrain and moving air masses.
>>> Winds striking a mountain barrier can create lasting fog or rain on the windward side.
>>> Inversions are downward-moving layers of stratus clouds, which trap cold air beneath warm air in valleys, typically creating mist.
>>> Thick fog may make travel nearly impossible. Compass, map, and altimeter can help.

LIGHTNING AND RAIN

>>> Mountain ridges and peaks contribute to updrafts that fuel thunderstorms. Storms are most common in the afternoon.
>>> Avoid ridges and peaks close to the clouds.
>>> If lightning approaches, descend as far and fast as you can before taking shelter.
>>> Avoid water, metal, and lone trees.
>>> Seek a place sheltered from direct strikes and ground currents.
>>> If caught in the open, crouch on top of pack.

DIFFERENT TYPES OF WIND

CANYON WIND, aka mountain valley wind. Created by uneven solar heating. Winds blow upslope during the day, downslope at night.

Anabatic wind cools while it rises, depositing moisture along the way.

Katabatic wind warms as it descends a slope, drying landscape as it goes.

Gap wind squeezes through openings in mountain ranges.

The uneven terrain and sharp altitude variations create mountain microclimates.

DESERT MOUNTAIN HAZARDS

PHYSICAL EXERTION IN desert mountains increases the dangers of dehydration. The regular stresses of traveling at high altitude are compounded by desiccated air and temperatures that reach above 100 degrees in the summer. Drying winds also chap lips and quickly raise a sunburn. Climbing will tire all except the most physically fit.

Natural water is scarce in desert mountains. Travelers should carry more water and food than they would in more temperate mountain ranges.

Novices to desert travel frequently are surprised by how quickly the landscape loses heat at night. This is particularly true in the mountains when the sun drops suddenly behind a western ridge. Pack a jacket, even in summer.

Mountain trails can be particularly treacherous in the desert. Lack of binding soils leaves a dusting of crumbling rock and gravel over many surfaces. Stepping onto a layer of eroded granite can be like stepping on a handful of ball bearings. In the absence of trees and other vegetation, trails may be hard to see and to follow. Know your route or risk getting lost in the desert.

High winds in desert mountains, like all winds, inhibit the ability to make fire and build shelter. They also are likely to carry grit and dust that make travel difficult. If you get caught amid blowing dust, get to shelter. In a pinch, the lee side of big rock will shield you from the most direct effects of abrasive, blowing grit. If you can find no shelter, sit on the ground facing away from the wind, cover mouth and nose, and close your eyes.

TERRAIN HAZARDS

>>> Canyons. They can be like a maze. Do not enter unless you know how to get out again.
>>> Slot canyons. Beware flash floods in summer, which may be touched off by a rainstorm many miles away.
>>> Bare rock. Hard terrain and exposed rock raise the risk of twisting or breaking an ankle.
>>> Loose rock. Losing your balance may pitch you into desert plants with spikes and thorns.

ANIMAL HAZARDS

>>> Gila monster. Neurotoxin is injected through a painful but rarely fatal bite.
>>> Scorpions. They hide during the day and come out at night. Shake out boots and clothes in the morning to check for any inside. Stings are seldom fatal.
>>> Rattlesnakes. Watch where you put your hands and feet as you ascend or descend a mountain. If you hear a telltale buzz, freeze, turn your head to locate the snake, and slowly retreat.

AVOID SURPRISING LARGE animals. Make noise, sing, talk. Most large mammals prefer to keep their distance from people and become aggressive only if you stumble upon them. Do not turn and run if you surprise a large animal. They consider such behavior appropriate for prey and may treat you as such. Try to back away slowly until safe.

Black bears zigzag as they approach their prey. Attack with teeth and claws. Must be fought—will not give up if you play dead. Hike in groups to reduce risk.

Grizzly bears bound straight at you if they are attacking. They bite at the head or neck, or shake their victims. May be fooled if you play dead. Hike in groups to reduce risk.

Cougars are secretive hunters that like hunting at night. Do not approach or corner a cougar. Attacks on humans are rare but becoming more common as development encroaches on their habitat.

Moose look docile but are aggressive in the presence of humans. Bulls can weigh 1,000 pounds.

SURVIVE BEAR ATTACKS

>>> Bears attack when surprised by intruder, feel space invaded by intruder, feel cornered, feel threatened for whatever reason, or are very hungry.
>>> Bears, especially females, need to protect cubs and food source. Stay away.
>>> If bear has been fed by humans, may expect handout, becoming aggressive if none is forthcoming.
>>> Bears have notoriously poor eyesight and may not recognize an intruder as human. Talk and shout.

SURVIVE MOOSE ATTACKS

>>> Bulls attack by kicking, stomping, and plowing with their antlers. If you get knocked down, try to roll out of the way before you are crushed by their hooves.
>>> Bulls are particularly aggressive during fall mating season.
>>> Cows with calves may attack in spring and summer. Stay away.
>>> Do not let dogs near moose; their barking makes moose very aggressive.
>>> Back off slowly and change direction if you encounter a moose on a path.

RECOGNIZE BEAR SIGNS

BEARS ARE BIG and bold animals. They do not try to hide their presence. They bite and claw trees to mark territory. They strip tree bark and dig massive, sloppy holes to look for food. They kill and bury game with dirt, tree limbs, and grass to save it for later, creating a stench that often attracts scavenger birds. They leave their hair stuck in trees where they rub themselves. They eat the heads off flowers and pick indelicately through berry patches. After digesting their meals they drop two-inch-wide scat that may contain bits of bone, hair, grass, leaves, and partially digested fruit.

THE BEST WAY to get along with bears is to avoid them. They're most dangerous when they're surprised or feel threatened. During drought and in fall after a dry summer, when they're hungry or need to store food for winter, bears are more of a potential problem.

Think about being seen, heard, and smelled over long distances as you travel in bear country. Hike only during the day. Talk, sing, or carry bells that clank as you walk. If you cross a loud, churning stream, realize that the sounds of your movement may be masked. The wind will carry your odor over great distances and alert bears of your presence, but sudden shifts may cut off the scent. Ideally, try to hike with the wind behind you, carrying your scent before you as an announcement. Be cautious as you go around blind corners and over the tops of mountain ridges, as a bear may be on the other side. Avoid breaking through thick brush and be careful wandering off trail if bears are in the vicinity.

As you walk in mountain woods, keep an eye out for claw marks on trees, droppings, footprints, and other physical signs of bears. If you encounter the carcass of an animal, give it a wide berth; a bear may have killed the game and may plan to return to it soon.

If starting from a trailhead, listen to the advice of rangers, who provide information on bears' whereabouts. Many bears in large parks are tagged with radio frequency devices to protect you—and them—from surprises.

essentials

ESCAPING BLACK BEARS AND GRIZZLY BEARS

These are the different steps you should take depending on which kind of bear attacks you.

IF A BLACK BEAR ATTACKS:

Do not play dead.

Fight with whatever is available—a fist in the snout, a stick in the eye, pepper spray in the face, stones thrown at the eyes.

Do not run or climb a tree. The bear is faster than you and a better climber.

IF A GRIZZLY ATTACKS:

Play dead, facedown.

Spread legs to keep grizzly from flipping you.

If grizzly rolls you faceup, keep rolling until face down.

Weave fingers of both hands together, place over neck.

Fight back only if you have exhausted other options. A grizzly licking your wounds is an indication of its being serious about eating you. Otherwise, do not move until bear goes away.

COUGAR POINTERS

>>> Cougars, also known as mountain lions, usually shy away from people.

>>> If confronting a cougar, don't yell, turn, and run away. This mimics the behavior of prey.

>>> Do try to make yourself look like a bigger animal. Raise your arms and spread your jacket.

>>> Make your group form one silhouette.

>>> Make noise and throw things, but do not bend to pick up any objects.

>>> Keep your dog securely at your side. Cougars eat dogs.

SIGNALING

Signals in the mountains vary with altitude and terrain. Snow itself can be arranged to send a signal to a rescue plane. You can write a simple message in large letters by walking back and forth in the snow to create trenches that cast shadows, contrasting dark and light areas to make the letters stand out. Arrange the message to take advantage of the position of the sun. At the Equator, a north-south message is best, as the sun will be east or west of that line except at noon. Farther north and south, a message should be arranged to take advantage of a sun lower in the sky. Snow also can be heaped into mounds to send one of the common international distress signals, such as SOS or groups of three. / Below the snow line, evergreen boughs or rocks can be piled to make similar messages. The trick is to create contrast with the background color, textures, and shapes. / Polished surfaces are effective as long-distance signals. Plane wreckage contains glass and polished metal, as well as bathroom mirrors. The U.S. Army used polished mirrors to flash signals from mountain to mountain during the 1880s, and the practice is still effective today, with signaling mirrors like the one above. Light signals work best when operated from open, high terrain, such as the top of a mountain ridge. Such sites are also good for lighting signal fires at night and smoke signals during the day. / In fog, mist, and whiteout, whistles are an excellent indicator of direction. Whistles also are easier to pinpoint than the human voice, and they don't give out under strain. Three blasts mean distress.

how to

SIGNAL WITH AN IMPROVISED MIRROR

① Hold a piece of glass, polished metal, or aluminum foil in one hand. Place your other hand at arm's length in front of it. Make a "V" with fingers of the extended hand. Wiggle the improvised mirror until reflected sunlight passes through your fingers, then sight along your arm.

② If the angle between the sun and the rescue plane is less than 90 degrees, the mirror will nearly face the plane.

③ If the angle between the sun and the rescue plane is between 90 and 180 degrees, hold the mirror at a shallower angle.

④ In both cases, aim the mirror at a point halfway between the sun and the intended target of reflected light.

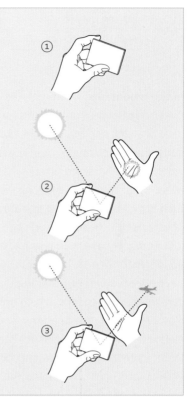

Steep and treacherous terrain requires gear and practice. Train with a pro, or hire a guide.

NAVIGATION

In the mountains, a straight line is seldom the quickest way between two points—unless, of course, the two points are the lip and base of a cliff, and the straight line is described by the plummeting body of an unfortunate hiker. / Steep slopes, avalanche zones, rock walls, talus and scree, glaciers, and ridgelines complicate travel. More often than not, the long way around—along a ridge rather than crossing gullies and streams, zigzagging up a slope instead of attacking it head-on—will take travelers to their destinations just as quickly and with less physical effort than a straight plunge up, down, or across. / Difficult ascents and descents should not be attempted without training in the use of ropes, knots, pitons, carabiners, and chocks, which are beyond the scope of this book. However, survival situations sometimes leave mountain travelers little choice, as Nando Parrado discovered in the Andes. Without technical equipment, he and two companions scaled a 17,000-foot peak. The secret, he said, was to "cut the mountain down to size." By that he meant to concentrate on moving a few feet within his field of vision rather than worry about what lay beyond. "Step-push, step-push. Nothing else mattered," he recalled.

In a group, position the most experienced hiker in front and least experienced second.

UNDERSTAND MOUNTAIN SURFACES

MOUNTAIN SURFACES challenge travelers' traction and balance. Paths often are covered with snow, ice, grit, gravel, or rocks that prove tricky for even the most sure-footed.

On slopes slickened by freezing rain, seek ledges and wear cleats.

On slopes with pebbles, step carefully. Pebbles can act like ball bearings.

Talus is formed by a buildup of fallen rocks at least the size of a fist. Step on the rock's highest part to maintain balance. Beware of rockfall; talus slopes accumulate in fall zones.

Scree—a layer of rocks ranging from pea gravel to golfballs and baseballs—requires a little extra work. To ascend, kick a toe of your boot into the scree to make a step for at least the ball of your foot. To descend, plunge your heel into the slope or take short, shuffling steps. Keep your knees slightly bent.

EXPERT TIP Studying the territory ahead will reveal what maps and guidebooks cannot—the conditions of the moment. Snow levels, vegetation, and weather conditions can have dramatic effects on potential routes. Experience and common sense come into play, too.

DANGERS OF CLIMBING

CLIMBING WITHOUT the aid of equipment such as ropes, crampons, and carabiners is known as "free solo climbing." It is one of the most dangerous sports. Falls of more than a couple of body lengths usually prove fatal, and getting stuck without a way down is equally dangerous.

Don't attempt to ascend or descend a cliff without a rope and an experienced guide. A National Park Service study found that 14 climbers died between 1970 and 1990 while unroped. You may choose to attempt an unroped climb if a short fall is an acceptable risk. Wear a helmet where rockfalls are possible.

Parrado had no mountain gear but nevertheless escaped from his Andes prison. "If we had known anything about climbing, we'd have seen we were already doomed," he said. "Luckily, we knew nothing."

HIKE SOLO VS. WITH A GROUP

>>> Solo hikers must pay attention to their route and minimize injury hazards. Broken bones are a greater danger to a single traveler than to a group member in mountains.

>>> In groups, an experienced leader should take the lead in mountains. The leader should choose the route and alter it as circumstances require.

>>> Routes must take account of the least experienced and weakest group members.

>>> Group members should monitor one another for exhaustion, frostbite, altitude sickness, etc. Solo travelers must remember to police themselves.

>>> Groups should not ascend or descend in vertical lines, to minimize danger of rockfall.

>>> Upper groups should pass through talus and scree while lower groups remain sheltered.

>>> Climbing routes should be mapped from start to finish for solos and for groups, according to level of skill and stamina.

Place your weight squarely over your feet to maintain balance. Don't lean back on slopes.

TECHNIQUES FOR ASCENDING AND DESCENDING SLOPES

STUDY TERRAIN for weaknesses in the rock strata or snowscape and use these to maximize ease of travel. When ascending, cross steep slopes at an angle instead of going straight up. If you must make a short, straight ascent, use a herringbone technique—keep heels in and splay your toes outward—to spread your weight over your feet.

When descending, go at a zigzag angle if the slope is grassy or slick. Descend directly if the slope is scree, hard, dry, and not too steep. Control your speed. Running down a slope may cause you to lose control and pitch forward.

In all situations, keep your weight centered over your feet and take short, easy steps. Stand with your head and feet aligned with center of the Earth, not perpendicular to the slope under your feet. Maintain as much contact between the soles of your boots and the ground as you can. Rest for five to ten minutes every hour as you ascend. If you gasp for breath, slow down and take more breaks. Do not attempt hard or technical climbs without expert instruction.

MANAGE A ROCKFALL

ROCKS HELD IN place by ice are released during a thaw. Water freezing in a crack or a gush of rainwater may split off a shower of stones. Avoid rock faces during temperature swings and heavy rains, particularly if you see rocky piles at their base. Other danger signs include collision scars on walls, rocks on snow, and fine grit on talus.

When climbing, test holds for sturdiness before shifting weight. A single dislodged rock may send you into space or start a chain reaction. If you drop a rock downslope, shout "Rock!"

Rockfalls make a crashing, whistling, or grinding sound. If you sense a fall and cannot get clear, hug the slope and cover your head.

A SLOPE COVERED with ice or snow compromises footing. You may need to kick toes or heels into snow to get a proper hold, just as if you were walking in scree. The hardness of snow cover will determine the best angle for plunging in a boot heel: A hard, steep cut may be needed in dense snow. Beware: Crampons, intended for gripping ice, may fail you in snow if they get covered with compacted crystals.

ENVIRONMENTAL IMPACT

MOUNT EVEREST, famous for its height and majesty, was long noted also for its trash.

Climbers discarded mounds of beverage containers and oxygen canisters high on its oxygen-starved slopes. Their lax attitude concerned environmentalists and the Nepalese government, which announced a ban on bottled drinks on Everest in 1998. Concerned climbers packed out more than a ton of trash in a cleanup effort lasting several weeks, focusing particularly on the dead batteries and spent fuel containers likely to pose the most serious hazards.

A spokesman for the cleanup crew told CNN, "It's a way to experience the mountains and, in a way, pay back for our use of the mountains."

Everest isn't the only mountain to have its beauty suffer after repeated human contact. Air at extremely high altitudes contains almost no bacteria. Discarded trash and organic material, including food scraps and, in the case of Everest, the bodies of some of its victims, remain on the slopes without decay for a long time. Unless mountain travelers are forced to take shortcuts because of a life-or-death situation, they should pack out all trash and leave no trace of their visit.

essentials

WHEN TRAVERSING ICE AND SNOW

Moving in ice and snow complicates mountain travel by making footing even more unsure.

TRAVERSE when climbing a steep, snow-covered slope. Traveling in a zigzag pattern not only is the easiest way up, it also spreads the stress of climbing over various leg and thigh muscles, minimizing strain.

TO CHANGE direction on a snow-covered slope, pivot on the downhill foot.

IF YOU START to slide on one foot, shift your weight to the other.

ON STEEP, snow-covered walls, face the rock and descend step by step by kicking your boots to form toeholds. Do not proceed until you are certain the holds will support your weight.

IF YOU SLIP, immediately head off a dangerous slide with a self-arrest using hands, knees, feet, or ice ax.

TRAVEL SAFELY: GLACIERS

SOME GLACIERS PROVIDE good routes through difficult terrain. However, be aware that glaciers may contain icefalls and deep crevasses. Travelers should rope together when crossing. Individuals should be no more than 30 feet apart and attempt to avoid obvious hazards. Deep crevasses create difficult rescue operations, and stranded hikers may suffer hypothermia while awaiting extraction unless properly insulated.

The leader of a group should be the most experienced in glacier travel, except when crevasses are hidden with snow and the least experienced member may be called upon to lead.

Apply sunburn cream to any exposed skin. Sunlight reflecting off glacial ice increases the chance of a burn.

TIPS FOR TRAVERSING GLACIERS

>>> Walking in high altitude or in snow, go at a steady, unrushed pace.
>>> Take a five- to ten-minute break every hour. Use the time to assess your route, your progress, and any adjustments you need to make.
>>> Keep groups together.
>>> Keep feet dry and healthy. Pack an extra pair of socks and carry bandages.
>>> Dry boots by a fire when camping for the night.
>>> On ice and snow, beware of extreme glare. Snow blindness and sunburn are risks of bright light reflected by white surfaces.
>>> When crossing ice-covered water, carry a pole in front of you. Use it to test ice, keep your balance, and deploy as a safety device should the ice break. It will give you a hold to pull yourself out.

how to
MAKE SNOWSHOES

1 For each shoe, take five straight branches a yard long and just under an inch thick and tie together at one end.

2 Secure other ends, leaving about two inches between tips in a narrow fan shape.

3 Attach two crosspieces in the center to support a boot's toe and heel.

4 Tie the boot to the crosspieces with toe pointing at narrow end.

5 Tie a cord to the tip and pull back to raise it above horizontal. Tie free end to boot.

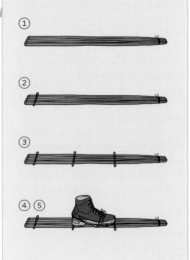

CROSSING MOUNTAIN STREAMS

CROSS MOUNTAIN STREAMS early in the day, when water typically is low. This is especially true if the stream originated at the base of a melting glacier. Look for a wide place where the stream is shallow and not as swift.

Remove socks to keep them dry, but wear shoes to maintain traction. Cross at an angle, heading upstream. As you wade in, drag your legs through the water instead of lifting your feet above the surface. This keeps an even pressure and helps in maintaining balance.

Avoid crossing near a waterfall, turbulence and eddies near big rocks, and places where you can't see bottom.

SELF-ARREST WITH AN ICE AX

IN THE HANDS of a skilled and well-practiced mountain traveler, an ice ax is a useful tool for halting a dangerous slide on a steep, snowy slope.

Use the ax like a waking stick in normal travel.

While traversing, hold the ax in the uphill hand with your grip on the head. When you feel yourself slipping, immediately turn to face the slope. Grab near the spike with your downhill hand and bring the shaft diagonally across your body. Drive the pick shoulder-high into the snow. Your head should be over the pick, your knees spread to create stability, your feet in the air, and back arched to maximize pressure on the pick and knees.

When descending, hold the head of the ax and keep the spike ready to plant into the snow. If the slope is extremely steep, face the slope, kick-step your toes into the snow, and continually plant the ice ax. If there is no risk of avalanche or going over a cliff, you can speed your descent by "glissading." Turn away from the slope, sit, bend your knees, put your boot soles (with no crampons) on the snow, and hold the ax handle across your body with the head in the snow to act as a brake.

MORE SELF-ARREST TECHNIQUES

>>> **If you have no ice ax, turn toward the mountain, facedown. As in the ice-ax self-arrest, try to maximize pressure on knees. Use hands for an upper-body anchor.**

>>> **Do not jam crampons into snow when you start to slide. If they stick, they may injure your ankles as you slide.**

>>> **Factors affecting the ability to self-arrest include the hardness of the snow, the angle of descent, and the swiftness with which the hiker attempts the maneuver. Delays cause a sliding body to pick up speed. Acceleration makes self-arrest much more difficult on a steep slope.**

During the spring season of 1998, I was hired to photograph and film the ascent of an expedition to Mount Everest through the South Col route in Nepal. A few days prior to my departure for Nepal, I met the family of Scott Fischer, a friend of mine who had died along with seven other climbers on

May 10, 1996—an infamously deadly day on Mount Everest. I asked his family members if they wanted me to bring something to Nepal or the mountain for them. They asked if I could retrieve some personal effects from Scott's body, which lay where he had died at roughly 27,000 feet two years earlier. The bodies of climbers who die at such altitudes are not often recovered, leaving visible and grisly reminders of the fragility of life and dangers of the environment. Of course I agreed.

Once on the mountain, I climbed along with the expedition team, while photographing and filming the group. As we began our descent, two renowned Sherpas—Babu Chiri Sherpa and his brother Dawa Sherpa—led me to where Scott Fischer's body rested. But then they continued down, frightened by my insistence on touching a body and convinced that harm would befall me.

When I reached Scott's body, I found him lying peacefully in a light blue

Tommy Heinrich is a climber, filmmaker, and photographer of National Geographic funded expeditions. He was the first person from Argentina to summit Mount Everest.

down suit, partially covered in snow, his legs and boots uncovered, his head protected by his backpack. I spent over one hour thinking, talking to him, and removing several personal effects from the body with great emotional difficulty. I took one of his crampons, a bracelet, a necklace holding his wedding ring, and a pouch containing personal objects, which I placed in my backpack to take home to his family.

As soon as I decided to continue my descent, I realized the rock ledge on which I crouched demanded a long step into the ridge that continued down. Snow had accumulated next to the rock wall, creating an icy step. I tested the step with one foot and it felt hard and solid, so I loaded my full body weight to take my first step down.

What happened next I can't explain, but suddenly I was hurtling, facedown, into the hard ice of the slope.

As I hit the ground a couple of times, I tried to stop myself with the ice ax, which instead plunged straight into my left forearm. I didn't even have time to notice the pain, instead watching in horror as the strap attaching the ax to me unleashed, unwinding itself with sickening swiftness, then suddenly disappearing, along with the ax. I continued plunging down the slope, quickly gaining speed. In despair and with no ax I tried to self-arrest with my feet and crampons, but that made things even worse as I began to spin, hitting against the hard ice with my back, then my forehead, over and over, faster and faster. Every time I spun facedown, I could see the ice getting closer, only to smack into it full force and watch it get farther away ... and closer again ... then draw away at high speed, while I catapulted helplessly over and over against it. Even worse than the pain of these bone-shocking blows was the feeling of helplessness—that nothing I did stopped the unending fall. Yet I did not want to give up trying. Out of desperation, I wrapped my arms and legs tightly together to protect myself, especially my head. In this position, I remember passing by a person very fast and seeing how the slope ahead was coming to an end. It then became clear that nothing I did would stop me from getting killed, that this would indeed be my last fall. Seconds felt like hours, with no hope of survival. Even as I thought this, I wanted so badly to survive.

Suddenly it all became pitch black and quiet, and I was no longer falling, hitting anything. As I pulled my head out of the snow, I saw in disbelief that I had come to rest in a relatively small section of soft ice that ramped up slightly at the edge of a ledge that plunged thousands of feet. Had I not hit this particular spot, I would have gone airborne, straight off the mountain. Instead, I lay alive, though injured, desperately gasping for air, at this elevation of 27,000 feet. I lay on the ground motionless for a couple of minutes, trying to breathe. I could move my arms, and my legs, which at least didn't feel broken. I was bleeding from my head, arm, and leg. I crawled to my oxygen mask, in desperate need to suck some oxygen and recover.

I had fallen over 700 feet from where I started. The people I passed during the fall, Thomas and Tina Sjogren from Sweden, came to my assistance and got me down the mountain to a doctor. I had broken my nose, and one rib, and partially cut a tendon in my left wrist. The greatest lesson of all was that no matter how experienced I was, no matter how good a climber I could be, a small mistake or distraction could take my life in a second.

I feel I was given a second chance to live, to enjoy life wisely, looking at what lies ahead with caution, wisdom, and humility.

When Captain James Riley entered the Sahara Desert after his merchant ship wrecked off the North African coast in August 1815, he weighed 240 pounds. / Upon his rescue that November, he weighed only 90 pounds. In between, his body suffered the tortures of the desert. Wind and sand ripped at his skin. Tremendous daytime heat—hot enough "to have roasted eggs" at nightfall, he said—alternated with cold after dark. Thirst parched him so badly that he drank camel urine just to wet his mouth. Hunger spared him more than his crewmen, one of whom he had to tie up to keep from chewing his own arms. Still, Riley gladly ate camel's blood, snails, and whatever small bits of vegetation he could find. / Indigenous Sahrawi tribesmen captured Riley and his crew and took them hundreds of miles for ransom. The Sahrawis knew the Sahara better than most. Yet even they remarked on its foul temper: snow-like hills of sand that slowed travel, fickle water sources, and the difficulty of navigation amid storms and shifting landmarks. / When a British consul finally purchased his freedom, Riley broke down. He knew he had had the narrowest of escapes.

IN THE DESERT

WITHIN THIS CHAPTER

168 172 174 181 186 191 193 197 199 202

Deserts cover one-fifth of the Earth's land. They range from rocky plateaus and high mountains to sand dunes, broken wadis, and salt marshes. Although definitions vary, deserts are generally dry, barren, and prone to temperature extremes. Earth's highest temperatures, in excess of 136°F, were recorded in the Sahara Desert. In contrast, the Gobi Desert has winter temperatures that dip as low as -40°F. / Rainfall of less than ten inches a year is common for deserts, with portions of the Atacama Desert in South America having gone centuries without a drop. In the driest regions, relative humidity as low as 5 percent kills bacteria, mummifies corpses, and preserves nearly anything. Tire tracks from World War II vehicles still mark the Sahara, and coins dropped there by Roman soldiers are unearthed in good condition. / In such climate, travelers are severely challenged but not outmatched. Humans have lived in deserts for centuries, adapting like native animals to conditions. They have learned to find and conserve water, make shelter, and travel at optimal times. Desert travelers today benefit from experience and should prepare accordingly.

The barbed spines of the cholla cactus can be removed from skin with tweezers or a comb.

KNOW YOUR DESERTS

DESERTS CONTAIN some of the harshest environments on Earth. Surviving unexpected emergencies in these environments involves ingenuity, contingency planning, and knowledge of the environment. The three main types of deserts—mountain, plateau, and sand dune—have distinctly different features.

What they have in common, besides climatic similiarities, is broken, irregular terrain. When rain arrives, it slices into sand and dry earth like a scimitar. Wadis/arroyos may be six feet deep and ten feet across, or several hundred feet both deep and wide. Flash floods carve gullies, deposit mounds of sand and rock, and sometimes make the desert bloom. When the water evaporates, however, deserts revert to stark, arid landscape. Travel in such land is difficult—not just from the heat, sun, and uninviting terrain, but also from the lack of defining landmarks.

MOUNTAIN DESERTS

>>> Ranges of scattered hills or mountains with dry basins in between.
>>> Prone to flash floods, cutting deep ravines and depositing piles of sand and gravel.
>>> Broken terrain gives choice of ridgelines, valleys, or climbs and descents for travelers.
>>> Rain prompts burst of vegetation and may create shallow lakes.
>>> Rapid evaporation dries plant life.
>>> Water in high basins, such as the Great Salt Lake, may be concentrated by evaporation and be too brackish to drink.

PLATEAU DESERTS

>>> Characterized by flat areas with extensive, broken rock surfaces.
>>> Steep canyon walls—wadis in the Middle East, arroyos in the Americas—constrain travel.
>>> Flat, barren areas and valley floors are prone to flash flooding and should not be used for camping.
>>> Dry lakebeds confuse navigation because of few landmarks.
>>> Heat and clear air make distances deceptive, with faraway objects seeming much closer.

SAND DUNE DESERTS

>>> Terrain with true dunes is unusual—less than a tenth of the Sahara.
>>> Generally flat, with windblown sand accumulating in waves and drifts.
>>> Dunes can reach as high as 1,200 feet and be 10 to 15 miles long.
>>> Plant life is limited by shifting sand, and scrub can grow as high as six feet tall.
>>> Rain and surface water are rare.
>>> Sand reduces traction, slows ground travel.
>>> Glare may blind travelers.
>>> Heat from sand-laden winds, direct sunlight, and reflection and conduction from the ground raise temperatures extremely high.
>>> Mirages are likely in bright sun and high heat.

essentials

PACKING FOR THE DESERT

Pack for arid heat, but remember that the desert can get cold after the sun goes down.

WATER, PLUS purifier system.

BOOTS. Lightweight, breathable, not waterproof.

SUNSCREEN. 30 SPF or higher. Apply even under light fabric.

SUNGLASSES/GOGGLES. Two pairs, in case one breaks.

HAT. With a wide brim. Chinstraps keep it secure in desert winds.

CLOTHING. Light-colored, loose, in layers. Desert colors are less likely to attract insects.

WINDBREAKER. And other cold-weather gear.

BACKPACK. With external frame, or one with a curved back that keeps pack from resting directly against your back, so there's breathing space for sweat to evaporate.

HIKING STICK. Useful for keeping balance, defending against animals.

FLASHLIGHT. Necessary for night hiking.

BANDANNA Or high-tech cool rag. Soaked and placed around the neck, it promotes evaporative cooling.

BINOCULARS. Useful in identifying landmarks at great distance.

EQUIPMENT CONCERNS

THE DESERT'S tremendous heat, especially with blowing sand, causes havoc with many types of equipment.

Heat during the day coupled with overnight condensation prompts the formation of rust on bare metal. Keep metal equipment protected from the elements. If you use such equipment in the desert, be sure to clean the metal surfaces after each use and apply a light coating of lubricant.

Glass surfaces are prone to scratching from windblown sand. Keep cameras, binoculars, and other items containing glass in plastic bags, particularly during sandstorms. Don't let dust build up on their surfaces. When in use, cameras and other equipment should be kept where air can circulate inside and around them to prevent the growth of mold. Goggles are a good way to protect the eyes. Blown sand will scratch eyeglasses. Contact lenses aren't a good option because they are difficult to keep in good condition in a hot, dry, gritty climate.

Metal objects placed in the blazing desert sun are likely to become warped by the tremendous heat. When one side of a metal object is in direct sunlight while its other side rests in shade, the metal will bend toward the cooler side. Rifle barrels are not immune to such "thermal bending."

Wooden objects shrink in the dry heat of the desert. Shovels, trowels, and axes may separate from their handles. This is particularly dangerous if the ax head flies off while the ax is being used. Leather coverings also are prone to cracking unless treated with oil to help them retain their moisture.

essentials

CARING FOR YOUR DESERT CLOTHING

Consider wearing fabrics specially made to absorb ultraviolet radiation, designated by a UPF (ultraviolet protection factor) rating. Choose clothes to perform two crucial functions: reflect heat and insulate the body. Follow the acronym COLDER:

CLEAN. Clothes lose their ability to create a cooling, insulating layer when they are dirty.

OVERHEATING. Avoid clothes that don't breathe. They trap in body heat.

LIGHT-COLORED. Choose light-colored clothing that is loose, layered, and long-sleeved. Increase insulation with multiple layers. Retard dehydration with long sleeves and pants.

DRY. Wet clothes lose their ability to insulate. Avoid sweating, and take along a rainproof outer shell.

EXAMINE. Check your clothes for rips and grime every day. Mend promptly, so that rips do not tear further.

REPAIR. Fix tears as they occur. Add a basic sewing kit to your desert survival pack.

how to

IMPROVISE SUNGLASSES

1 Slice a piece of cloth, leather, tree bark, etc., to fit over the eyes like a mask.

2 Cut narrow horizontal slits for each eye. Make sure they're big enough to see out of yet let in the least possible light.

3 Apply soot under the eyes to cut glare. The sun's ultraviolet light, reflecting off sand and light-colored rocks, can burn the surface of the eyes from below.

4 Tie the mask in place with string or cord.

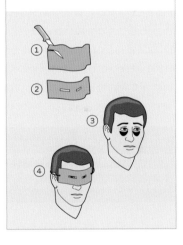

REMOVE WASTE PROPERLY

DESPITE THEIR RUGGED appearance, many desert surfaces are fragile. In proper soil, human waste should be buried at least six to eight inches deep and at least 200 yards from a water source or arroyo. Otherwise, a sudden storm could uncover it, contaminate a precious water hole, and endanger you or the animals that must drink from it.

In rocky or thin, sandy soils, or when in doubt about the impact of burial, pack the waste out.

FIRE

You may not need a fire in the desert. If you've prepared shelter and clothing adequately for the nighttime and you've got an adequate supply of clean water, you could get by without the heat and purifying properties of fire. / However, deserts lose heat quickly after sunset because of their lack of insulating ground cover. Nights may be surprisingly chilly. Nighttime blazes provide warmth as well as signal lights that can be seen at great distances. Fires can dry clothes dampened by sweat or soaked by a rainstorm. A night fire in the desert also drives off animals that hunt at night, and lends comfort to those who gather around it. / Deserts contain little fuel. Travelers should consider packing a lightweight stove, lantern, or charcoal. / Combustible vegetable matter on the desert floor may include dead cacti and brush. Examine them closely before burning. In the desert ecosystem, they may provide homes for birds and small animals. Many desert parks prohibit collection of firewood or open flames. / Leave no trace in the desert. Bury ashes or pack them out.

> **EXPERT TIP** Convex lens: Use this method only on bright, sunny days. The lens can come from binoculars, camera, telescopic sights, or magnifying glasses. Angle the lens to concentrate the sun's rays on the tinder. Hold the lens over the same spot until the tinder begins to smolder. Gently blow or fan.

BUILD A FIRE IN THE DESERT

DESERTS ARE ONE of the most hazardous environments for building fires. Due to the dry climate, sparks from a fire easily ignite ground cover. Native desert plants are easily damaged by fire. Though fire plays a healthy role in the ecosystem of many deserts, such as the Rincon Mountains near Tucson,

Arizona, where fire burns off excess fuels every 5 to 15 years, you do not want to be there when one starts. If you are in a true survival situation and require fire for warmth, signaling, food, or purified water, use a windbreak, clear a wide area of ground growth, and keep the fire as small as possible.

A primitive form of firemaking uses a bow-drill and spindle on a fireboard to make a spark.

CARRY FUEL INTO DESERT

NO FUEL IN THE DESERT? No problem. Travelers can carry small, manufactured fuel sources with them.

Portable stoves and cans of Sterno, a jellied form of alcohol, provide light and enough heat to boil water or warm a small shelter. Canister stoves burn cartridges of butane, isobutane, or propane. White gas and kerosene are commonly burned in liquid-fuel stoves.

Fuel tablets such as Esbit, hexamine, and trioxane also produce bursts of heat lasting several minutes.

Candles and hurricane lamps are useful for providing light at night.

If you are stranded as a result of an airplane or car crash, you can use gasoline and oil for fuel. Mix with sand and light carefully. Be cautious when adding new fuel to the fire in order to avoid flashing.

Candles and hurricane lamps are useful for providing a welcome light at night. For signaling purposes, handheld red flares can be seen over great distances at night.

FIND FUEL IN THE DESERT

NATURAL TYPES of fuel exist in the desert. It's just a matter of identifying and locating them. Cacti and other desert-hardy plants are a likely source of fuel for fires. Unless you are in a life-threatening emergency, however, do not gather dead or dry plants for fuel if birds or other animals are living in them.

DESERT FUEL SOURCES

>>> Dead sagebrush and other scrub brush
>>> Dry grasses twisted into bunches
>>> Dried buffalo, cow, donkey, or camel dung
>>> Dead cacti, if not used for animal homes
>>> Mesquite branches
>>> Cottonwood and willow branches
>>> Acacia branches
>>> Bark from the base of old ocotillos—it contains a waxy substance that readily burns, making it ideal for tinder
>>> Inner bark of cottonwoods and junipers also makes good tinder
>>> Abandoned bird and mouse nests

WATER

"Water is not necessary to life in the desert," wrote Antoine de Saint-Exupéry after surviving a plane crash in the Sahara. "Water *is* life." / "Of the riches that exist in the world, thou art the rarest and also the most delicate," he said. "For thou, water, art a proud divinity, allowing no alteration, no foreignness in thy being. And the joy that thou spreadest is an infinitely simple joy." / Nothing is more important to staying alive in the desert. Water can be as rare as a Mojave rainstorm, and drinkable water rarer still. Yet without it, survival becomes a race against the clock. / Desert travelers use water at an accelerated rate. They must carry most, if not all, of what they need. Unfortunately, water is heavy. A gallon weighs just over eight pounds, and two days' supply 50 pounds. Desert gear should be stripped to bare necessities to make room for water. / Trips lasting longer than a couple of days will require you to find water sources or to cache supplies along your route and recover them as needed. But don't be forced to rely on cached water for survival. Desert animals and other travelers may break into cached supplies. They need water, too.

EXPERT TIP Drink plenty of fluids even if you do not feel thirsty. Injury and death can occur from dehydration, which can happen quickly and unnoticed. Symptoms of dehydration are often confused with other causes.

American Red Cross

DON'T EAT IF YOU HAVE NOTHING TO DRINK

THE BODY SWEATS to rid itself of excess heat. The greater the heat, the more sweat is needed to keep cool.

Sweating is the body's primary source of lost water. To reduce water loss through perspiration, completely cover your body. Reduce your physical exertion, particularly in full sun. Get out of the wind—it dries the skin and robs the body of moisture.

If you don't have water to drink, don't eat. Digestion requires water.

CHECK CONTAINERS for leaks. Opening a water bottle to find it half empty is a terrible surprise.

Don't keep water in just one container. Carry a bottle and drink from it as you go. Or tote water conveniently on your back, in a CamelBak or similar device that allows you to drink from a tube near your mouth. Water kept in an inconvenient place is less likely to be drunk regularly and can cause "voluntary dehydration." Take a lot of small drinks—even just small sips—rather than a few large ones.

Try to keep water at 50° to 60°F, the optimal temperature for absorption. Water can be frozen in unbreakable containers before departing for the desert or kept inside insulated material. Placing a wet cloth cover around a bottle cools the contents through evaporation. Canvas water bags slowly ooze water through their sides, losing about a tenth of their contents while shedding heat. Once empty, bags weigh very little and can be rolled into a small shape. Don't wait to feel thirsty before drinking; you may already be dehydrated.

essentials

TREATING ELECTROLYTE IMBALANCE

Extreme, prolonged sweating coupled with drinking pure water creates electrolyte imbalance giving victims hyponatremia. This is marked by dizziness, disorientation, nausea, and cramps. Victims should rest and rehydrate. The World Health Organization recommends the following as a simple rehydration mix:

ONE LITER (just over one quart) of clear, treated water.

TWO TEASPOONS sugar or honey.

ONE-HALF TEASPOON salt.

ONE-HALF TEASPOON baking soda, if available. If not, this ingredient can be omitted from the mixture.

BLEND AND DRINK to rehydrate.

RECOGNIZE THE FIVE STAGES OF DEHYDRATION

THIRST ISN'T A GOOD indicator of the onset of dehydration; when you crave water, you're already dehydrated by a quart or more. Replace water as you lose it by drinking regularly and conserving sweat.

In the early 1900s, W. J. McGee, a researcher at the St. Louis Public Museum, developed a widely used scale of thirst in five stages: clamorous, cottonmouth, swollen tongue, shriveled tongue, and body sweat. Each accompanies a roughly 5 percent loss of body weight. "Clamorousness" includes complaining, emotional instability, fatigue, and discomfort.

OTHER WARNING SIGNS

>>> Dark, sunken eyes
>>> Trench line along the center of the tongue
>>> Low urine output
>>> Urine darker than diluted lemonade
>>> Very dark, odorous urine

KNOW HOW MUCH TO DRINK

THOUGH THERE ARE general guidelines for how much to drink, there is no precise formula for fluid intake for all individuals. Hydration varies by how much you sweat, your percentage of body fat, metabolism, gastric emptying, and what you are drinking, among other things. Make sure you are familiar with your own fluid needs.

POINTERS FOR DRINKING

>>> According to the U.S. Army, when air temperature is below 100°F (38°C), drink a pint of water every hour.
>>> When the air temperature is above 100°F, drink a quart of water every hour.
>>> Drink more if you exert yourself.
>>> Don't wait until you feel thirsty to drink. You're already dehydrated.

RECOGNIZE POTABLE WATER

STANDING WATER in the desert may be more bane than boon. Pollution from mines, farm fertilizer, and natural chemicals in desert terrain may make water too dangerous to drink. Arsenic, sulfur, lead, selenium, and other toxins are not uncommon.

Native animals know good water. Look for tracks around a pool. Also check for a variety of healthy plant life. Weeds alone aren't enough to guarantee freshness, as many species have a high tolerance for pollution. Sniff for odors such as petroleum, and watch

essentials

FINDING WATER

Know these sources for water in the desert:

CUT into vegetation like cactus and century plants ("How to," opposite page).

DIG into moist soil. This may indicate a dry riverbed or a high water table, with water below the surface.

SEEK depressions and seepage in porous rock, such as limestone.

LOOK for seepage in lava flows and canyon walls.

FOLLOW a dry riverbed to its source; water may still drip there.

DIG in the outer bend of a dry riverbed.

DIG at the base of dunes on the leeward side of prevailing winds.

SOP up dew with a cloth and wring it.

LOOK for cottonwoods and willows; they have greater moisture needs than cactus, and their presence indicates water.

for telltale rainbow slicks. Beware: Rain is clean as it falls, but it begins to collect impurities on the ground.

Extreme thirst will tempt you to drink any liquid you can find; however, consuming contaminated water will weaken you, making travel to cleaner water more difficult. Within reason, try to travel thirsty than risk debilitating illness.

how to

GET WATER FROM A CACTUS

1. Identify a barrel cactus: These are spiny cylindrical, short cacti with pink or yellow flowers growing out of the top. Cut off the top of the cactus with a knife; avoid contact with the spiky outer skin.

2. Mash insides with a stick or spoon until reduced to a pulp.

3. Strain the pulp through a thin cloth, such as a bandanna, catching liquid in your mouth or a cup. The fluid may have an unpleasant taste. If you don't have a cloth, chew the pulp for the liquid. Don't eat the pulp.

GET WATER FROM PLANTS

PLANT JUICE WON'T TASTE pure. Be sure you have a nontoxic plant and add powdered drink to cover any bad taste. Chewing the pulp to release liquid will rehydrate you faster than eating the plant itself. Don't chew the pith of organ pipe, saguaro, or other cactus as it will likely make you sick.

GET WATER FROM ROCKS

STAND ON A HIGH POINT and look for water pockets in shaded, eroded sandstone. Also check cracks in granite. Lick the dew off rocks in the early morning.

PLANT WATER SOURCES

>>> Broad-leafed plants. Look for water at broad bottom of yucca and bromeliad leaves.
>>> Century plant (agave). Cut stalk at base of green stem. Slice stalk into sections. Remove casing and chew pith.
>>> Prickly pear fruit. Remove tiny barbs (glochids) with knife or open flame. Peel.
>>> Wild desert gourd. Found in the Sahara; look for ground vines and fruit the size of an orange. Eat seeds, flowers; chew the shoots.
>>> Dig up roots of desert plants. Cut into two- to three-foot lengths, peel, and suck the water.

TRY HIDDEN SOURCES

>>> In erg formations, dig at a low point.
>>> Look for oases at the base of the leeward side of mountains.
>>> Tinajas are catchbasins carved in rock. Use a shirt to skim off algae.
>>> Don't overlook wells and windmills.

FOLLOW CREATURES TO WATER

WATCH AND LISTEN for flying insects. Bees, wasps, and hornets live within flying range of water. Mark their direction as they fly, as it may lead you to water.

Recent sources of surface water may be indicated by buzzing flies and animal scratches in damp soil.

Grazing animals usually seek water at dawn and dusk. If you don't see the animals, look for their tracks. They may be well worn in desert soil from longtime habit.

Birds fly to and from water, except carrion and birds of prey that take much of their water from their food. A thirsty bird saved explorer Richard Francis Burton's life in the East African desert in 1855. After wandering for 36 hours with no water, at twilight he spotted a katta, or sand grouse, streaking toward a hill. "These birds must drink at least once a day," he recalled. "I cried out, 'See, the katta!'" The bird zoomed to earth near a small spring. Burton followed to sate his thirst. "I have never since shot a katta," he said.

DECIDE TO STAY OR GO

IF YOU ARE LOST in the desert, the easiest ways to get found are to stay where you are and signal for rescue, walk out if you know the way, or retrace your steps and leave the way you entered. The "X" factor in your calculation is water. Do you have enough to move—or to stay?

Staying probably is the best bet, especially if you have left a travel plan with a friend of family member before departing. You'll need a minimum of a gallon of water per person per day while waiting, and that's effective only when everyone rests in the shade without doing any physical activity. If you know nobody is likely to rescue you in time, if you have deviated substantially from your filed route plan, or if someone is badly injured, you may choose to leave.

Plot distances and hike times for legs of the trip. Figure your water needs. Going at night is cooler but slower.

PLAN YOUR STEPS

>>> Walking 20 miles in daytime requires at least two gallons of water.
>>> Walking the same distance at night requires at least one gallon.
>>> Walking without water at night may cause physical collapse after 20 miles.
>>> Walking in daytime without water is foolhardy.
>>> If you have no water, calculate your odds: Is it better to walk 20 miles at night and risk death in a day or two, or to sit tight, extend your life three days, and hope for rescue?

EXPERT TIP Large, heavy meals are more difficult to digest and cause your body to increase internal heat to aid digestion, worsening overall conditions. Avoid foods high in protein, such as meats and nuts, which increase metabolic heat.

American Red Cross

HOW TO CONSERVE WATER IN AN EMERGENCY

Ideally, you should have enough for frequent, small drinks. If not...

STAY out of the sun.

WALK and work only at night, or at dusk and dawn, staying still and covered during the day.

DON'T RATION water. Drink it as you need it; reducing consumption does not cut the body's need, or the rate at which it consumes water.

DON'T DRINK urine or water contaminated by minerals. Use unpotable water to cool the skin.

KEEP your clothes on. Stripping them off invites sunburn and speeds dehydration by allowing sweat to freely leave the body.

STAY OUT of the wind. Breezes increase evaporation and thus dehydration.

DON'T EAT. Digestion requires water, stealing it from elsewhere in the body.

PURIFY DRINKING WATER

DESERT WATER usually is not as clean as mountain sources. Parasites, feces, contamination from animal carcasses, and mineral and chemical pollution raise the risks if you drink untreated water in desert terrain.

TYPES OF PURIFIERS

>>> Use a coarse strainer to remove grit before treatment.
>>> Chemical treatments include iodine, chlorine, potassium permanganate, and chlorine dioxide. They are easy to carry but require time to work and are not always effective against tough parasites.
>>> Microfiltering systems produce drinkable water quickly. Combination filters, such as ceramic and carbon, eliminate parasites and chemicals.
>>> Boiling concentrates pollutants. Steam from heating polluted water may be impure, as some toxins have a low boiling point. Steam from boiled saltwater is drinkable and can be collected by draping a rag over the top of a boiling pot.

Carefully scrutinize standing pools of water. Rainwater gathers contaminants as it sits.

CONSIDER A SOLAR STILL

LITERATURE ON the effectiveness of solar stills is inconclusive. Some sources, such as the *U.S. Army Survival Manual*, endorse them, while others say any water they yield is likely to be less than that expended in construction. Mark Johnson, author of *The Ultimate Desert Handbook*, reports experimenting with desert solar stills for years but finding all but one or two to be failures.

In any case, solar stills require time to build and even more time to extract even a small amount of water. However, in a survival situation, time may be something you have to invest. Do the digging and construction of the still (see below) after dark to minimize exertion and water loss through sweating.

A solar still is a pit covered by a sheet of clear plastic. Water vapor in the enclosed space is heated by the sun and condenses on the plastic.

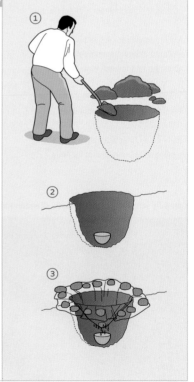

how to

CONSTRUCT A SOLAR STILL

1. Choose a damp site, streambed, or low spot in full sun and dig a pit about two feet deep and two feet wide.

2. Place a container in the center of the pit. If you have a drinking tube, extending it from the container to the surface makes it easier to get to the water without disassembling the still; however, you can get by without a tube in a survival situation.

3. Cover the pit with a plastic sheet and secure it with rocks or sand. Weight the middle so that it dips down toward the container in a cone shape. The point of the cone should hang just above the middle of the container. Sunlight causes water vapor to condense on the underside of the plastic. Gravity draws water droplets toward the rock-weighted point of the plastic "cone" above the container. The container collects the water as it drips off the plastic.

SHELTER

Shelter in the desert need not be elaborate. Temperatures at night in most deserts are cool but not life-threatening. Nighttime pests such as mosquitoes and flies don't pose much of a problem in extremely dry air, and scorpions, snakes and other desert denizens generally stay clear of sleeping humans unless a bag or tent layer covers their home. / A tent screens out sun, sand, rain, and wind. A sleeping bag, tarp, or blankets may be all you need for a comfortable night's rest. A tube tent made of fine-mesh material, screened by natural shade or a tarp, will promote a comfortable internal temperature in spring, summer, and fall. In winter, particularly in the high deserts of the Great Basin, a thick blanket, sleeping bag, and pad may be necessary. / Shelters may be improvised with brush, stones, and sand. Don't expect to find enough wood for a platform and roof. However, grasses and other vegetation can provide an insulation layer. / Locate your shelter in a safe place. Flash floods, lightning, and windstorms can strike with little warning. / Whatever you carry into the desert, keep it light so you can carry enough water, your most precious resource.

Use rock formations as a barrier against wind, but beware flash flooding at lower levels.

YOU'LL FEEL A LOT COOLER in a shelter in the desert. The temperature in the shade will be 20 to 40°F cooler than air in direct sunlight. Shade also cuts the conductive heat of sand and rock. When heated by the sun, they average 30 to 40 degrees warmer than the surrounding air. Without shelter, desert heat accelerates dehydration and increases the risk of heat illnesses.

Sheltering in a high spot has its advantages. The ground is often cooler, and high country picks up the occasional cooling breeze. Hot winds and sandstorms should be avoided, however, by building wind breaks or situating your shelter in the lee of a boulder.

SHELTER FACTS

>>> Shelter keeps you out of direct sunlight. In a "desert shade shelter"—a covered trench—the air temperature may be 30 to 40 degrees cooler than in sun.
>>> Shelter slows dehydration. Sun and wind rob the body of moisture.
>>> Shade with air circulation promotes cooling of the body.
>>> Shelter at night and from sudden rainstorms helps prevent hypothermia. "I suffer from the cold a great deal more than from the sun," desert adventurer Michel Vieuchange wrote in 1933 of his experiences in the Sahara.

essentials

SAND AS SHELTER

Deserts don't have an abundance of shelter-building materials, but they likely have sand and rock.

SAND is an insulating material. It helps keep you cool or warm.

DIGGING into sand and covering your body gives relief from heat or cold. "I dug a pit in the sand, lay down in it, and flung handfuls of sand over me until all but my face was buried in it," French pilot Antoine de Saint-Exupéry wrote of his surviving a frigid night in the Sahara.

SAND COVER slows dehydration by keeping sweat near the skin.

SAND'S WEIGHT will hold the edges of a tarp in place. This is useful in creating a trench shelter.

SAND AND ROCKS also will anchor a parachute cover draped over desert vegetation to create shade.

SAND DUNES act as windbreaks. Seek or build shelter at the base of the leeward side.

WIND will work against you to move sand shelters and sand-aided constructions. When making shelter, take wind direction into consideration. You may also need to regularly rebuild your shelter and sand piles holding down tarps, etc.

EXPERT TIP Protect face and head by wearing a wide-brimmed hat. A hat will keep direct sunlight off your head and face. Sunlight can burn and warm the inner core of your body.

American Red Cross

BRUSH SHELTERS ARE traditional dwellings of natives of the American Southwest. Brush can be fashioned into simple or elaborate designs. Thatched walls allow air to circulate.

Conical shelters resist shifts in wind direction. They can be covered with reflective material to catch the attention of search-and-rescue teams in any direction.

how to

BUILD AN APACHE BRUSH SHELTER

1 Gather five or six ten-foot branches and arrange in a circle with tops leaning together at a 45-degree angle.

2 Add more support poles, leaning them together in the same manner.

3 Brace with flexible, horizontal willow branches.

4 Gather thatching—dried leaves from desert plants—and attach from the bottom up.

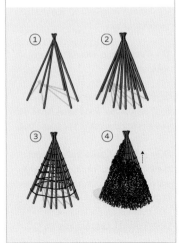

how to

DIG A TRENCH SHELTER

1 Dig a trench 18 to 24 inches deep and long enough for you to lie in comfortably. Pile sand around three of the four sides.

2 Place a tarp or brush over trench, leaving a hole for air, and weigh down the edges with sand or rocks.

3 If a second tarp is available, pile additional rocks or objects around the edges of the first tarp and pull the second tarp tight across them, then anchor with more rocks or dirt to hold it. This creates an insulating space between the two tarps, ideally a foot above the first. Crawl into the trench to wait out the hot part of the day.

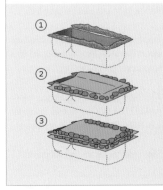

IN THE DESERT

CHAPTER

6

183

USED WISELY, a car that won't run can provide excellent shelter.

In direct sun, the metal and glass body will heat the interior like an oven. However, the seats can be used as a nighttime bed, and the interior provides a warm, dry place to wait out a rainstorm.

During the heat of the day, a car or truck projects a solid rectangle of shade beneath its chassis. To take advantage of it, wait until the car's engine and exhaust system have cooled.

Your car will be conspicuous to search-and-rescue teams that are combing the desert. You can make it more so by detaching its mirrors and using them as signaling devices.

how to
MAKE A CAR SHELTER

1 Remove hubcap to use as digging tool.

2 Start between the back wheels (as the front axle of the car has less clearance), and dig a space under the vehicle.

3 Keep digging until you've made your trench parallel to the car's length, deep enough for your body with several inches of clearance.

4 Slide under the car and wait out the day.

essentials
DOS AND DONT'S FOR DESERT SHELTER

Attractive shelters may already be inhabited. Be watchful for returning occupants.

DO: GET out of the sun.

DO: REDUCE the sun's impact by situating shelter with a northern exposure in the Northern Hemisphere, and the opposite in the Southern Hemisphere.

DO: REDUCE the bite of wind by positioning shelter openings at a 90-degree angle to prevailing air flow.

DO: MAKE shelter within a short walk of a water source.

DON'T: PLACE shelter in a riverbed or flood plain; in cool, damp places (favored by snakes and scorpions); or along game trails.

DON'T: SETTLE into a shelter without checking for pests. They may appear after you've settled in, so stay alert until you've been there for awhile.

DON'T: MAKE camp in a mine shaft.

DANGERS OF MINE SHAFTS

YOU SEE A NATURAL or excavated hole in the ground and think, "There's a safe shelter." Think again.

The cool, dark interior of a cave attracts animals such as mice, bees, and rattlesnakes, as well as bears and other predators. The air inside a cave may be thick and contain toxic gases. And the cave floor may drop away unexpectedly. Abandoned mine shafts may look safe, particularly if they have wooden supports. However, the wood may be ancient and ready to give way, and the floor may contain sharp and rusty scraps of metal. Water around mine shafts may pick up pollutants from underground. And even if the shaft itself is safe, denizens may include snakes and scorpions.

Take advantage of shade where you can, but investigate caves and crevices for inhabitants.

FOOD

Don't expect to find, or need, much food in the desert. In the most extreme environments, plant and animal life virtually disappears. In friendlier desert surroundings, hunting for animals and searching for edible plants might expend more energy than you could expect to recoup. Thus, the decision to search for desert food can become a strategic gamble. Add to the equation your body's more pressing need for hydration and the knowledge that digestion requires water, and you may choose to reduce the amount of food you eat. You might even fast for a few days. Desert heat makes it easy, as heat kills the appetite. / A good rule of thumb: If you don't have enough water to drink, don't eat anything. However, if you carry or find enough potable water, eating helps maintain energy and a positive attitude. / Be especially careful of any native foods you do eat. Consuming the wrong vegetable matter or drinking contaminated fluids may induce vomiting and diarrhea. Both speed dehydration. / Try to carry food you need, favoring lightweight, nonperishable items. Avoid meals that require a lot of water for preparation. Pack a small stove and fuel sources, too, as the desert may not provide enough dry vegetation for you to make and sustain a fire.

Wait until after the heat of the day to make a cooking fire, and then only if necessary.

TRAVELERS ARE challenged in selecting and protecting their food. Extreme heat spoils fresh food quickly. Freeze-dried food won't go bad and is light and easy to carry, but it requires precious water to reconstitute. Canned food is safe but adds a lot of weight ot a backpack. Any food carried in a bag or cloth container invites pests to make a nighttime raid.

Given the options, it makes sense to carry a variety of lightweight, spoil-resistant foods that require little water for cooking. Foods can be frozen before departure, which allows them time to thaw in a backpack before mealtime. Frozen bean dishes, such as burritos, are a favorite of many desert backpackers. They can be warmed on a dark surface or aluminum foil in full sun.

FOOD TIPS

>>> Fresh foods are refreshing and nutritious, but desert heat spoils them quickly. Be especially careful with fresh fruit, dairy products, and meat.

>>> Travelers can prevent spoilage by packing dehydrated and freeze-dried foods, but they require precious water to reconstitute.

>>> Canned foods and military MRE (meal, ready to eat) rations won't spoil or require water, but they are heavy.

>>> Protect food from desert mice, coyotes, and other thieves. Cloth bags are not strong enough to keep out biting and burrowing animals. Try suspending your food in a bag well off the ground.

MAKE AN ANTI-RODENT BAG

1 Secure food in airtight or sturdy bag. The less porous the bag material, the better.

2 Tie a knot in the cord well above the bag.

3 Punch a hole in a wide can and slide it down the cord until it stops at the knot. If the knot slips through the hole, tie the knot multiple times until it is big enough to stop the can.

4 Hang the bag several feet off the ground. The can acts as a barrier to prevent rodents from climbing down the cord.

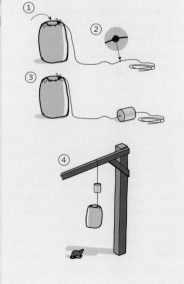

BRING THIS FOOD

THERE ARE A VARIETY of prepared foods that travel well, don't easily spoil or melt, and are hearty and nutritious. Consider stocking your bags with a selection of these in the event you need a quick snack or survival rations.

GOOD PORTABLE FOODS

>>> Granola bars, fruit bars, trail mix, and nuts.
>>> Peanut butter.
>>> Hard breads, such as bagels and tortillas.
>>> Small bags of vacuum-sealed chicken, tuna
>>> Hard, dry, or reduced-fat cheeses, such as cheddar, Swiss, manchego, or pecorino romano. Blocks resist spoilage longer.
>>> Hard candies.
>>> Prepared beans. Frozen burritos are popular. Dried beans and pasta require water for cooking; couscous uses less.
>>> Drink mixes to keep electrolytes in balance and cover taste of treated water.
>>> Avoid chips and salty foods, as high salt content provokes thirst.

FIND THIS FOOD

IF YOU FIND yourself stranded, isolated, and uprepared, you will need to find food. That can be difficult as desert conditions are among the planet's harshest. Yet, with ingenuity and the will to survive, you can find food to sustain you.

DESERT EDIBLES

>>> Insects. Many adults and larvae can be eaten and are high in protein. Cook them to kill parasites.
>>> Reptiles. Lizards and snakes are among the most common desert vertebrates.
>>> Crustaceans and mollusks. Look for them in shallow water along desert shorelines. Avoid mollusks from April to October.
>>> Rodents.
>>> Cactus fruits. Beware hair-thin barbs and bristles.
>>> Grasses in dry riverbeds and drainage systems.
>>> Water.

EDIBLE PLANTS

EATING REQUIRES WATER for digestion and preparing food. Many plants classified as "edible" are hard to stomach unless properly cooked. Even cooked desert plants may induce vomiting, which will dehydrate you further.

Gather plant foods if you know what you're looking for, and if you won't dehydrate yourself in the process of collecting and preparing them.

BEST BETS: PLANTS

>>> Mature fruit of the pricky pear, organ pipe, saguaro, Mojave yucca, and cholla cactus.
>>> Base ends of ocotillo buds.
>>> Grasses. Eat young stems, shoots, and leaves raw or cooked; boil to make tea.
>>> Yucca. Eat flowers raw or cooked; boil, peel, and deseed fruit. Do not eat roots.
>>> Date palm fruit.
>>> Desert amaranth shoots and leaves. Eat them raw or cooked.

EDIBLE ANIMALS

BIRDS, SNAKES, insects, and rodents are the most common edible animals of the desert. Rocks and sticks make effective weapons against such small animals. Stun the animal, then kill it.

Pluck and gut birds, although the heart, gizzard, liver, and neck are edible. Other animals should be skinned and gutted. Cook to kill harmful parasites.

BEST BETS: ANIMALS

>>> Lizards. Catch with noose. Skin, gut, and cook.
>>> Snakes. Stun with rock or stick. Pin head with forked stick before trying to make sure it's dead. Skin, gut, and cook.
>>> Rabbits. Stun with throwing stick.
>>> Locusts. Treat them as a gift instead of a plague. John the Baptist is said to have eaten them. Roast; remove heads, legs, and wings; eat the bodies.
>>> Quail and grouse. Stun with throwing stick.

how to

MAKE A SOLAR OVEN

1 Get a cardboard box, clear plastic, and aluminum foil. Cut around three sides of the top to make a lid. Space the cuts an inch in from the top edges of the box. Fold lid back.

2 Cover underside of the open lid with taped or glued aluminum foil. Cover the insides of the box with more aluminum foil. Place rocks in the bottom of the box to absorb more heat and raise the oven's efficiency.

3 When the sun is high in the sky, place food in a cooking bag or metal container on top of the rocks on the box floor. Tape clear plastic across the opening at the top of the box. Angle the box so the sun's rays strike the clear plastic directly and are reflected off the aluminum foil on the underside of the open lid. Leave the food for at least an hour, to allow the box to heat and begin to cook the food. Watch for bubbles as a sign that your food is cooking.

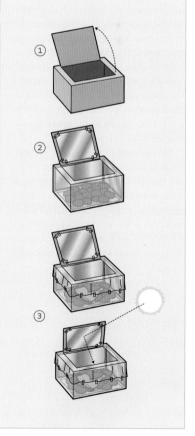

COOKING DESERT FOOD

EATING IS A SECONDARY need in the desert, well behind drinking enough water. Because much of a traveler's pack must be reserved for water, any cooking stoves, containers, and utensils should be kept to a minimum weight. Small, simple folding stoves, designed to sit on the ground and hold a cup or tin on a metal stand, are ideal for heating enough water for tea or a bowl of soup.

Folding stoves are designed to work with compressed fuels such as Sterno. Natural fuels such as wood and brush may be scarce in the desert, but piles of grass and sticks ignited beneath a stove platform can provide enough heat to cook a small meal. Use a candle to simmer contents already hot. A lightweight aluminum pot with a lid, cup, and fork and spoon may be all the cooking gear you need.

Boiling food in the desert is best because it provides not only hot solids but also nutritious broth. Baking atop rocks in a hole in the ground is a good alternative. You also can position a flat rock near a fire and fry your dinner on top as if the rock were a skillet. Drying preserves meat by reducing moisture content, which feeds mold and bacteria.

Building a fire and using smoke hastens dehydration and coats meat with a protective layer. Sun, wind, and heat from a fire will dry meat.

Large stoves requiring bottled gas may be appropriate when cooking for groups, but they add substantial weight to backpacks and are likely to be subject to airline baggage restrictions.

how to

SUN-DRY MEAT

1. Cut the meat into long, thin strips. Aim for a quarter-inch thickness.

2. String a cord between two supports, out of reach of animals.

3. Skewer pieces of meat on the cord, or drape them over it.

4. Keep pieces from touching each other or from touching themselves if folded.

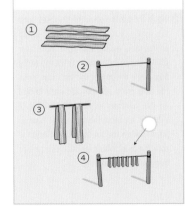

FIRST AID

The best medical advice for desert travelers is to prevent problems before they happen. Drink plenty of water to avert dehydration and resulting heat illness. Avoid animals that sting and bite, as well as the sharp spines of cactus and cholla.

Choose the right footwear to reduce the risk of falls and blisters. But, be prepared to respond to medical problems if they arise. Carry rehydration salts, antihistamines, antidiarrheal tablets, and other first aid items to deal with the unexpected. / Treating heat illness is absolutely crucial. Heat illness progresses through the following stages: Cramps. Stretch affected muscles and drink water. Rest if possible. / Heat exhaustion. Results from heat and lack of proper hydration. Victims may complain of feeling faint, cold, or nauseous, or seem confused. Heat exhaustion is a form of shock, so treat it as such. The victim should lie in the shade with feet elevated a few inches and drink cool—not cold—water with a pinch of salt. Physical exertion should be avoided for 12 to 24 hours. / Heatstroke. A medical emergency that occurs when the body cannot shed heat. Elevated temperatures threaten cells in the brain and vital organs. Look for dry, flushed skin; rapid pulse; and loss of motor skills ranging from lightheadedness to convulsions and unconsciousness. Treat by removing the victim's clothes, pouring water on limbs, and fanning the skin. Immersing the victim in a pool of cool water is helpful. Apply damp cloths if water supplies are limited. Give the victim cool water containing a pinch of salt to drink. If possible, get a victim of heatstroke to a hospital as soon as you can.

COMMON DESERT ILLNESSES can be annoyances or killers. Learn to recognize the signs and understand the symptoms.

COMMON ILLNESSES

>>> **Sunburn.** Caused by direct sunlight and reflection off sand and light-colored rock.

>>> **Cramps, heat exhaustion, and heatstroke.** Caused by dehydration.

>>> **Hyponatremia.** Caused by failure to replace sodium lost through sweat.

>>> **Eye irritations.** Bright light can blind; blown grit can cause conjunctivitis.

>>> **Diarrhea.** Caused by parasites in food and water.

essentials

MUST-HAVE ITEMS

Pack your first aid kit with additional items for desert environments.

WATER PURIFICATION TABLETS

MOLESKIN /tape for blisters

ANTIBIOTIC OINTMENT for bites, scrapes, punctures, and stings

ANTIHISTAMINE

SUNBLOCK

SUNBURN LOTION

ADHESIVE BANDAGES

ELASTIC BANDAGES for treating sprains and snakebites

how to

TREAT A RATTLESNAKE BITE

1 Get the victim to a hospital as soon as possible because hemotoxin, injected by rattlesnakes, attacks the blood. In the meantime, follow these steps:

2 Have the victim lie down and not move.

3 Clean, bandage, and disinfect the wound.

4 Immobilize the limb and keep it slightly below heart level.

5 Keep air passages open. Treat as if for anaphylactic shock, if necessary.

6 Do not cut around the wound, apply heat or cold, use a tourniquet, or give the victim food, alcohol, or painkillers.

7 Use a suction device to extract venom. (Experts debate the efficacy of this technique, but it may still calm the victim by giving some peace of mind.)

HAZARDS

Deserts are lands of paradox. / Sun-scorched sand and rock conjure images of fiery furnaces, but empty desert landscapes can be uncommonly cold at night. Lack of water raises fears among travelers, yet flash floods remain one of the most common dangers. High temperatures that seem an invitation to strip off hot clothes are best parried by wrapping in multiple layers to trap precious sweat. Sun and wind mimic similar hazards of mountains and polar regions, burning exposed skin and blinding unprotected eyes. / Captain James Riley struggled to hold onto his sanity amid the trials of sand, wind, heat, thirst, and hunger, not to mention the slavery forced on him by his captors. For a while, he considered bashing his brains out with a stone until his "paroxysm" ended. Then, like many who venture into the desert to seek something they can find nowhere else, he decided to place his life "in the hand of the power that gave it." The empty forge of the desert long has tempered poets, mystics, and visionaries. / Deserts are not conquered. To be survived, they must be understood—and embraced. Desert creatures show the way. They stay cool, save water, and travel at night.

If caught in a sandstorm like this Navajo in the Southwest, cover mouth and nose.

KNOW DESERT HAZARDS

GIVE THE DESERT due respect.

If you know the potential hazards of the desert, you can prepare for them. If you don't realize the dangers of sandstorms, flooding, dehydration, and other potential problems, the desert can easily kill you.

While most travelers probably are aware of major desert hazards, it's easy to overlook one of the worst: falling. Take caution hiking steep trails, especially when alone. Keep your walking speed under control, and don't push yourself too hard when tired. A fall of 15 feet may be enough to crush a skull.

DANGER POINTS

>>> **Blisters.** Wear the right boots, well broken in before hiking.
>>> **Spiny vegetation punctures.** Cholla and cactus inflict painful wounds.
>>> **Sunburn.**
>>> **Heat-related injuries.**
>>> **Dehydration.**
>>> **Illnesses from bad water.**
>>> **Falls.** Keep solid footing on gravel.
>>> **Bites and stings.** Treat them to prevent infection. Beware of anaphylactic shock.
>>> **Rainstorm hazards:** flash floods, lightning strikes, hypothermia.
>>> **Sandstorm hazards:** Eye injuries, dehydration, injuries to exposed skin.

EXPERT TIP A flash flood occurs when a thunderstorm becomes stalled and the extremely saturated clouds dump moisture over one area. These are very difficult to predict because it's never certain where a storm will stall....go to safety immediately. Don't wait for an official warning.

American Red Cross

UNEXPECTED WEATHER

FLASH FLOODS are appropriately named. They surprise travelers in desert country, seeming to appear out of nowhere.

Blame the desert terrain. The storm that generates a flood may occur 100 miles away, well out of the traveler's circle of vision and hearing. Summer thunderstorms often form rapidly and saturate a small section of desert. The ground's lack of vegetation causes swift runoff. Water collects and flows in channels cut into the rocky surface by previous storms. Surges of water choked with sand and gravel roar through canyons and across dry washes like freight trains.

STORM PRECAUTIONS

>>> Obtain the regional weather forecast from local stations or newpapers before you set out. Get as local a forecast as possible. Some microclimates differ greatly.
>>> Learn the seasonal weather patterns for your region and watch the skies for signs of rain falling nearby or far away.
>>> Never park a car in a dry wash.
>>> If floods strike when you're in a drainage area, get to higher ground immediately. Abandon equipment if you must.
>>> Stay out of swift water, no matter how shallow.
>>> Hike in slot canyons and steep-sided arroyos only during stable, high-pressure weather systems to avoid getting caught by flash flooding.

UNDERSTAND SAND

TRAVELING ACROSS SAND is very different than traveling across other terrains. Sand travel requires a great deal of energy. Understanding how to travel in sand without exhausting or hurting yourself is vital to desert survival.

ENDURING SAND

>>> **Plan to expend twice as much energy when walking in sand.**

>>> **Wear smooth-soled boots to stay atop soft sand. (Sandals give traction but may cause sunburn on the tops of your feet.)**

>>> **Avoid the softest sand by walking in hollows or on high, windward slopes where breezes have compacted grit.**

>>> **Sand reflects sunlight and can contribute to desert blindness and sunburn.**

>>> **Shifting sand dunes prevent plants from growing.**

>>> **Driving in soft sand is an invitation to get stuck far from civilization. If you must drive, do so at night or early morning, when the sand is damp.**

WEATHER SANDSTORMS

A SANDSTORM is nothing to sneeze at. Twenty-five hundred years ago, the army of King Cambyses vanished in a Sahara sandstorm. Modern storms have winds as high as 100 miles per hour. Their heat and grit can suffocate and rasp at flesh. Lawrence of Arabia described the khamsin sandstorm of northern Arabia as a breathless furnace. "By noon it blew a half-gale," he wrote, "so dry that our shriveled lips cracked open, and the skin of our faces cracked; while our eyelids, gone granular, seemed to creep back and bare our shrinking eyes."

essentials
SURVIVING A SANDSTORM

Take shelter from wind and wait.

PITCH a tent or make shelter if you have time. Do so behind a solid windbreak.

IF CAUGHT in the open, lie on your side at the base of a hill opposite the wind.

WRAP all flesh in cloth to protect against blown sand.

COVER MOUTH and nose to prevent inhaling grit.

REMOVE GLASSES and contacts. Blown grit will sandblast them.

PUT ON goggles if you have them.

MARK the direction of travel with piles of stones, as landmark dunes may change.

Coyotes, like this one in the Sonoran Desert, Arizona, may pilfer your food or water.

BEWARE ANIMAL HAZARDS

ANIMALS OF THE desert have adapted to the lack of moisture. Most are harmless, but a few pose hazards to humans.

Rattlesnakes typically hunt in the cool of night, attracted by the warmth of their prey. About 60 percent of bites occur when a snake is cornered or provoked, or is foolishly handled. Most of the remaining bites result from carelessness, such as putting a hand or foot into a blind spot or touching a snake that is playing dead. They typically strike within two-thirds of their body length. Beware of taking a dog into the desert if it hasn't been trained to shy away from snakes.

Scorpion stings are painful but rarely deadly. The most dangerous North American variety is the translucent yellow or brown Arizona bark scorpion, which injects a powerful neurotoxin. Scorpions like shade, and may inhabit old buildings and boots left untended.

Beware of stinging insects as well as biting species that may spread diseases.

DANGEROUS CREATURES

>>> **Bees and wasps.** Don't disturb nests. Multiple stings pose a danger.
>>> **Flies, fleas, lice, and mites.** They seek moisture and spread disease. Beware of wild dogs and rats, which may be infested.
>>> **Black widow and brown recluse spiders.** Painful bites. They often live in dead wood and abandoned dwellings. Tarantulas look fierce but are relatively harmless.
>>> **Coyotes.** Thieves of food and water.
>>> **Javelinas.** Dangerous if threatened.
>>> **Pit vipers,** including rattlers.
>>> **Gila monsters.** Sluggish and not usually a threat unless harassed or handled.

SIGNALING

Signals are particularly important in desert terrain, where survival usually depends on staying in one place and awaiting rescue. Long-distance communication methods help direct rescuers to your general location, then pinpoint where you are. Annual search-and-rescue operations are significant; the U.S. National Park Service typically conducts 4,000 every year, including half that involve injury or illness. Helping rescuers find you quickly increases your chances of survival. / Bright sunlight and transparent desert air make light signals carry over great distances. Mirrors and reflective metal are the most important signaling devices. At night, signal fires shine across miles of darkness. Groups of three indicate distress. / Signals should be set up with maximum line of sight. Ridgelines, hilltops, and the center of flat spaces increase the odds of being spotted. / Some signal devices, such as colored smoke flares, can be used only once and should be ready to go as soon as potential rescuers are seen or heard. Prepare bonfires in advance, ready to light at a moment's notice. Practice aiming the sun's reflected rays on a specific target before you need to do it for real on a moving plane. / When using ground signals, choose hues and surfaces for contrast against the desert's dominant colors.

USE A PERSONAL LOCATOR BEACON

PERSONAL LOCATOR beacons have been used by boaters and pilots for years in noncommercial form but are now more widely available. They weigh as little as a pound and some can fit in a pocket. They operate by broadcasting a coded distress signal when activated. The signal is bounced off a satellite to receivers operated by emergency crews. The decoded signal indicates your position on the ground.

Rescuers check a database for information about who sent the message. Data may include preexisting medical concerns. Activate the beacon only when you're truly in trouble.

BEST METHODS OF DESERT SIGNALING

WHEN YOU'RE STUCK, consider everyday items you may be carrying with you as signaling aids. Be innovative: Your goal is to attract the attention of rescuers. Consider what you carry in your pack or vehicle. A camera flash emits a powerful white light. A cell phone might work from the highest point you see. The sound of a car horn carries far in still air, and car headlights can be used for short intervals at night. Metal from plane or car wreckage can substitute for a glass mirror.

SIGNALING STAPLES

>>> **Handheld mirrors.** When reflecting the stark desert sun, they can bounce up to seven million candlepower. Detach car mirrors if necessary.
>>> **Shiny or bright orange cloths.** Spread them on your shelter or on the ground to attract attention. Fashion the letter "X" to indicate distress.
>>> **Signal fires.** In a huge circle of darkness, they act as beacons.
>>> **Flashlights.** Operate them at a high point. Click out S-O-S.
>>> **Ground flares.** Light them when you hear planes.
>>> **Black smoke.** Set fire to tires or oil and gas mixed with sand.

USE AN AM RADIO

IT'S A HIGH-TECH AGE. Funny that one of the most valuable desert communication tools is straight out of the 1920s.

AM band radio broadcasts are an important news source. AM signals bounce off the atmosphere and travel great distances at night. The National Oceanic and Atmospheric Adminis-tration forecasts alert travelers to bad weather. Knowing in advance about thunderstorms many miles away could save your life by keeping you clear of flash flooding.

Overseas, AM radio can pair with shortwave receivers to pick up English-language weather news.

EXPERT TIP Sandstorms (sand-laden winds) occur frequently in most deserts. The greatest danger is getting lost in a swirling wall of sand. Wear goggles and cover your mouth and nose with cloth. If natural shelter is unavailable, mark your direction of travel, lie down, and wait out the storm.

NAVIGATION

Traveling in the desert can be as easy as just saying "no." / In a survival situation, don't travel unless you feel you must. Walking uses energy and water, and it significantly raises your risk of heat illness. Move along only when you don't believe rescuers will find you in time, and you know how to navigate toward your intended destination. / If you must travel, do so only at night if you can see adequately, or in the cool hours just after sunrise and before sunset. Stay in shade during the hottest part of the day in shelter you carry or construct. / Keep hydrated. Don't ration water as you travel. / Cover your body with layers of clothing, including long sleeves and pants. Wear a wide-brimmed hat. Protect your eyes from glare and your skin from sunburn. Take care of your feet and boots. / Indicate your route of travel for anyone who finds the site you left. Leave a note in a conspicuous place; fashion sticks to make arrows on the ground showing where you went; tie flags to branches or cacti. / Learning to use GPS and compass simplifies your travel when the world looks much the same in every direction. But beware of routes that take you across flood zones and other potential hazards.

If you must move in the desert during the day, stay hydrated and plan your route carefully.

DESERT CHALLENGES

THE LACK OF significant landmarks increases your reliance on compass, GPS, and maps. However, without solid reference points or obvious trails, you may have difficulty staying on a true course. Try to orient your route with any objects along your line of sight, or use dead reckoning to navigate. Pace off detours around hills and ridges.

Don't rely too heavily on topographic maps; they may be inaccurate for remote deserts and of no use in shifting dunes.

Daytime travel courts heat illness. Learn to read stars and travel by night.

ACCLIMATE TO THE HEAT

>>> **Be as fit as you can be before traveling in the desert.**

>>> **Increase physical activity slowly to acclimate to the heat. A prior healthy level of fitness promotes swifter acclimation.**

>>> **Significant acclimation may occur in four to five days; fuller acclimation takes a week or two.**

>>> **Beware: Acclimation may actually increase your need for water.**

USE DEAD RECKONING

REFERENCE POINTS for desert navigation may be few and far between. Sand dunes and flat, empty plains offer few visual clues to distinguish one location from another. Under such conditions, an old system of navigation known as dead reckoning allows you to make a close estimate of distance and direction traveled. Though dead reckoning is dwarfed in accuracy and speed by GPS, the skill is useful in case you are stranded without electronic equipment. It is also useful as a backup, to double-check the accuracy of your electronic equipment.

The system combines reading compass bearings with walking in straight lines and keeping track of paces. Distance traveled in each direction should be recorded in a log. Without solid reference points, such as mountains or trees, walkers must find other ways to correct

for their natural tendency to drift left or right.

Start by taking an initial bearing. Move along that direction, counting paces. Alternatively, time your movement in each direction or measure your pace count over a fixed length of ground and then convert the count to yards or miles. Mark your count at each stop. When changing direction, record a new bearing and begin a new pace count. Try to take account of how your pace changes as you go uphill or down, or cross soft sand or broken rocks.

Dead reckoning is best used when covering short distances in featureless terrain, as well as retracing your steps if you must.

SOURCES OF HEAT GAIN

You are subjected to a variety of
heat sources in the desert.

YOU absorb heat directly from sunlight.

SUNLIGHT also reflects off the ground,
giving your body a second dose.

HOT ground transfers energy to the air above
it, which heats you as you pass through it.

RADIANT heat from sand and rocks gets
transferred to your body parts on contact.

YOU ALSO create your own heat as you
exert energy.

PROTECT BOOTS, FEET

DESERT HIKING punishes boots and
feet. Radiant heat from the ground can
burn feet through boots and socks. Sand
in your boots causes chafing and blisters. One quick fix when you're wearing
shorts is to make puttees: Wrap bands
of cloth around your legs from knee to
ankle to block sand and radiant heat.

BOOT-CARE TIPS

>>> Protect leather footgear by treating with
saddle soap to prevent drying and cracking.
>>> Wear thick socks to block the ground's
radiant heat.
>>> If your boots have air holes, seal them with
epoxy to keep out sand and grit.
>>> Remove your boots to dry your feet and
socks when you stop to rest in shade.

DON'T BE FOOLED: MIRAGES

MIRAGES ARE TRICKS of light and
heat that make distant objects seem to
move. Light refracted through heated
air ascending from sand or hot stone
causes odd reflections. It distorts
objects along the horizon, sometimes
causing desert travelers to feel as if
they are surrounded by water.

To eliminate the distortion, climb
to a high point above the superheated
desert floor, or take sightings at night or
in the cool of dawn or twilight.

NAVIGATE BY THE STARS

Navigating by stars makes sense. You
may do much of your traveling by night,
and the clear desert air lets stars shine
most of the year.

STAR-HIKING TIPS

>>> Stop hiking to take a sighting. It's easy to trip.
>>> In the Northern Hemisphere, use the
front edge of the Big Dipper as a pointer
toward Polaris, the North Star. Polaris
also is the first star in the handle of the
Little Dipper.
>>> As night progresses, the Big Dipper circles
Polaris counterclockwise.
>>> In the Southern Hemisphere, find the
Southern Cross's long axis. When that line is
extended down four and a half lengths, the
endpoint is south.
>>> Navigate by picking out stars near the
southern or northern horizon to guide your
way. Because of Earth's rotation, pick out
a new star every 15 to 30 minutes.

A s we settled down to sleep near the southern shore of the dried-up lake of Lop Nur in China's Xinjiang Province, a long-predicted sandstorm sprang up. Lop Nur lies in the heartland of the Gashun Gobi desert, which for almost 50 years was the nuclear test area of China. Indeed, I had been the first foreigner permitted to enter the area since atmospheric nuclear testing had been abandoned 18 years previously. The Gashun Gobi encompasses one of the harshest landscapes in the world and furthermore holds no fresh water, only saltwater, which has a higher salt content than seawater. We were there to survey the southern boundary of a proposed nature reserve to protect the critically endangered wild Bactrian camel, which incredibly has adapted to drinking the saline slush.

Before our arrival at Lop Nur, the expedition had not been without drama. The melting snows prevented our two vehicles from crossing the 18,000-foot Arjin Mountains as planned. So we had crossed with our 20 domestic camels, taking them up to a pass of 12,000 feet in temperatures of –10°F. On our descent, in a howling blizzard, the camels slithered down frozen riverbeds, their woolly coats covered with icicles. In one valley, a camel fell into a crevasse

John Hare, explorer and National Geographic grantee, works to protect the endangered wild camels of the Sahara.

in the ice and had to be hauled out. In another, we had to construct a stepladder of rocks to get the camels through a narrow gorge.

Now on the shore of Lop Nur, as the strength of the wind increased, we all left the comparative warmth of our kitchen tent and ran out into the howling gale to check on ropes, pegs, and wildly flapping canvas. Huddled in my tent, it seemed that the full blast of the storm, which was sweeping over hundreds of miles of desert, was expending all its energy on my few feet of canvas. The wind howled and ripped at the fabric with ferocity. When, in spite of precautionary piles of rocks and stones, the cords on one side of the tent suddenly freed themselves from their moorings, my tiny living space was transformed from comparative order to utter chaos.

Loose ends of canvas smacked at everything. Dust flew everywhere. No one could leave their battered stronghold to help the other. It was every man for himself in a swirling mass of blinding grit and sand. Having ensured that knife and flashlight were in reach, I covered my head with a large cloth in a feeble attempt to keep dust out of eyes, ears, nose, and mouth, pulled the sleeping bag tightly around me, curled up my knees, and waited for the worst. The full frontal attack kept going all through that very cold night.

The next morning, after the winds had ceased, we discovered to our great dismay, 19 of our domestic camels had fled. Their tracks led back to the Arjin Mountains, more than 100 miles to the south. Two of our herdsmen were sent off to follow them. Terrified by the storm, they could have galloped far beyond our ability to pursue and return them before we died of thirst or hunger.

We checked out provisions and stores. We calculated that we could sit it out for three days. If the camels had not been recovered by the morning of the fourth day, then we would have to set off by foot to our vehicles, which had

been left in a riverbed more than 250 miles away. The crossing would have to be made across a flat, waterless plateau at a time of year when sandstorms can spring up with very little warning.

Each member of the six-man team was instructed to take only what he could carry. There was one sick camel that had not run away and it was planned to load him with as much water as he could manage. We were each responsible for our own food, and we had already begun to eke out our rations by making a disgusting porridge from the camels' rock-hard maize. There were tins of meat and fish, rubbery processed sausages, and instant noodles. In addition, each member took four liters of water, easily the most important item, in case the sick camel broke down or jettisoned his load.

Knives, matches, and very basic cooking utensils were evenly distributed among the team. Tents and all other equipment were to be left behind. We planned to take only the clothing, which would keep us warm, but no more than we stood up in. I took extra pairs of socks to keep my feet in good shape.

Photographic equipment was a concern. I decided to take my camera. I felt that a record of a journey that might be my last must be kept. Pencils and notebooks, flashlights, and spare batteries were all classed as essentials.

And then, on the evening of the third day, just as we were summoning up the strength to undertake our long march, the herdsmen reappeared with the lost camels. As we carefully loaded them up the next day, I uttered prayers of thanks that we had not had to undertake the return journey with only a sick camel for support in terra incognita.

"WE TOOK RISKS, we knew we took them....Had we lived, I should have had a tale to tell of the hardihood, endurance, and courage of my companions which would have stirred the heart of every Englishman." / So wrote Antarctic explorer Robert Scott in his "Message to the Public." The words he penned in 1912 were found near his frozen body. / Scott's death only 11 miles from salvation can be interpreted two ways. It ranks as evidence of hubris among those who venture into regions of extreme cold without proper preparation, or as testimony to Scott's near success against all odds. / Scott courted disaster by exhausting his men in sledge-hauling; failing to position supply caches properly; burdening his four-member team with a fifth man for its final push to the South Pole; and wearing woolens instead of lighter furs. Scott's rival, the better-prepared Roald Amundsen, who won the race to the Pole, used dogsleds, wore furs, and traveled lightly and swiftly on skis. / Polar conditions give no quarter. Lack of resources coupled with extreme weather and difficult terrain led Scott to declare, "Great God, this is an awful place." Yet humans have learned to adapt—and survive.

POLAR & SUBPOLAR

W I T H I N   T H I S   C H A P T E R

Explorer Vilhjalmur Stefansson liked to tell audiences in the 1920s that nearly anyone could thrive in the Arctic. "A family can now live at the North Pole as comfortably as it can in Hawaii," he said. All they needed were good eyesight and a rifle. / His hyperbole proved false when four of five young explorers he placed on frozen Wrangel Island died or disappeared. Yet Stefansson got one thing right: attitude. Preparation for survival starts with belief. Confidence grows with knowing how to fit into a land of few or no trees, few resources, and cold that on occasion plummets to -70°F—and beyond. / Those who deliberately enter polar and subpolar regions must have plenty of food, as well as the skills and means to obtain more. Native plants and game may be scarce or nonexistent; harvesting animals to supply meat likely will require a gun and fishing equipment. Survivors need proper clothing and shelter to protect against deadly cold and violent winds; the means to create fire for warmth and ice-melting; and specialized equipment to cross snow and ice fields. / Without them, they must learn to live carefully. Nature forgives few mistakes at 70 below.

National Geographic grantee Børge Ousland on the Southern Patagonia Ice Field in Chile.

POLAR ENVIRONMENTS

EARTH'S COLDEST REGIONS contain a variety of climates and terrain, and fall into three major categories: tundra, polar, and subpolar. All are ecologically delicate. Survival techniques should be used only in emergencies, in order not to upset the balance of nature.

"Arctic" refers only to the North Pole, while "Antarctic" refers to the South Pole. In the north, subarctic zones stretch longitudinally from Siberia to Scandinavia to Alaska, and the Arctic Circle starts at about 66°30' N. In the Southern Hemisphere, the Antarctic Circle starts at about 66°30'. Their climates, like that of tundra zones, are driven by the weak power of low-angle sunlight. Temperature extremes can be up to 200 degrees apart. Vegetation is sparse amid shallow snow cover.

Tundra extends from north of 55° in the Northern Hemisphere and south of 50° in the Southern Hemisphere. The cloudy, cold, and moist tundra plains may include some shrubs, mosses,

TYPES OF SEA ICE

>>> **Milky or gray when new, blue when old**
>>> **Salty when new, fresh or nearly so when old**
>>> **Hard to break when new, brittle when old**
>>> **Sharp-edged when new, soft-edged when old**

and bogs. Permafrost exists where soil never warms above the freezing point. A top layer may thaw, but the water is trapped by a frozen layer beneath.

Permanent ice caps cover Antarctica, the North Pole, and Greenland. A layer of moving sea ice expands and contracts atop the Arctic Ocean.

SURVIVING COLD CLIMATES

LIFE IN THE POLAR REGIONS doesn't change the equation of survival as much as it adds a variable: cold. As with the arid heat of the desert, the cold of Arctic regions demands adaptation as the price of survival. Humans who fight the cold instead of trying to live with it are doomed to failure.

Living in an extremely cold climate is possible. The Inuit have lived in the Arctic for millennia. They have learned to gather food in times of abundance,

such as the thaw and extended daylight of summer. They hunt and fish. They find ways to turn the snow and ice to their advantage in building shelter and simplifying their transportation.

Warmth can be cultivated behind walls of snow, which is an excellent insulator; in multiple layers of clothing; with fires for cooking and heating shelter; and with sunlight. Warmth also is a state of mind. Staying clear-headed and calm is crucial to survival.

DRESS FOR THE COLD

PROPER COVERINGS serve as the primary defense against cold. They must trap body heat, protect against wind and sun, wick away moisture, and dry quickly.

Synthetic fabrics are best for insulation. Polyester and polypropylene are light and warm, and they continue to work even when wet. So-called technical fabrics, including brand names Capilene, Gore-Duratherm, and Thinsulate, are light synthetics that work well in layers. As they do not protect against wind, they work best under an outer shell, such as waterproof nylon. Waterproof designs such as Gore-Tex and Supplex allow air transfer but must be kept clean.

Technical fabrics outperform even most woolen garments. Avoid cotton, which is useless when wet.

Clothing layers worn next to the skin must be kept dry and clean. Sweat and dirt clog the air spaces in fabrics and interfere with their insulating and wicking properties. Wash your inner layer frequently, hang dry, and then beat out any ice particles or dry them near fire.

PACKING POLAR GEAR

>>> Bed pad. Do not sleep on snow or ice.
>>> Insulated, mummy-shaped sleeping bag.
>>> Tent and sewing kit for repairs.
>>> Ice ax and telescoping probe.
>>> Snowshoes and/or cross-country skis.
>>> Sled or internal-frame backpack.
>>> Stove and pots with bottled fuel.
>>> Tools to cut wood or blocks of snow.
>>> Headlamp for long nights. Keep batteries warm.
>>> Duct tape, screwdriver, extra screws for boots/poles/ski bindings.

essentials

PACKING CLOTHES FOR COLD

Choose clothes carefully before venturing into polar regions.

LEATHER BOOTS for all-purpose traveling.

WATERPROOF coatings or synthetic liners.

PLASTIC BOOTS for hard snow.

TWO pairs of socks.

UNDERGARMENTS of technical fabric to wick away moisture.

ONE or two insulating layers to trap warm air.

GAITERS for wet regions.

PARKA and pants with breathable, waterproof coatings. Seams should be sealed.

TECHNICAL fabric hand coverings. Consider gloves inside mittens.

HEAD coverings. Balaclavas protect neck and head, leaving an opening in front of the eyes.

SUNGLASSES or goggles. Protect against snow blindness.

FACE MASK of synthetic material such as neoprene to protect nose and cheeks.

FIRE

Fire ranks behind shelter and clothing as a necessity in cold regions. The body makes its own heat. Capturing it and keeping it from being stolen by the elements may be enough for survival. Thus, skin-covering layers of warm, dry clothes and a stout igloo may be all you need to stay comfortable. However, fire has other functions besides providing warmth. It provides comfort during the polar dark seasons, energy for cooking meals and killing microorganisms in drinking water, smoke and light to signal rescuers, and crucial heat for drying clothes. / Conifer forests provide wood in the subarctic region. North of the tree line, little fuel is likely to be available. Scrub willows, shrubs, grass, and moss may be the only combustible plant matter. On sea ice, glaciers, and barren shorelines, driftwood, and animal blubber may be the only things that will burn. / Fires inside snow shelters must be small. Too much heat will cause a shelter's interior surfaces to drip, soaking the occupants. A candle likely will provide all the necessary heat in a well-built shelter. Ice and snow shelters should never be too tightly sealed, however, in order to prevent the buildup of dangerous gases.

Fires provide more than just warmth; they dry wet clothes, heat food, and lift morale.

FINDING WOOD IN SUBPOLAR REGIONS

WITHIN THE TREE line, conifers dominate. Spruce makes excellent firewood. Spruce branches and logs smoke heavily in spring and summer but burn nearly smoke free in late fall and winter. Tamarack trees also produce excellent smoke for signaling. Bark moisture often causes smoke. Among deciduous trees, the wood of the birch, which grows near water, easily catches fire. Junipers and birch scrub grow north of the northernmost forests.

Look for dead trees with dry wood that you can snap or cut. Beware when snapping branches off trees. They may be merely frozen instead of dead. Cut off a piece of bark to check for live wood tissue underneath.

The best fuel logs are bare of bark. However, birch bark makes excellent tinder e v e n when wet because of its flammable resin. Try feathering it with a knife before applying a spark or a match. Dry pine needles also catch fire easily.

In the tundra, mats of dwarf, arctic willows dominate vegetation in North America, Europe, and Asia. The low-growing shrub—never getting taller than about two feet—thrives in dense clumps as well as mountainous regions farther south. Although there's not much woody material in arctic willows, they grow so profusely that collecting enough for a fire should not be difficult.

Above the tree line, driftwood may be available. Vilhjalmur Stefansson's Wrangel exploration team of 1921-23 found enough driftwood on the treeless island in the Arctic Ocean to build a shelter's walls and ceiling, with enough left over to keep fires burning. In the Atlantic, Greenland residents once built homes out of wood that drifted across down from the mouths of Siberian rivers.

FUEL IN POLAR REGIONS

>>> Branches and driftwood.
>>> Peat. Found in bogs in certain regions; can be cut with a knife. Needs good ventilation. Bogs are a shrinking natural resource.
>>> Grasses, tied in bundles.
>>> Animal dung. Dry, mix with grass. Old West variety included "buffalo chips."
>>> Blubber. Robert Scott's Antarctic team used blubber stoves to melt water and cook mash for horses.
>>> Compressed gases and jellied fuels carried by travelers.

EXPERT TIP Give a good deal of thought to selecting the right equipment for survival in the cold. If unsure of an item you have never used, test it in an "overnight backyard" environment before venturing farther.

Be aware of factors that could extinguish your fire. Shelter it from wind, hail and snow.

BUILD FIRES AMID SNOW AND ICE

BUILDING A FIRE IN SNOW or ice requires a dry base; igniting fuel directly atop snow or ice will melt the water and extinguish the flames. Fire can be built on a platform of green logs, if any are available. A small metal platform, such as a license plate or trash can lid, can serve a similar purpose for a portable gas stove amid snow. The plate prevents the stove from tipping and going out as it heats the surrounding snow.

When building a fire from wood or other available fuels, gather enough tinder, kindling, and main fuel for three fires. This allows you to keep the fire going if the flames start to die or if you need to gather more fuel. In wet weather, remove bark and lichens and split sticks to expose their dry cores.

Shelter your fire from the wind with rocks stacked into a wall, or blocks of snow. In enclosed areas, beware of carbon monoxide poisoning—you may not notice the effects until too late. Leave a ventilation hole in all shelters.

If you find a deposit of sand at the mouth of a river, collect a few pounds. Do the same for baseball- and softball-size rocks. Heat the sand by building a fire on top of it. Use hot sand to dry wet boots or, when placed in a small container, to warm your hands while traveling. Rocks heated near a fire can be moved under a bed pad inside an polar shelter to provide a safe source of warmth.

BEWARE CARBON MONOXIDE POISONING

>>> **Gas, produced by combustion, is odorless and colorless. Victims may not know they're being poisoned.**
>>> **Danger signs may include nausea, headache, dizziness, and lethargy. Or there may be no symptoms.**
>>> **Legs may fail. Victims who collapse should immediately get fresh air and warmth.**
>>> **Give mouth-to-mouth resuscitation if victim stops breathing or can only gasp.**
>>> **Victims may die in their sleep.**
>>> **Recovery may require a day of rest and warmth.**

WATER

If you are stuck in the extreme North or South you'll likely be surrounded by water. But it's locked up in snow and ice—the one resource likely to be abundant the closer you get to the Poles. / Survival hinges on creating drinkable water. Do not consume ice and snow directly. "The result of eating snow is death," wrote Matthew Henson, who accompanied Robert Peary's Arctic expedition. Metabolic loss from body heat melting snow in the stomach is never offset by the hydration gain. / Water should be drawn from open streams or from holes cut in ice. Melting ice is acceptable, but avoid melting snow except in an emergency. Seventeen cubic inches of loose snow yields only one cubic inch of water, at a considerable expenditure of fuel. Boil water to purify it; filters freeze and fail, and chemical treatments lose their effectiveness in extreme cold. / Cold, wind, and often-dry polar and subpolar air hasten dehydration, as does exertion required to move across snow and ice. Add to those conditions the thin atmosphere above Antarctica's plateau and the planet's northernmost mountain ranges, and the body screams for food and water.

USE THESE SOURCES FOR WATER

DRAW WATER from the downwind side of lakes and rivers. It usually is clearer than water from windward sides, and the snow cover is shallower. At an ice-covered lake, draw water away from shore if the ice is thick enough to support your weight. Open a hole with an auger. Cover a hole with snow blocks and loose snow to keep it open. Water also can be obtained by melting ice or, in a pinch (though less efficient), snow.

Fresh sea ice tastes salty, but sea ice a year old—blue with rounded edges—has lost its salt through leaching and can be melted for drinking. Also, fresh water sometimes accumulates atop ice where tides and currents are weak.

In warm weather, tundra may be covered with brown surface water, which should be fine when boiled.

KEEP WATER LIQUID

ICE AND SNOW yield water but require a lot of fuel for melting and boiling. Collect ice and snow from areas free of animal contamination. Put a little water in the bottom of a pot before adding clean snow or ice in order to avoid burning the exterior surface.

If you need to conserve heating fuel, you can melt snow with solar power in high-latitude summers. Open a large piece of dark plastic or a dark tarpaulin, place it atop a layer of pebbles or sticks, and make a depression in the center. Dark materials absorb light, raising their temperature. Once the dark material gets warm in the sun, throw a thin layer of snow onto the plastic to melt and collect in the depression.

Carry your water in containers that are vacuum-insulated with separate inner and outer stainless-steel shells and a mouthpiece that won't freeze your lips. Wrap the outside in fabric. You may choose to carry warm water at the start of a day's journey, cooling it as you travel. If there is risk of freezing, never fill the container beyond the two-thirds mark to allow for ice expansion, as well as because the movement of the water will help keep it from freezing.

You may be able to keep water from freezing overnight by storing it in a snow chamber. The container should be completely surrounded by snow a foot thick and set on its lid to avoid freezing shut.

MELT ICE BEFORE SNOW

>>> Melt ice instead of snow if both are available. Ice yields more water with less effort.
>>> Choose ice that is salt free. Salty sea ice is milky and hard.
>>> Choose snow that is the most compacted, often found on the windward side of rocks formations. It contains the least air and yields the most water.
>>> Mix snow with a bit of water from a canteen for most efficient melting in a pot. Otherwise, pot may scorch.
>>> Melt snow in a container inside your clothing layers (not against skin) or in a porous bag above a collector near a fire.
>>> Place snow on a dark surface in full sun to promote melting.
>>> In an emergency, snow can be eaten by bringing it to the melting point in a bare hand. This could lead to frostbite.

EXPERT TIP Fire not only provides a means to prepare food, but also to get warm and to melt snow or ice for water. It also provides you with a significant psychological boost by making you feel a little more secure in your situation.

U.S.ARMY

SHELTER

Your surroundings are the key factor in determining the best form of shelter. Forested areas may offer protection from wind and enough wood to build a structure and light a fire. Barren regions of tundra may have little except snow with which to fashion a shelter. Fortunately, snow is a natural insulator. Loose snow contains air pockets trapped between the flakes. Creating shelter near the Poles can be as basic as digging or shaping snow to take advantage of its natural insulating properties, or pitching a tent and packing snow around its exterior to deflect wind and trap heat. Shelters should be situated to catch any sun that is available and to take advantage of terrain to minimize the impact of wind. / Choosing the right kind of shelter also depends on what you carry and how quickly you can use it. Sawing blocks of compacted snow and fashioning them into an igloo requires not only a cutting tool such as a snow saw, but also a considerable investment in time. Pitching a tent or building a tree pit, trench, or snow cave makes more sense if shelter is an immediate priority. Long-term shelters can be made to replace or shore up temporary structures.

Cover your shelter's floor with mats, bags, or natural materials. Don't lie directly on snow or ice.

essentials

TENT FEATURES

Tents are relatively light and easily transported. They need special characteristics to keep occupants warm and dry in polar and subpolar cold.

NYLON, the most common tent fabric, must be treated to create a waterproof exterior.

HOWEVER, waterproofing must not make the tent airtight. Air-permeable fabric prevents condensation from building up and dripping on interior walls. Moisture should leave but not enter.

CHOOSE double-walled tents for insulation and lower interior condensation.

SEAMS should be sealed with a water-based urethane sealer or tape-welded.

ALUMINUM poles should be at least 8.5 millimeters in diameter to stand up to blizzards.

CALCULATE expected weather conditions, ease of transportation, and number of occupants to find the right balance between a tent's strength and weight.

A TENT may be rated for three or four seasons, or a hybrid. Four-season models are strong but heavy.

USE a dome tent in extreme cold. Packing snow around the dome increases stability and insulation.

TO MAKE the most of body heat, a tent should not be too big for its occupants.

NO TENT? TRY THESE

WIND AND COLD are killers when you have no shelter. When stuck in extreme cold, your first task is to get out of the elements. A variety of snow shelters, relatively easy to make, offer basic protection.

Fashion an igloo from a hemisphere of hard, dry snow cut from blocks.

Snow caves are basically a hollow into a snowbank. Wall off the entrance, and poke holes for ventilation.

Rock overhangs are quick and easy shelter. Wall off openings to cut wind.

Dig a Snow trench—a pit large enough for you to sleep and sit in. Cover with snow or brush.

Make a brushy A-frame shelter and cover it with snow for insulation.

Dig a tree pit around the base of a tree with low branches until you reach ground. Remove branches to use as an insulating overhead cover.

Quinze (pronounced "kwinzee") is fashioned as a snow dome over your gear. Remove gear to leave a hollow.

GEAR FOR YOUR SHELTER
>>> Vinyl tent-repair patches.
>>> Shovel, snow saw, or knife to cut and pack snow for makeshift shelter or add insulation around tent.
>>> "Mummy" sleeping bag for maximum warmth. The drawstring closes over head and neck.
>>> Rounded-foot bag with baffled zipper is a good alternative.
>>> Modern synthetic fillers for sleeping gear. Unlike down, they still insulate when wet.
>>> Cotton sleeping bag liner. Extra insulation that can be removed and washed.
>>> Pad to place under sleeping bag.

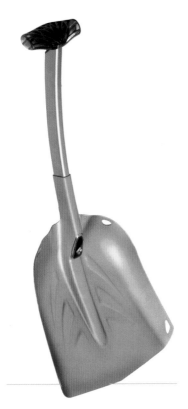

how to

BUILD A QUINZE

1. Stack backpacks, equipment, and brush or branches into a large pile.

2. Shovel snow on top, let it harden, and add more snow until it forms a dome with walls three feet thick.

3. Push two-foot sticks into the walls to use as guides for wall thickness.

4. Remove backpacks and dig at the inside surface to expand the hollow interior until you see tips of sticks.

VENTILATE YOUR SHELTER

>>> Snow shelters must have at least one roof hole to prevent potentially fatal carbon monoxide buildup from heat sources.

>>> Site vent holes at 45-degree angle between roof and opening.

>>> Cut holes with ice ax in hard snow walls.

>>> Check the holes periodically to ensure they're open.

>>> Extinguish heaters while sleeping as a safety precaution.

>>> Allow ventilation from door or tunnel to let air mix. A U-shaped igloo entrance tunnel drains away cold air.

>>> Do not completely block doorway. Build snow walls to act as wind barriers.

INSULATION INFORMATION

Dead air spaces trap warmth. Insulating materials that retain air pockets, are easy to pack and carry, and don't quit working when exposed to water are ideal for sleeping bags and pads.

GOOSE DOWN. It still rates as the warmest insulation material per ounce, giving a third more insulation than a similar amount of synthetic fiber. Down is light and compact. Its biggest drawback is the collapse of its air pockets into a feathery mess when wet.

SYNTHETIC FIBERS. They best retain insulation properties when wet, and they dry quickly. Expect to carry a third more weight to get the same insulation rating as down. Polarguard, Hollofil, and Quallofil are used in parkas and sleeping bags. Polarguard has sheets of insulating material. The other fabrics expand the sheets' dead air space. Thinsulate, Microloft, and Primaloft are thin and allow room for multiple layers. Nylon often is used as a shell material but must be made waterproof.

SHINGLED BAFFLES of insulation material. Overlapping design creates a barrier.

QUILTED BAFFLES. Oval tubes contain filling material. Stitches that edge the tubes may act as channels for heat loss.

OFFSET, overlapping, and V-tube quilted baffles. Multiple layering patterns, with tubes overlapping seams, minimize heat loss.

WOOL. High-grade wool is still accepted as an insulating fabric because it keeps working when wet. Experienced polar travelers prefer high-performance synthetics.

GET OFF THE GROUND AND SNOW

PLACE INSULATION between your sleeping bag and cold ground or snow to minimize heat loss. Options include pads, materials you gather, and materials you carry.

Open-cell foam pads easily compress for travel, but closed-cell designs are warmer and repel moisture. Pads also come in inflatable varieties; their trapped air acts as insulation between ground and bag.

Evergreen boughs and other vegetable matter contain air spaces. Using a cross-hatched pattern, make a thick layer of branches on the ground or the snow and place your sleeping bag on top.

Don't forget that backpacks and spare clothing also contain air pockets. Place backpack under your knees and a mound of clothes under your head for comfort and warmth. Or place feet and legs inside empty pack for warmth.

INSULATE YOURSELF IN AN EMERGENCY

>>> Milkweed and cattail can be stuffed into sleeping bags to increase insulation.
>>> Dry grass, cattail fluff, and milkweed also can be stuffed into clothing layers, such as an extra pair of socks.
>>> Stuff dry plant matter into parachute or other type of cloth to create a makeshift sleeping bag.
>>> Place your sleeping bag on branches to insulate yourself from the cold ground. Never lie directly on top of ice or snow.

SLEEPING BAG OPTIONS

DON'T USE old-style rectangle bags in extreme cold. They are too light and too bulky. They lack hoods to protect head and shoulders and allow cold to penetrate through zippers. Weak insulation can be improved by the insertion of liners.

Semi-rectangular and semi-mummy bags trap more body heat than rectangular bags because of their constricted space. Those with curved backing for upper bodies and baffled zippers increase warmth.

Mummy bags have tapered feet and a small entrance hole at the head. The tight space minimizes the air the occupant's body must heat. Mummy bags may be hard to enter and exit through their drawstring openings.

Restricted movement may cause muscle cramps. However, a well-insulated mummy bag provides the best defense of all sleeping options against polar cold.

KEEP YOUR BAG DRY

>>> **Waterproof mat between bag and ground cuts moisture transfer.**
>>> **Keep bags clean.**
>>> **Remove bag from tent and shake.**
>>> **Aerate and dry bag thoroughly before rolling and storing.**
>>> **Carry bag in waterproof cover.**

EXPERT TIP The snow cave shelter is a most effective shelter because of the insulating qualities of snow. Remember that it takes time and energy to build and that you will get wet while building this shelter.

SHARE YOUR BODY HEAT

IF YOU TRAVEL in a group, you and your companions are blessed with handy portable heaters: each other.

In a survival situation, you may need to forget your inhibitions and huddle with others in a shelter or under a tarp to stay alive. In groups, place children, the elderly, and very thin people at the center of any collection of bodies, as they will lose body heat fastest.

For emergency shelter, dig a snow pit and line the inside with evergreen boughs.

SLEEPING WELL IN POLAR AND SUBPOLAR REGIONS

GETTING A GOOD NIGHT'S SLEEP in the high latitudes may not be much different than doing so in the suburbs. You should exercise your muscles during the day to warm them up and make your body tired, but not so much that you perspire heavily and get your clothes wet. Take a trip to relieve yourself before you bed down so you don't have to face the cold in the middle of the night—or, worse, lie awake because you can't stomach the thought of getting out of your sleeping bag. Eat your biggest meal before bedding down.

Wear extra clothes, particularly socks and hat, to bed. Make sure these are not the clothes you wore around the campfire or while eating, so as not to attract predators while you sleep. As the majority of body heat escapes from your head, a comfortable knit cap will insulate you well. Warm feet and head will help you sleep.

Keep the wind and cold out of your shelter. If you have a fire going—as well as good ventilation to keep from suffocating—keep a supply of fuel handy to maintain heat throughout the night.

In long polar nights, you may find yourself sleeping 12 hours or more. As long as you stay warm, this should not be a problem and may help you overcome exhaustion associated with working under difficult conditions.

NIGHTTIME TIPS

>>> If you have a gun, keep it outdoors at night nearby. Avoiding temperature changes will lower the risk of condensation.
>>> Keep ammunition with you to keep it warm.
>>> In a snow shelter, sleep with your digging tool. You may need it to dig your way out if the snow shifts or collapses.
>>> Warm stones left in wet boots overnight will dry them. Don't burn the boots by putting in stones that are too hot.
>>> Hang up wet clothes where they can freeze. In the morning, beat the ice out of them.

FOOD

Your body needs more food in extreme cold. If you plan a trip, pack light and take dry foods such as pasta and oatmeal, as well as dried fruit, nuts, and meats. Eating protein before going to sleep helps keep you warm through the night. / Native foods include fish, birds, mammals, and plants such as hardy foliose or tripe de roche lichens, which grow on rocks, and reindeer moss can be eaten after soaking and boiling. / In barren lands and on ice caps, a diet of animal flesh may be all that's available. Humans can live for a long time on nothing but fresh fish and meat. They long have been the standard diet of the Inuit, who have little access to vegetables and fruit. However, the Inuit shun the livers of polar bears and husky dogs, which contain vitamin A in toxic concentrations. Vitamin A poisoning from a steady diet of dog liver killed Antarctic explorer Xavier Mertz in 1913 after he suffered delirium, dementia, convulsions, and brain hemorrhage.

BASIC CALORIC REQUIREMENTS

COLD WEATHER taxes the body, making it burn more calories to keep warm. Difficult travel conditions across snow and broken ice terrain, complicated by the weight of clothes and supplies, put more stress on the body's fuel-burning engine. Dry air, like that in the desert of Antarctica, adds even more. Not surprisingly, starvation is a common cause of death in polar regions.

Plan to consume up to 5,000 calories a day in polar regions. Compare this with 1,600 to 2,800 calories a day for adults in temperate zones.

Caloric needs rise with the level of physical exertion. Climbing at high altitude in polar regions burns a phenomenal amount of body fuel.

HIGH-CALORIE FOODS

- ››› **High-energy bars**
- ››› **Hard candy**
- ››› **Fats (includes blubber, but avoid seal fat)**
- ››› **Nuts and chocolates; trail mix, gorp**
- ››› **Honey, syrup**

PLANT WISDOM

THE SHORT GROWING season stunts plant life. Shrubs and ground cover plants replace trees at high latitudes. Lichens cling to rocks.

A few Arctic plants are poisonous, such as arctic poppy, Baneberry fruit, and others (see list below), but none is known to irritate skin.

For best health, don't eat one plant exclusively, and remember that just because one part of a plant is edible, other parts may be poisonous. For long-term survival, you probably will need to supplement plants with animal protein to survive. You also are likely to eat more than normal to get enough calories.

AVOID THESE PLANTS

>>> Arctic poppy: poisonous flower.
>>> Baneberry fruit.
>>> Bearded lichen. Grows on trees. Acid causes stomach irritation.
>>> Fungi. Make sure you can distinguish edible lichens from poisonous varieties of fungus.
>>> Lupine and larkspur—showy wildflowers that are toxic.
>>> Water hemlock. Look for small, white flowers and a hollow, sectioned, bamboo-like stem. Even small amounts are fatal.

BEST BETS: PLANTS

>>> Arctic raspberry. Nearly all aggregate berries are edible.
>>> Arctic willow. Typically grow thick, one to two feet high, on tundra. Young leaves and peeled shoots are edible; leaves have more vitamin C than an orange.
>>> Iceland moss. Grows only a few inches high and only in Arctic regions. All parts are edible. Boil to rid of bitterness or dry for storage.
>>> Reindeer moss. Lichen prefers open, dry territory. Soak it with wood ash to remove bitterness.
>>> Foliose lichen (tripe de roche). Dark on top, light on the bottom. Scrape this lichen off rocks and wash it to remove grit.
>>> Spruce needles. Steep them for tea.

When ice-fishing, keep the hole from freezing shut by covering with a layer of brush.

ANIMALS TO EAT IN AN EMERGENCY

FISH, CRABS, CLAMS, and oysters abound in coastal waters at high latitudes. A few bird species remain in subarctic regions all year. Large mammals such as seals move from region to region in search of food. Dangerous predators such as leopard seals, whales, and polar bears likely are not far behind.

For survival situations, when you have no food and are faced with starvation, look to the seal as a key source of food and fuel. They live in the water most of the time but must surface to breathe. Females crawl onto land to give birth in spring. If you have exhausted all other food resources and possibilities and must kill a seal to survive, find a breathing hole in the ice and wait beside it with a club. A heavy blow to the head will kill a small seal, which then can be dragged onto the ice. Do not eat the meat raw, and do not eat the liver. The skin can be used as a waterproof covering and the blubber as a fuel for fire.

To preserve leftover meat, cut it into strips and freeze or dry in the sun (see "How to Sun-Dry Meat" in Chapter Six).

BEST BETS: ANIMALS

>>> Most fish and fish eggs are good. Fish are relatively low in calories.
>>> Bivalves such as clams and mussels.
>>> Ptarmigans and owls in wooded regions. Birds cannot fly while molting in the summer, making them easier to catch.
>>> Bird eggs.
>>> Porcupines in wooded regions. They eat bark; look for strips peeled from low limbs.
>>> Foxes and weasels.
>>> Reindeer/caribou, if you have weapons to hunt them.
>>> Seal meat. Seals are hard to catch. Inuit hunt them by sliding slowly across the ice toward them, then shooting them before they can slide into the water. A dead seal will float but likely will be difficult to retrieve without a boat.
>>> Penguins (found only in Antarctic regions).

AVOID THESE ANIMALS

>>> Black mussels. They are likely to contain powerful toxins.
>>> Greenland shark. The meat is toxic.
>>> Polar bears. Best advice is to avoid bear country. These carnivores are fierce and fearless and have been known to eat humans. Without a gun or pepper spray, you're unlikely to survive a close encounter with an aggressive polar bear. If you have a gun, shoot into the brain. If you manage a kill, do not eat the poisonous liver.
>>> Ravens. They lack enough meat to be worth the trouble.
>>> Sculpin eggs. They're poisonous.
>>> Walruses. Sluggish-looking, they're actually quite dangerous.

ICE-FISHING AT THE POLES

YOU CAN CATCH FISH by cutting a six- to eight-inch hole in ice and dropping a line through the opening. A hand-turned auger should cut through ice a foot thick. Don't walk onto ice unless it is at least three to four inches thick, the minimum for supporting body weight If you have doubts, stay off. Be aware that ice is weaker over moving water.

You can fish through several holes at once by baiting lines and hooks and rigging each to a pair of crossed sticks. The first stick spans the width of the hole. The second stick, attached perpendicularly, is tied to the end of the fishing line. When the fish strikes the hook, it pulls the stick. The second stick rotates like a turning wheel until it stands up. Check the holes regularly to make sure they don't freeze over.

If you see a fish beneath you, bang the ice with a rock or log. This may stun the fish, giving you time to drill a hole and grab it.

You can cook fish on a fire or do as the Inuit do: Debone it on the spot and freeze fillets on the ice. Frozen fillets are sliced and eaten raw.

EXPERT TIP There are several sources of food in the Arctic and subarctic regions. The type of food—fish, animal, fowl, or plant—and the ease in obtaining it depend on the time of the year and your location.

★ U.S.ARMY

how to
ICE-FISH

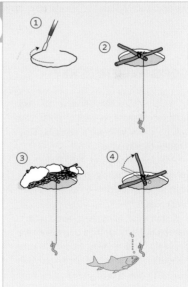

1. Use an auger or ice chisel to cut holes in ice over water.

2. Rig line and bait to the end of one of a pair of sticks that are crossed in a "plus sign" shape and tied tightly at their intersection. Set the sticks over the hole to rotate when the bait is pulled down.

3. Keep holes from freezing shut by covering them at night with brush and snow.

4. Baited stick pops up when fish bites.

FIRST AID

It's no surprise that common polar health problems involve reactions to cold and light. / Frostbite results when flesh freezes. It often happens to exposed skin, particularly during a strong wind. Dry layers with no gaps provide the best protection. Treatments include pressing affected skin against warm flesh. Do not rub. Hospitalization is necessary in extreme cases, as thawing frozen limbs leads to pain and infection. / Hypothermia occurs when the body loses heat and cannot replace it. Take immediate action if you observe someone beginning to shiver uncontrollably, use slurred speech, become confused, or grow drowsy. Get the victim inside shelter. Warm the body trunk with a blanket or skin contact. Give warm liquids, but avoid alcohol. Keep the victim dry and warm. / Snow blindness is sunburn to the eyeballs caused by the reflection of ultraviolet rays. One victim likened it to "driving thumbtacks into my eyes." Prevention is as simple as wearing sunglasses. Treatment options include rest and blindfolding.

GOOD HYGIENE IS KEY

IF YOU WEAKEN because of bad nutrition, disease, or lack of sleep, you will be more vulnerable to cold. Stay healthy to stay alive.

Replace water and salt. Failure to rehydrate can result in symptoms as light as constipation or as serious as blackouts.

Clean your body, hair, and clothes regularly. Dirty clothes don't breathe properly, and a dirty body attracts parasites. If water is scarce, rub your skin with one cup of soapy water and rinse with one cup of clean water.

Rubbing with a dry cloth is better than nothing.

ADD THESE TO A FIRST AID KIT

>>> **Chemical heat packs**
>>> **Foot powder**
>>> **Lip balm**
>>> **Razor. Remove facial hair; it collects frost.**
>>> **Sunburn treatment and sunscreen**
>>> **Vitamins**
>>> **Space (emergency) blanket.**

INSULATING YOURSELF

In extreme cold, covering every square inch of skin will protect against the pain of frostbite. Try these tips:

WEAR GLOVES with high cuffs to keep snow off wrists.

COVER HEAD and face with goggles and scarf, hat, and/or balaclava. Avoid exposing any part of your face to the air. The U.S. Army advises against smearing your face with petroleum jelly, saying it encourages frostbite.

WEAR BOOTS with waterproof soles.

CHOOSE clothing with sealed seams and zippers that zip at both ends. Parkas should close with overlapping flaps to keep out wind.

AVOID trenchfoot from prolonged exposure to cool dampness if the temperature is above freezing. Numbness leads to pain. Prevent/treat by drying and cleaning feet dry and applying foot powder. Do not rub.

COLD AND FIRST AID

EXTREME COLD changes the physical properties of many materials, including some in your first aid kit. Typically, cold weakens materials and reduces their capacity to bend. Any objects that have moving parts are subject to freezing up or working sluggishly.

Rubber stiffens with cold and may crack or break when subjected to pressure. Thaw rubber before use.

Canvas resists folding and may tear when frozen.

Glass will shatter if abruptly heated or chilled.

Oils become thicker at low temperatures. However, alcohol won't freeze until well below -100°F.

Water expands as it freezes and may crack any full or nearly full container.

Leather cracks unless it is treated with neatsfoot oil.

Metal, when very cold, may freeze to bare skin because of its moisture. Do not touch bare metal with naked fingers in extremely low temperatures.

In polar regions, the extreme cold can quickly exacerbate minor injuries; treat promptly.

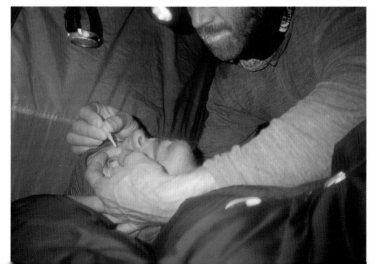

HAZARDS

Polar hazards are sneaky. / You expect cold, yet a common hazard is sweating. Arctic travelers often get dehydrated because they don't realize they're losing water through perspiration. Daytime exertion also soaks the bottom clothing layers, while respiration and sweating pour a pint of water into a sleeping bag every night. Unless dried, wet materials freeze solid. They lose their insulating ability and contribute to frostbite and hypothermia. / Hidden crevasses and rotten or thin ice trap unwary travelers, plunging them to death or serious injury. And one of the most common predators of the North, the polar bear, blends in with its environment so well it can virtually disappear. / Just living amid the cold can be sneaky, too. Simple tasks become complicated while wearing heavy clothes and gloves. Glasses fog over. And unprotected eyes eventually scream for rest from sunlight on snow.

AVOID DEHYDRATION

IN THE TROPICS, you know you're sweating when you feel sweat on your skin. In cold regions, you may realize you're losing water in your frosty exhaled breath. But when sweat is wicked away from skin under multiple layers of clothing, you may not realize just how much you need to replace. The South Pole standard is a gallon and a half per day per person.

Like snow blindness creeping up on unwary travelers, dehydration may hit suddenly. Mouth and tongue go dry; swallowing becomes difficult; and cramps and weakness follow. Treat as usual (see Appendix). Make sure clothes are loose enough to allow free circulation.

TREAT SNOW BLINDNESS

>>> **Prevent with sunglasses or Inuit slit glasses.**
>>> **Highest risk is at high altitudes and after fresh snowfall.**
>>> **Onset of pain occurs after significant injury.**
>>> **Symptoms include gritty feeling, pain, headache, redness.**
>>> **Rest and darkness return eyes to normal.**

KEEPING DRY

Water, so crucial to survival, can take on a sinister role in the polar regions by attacking clothes from within and without. Keep clothes dry to stay healthy—and alive.

WEAR waterproof outer garments.

WATERPROOF your boots, or use plastic footwear akin to ski boots for snow travel.

BRUSH or shake snow off clothes before entering places where it will melt.

AVOID rubbing snow into fabrics.

REMOVE LAYERS to prevent sweating from overheating. Aim to be a bit chilled rather than too warm.

USE a sleeping bag with a water-repellent cover and insulated pad.

VENTILATE sleeping bags and air them in sunlight to rid them of moisture after use.

TRANSPORT sleeping bags in waterproof bags.

DRY DAMP SOCKS and mittens with body heat. Use drying racks inside shelter for other clothes.

DRY LEATHER BOOTS slowly to avoid cracking.

NEVER ASSUME a sheet of ice atop a lake or river is safe for you to traverse, particularly in spring. Test its thickness and strength.

NAVIGATING DARKNESS

YOU CAN'T PICK when you may find yourself in a survival situation. In the polar regions, chances are you'll have to survive most of the time in the dark.

Don't panic. Check to see if you have any sort of light. If you must move, rope group members together, with weakest members in the center. Plant feet firmly in snow, check footing with each step before proceeding. On uncertain ground, you may need to drop to hands and knees, protecting skin from direct contact with ice and snow. If you hear water, it may indicate a dangerous falls. Do not try to cross a river in the dark, as it is extremely dangerous.

SURVIVE A FALL THROUGH ICE

>>> Snap off as much thin ice as you can in the direction you wish to emerge.
>>> Pull yourself out when you reach a thickness that will support your weight.
>>> A knife or hook plunged into the ice may help.
>>> If in a group, have someone toss you a rope and/or slide a stick along the broken ice edge to assist in escape.
>>> Squirm and roll horizontally until safe. Standing may recrack the ice.
>>> Blot yourself by rolling in snow.
>>> Change clothes, get dry, get warm.

KNOW YOUR POLAR PREDATORS

SOME POLAR animals look at humans and think, "Dinner." They range from the tiny—mosquitoes and blackflies—to thousand-pound polar bears.

Polar bears are an Arctic menace. They generally frequent coastlines in search of seals and are rarely found inland. Polar bears also gather on pressure ridges, icebergs, small islands near shorelines, and boulders. They are aggressive and dangerous to humans.

Grizzlies also frequent cold regions but are seldom aggressive toward humans.

Likewise, gray wolves have an undeserved reputation. They prefer large, hooved animals as well as the occasional rabbit. They tend to shy away from human encounters.

Musk oxen, while not predators, react to threats by forming a defensive circle. Typically a bull or two charges out of the circle to confront an approaching threat. While Inuit hunt them for meat, unarmed humans should leave them alone. Simi-larly, walruses pose no threat unless they feel threatened. Walruses, recognized by their long, straight tusks among the males, live throughout shallow Arctic waters. The largest may weigh two tons and stretch more than ten feet long. Do not approach a walrus without a powerful rifle; they are dangerous animals.

LOWDOWN ON BLACKFLIES

>>> They grow to five millimeters in length.
>>> You should avoid campsites near water, where larvae breed.
>>> Swarms arise in subarctic regions in late spring/early summer.
>>> Churning, swift water is favored breeding ground for larvae.
>>> Painful bites torment animals and humans, affecting subarctic settlement patterns.
>>> Wear a net over the head.
>>> Burn green wood and leaves; smoke acts as repellent.

A fierce, strong-jawed leopard seal prowls beneath bobbing sea ice for a 3 a.m. meal.

AVOID BECOMING POLAR BEAR PREY

POLAR BEARS are curious and keen-nosed; they are likely to consider odors from food, garbage, and dirty clothing an invitation to investigate. Polar bears have been known to stick their heads inside occupied tents, looking for food. Store food in bear-proof containers and eliminate attractive nuisances.

If a polar bear enters your camp, get away to a secure spot.

Try to see the bear before it sees you. Polar bears are stealthy hunters and can make themselves difficult to see by sliding along ice and covering their black noses with their paws.

Use dogs to warn of bears' approach. If you must face a polar bear, use bear spray and a gun. An unarmed human stands little chance of survival.

Signs of polar bear aggression include a growl, hiss, or jaw motion that looks like a yawn. If the bear has foam at its mouth, it is highly upset. However, you may never see a bear before it attacks because of its camouflage. Young bears are the most dangerous.

UNDERSTANDING WIND AND COLD

POLAR AND SUBPOLAR regions brew some of the worst weather on the planet. Heavy snowfall is atypical. Strong winds combined with snow and cold create terrible survival conditions.

Earth's lowest recorded temperature was -129°F at Vostok, Antarctica, in 1983. Winter temperatures at the Poles generally bottom out scores of degrees warmer than that. However, wind and low visibility from blowing snow sometimes make travel impossible. "Hell is on the other side of the thin sheet of canvas that protects us," Robert Scott wrote during an Antarctic blizzard. One of his companions noted that taking more than a few steps from the tent would have been fatal.

Windchill, a measure of how wind and cold affect exposed skin, is negated by clothing layers that cover all flesh. Losing a glove in high wind is certain to flash-freeze skin, so pack an extra pair in an easily-accessible outer pocket of your gear. At the freezing point of water, 32°F, a 40-mph wind makes skin feel as if it were about 13°F. At -20°F, that same wind would create a windchill of -57°F.

Blowing snow can create a whiteout. Contrast drains from all objects and an observer feels lost in a sphere of uniform whiteness. A similar phenomenon may occur when there is a solid blanket of snow on the ground and a hazy, completely overcast sky.

NAVIGATION

Navigation raises a new set of challenges in polar regions. A dearth of landmarks, proximity to magnetic poles, and days without sun cause confusion about routes and compass directions. Blowing snow can cause whiteouts, making travel virtually impossible. Restricted visibility at sea level makes getting through ice pack and across pressure ridges difficult. Atmospheric phenomena caused by reflected light play tricks on the mind, making objects appear closer or more distant. Bright light can eliminate shadows that normally help observers judge shape and distance. Reflections also cause snow blindness. / Lack of natural resources requires travelers to carry or drag everything they need, which may weigh hundreds of pounds for extended trips. Humans have devised ways to cope. Old-school methods include cross-country skis, snowshoes, animal-skin boats, and dogsled teams pulling sleds and sledges. Crampons and ice axes improve traction for both everyday travel and emergencies. / Travel surfaces become problematic during spring and fall, when ice formations thaw and freeze. Sudden floods are almost guaranteed after a warm spell. Somewhat counterintuitively, the best time for travel often is early winter. Ground and waterways freeze solid in imitation of paved highways. Unless extreme cold, deep snow, high winds, and glacial crevasses interfere, winter simplifies movement. Decrease your speed when traveling during the long hours of polar winter darkness.

READING EDGES AND SURFACES OF ICE FLOES

FLOATING MASSES of ice are called ice floes if they are less than a few miles across, and ice fields if larger. Leads are the long cracks that form water channels when floes split or shear. If you are traveling by raft, canoe, or skin boat, ice floes present an opportunity and a challenge. The challenge arises from floes that jam together near shorelines and close water channels. The opportunity lies in landing on a floe and riding it as a natural float. If your raft is inflated, keep it away from sharp ice edges to avoid punctures and weight it down to prevent it from blowing away.

Learn to read the edges and surfaces of ice floes to get clues to land's distance. Sharp edges and plates of ice close together indicate land close by. Low and flat ice forms over protected bays. "Ice blink," a spot of light in a gray sky, may be a reflection off an ice floe or berg. "Water sky" is just the opposite. A cloud layer over open water may show a dark underside visible from a distance.

Similarly, "land sky" indicates land. Land sky appears as a dark layer on the bottom of cloud cover above land that is not blanketed with snow; it is darker than ice blink but lighter than water sky.

Use ice floes as a source of fresh water when traveling on the ocean. Carve out a piece of ice from the highest part of an ice floe. If the floe is old, the chunk likely will lack salt.

If you're on ice or snow and the wind becomes warmer than your surroundings, it may be a sign of water nearby in the wind's direction.

ALLOW ICE THICKNESS OF:

>>> At least two to three inches of ice when wearing skis.
>>> At least four inches for ice fishing, skating, drawing water.
>>> At least seven inches for snowmobiles.
>>> At least eight inches for larger vehicles.

When moving across ice, make sure it is thick enough to support you and all of your gear.

Blizzards, like this one at Butson Point, a northeast glacier in Antarctica, limit visibility.

TAKE DIRECTIONAL CLUES FROM SUN, SNOW, AND WIND

THE ELEMENTS can be unforgiving and treacherous near or at the Poles, but let them assist you in finding your way.

The sun's rays warm dark objects such as tree trunks in snow. Absorbed heat melts some of the snow. That allows more sun to strike the object and deepen the hole. The shape of the hole typically is a half-circle. The rounded front edge points south. Shadows at midday point north. (Note: This method doesn't work north of the Arctic Circle, where the sun's summer path describes a great arc around the horizon.)

Snow is shallower and erosion greater on the southern side of hills, thanks to greater sunshine and temperature changes. Extra solar energy also influences the growth of conifers. Their southernmost, sunward sides tend to have more branches and needles. Where winds are strong and favor one direction, however, a tree's leeward side may have the most green.

If you know the wind's dominant direction, you can use that to help navigate. Keeping that direction at a constant angle helps keep travelers on a steady line. Dominant winds shape snow features and bend plant life. However, take the local terrain into account. At land's edge, winds tend to blow offshore during the day and change direction in the evening to blow onshore. Mountains also are likely to have their own local wind patterns.

MAKE A SHADOW STICK TO FIND DIRECTION

>>> Shove a pole at a slight angle into the ground or snow.
>>> Tie a piece of long string to the top.
>>> Lie down with your head under the string. Pull it taut next to your eye.
>>> Wriggle your body and head until the line points at a star or planet well away from the North Star.
>>> The line traces the star's "shadow." Mark its contact point with a stone.
>>> Wait at least 10 minutes. Repeat.
>>> Connect the points. They mark west (first stone) and east (last stone).

NAVIGATE BY DEAD RECKONING AT THE POLES

POLAR REGIONS offer few landmarks to fix on a map. Without a GPS, the only practical guide for your progress while traveling may be dead reckoning—calculating your position by figuring distance and direction from a previous fixed point.

It's more difficult in the high latitudes. Earth's magnetic field plays havoc with compasses near the Poles, and moving across ice and snow affects a normal pace count.

Keep a log of daily travels. If you can, count your paces to measure distance. Doing so in snowshoes is possible, though such large footgear will cause you to take smaller steps than usual. With care, you can also determine your "paces" on skis.

essentials

METHODS OF NAVIGATION POLAR, SUBPOLAR TRAVEL

You'll need help finding your way and getting across ice and snow.

SNOWSHOES allow bodies to float atop snow.

CROSS-COUNTRY SKIS, another flotation method, work better in open country.

ICE AX and crampons help with footing and traction. Get training for proper use.

GPS operates at the Poles, but the cold saps battery life. Keep batteries warm when not in use.

MAPS and compasses play the same role as in other regions. Adjust for magnetic variations and be aware that maps may lack detail in polar regions.

CALCULATE heading, count paces when leaving camp. Use the count to retrace your steps.

USE YOUR SHADOW over short periods as a general directional indicator.

OPTICAL TRICKS: OBJECTS IN THE SNOW...

>>> **Appear nearer: in bright sun.**
>>> **Appear nearer: in clear air.**
>>> **Appear nearer: across flat snow or water.**
>>> **Appear farther: little variation in color.**
>>> **Appear farther: across snow drifts.**
>>> **Appear farther: in dim light.**
>>> **Appear higher: overcast sky above snow reflects distant objects.**

TRAVEL AND NAVIGATION present difficulties ranging from simple to complex in high latitudes.

The simplest may be the cold. It's hard to pull out and read a map or a GPS while wearing gloves, but removing them may cause exposure injuries.

Monotonous tundra presents few landmarks on a map, and even if trails and other elements of terrain are marked, they may be covered with snow and impossible to see. Furthermore, detailed maps may not be available for much of the polar regions.

Aerial or satellite photographs of terrain are likely to offer few recognizable features because of the lack of contrast in places.

The most complex navigation difficulty may be magnetic. Magnetic variation varies a great deal. Magnetic disturbances also occur near the Poles. Both complicate use of a compass needle to find "north."

ADJUST COMPASS AT POLES

>>> At the poles, a compass needle points at magnetic north, not geographic (polar) north.

>>> The northern magnetic pole lies near Bathurst Island, Canada, but has minor shifts.

>>> Adjust for variation in high latitudes. Greenland's is as much as 50 degrees east.

>>> "Agonic line" divides magnetic east and west. East of line, variation is east. There is no variation on the line itself.

>>> Compass readings become complicated near magnetic poles.

>>> Above the magnetic pole, compass needles point down.

essentials

DOS AND DON'TS FOR NAVIGATING POLAR REGIONS

Let polar and subpolar terrain help you instead of hinder you.

DO: CROSS streams at their lowest point.

DO: WALK on ice only when it is 4 inches thick or more. If crossing shallower ice, consider lying flat and crawling to distribute body weight.

DO: FOLLOW frozen rivers if covered by thick ice. Beware of snow cover, which insulates and may make river ice soft or unreliable.

DO: READ the air for weather changes that may affect travel. Thin, rising smoke means good weather. Shifting winds or heavy, humid air indicates a possible storm.

DON'T: TRAVEL in a blizzard or whiteout.

DON'T: SLOG through deep snow without snowshoes or skis.

DON'T: STEP near cornices.

THE MULTIPLE USES OF SNOWSHOES

Snowshoes simplify walking and pulling loads in deep snow. They allow your body to float instead of sink.

STRIDE by lifting the toe up above snow, then pushing foot forward.

CONSERVE energy by lifting toes only enough to clear snow.

CHOOSE shoes that allow feet to bend in an approximation of walking, without allowing tips to hit your shins. Maintain a loose, rocking gait.

CLIMB straight up gentle slopes and zigzag up steeper ones. On traverses, try to keep snowshoes horizontal.

TURN by swinging one leg, as in a skier's kick turn.

TAKE a five- to ten-minute break every hour to rest, plan, and make repairs.

REMOVE snow buildup.

CHOOSE the lightest model that supports your weight. Heavy shoes sap strength.

TRAVELERS in snowshoes usually underestimate distance, often, arriving much more tired and later than expected.

MAKE SNOWSHOES

1 Find two densely needled pine branches of equal size, about 2.5 to 3 feet in length.

2 For each branch, tie a long cord or strong grasses around the thickest part of the branch, about an inch or two from the end. Leave enough rope loose to attach your boot to the branch.

3 Loop the cord on both sides underneath the first boughs. Put your foot on the body of the branch, with the closest to the end where the knot is tied. Tie your boot into place by looping the rope around your toe and heel and knotting securely.

4 Put green wood below your feet.

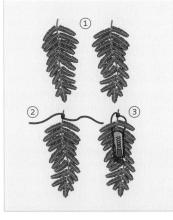

POLAR & SUBPOLAR

CHAPTER

7

235

Borge Ousland's and my goal: to ski to the North Pole in winter. Starting from the extreme north Siberian Cape Arkticheskiy, we planned to cross 600 miles, across moving islands of ice separated by water canals (leads) and pack ice, through whiteout conditions, -40°F temperatures, and polar bear territory.

236

Every morning, after we broke down our tent, I would lead for the first two hours to set the general direction we would take for the day. After that, we'd alternate (leading and following) every two hours. Based on my two years' experience traveling in and around the Arctic Circle, I had agreed to take responsibility for navigation during our expedition. Borge had, in turn, agreed to be responsible for finding safe paths across the snow and ice, a terrain on which he has great expertise.

We continued in this manner for more than a month. About five weeks into the trek, a bitter storm raged for three days, cracking the ice under strong winds. As blocks of ice collided with each other, they created an increasing number of treacherous leads (pronounced "leeds"—water channels between thick ice floes), which lie hidden under blowing snow. We proceeded with increasing caution, knowing that any minute, we could find ourselves skiing off a solid ice

Mike Horn is a National Geographic grantee whose trek to the North Pole in winter was featured in National Geographic's *Adventure* magazine.

floe onto nothing but snow floating on top of the Arctic Ocean.

After three days of these stormy, blowing conditions, we became even more uncertain of our footing, as we skied across a minefield of snow-masked leads. That night, we earnestly discussed the growing danger of skiing off the ice into salt water, whose temperature hovered slightly below 32°F. Despite the danger, we decided to persevere so as not to fall farther behind schedule. We'd already lost two weeks at the start of our expedition due to the negative drift of floes across which we skied—they moved in a direction opposite to the one in which we were headed—and were at risk of not making our goal of reaching the North Pole before the last day of winter, or—far worse—running out of food.

The next morning, the storm continued its snowy gusts, as we ventured out into the darkness using our headlamps to light the way. I led, making good time on my two-yard-long telemark skis, while Borge followed about ten yards behind. I continued making steady glides forward, when suddenly, I skied onto what appeared to be solid ice, but turned out to be a thick layer of snow atop seawater. The snow gave way beneath me, enveloping my skis in a kind of heavy icy slush that threatened to drag me under. I knew if I became fully submerged I would have to release my skis, ending my expedition—and possibly my life. To avoid getting my skis caught further under the slush, I managed to throw myself backward, wildly lunging for a solid piece of ice. Though my ski tips were still caught underneath some of the slush, I managed to gain purchase on the ice behind me and stop myself from sliding under.

Borge saw all of this happen and rushed to close the ten feet between us. Normally, when someone falls through the ice it's on a lake or a river where the ice is very thin all around the hole, making rescue at the point of entry impossible. In those situations, ropes are required to drag the person out. But because the ice at the North Pole was in floes, it was quite strong all the way to its edges. Borge could approach me without putting his own life in danger.

As Borge moved toward me, I struggled against the moving water and heavy slush trying to pull me under. I managed to free one ski by leaning back against the ice, which then gave me some leverage to pull the other ski out of the water. By that point, Borge had reached me and helped me the rest of the way out of the frigid water, back onto solid ice. I immediately found a pile of snow and rolled back and forth, so that the snow would aborb some of the moisture in my soaked clothing.

I had been in subzero temperatures enough to know that my condition was quite serious—my soaked clothes were quickly freezing in the snowy gale. Frostbite would start to set in if I didn't get dry—fast. We decided to pitch the tent so I could change into dry clothing. It took a long time to pitch the tent, but we did it anyway. I changed everything, down to dry underwear and shoes. I then piled snow in my discarded, wet clothing, which quickly froze stiff as the snow absorbed the moisture. I broke the ice out of the fabric, shook it out and repacked the clothes in more fresh snow. I repeated this process over and over. Ultimately, it was impossible to dry them completely because the Arctic Ocean water left a salt residue that retained moisture. I contemplated putting on the damp clothes, but I couldn't feel my feet, so I knew I had to warm up.

We lost an hour and a half in this process, but it meant that I survived. And, though a little behind schedule, we eventually reached the North Pole.

Fletcher Christian stands tall in public memory for his seizure of the H.M.S. *Bounty* in 1789. What happened next is not so well known. / Christian set Captain William Bligh and 18 crew members adrift in an open launch 23 feet long. On board were some canvas, twine, sails, 28 gallons of water, 150 pounds of bread, a bit of rum and wine, a compass, and a quadrant to measure latitude. Against incredible odds, Bligh navigated 3,618 nautical miles in 47 days to safe landing at Timor. / Bligh formulated a plan and executed it. He organized the men to sit and lie down in shifts. He strictly rationed water and food. "We now returned God thanks for His protection," Bligh wrote, "and with much content took our miserable allowance of a twenty-fifth of a pound of bread, and a quarter of a pint of water, for dinner." / He collected rainwater and doled out meat from captured sea birds. Thirst and hunger tormented the men, but none died on the open sea. / Water can be a hostile environment. Waterways pose unique challenges of staying warm, getting enough to eat and drink, and finding one's way— while staving off the effects of sun, wind, and water.

ON THE WATER

WITHIN THIS CHAPTER

PREPARATION

The biggest threats to survival on water are dehydration, drowning, and loss of body heat. / Only a fraction of Earth's surface water is warm enough to support prolonged exposure. If you are dunked in an ocean or river, you'll need to get out, get dry, and get warm. Cold shock is a major factor in drowning. / Once you're out, your biggest problem likely will be obtaining enough good water to drink. Smart preparation includes packing a supply of fresh water and the means—such as a solar still—to obtain more. / This chapter covers skills for surviving on oceans and rivers. On the ocean, know the currents, weather patterns, shipping lanes, and location of land. On streams and rivers, scout your route to portage around falls and rapids. In both cases, take the proper equipment to navigate, signal, and get food and water. According to Steven Callahan, who lived for 76 days in a raft on the Atlantic, water survival depends upon experience, preparation, equipment, and luck. And luck always favors the well prepared.

READING THE WATER

WATER IN MOTION is a powerful force. In a channel, such as a riverbed, water creates drag as it flows over a variety of objects and surfaces. This so-called laminar flow results in layers moving at different speeds. Water near the bottom and banks crawls the most slowly. Water just below the surface in the channel's center moves with greatest speed. In oceans and seas, currents act like huge rivers. Churned by heat, air, and the planet's spin, currents move along the ocean surface, at great depth, in parallel with wind, and in tides. At four to five knots, currents begin to create turbulence, complicating water travel.

KNOW RIVER WATER TERMS

>>> **Eddies: Circular currents**
>>> **Rapids: Fast currents**
>>> **Strainers: Objects such as logs that allow water through but snag boats**
>>> **Suction holes: Traps at bottom of falls**
>>> **Waterfalls: Drops of more than a few feet**

UNDERSTAND CURRENTS

OCEAN CURRENTS generally move clockwise in the Northern Hemisphere and counterclockwise in the Southern Hemisphere. Where warm and cold currents mix, they often generate fog, wind, and large waves.

Survival rafts do not sail like ships, but they can take advantage of sea currents by means of a sea anchor (attached to the bow, it keeps the raft pointed into the waves, lessening capsizing risk). Direction and velocity of surface currents are marked on nautical charts. Strong winds have a slight impact on a current's direction. Near shorelines, tidal currents affect a watercraft's approach to land. Four maximum tidal currents, pulled by the orbit of the moon, occur every 24 hours, 50 minutes.

RESCUE ON OPEN WATER

>>> Rescue ships approach from raft's windward side and drift toward it.
>>> Helicopters drop baskets or slings to pull up survivors, or they lower litters for those too injured to get into the basket or sling.
>>> Do not touch helicopter cable until it hits water or raft; its static charge can give an electric shock.
>>> Rescuers may ask raft inhabitants to get in the water before attempting rescue.
>>> U.S. Coast Guard commonly uses a rescue basket. Climb in and sit.

essentials

WHAT TO PACK

On the water, you must pack a lot into a small space. Secure all items to craft.

FIRST AID KIT in watertight container

HELMETS for canoeists and kayakers

PADDLES OR OARS in correct sizes

HIGH-CALORIE FOOD and snacks

FLOTATION DEVICES for all travelers

WATER PURIFIER such as a solar still (recommended)

UP TO 100 FEET of throwing rope

KNIFE of the all-purpose variety

ONE PINT OF WATER per person minimum; more is better

FLARES for signaling

SIGNAL MIRROR in case of emergency

FISHING KIT for recreation/survival

EPIRB (Emergency Position Indicating Radio Beacon) for communicating your location

GPS AND COMPASS for navigation

PATCH KIT for inflatable raft

IMMERSION SUITS for all passengers if the craft is in very cold water

PREPARE FOR A TRIP ON RIVER OR SEA

CHECK YOUR CRAFT before you set out. Make sure it is an adequate size for the number who will occupy it. Steve Callahan's raft was rated for six, but he felt cramped within its diameter of five feet, six inches. It's wise if you can share a vessel or boat in groups for safety. Just make sure everyone knows emergency procedures.

Ensure your craft is certified by the U.S. Coast Guard, is in good condition, and includes all required safety equipment. Know how to launch the craft, and how to enter and exit.

If you can choose, boat only in waters that match your abilities. Know how to right a capsized craft, and how to reenter it. Become familiar with all emergency gear.

File a travel plan with a friend so authorities can launch a search if your return is overdue.

SECURE ITEMS TO CRAFT; WATERPROOF YOUR GEAR

REMOVE ANY ITEMS that may cause difficulties if you capsize. You will need a knife, but secure it so it cannot puncture anything or injure any occupants. Lash all gear to the inside of the craft.

Make sure you have easily accessible rope to throw to anyone outside the craft or to cling to if you go overboard.

Make sure that the craft is waterproof and contains a repair kit more elaborate than just a patch and adhesive.

Seal gear tightly in plastic bags to help keep it dry in the event of capsizing.

HOW TO ABANDON SHIP

AT LEAST IN peacetime, nobody goes to sea on a ship expecting it to sink. In fact, two of the most significant sinkings in modern history occurred on vessels designed to inspire confidence. The R.M.S. *Titanic* was advertised as "virtually unsinkable" before its 1912 voyage. Seventy-five years later, the *Doña Paz*, a Philippine passenger ferry, sank on a calm night and set the maritime record for accidental deaths with more than 3,100.

Therefore, it pays to plan, prepare, and run drills for the worst, even when the worst is unthinkable.

Every vessel at sea should have an emergency escape plan. The crew should conduct frequent drills, including entering survival craft and putting on survival gear such as immersion suits. Survival craft should be kept well stocked with

water, food rations, signaling gear, and an emergency kit. It should be ready for launch at a moment's notice.

Figure your geographic position before you abandon ship. Take along any emergency location beacons, and activate them as you enter survival craft. If the ship is merely capsized and not sunk, stay near as it will be easier to spot from a plane than smaller craft. Cut free and stand off if the ship begins to sink so it doesn't drag you under.

PROPERTIES OF SALT WATER VS. FRESH WATER

SEAWATER is about 3.4 percent salt, making it distinctly different from fresh. Currents keep the percentage roughly the same all over the world, but the salt level is highest in the Red Sea and lowest in the Arctic Ocean. Salt is heavier than water, so seawater is heavier than the same amount of fresh, thus a sealed bottle of water will float.

The higher density of ocean water causes it to freeze at about 28.6°F. Salt leaches out, turning old sea ice blue and drinkable. Likewise, evaporating seawater separates pure water gas from salt. Condensing the vapor, as in a solar still, produces fresh water. The salt

left behind attaches itself to the surface from which the water evaporated.

Nature makes pure water available even on the open ocean. Rain is fresh water, as is dew. Wipe up dew when it forms. Collect rain in containers such as cans or the bladder of a life preserver. If the containers are encrusted with sea salt, rinse them in the ocean before collecting rain. Do not worry if a small amount of salt gets in the fresh water. The water will still be drinkable and will replace lost body water if its salty content is below the salt concentration of the fluids in body tissue, which is about 0.9 percent.

READING THE WEATHER

AIR PRESSURE at sea level normally displaces 29.92 inches of mercury in a glass tube. In general, when pressure falls, as measured on a barometer, bad weather is likely soon.

You don't need instruments to read the clouds. Variation in cloud shape and height indicates changes in weather. Cirrostratus clouds, milky-white sheets that form above 20,000 feet and cover the sky, indicate the approach of rain or snow within 24 hours. Altostratus clouds, formed of grayer sheets that partially obscure the sun, point to storms and heavy precipitation. Altocumulus clouds, composed of groups of fluffy, flat-bottomed cumulus formations, usually indicate good weather, although summer storms are possible in the afternoon. Cumulonimbus clouds, the towering mountains of the atmosphere, spell thunderstorms.

Wind direction may indicate the presence of land. Sunlight heats land more quickly than water, and after dark land quickly loses its heat to the atmosphere. Thus, the air over land tends to be warmer than ocean air during the day, and colder than ocean air at night. This difference in local temperature causes changes in air pressure, as cold air is heavier than warm air. Winds tend to blow landward during the day and seaward at night.

THE BEAUFORT WIND SCALE

>>> **Force 0. Calm. 1 knot. Sea surface like a mirror.**
>>> **Force 1. Light air. 1 to 3 knots. Scaly ripples, no foam crests.**
>>> **Force 2. Light breeze. 4 to 6 knots. Small wavelets; no breaking.**
>>> **Force 3. Gentle breeze. 7 to 10 knots. Large wavelets.**
>>> **Force 4. Moderate breeze. 11 to 16 knots. Waves 1 to 4 feet, becoming longer; many whitecaps.**
>>> **Force 5. Fresh breeze. 17 to 21 knots. Waves 4 to 8 feet, taking longer form; some spray.**
>>> **Force 6. Strong breeze. 22 to 27 knots. Waves 13 to 20 feet; whitecaps everywhere, more spray.**
>>> **Force 7. Near gale. 28 to 33 knots. Foam forms streaks off breakers.**
>>> **Force 8. Gale. 34 to 40 knots. Waves 13 to 20 feet; edges of crests begin to break into spindrift.**
>>> **Force 9. Strong gale. 41 to 47 knots. Waves 20 feet. Sea begins to roll. Dense foam streaks and spray.**
>>> **Force 10. Storm. 48 to 55 knots. Waves 20 to 30 feet with overhanging crests. Heavy rolling.**
>>> **Force 11. Violent storm. 56 to 63 knots. Waves 30 to 45 feet. Foam patches cover sea.**
>>> **Force 12. Hurricane. 64 knots or more. Air full of foam, spray; waves higher than 45 feet. Sea is white.**

LOST? STAY ON THE BEACH

AIRBORNE SEARCHERS are probably more likely to spot you on the coast than in open water. However, landing in surf carries a risk of injury. Pick a good spot, ideally on the lee side of an island or a spit of land. Avoid coral and rocks. If you must land in surf, wear shoes and clothes to protect your body. Adjust the sea anchor on a tight line behind the stern and paddle toward shore in order to lessen the chance of capsizing. Try to avoid rip currents and ride in on the seaward side of a wave. If caught in a rip current, don't fight it—swim with it.

On the beach, obtaining food, water, and shelter is easier. Edible animals and plants live in the shallows and the sand dunes, and fresh water may be as near as digging a hole on the landward side of a dune.

You can make a shelter above the high tide line by using your survival raft as a wall. Bury a fifth of the raft in the sand and stand it straight up. Attach a tarp to the top edge of the shelter and slope it toward the ground. Secure the bottom edge. No tarp? Tip the survival craft and prop it up with a paddle.

SEEK OUT RESOURCES IN SAND AND DUNES

COASTAL FORMATIONS range from cliffs to rolling and sloping sand. Nearly all offer resources for survival; in fact, after an ocean voyage on a small survival craft, a sandy shoreline will seem like a treasure of food and water.

On sandy beaches, receding tides reveal expanses of wet sand that are home to burrowing animals such as mollusks. The siphons of mollusks at the water's edge are easily seen when covered with a thin layer of water. Exposed marine life attracts birds, which can be caught for food. Dunes often are sources of fresh water, marked by green plant life. However, they also tend to attract biting insects, making them less than ideal for shelter.

Muddy shores at river mouths support a rich variety of plant and animal life.

Rocky shores may contain tidal pools of trapped marine life and nesting sites for birds. Beaches made up of shifting

pebbles, however, are least likely to support life.

Wind picks up particles of sand along the seashore and blows it into every conceivable opening. If you store food or have sensitive electronic equipment, seal it completely to prevent sand and grit from penetrating.

TIDES

>>> Time the high and low tides and plan activities accordingly.
>>> Avoid getting isolated or swept away.
>>> Look for strong currents where a beach meets deep water.
>>> Look for signs of high tide line: debris, a change in surface appearance, and color changes on rock faces.
>>> Scour rocky pools after the tide has gone out for food fish.
>>> Check for valuable tide-borne flotsam, such as driftwood.

USING DRIFTWOOD AND OTHER BEACH MATERIALS

EVEN IN TREELESS LANDS, seashores are likely to attract driftwood. You can use it as construction material to make a long- or short-term shelter, as fuel for a warm fire, or as combustible material to make smoke signals. Sun-dried driftwood is easily collected and quick to burn. Seaborne driftwood may emit toxic fumes during combustion, so it is best as an outdoor fire. A stout knife can be used to carve driftwood into tools useful around a campsite.

Driftwood isn't the only material that washes up on the beach. Items ranging from ship's cargo lost at sea to household garbage are cast ashore with regularity. Other materials are dropped by previous shoreline visitors. Use your imagination when you find a human artifact on the beach. Metal objects can be used to hunt and fish, or to cut, scrape, or puncture. Rope and cord, such as the laces of a shoe, can be used for fishing. Shiny objects aimed at the sun can function as signal mirrors.

Dense mats of seaweed are often found near the shoreline. Check seaweed and fresh driftwood for small barnacles, crabs, and other possible sources of animal protein. The seaweed itself is edible.

In short, though the ocean is vast, forbidding, and likely to test your endurance, the shoreline is a good place to wait for rescue. If you feel you must move, travel along the beach unless you encounter signs of civilization inland.

USES OF DRIFTWOOD

>>> Fuel for signal fires. Smoke during the day, light at night.
>>> Fuel for fire to provide warmth and dry wet clothes.
>>> Construction material for beach shelter. Dig a hole on the lee side of a dune, frame it with driftwood, and top it with a tarp and insulating sand.
>>> Roofing material for a survival hole. Dig a trench well above the high-water mark and top with driftwood and canvas or leaves. Top with sand.

Use driftwood to build signal fires on the shore, where they will more easily be seen.

PREPARING FOR
SURVIVAL ON WATER

SURVIVAL ON THE OPEN ocean starts with mental toughness.

Steve Callahan, who survived two and a half months at sea on a six-foot raft, fought against panic as he first realized he was cast into some of the Atlantic Ocean's emptiest waters. "I am lost halfway between western Oshkosh and Nowhere City," he thought. Instead of fixating on the fact that his most likely landfall lay 1,800 miles to the west, in the Caribbean, he focused on what to do the next day, and then the day after that. Survival became a long-term goal accomplished one day at a time. He kept things in perspective, telling himself he could rely only on himself. Callahan spotted nine ships on his voyage, but none responded to his signals. He told himself rescue comes when it comes.

Confidence begins with the knowledge of how to use survival equipment on a life raft, the ability to improvise when things go wrong, and the will to live. Waves, wind, sun, cold, and the hazards and challenges of marine life test all survivors on the open sea. As survivors are at the mercy of the elements, they must be patient, resourceful, and determined to ride out their ordeal as long as it takes.

When going to sea in groups, make sure every passenger knows basic survival procedures. These include what to do if someone goes overboard, where emergency gear and life rafts are located, use of emergency locator beacons, how to deploy the anchor and launch a life raft, and your route and destination.

essentials

ABANDONING SHIP

Know exactly what to do when the time comes. Demand total compliance with regular abandon-ship drills.

IF YOUR SHIP is threatened, radio the coast guard. Its expertise may help you slow or avoid sinking. However, if the ship is doomed, sound the abandon-ship alarm and take the following steps:

BROADCAST and repeat a Mayday signal. Say "Mayday" (from the French "M'aidez"— "Help me") three times, along with the ship's name and call sign. State location, nature of emergency, and number of people aboard.

DRESS in clothing layers that wick away moisture. Waterproof shell, hat, and gloves are good for trapping body heat.

PUT on your life jacket or immersion suit. Treading water speeds heat loss.

MAKE SURE the life raft has emergency survival gear, then launch it.

BOARD the raft. Try not to get wet.

IF THE SHIP SINKS, cut any lines connecting it to the raft.

DEPLOY the stabilizing sea anchor.

ATTEND to medical needs. Keep everyone warm and dry.

FAMILIARIZE yourself with all contents of the craft, including survival manuals.

SAFELY EXIT A BOAT OR SHIP

LAUNCH THE LIFE RAFT. If it's a canister type, inflate the raft in the water; inflation on deck could cause injury from canister halves explosively flying off. If you cannot deploy before the ship sinks, wait to see if the raft is automatically released by hydrostatic pressure.

Try not to get wet as you board the raft. You may be able to board from a ladder or net. Jump into the canopy entrance if you have no other options.

If you must go into the water, do so as close to the survival craft as possible. Hold the painter to keep from being swept away. Two people on the raft should haul a third person aboard by turning the person's back to the raft, grabbing the arms and life jacket, pushing down slightly, and then pulling across the buoyancy tubes.

INFLATING A DINGHY

THE BEST SURVIVAL RAFTS have two inflation tubes, one atop the other, along the craft's outer edge. The inflated tubes should be at least a foot in diameter in order to provide maximum stability. To inflate, pull the operating cord attached to the cylinder of compressed gas, usually carbon dioxide, attached to the bottom of the raft. Note that inflated tubes let gas escape from time to time. Gas expands on warm days, and pressure relief valves allow the excess to escape. As the craft cools and the gas contracts, you may have to hand-pump air into the tube to compensate.

MAKE A CALL FOR HELP

VHF RADIO provides an easy way to make a distress call. Reception is limited to 20 to 60 miles, but calls can be relayed over far greater distances by repeaters. Three signal calls are recognized internationally: Mayday, Pan-pan, and Security. Broadcast Mayday in groups of three on Channel 16, which is reserved for emergencies, and give information to help rescuers find you. Mayday calls should be repeated until answered or you are forced to abandon ship. Pan-pan calls alert outsiders to potential threats that do not pose an immediate danger. Low-priority security calls direct vessels to monitor other stations.

Emergency Position Indicating Radio Beacons (EPIRBs) send out satellite signals that allow rescuers to pinpoint your location. Register your unit before setting out. EPIRB signals are monitored around the clock. When you register, provide personal medical information so that search-and-rescue teams can try to provide specific medication upon rescue.

NAVIGATION

Navigating on water can be simple or complicated. Canoeing or kayaking may be simply a matter of following nature's highways toward lower ground and, generally, toward civilization. However, travelers should scout their routes in advance and always be on the lookout for rapids, strainers, and other hazards. When in doubt about traversing potentially dangerous water, the best course is to err on the side of safety and portage around any obstacles. / On the open sea, a survival craft is virtually at the command of wind and wave. You may rig a sail or set a sea anchor to make minor adjustments in direction, but forcing a major course correction is out of the question. You can get a fix on latitude by estimating the height of Polaris above the horizon. Steve Callahan tied three pencils together to form a crude sextant, measured the angle of Polaris, and found that since it was about 18 degrees above the horizon he was at about 18 degrees north latitude. He figured longitude by dead reckoning.

CROSS A RIVER ON FOOT

IT'S HARD TO KNOW the best place to cross a river. Most rivers meander as they flow to the sea, making it hard to see more than just the section in front of you. Better crossing places could lie out of view, and you would not know.

If you choose to cross, have a strategy. Choose the right footwear, such as rubber-soled canvas shoes. Then choose a path. Straight across is shortest, but it will subject you to the full strength of the current. A better route may be diagonally into the current, which will give you better traction and balance.

If the water reaches your knees and churns around you, you likely will be swept off your feet. Log rafts or other flotation devices might serve you better.

CROSS A STREAM

>>> **High in its course, where it has lower water volume and is narrower**
>>> **Above any confluence of streams**
>>> **Where current is weak**
>>> **Where the opposite bank provides an easy exit**

CARRYING GEAR ACROSS A RIVER OR STREAM

PUT YOUR CLOTHING and sleeping gear inside a waterproof bag. Tie the bag shut with an air pocket inside. Balance the contents of the bag so it won't shift as you carry it. If you lose your footing, let go of the waterproof bag.

Another option is to lay your gear flat on a poncho. Place the gear between two long sticks slightly shorter than the poncho's length. Roll the poncho from both sides around the sticks. Then roll the first poncho inside a second one. Tie the poncho bag shut and pull it or push it across deep water like a raft. To avoid small tears, do not drag the ponchos on the ground.

If you carry gear in a backpack and are crossing a rapid stream, you might take off the pack, attach it to a flotation device, and push or pull the pack across as you wade.

FLOTATION AIDS

>>> Wet trousers, inflated and tied off
>>> Air mattress
>>> Log raft
>>> Waterproof bag, tied shut with air inside
>>> Waterproof material wrapped and tied around dry branches and vegetation
>>> Airy plants, such as water hyacinth, stuffed inside a plastic bag
>>> Boards, logs, etc., tied together

essentials

TRAVEL BY WATER'S EDGE

Footing and route selection are issues.

SHORELINES may contain swampy terrain, especially near the mouth of a river.

RIVERBANKS may be impassable with thick, sticky, shoe-swallowing mud.

VEGETATION flourishing in rich river soil may grow so densely out into the water that it makes it difficult to approach a riverbank. When traveling under overhanging branches near shorelines, keep an eye out for tree-dwelling creatures that may drop into your boat.

RAINFALL may cause a river to surge out of its banks.

WET SAND often makes an excellent surface for walking, but beware of sudden waves that catch at your feet and drag you toward open water.

LOW RIVERBANKS are best for crossing a river, unless the shoreline is impassible with mud or thick plant growth.

TRAVEL on a shore or river edge makes you easier to spot from an airplane.

EXPERT TIP You must not try to swim or wade across a stream or river when the water is at very low temperatures. This swim could be fatal. Try to make a raft of some type. Wade across if you can get only your feet wet. Dry them vigorously as soon as you reach the other bank.

U.S.ARMY

USING ROPES

ROPES PROVIDE ANCHORS for hands and feet for difficult water crossings.

A one-rope bridge can be set up at or above water level. It should be carried across by the group's strongest member and secured to a tree or rock. The near side should be held in place with a slipknot and pulled tight. The last person crossing should undo the knot and be pulled across or carry the rope's end.

For extra safety, a bridge can be made of two ropes, spaced 5 feet apart vertically, for hands and feet. Keep the ropes the same distance apart by tying them together with spreader ropes every 15 feet. Step on the lower rope while holding the upper one.

When crossing at water level, hold rope with both hands and walk into the water while facing upstream. For added safety, connect to rope bridge with a snaplink at the end of a 3- to 4-foot cord. If the rope is elevated, commando-crawl or monkey-crawl—right side up, or upside down—along the tightrope. Allow for stretching of nylon rope.

BUILD A LOG BRIDGE

MOTHER NATURE may already have provided you with a natural bridge. Look for downed trees that span all or part of the river. Cross on the tree trunk if it appears to be well anchored. If it is wet, sprinkle dry sand on the trunk before stepping onto it in order to increase traction, or sit on the log and scoot across it on your bottom.

As you scoot, beware of submerged branches that could catch on clothing. Carry a walking stick for extra stability. Take care if you leap from the log to the shore. Jumping puts extra pressure on the log beneath your feet and may cause it to roll or topple into the river below you. Make sure your packs and gear are well fastened before crossing.

STABILITY DURING RIVER CROSSINGS

>>> **Pivot method: Three or more people form a circle and hold onto one another's clothing at shoulder height. One person moves at a time, as others provide stability.**
>>> **Pole method: A group holds a pole about five inches wide and eight feet long, with the heaviest person at downstream end. Keeping the pole parallel to the current, move together downstream.**
>>> **Single-person pole method: Carry a pole on the upstream side and probe the riverbed. Move only one of your three supports— foot, foot, or pole—at a time.**

KAYAKING, CANOEING, AND RAFTING

PERSONAL WATERCRAFT include canoes, kayaks, and rafts. Each type has its advantages.

Canoes are extremely versatile. They can be paddled, rowed, poled, sailed, or outfitted with a motor. They are light enough to be portaged around rough or dangerous water, yet strong enough to carry 20 times their weight and stand up to strong currents. Long canoes go fast on open, flat water and glide longer between strokes, whereas short ones have more maneuverability at a cost of less glide. The most versatile are around 16 feet long.

Kayaks are canoe-like craft in which the paddler usually sits within a spray skirt. As with canoes, length adds speed and reduces maneuverability, and the mid-length varieties are the most versatile. A medium kayak can store about two weeks' provisions for one person. Kayak paddles are bladed at both ends for efficiency. Kayaks can be rolled without swamping.

Rafts take up little room until inflated. They can be paddled like canoes and respond similarly, once they have been trimmed by taking in their ballast buckets and sea anchors. Poling a raft is most efficient in shallow water, while sweep strokes with an oar or paddle are best in greater depth. Weight must be balanced in rafts, particularly if there are several passengers, in order to avoid capsizing.

Paddling and poling exercise arm, chest, shoulder, and back muscles long accustomed to having the legs do all the work. Build your upper-body strength before voyaging on a canoe, kayak, or raft.

Don't expect a personal watercraft to keep you out of the water. They tip all too often, from hazards in the water, unexpected waves, and human error. You must know how to swim before getting into any personal watercraft. Wear a helmet and a life jacket—even if you can swim—every time you are in a canoe or kakak. Wear clothes that are not liable to get tangled in the craft and allow enough room to move your arms and legs without restriction.

Kayaking provides ideal water passage through this Chesapeake Bay salt marsh.

CANOEING BASICS

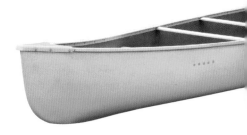

CANOE DESIGN is tailored to specific types of water. Canoes fashioned for whitewater don't perform well in quiet pools, and vice versa. Important design considerations include length, hull cross section (whether the bottom is flat, slightly rounded, or resting on a shallow V shape), keel line, and shape when viewed from above.

All canoes must be kept in careful balance. Although canoes can carry a tremendous amount of weight, they tip easily if their center of gravity shifts too much to one side. Distribute gear accordingly, and always keep your weight low and evenly distributed while the canoe is on the water. Wear a correctly sized personal flotation device and shoes.

If you fall out of the canoe or it capsizes, stay on the upstream side of the boat to avoid having the current push the canoe into your body with crushing force. Salvage equipment that spills out only if you can do so without risk. As with kayaks and rafts, if you are thrown free and float freely in midstream, float on your back, facing downstream with your feet up, so you can push off rocks.

Abandon your canoe before it gets caught in a strainer—an object, such as a tree or bridge pilings, that lets water through but stops a watercraft. Wedged canoes can be pulled free with ropes.

If you are in a group and your canoe appears about to capsize, warn the others by shouting, "Prepare to capsize!" All should remove their paddles from the water and hold them with the blades facing out. When a canoe overturns, rescue people in the water before attempting to retrieve any spilled gear.

CANOE-BOTTOM OPTIONS

>>> Flat bottom. Adds maneuverability and reduces stability as it carries more and more weight. It may also react poorly to high waves. For rough water, use a canoe with a V-shaped bottom, below.

>>> Bottom with shallow arch. Adds speed when paddled in calm waters, but performance declines in rough water.

>>> Bottom with shallow V shape. Adds stability and control, especially in rough weather, but the V may slow the canoe in calm water and take on extra wear.

how to

GET INTO A CANOE

1 Place one foot in center of canoe while keeping a low center of gravity.

2 Grasp both sides of canoe while continuing to stoop, and distribute body weight evenly on both arms.

3 Lift outside foot into canoe. Kneel or sit inside the canoe.

PADDLING A CANOE

IN A TWO-PERSON CANOE, the bow (front) paddler sets a regular rhythm with the bow stroke and calls out directional suggestions as well as hazards. The stern (rear) paddler is responsible for steering and giving paddling commands if assistance is needed (such as the forward sweep for additional turning speed and power). Novices often try to steer by switching sides; however, this is inefficient, accumulates water in the craft and on your gear, and can be deadly if you're caught in a sudden squall or in rapids since it does not allow for quick and efficient maneuvering.

Don't take on more than you can handle. Know your route, or scout ahead for hazards such as rapids. If you come to swift currents, examine the water, rocks and submerged obstacles, and the shoreline before deciding whether to try to paddle through. Know whether you can safely float the entire rapid if you capsize. If you canoe in groups, signal from boat to boat with your paddles. Holding the paddle with blade upright and wiggling it back and fourth signals an emergency. A lead canoeist signals "stop" by removing the paddle from the water and holding it overhead, parallel to the water. The "all clear" sign is made by holding the paddle straight up, with the blade highest. Signaling "all clear" and then pointing indicates it is safe to proceed in that direction.

essentials

BASICS OF CANOE STROKES

Especially in rough water, it is essential to be able to paddle and steer effectively. For efficient paddling, learn the following essential strokes.

BOW (FORWARD) STROKE: Put right hand on grip if paddling on left side, and vice versa. Lower hand holds the paddle shaft a few inches above the blade. Stroke front to back, close to the center line of the canoe.

BACKWARD STROKE: Reverse the motion of the bow stroke. Slows the canoe, halts it, and then makes it go backward.

FORWARD SWEEP and backward sweep: Turns the canoe. For forward sweep, hold blade at 45-degree angle with top half of paddle entering water, and paddle front to back in semi-circular motion. Reverse for backward sweep.

J-STROKE: Essential for solo canoers or stern paddler in two-person canoe. Most important steering stroke, since it allows simultaneous steering and forward propulsion. Turns the canoe toward the side on which you are paddling. Start by performing the bow stroke, but three-quarters of the way through, rotate and push the back of the paddle away from the canoe, forming the letter J.

DRAW STROKE: Changes the direction or rotates the canoe. Lean out over water, make a deep stroke, and pull the paddle inward toward the canoe.

RUDDER: Stern paddler dips the blade behind the canoe and maneuvers it like a rudder. Useful for maneuvering in tight spaces.

KAYAKING BASICS

KAYAKS RIDE LOWER in the water than canoes. Paddlers ordinarily sit amid a spray skirt fastened to the cockpit edges, which keeps wave water and spray from entering and may allow the paddler to right the craft after capsizing through a maneuver known as an Eskimo roll. Cargo capacity is much smaller than in a canoe. Like canoes, kayaks are faster when longer and more easily controlled when shorter. A good all-purpose length is 15 to 17 feet.

Stability is enhanced by greater width. A cross section of 23 to 25 inches is appropriate for general use. Hulls that terminate in a "V" or rounded shape have the most stability except in calm water.

Paddles are double-bladed, allowing paddlers to alternate strokes on the left and right side of the kayak to keep moving forward in a straight line. Paddles come in a variety of materials and weights, with fiberglass the best option. Some "feathered" varieties have the blades offset by angles of 60 to 90 degrees for optimizing power and control for certain paddlers' strengths. Try out a kayak and paddle before making a purchase.

Avoid launching and exiting a kayak in surf. If you have no choice, launch perpendicularly into a wave that spills foam at the front, and not one that curls and breaks. Do not attempt to launch into a wave that is six feet or taller.

PRINCIPLES OF PADDLING AND FLIPPING

Inability to right or exit a kayak could prove fatal. Know and practice the essentials.

CHOOSE PADDLES of the right length. Stand the paddle next to you; if you can curl your fingers over the top blade, it's the right length. Whitewater paddles should be shorter.

START STROKING with good posture—a straight back, leaning slightly forward. Power comes from the torso.

BOTTOM BLADE is just below water level and upper hand is eyeball height.

A RIGHT-HANDED PADDLER'S right wrist does not rotate during a stroke on the right side, but rotates backward for a stroke on the left.

DRIVE THE BLADE into the water near the feet. The paddle's power comes from rotating the torso. Do not attempt to push the stroke through the biceps.

WHEN KAYAK CAPSIZES, exit or perform Eskimo roll. This move is potentially fatal if not performed correctly; learn under supervision and practice in still water or a swimming pool. Take classes to practice and perfect the roll's three parts: the setup, sweeping brace stroke, and hip flick.

ON THE WATER

CHAPTER

8

EXPERT TIP Surviving along the seashore is different from open sea survival. Food and water are more abundant and shelter is obviously easier to locate and construct. If you decide to travel, it is better to move along the coast than to go inland.

U.S.ARMY

CHOOSE THE RIGHT KAYAK

SEA KAYAKS are made for open water. Their cargo capacity, seaworthiness, and stability are more important than their maneuverability. They may have rudders to enhance straight-line movement. They may be built for as many as three paddlers, but be aware that a three-person kayak has less carrying capacity than that three individual sea kayaks.

Whitewater kayaks are smaller, to maneuver in the fast water of rivers and streams. They have a lower hull designed for speed and a flared upper hull for stability in rough water.

Surf kayaks are long, narrow boats designed for use amid breakers at the shoreline and rescue operations within the surf zone. Their narrow hulls make them difficult to control except when handled by experts.

Racing kayaks are designed for speed competitions on flat water.

As you choose your kayak, consider not only where you intend to use it, but also how long you must occupy it. Proper storage capacity may support life for a few days or a few weeks.

"WET EXIT" FROM A CAPSIZED KAYAK

>>> Hold paddle parallel to kayak with one hand.
>>> Release spray skirt with other hand by pulling the release strap.
>>> Grab cockpit next to hips.
>>> Straighten legs.
>>> Lean forward; use arms to push lower body free.
>>> Always hold onto kayak and paddle.
>>> Go ashore to empty water inside the vessel. If you cannot reach shore, reach under the cockpit, grab the far side, and pull toward you while pushing up on the near side.

If you fall out of a raft on whitewater, float on your back with your feet downstream.

RAFTING BASICS

THE PRINCIPLES of riding an inflatable raft vary greatly according to your surroundings.

On a raft in mid-ocean, you must conserve energy. Move slowly and deliberately, and do not bother to paddle unless you need to avoid obstacles or approach land or rescue. Set the canopy, or rig a sail or tarp to protect you from the sun. Try to stay dry, as prolonged exposure to wet conditions will speed hypothermia.

River rafting, particularly in whitewater, is wet and likely unpredictable. Rafts must be steered by oars and poles. On slow-moving water, a homemade sea anchor, such as a waterlogged piece of wood suspended by a cord, will automatically position the raft in the center of the main channel without need for steering. In calm water, you may want to paddle from a position in which you straddle the upper buoyancy ring. On faster water, use paddles while sitting sidesaddle on the upper buoyancy ring, or sit inside and reach over the tube. Be on constant alert for rapids, strainers, and other hazards. If the river bends a lot and has few places to survey it, make frequent stops to avoid being caught suddenly in a tight spot. Use all your senses—you may hear rapids and waterfalls long before you see them.

CHOOSE THE RIGHT RAFT

>>> **Buoyant apparatus. Designed for rapid deployment and short-term use. Rigid construction, reversible sides, and lifelines on the outside.**
>>> **Inflatable buoyant apparatus. For use on vessels close to shore. Not as good as an inflatable life raft. Normally deploys with only one buoyancy tube.**
>>> **Inflatable life raft. Vary in shape and capacity. They should have two inflation tubes, a double floor with air space insulation, canopy, ballast and sea anchor for stability, and survival kit.**

PADDLING A RAFT

PADDLING A RAFT is much like working a canoe. The forward (bow) stroke and backward stroke are the same. Three alternative strokes are added: draw, pry, and the calm-water crawl.

To execute the draw stroke, drop the paddle blade away from the raft, parallel to the craft's longitudinal line. Pull the shaft and push the grip. This stroke pulls the raft in the direction of the paddle.

For a pry stroke, push the blade near the raft, parallel to the longitudinal line. Push the shaft while pulling the grip. This pushes the raft away from the paddle side.

In calm, open water, a rafter may choose to sit facing the stern to execute the calm-water crawl. Drop the blade in the water behind you—to the front of the boat—and pull on the grip using the hips and back to gain leverage. This stroke provides a lot of power without a lot of energy spent.

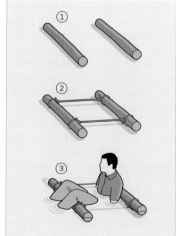

how to
MAKE A LOG FLOAT

① Cut or find two logs (the drier, the better to increase buoyancy) at least six to eight inches thick and about three to four feet long. Trim branches from the logs.

② Tie the logs together with two ropes so that the logs lie parallel to each other about two feet apart.

③ Wade into the water until it comes up over your knees. Place the logs in the water and sit between them, with your knees over the front log and your back resting against the rear log.

BEACH A RAFT IN SURF

>>> Scout the shoreline for a spot free of rocks, coral, and other obstacles, then set out sea anchor and take down sail. Use your paddle as a rudder.
>>> Time approach to begin on a small wave. Paddle backward as the wave reaches you, then forward, hard, when the front of the raft drops as the wave passes beneath you.
>>> If raft capsizes, hold tight and ride it in.

USE A THROW ROPE

A THROW ROPE is designed for water rescue. It is strong and water resistant. It may be coiled in a bag, making it easier to throw, with a clip at the end for securing to a victim. Tossing the rope accurately requires practice. Clip on the carabiner at rope's end so you don't lose it and practice tossing the bag to a particular point in the water. With throw rope attached, it can be hauled in.

SURVIVE WHILE SUBMERGED

WITH YOUR LUNGS INFLATED, your body is quite buoyant. If you find yourself in deep water far from shore and with no flotation aids, practice the dead man's float to expend the least energy while continuing to breathe regularly. This technique is especially good for awaiting help that you know is coming.

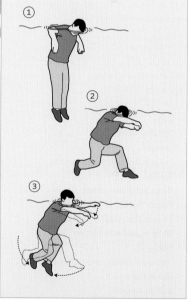

how to

DO DEAD MAN'S FLOAT

① Start by floating facedown. Raise your head, take a breath and immediately lower your head back into the water. Stay relaxed, letting your limbs dangle.

② Before you need a new lungful of air, cross your arms in front of your head. Raise one leg, with knee toward chest, and extend the other behind you.

③ Raise your head just enough to keep your chin in the water. Exhale through your nose. Gently push your arms outward and bring your legs together beneath you as you inhale through your mouth.

EXPERT TIP If you must ride out a rapid before swimming to safety or catching a rescue line, go down stream feet first, with your legs acting as shock absorbers to fend off rocks. Use a backstroke to maneuver past obstacles, and watch for eddies that might protect you.

SURVIVE IN A LIFE RAFT

LIFE RAFTS ARE BUILT to be small, self-contained survival shelters. They contain small amounts of high-calorie food, fresh water, and signaling devices. They are notoriously cramped, yet survivors have ridden them for months at a time. Knowing how to take advantage of wind and current, as well as how to augment food and water supplies, will increase your chances of survival.

Life rafts do not sit deeply in the water, and so are easily influenced by surface currents and, to a lesser extent, wind. Sailing is ill advised unless land is near. Then, a sail can be rigged and paddles used for steering.

The raft probably comes with a sea anchor, but you can improvise one if needed. The sea anchor's aperture can be opened or closed. When opened, the sea anchor acts as a drag, slowing the life raft but providing stability in waves. Closing the aperture catches the current and pulls the craft in the direction of the moving water.

Collect rainwater and deploy a solar still to distill fresh water from seawater. Look for edible barnacles on submerged surfaces. Catch fish and sea birds. Check for seaweed, most of which is highly nutritious and supports marine life such as crabs.

STANDARD SUPPLIES FOR MOST RAFTS

>>> **Bailer**
>>> **Signaling mirror**
>>> **Sponges**
>>> **Pump, leak stoppers, and repair kit**
>>> **Paddles**
>>> **Flares and smoke devices**
>>> **Rations that do not promote thirst**
>>> **Six seasickness pills per person**
>>> **Water—usually one pint per person**
>>> **Fishing kit**
>>> **Graduated drinking vessel (for rationing)**
>>> **Rescue line**
>>> **Instruction cards**
>>> **Radar reflector**
>>> **Whistle**

SITTING SAFELY

MODIFY THE RAFT INTERIOR and your posture to help you stay warm and dry. Start by inflating the floor to provide an insulating layer between you and the surface of the ocean.

When you are sure the raft will not collapse, remove your personal flotation device, fold it up, and use it as a seat cushion to cut heat loss through conduction, caused by your warm body in contact with water-chilled rubber or plastic.

If your clothes are wet, take them off, squeeze them out, and put them back on. Better yet, wear a survival suit over layers of clothes. While seated, fold your arms close to your chest and place your hands in your armpits to minimize radiative heat loss. If the raft has a canopy seal, your body heat should be enough to make the interior comfortable.

ESTABLISH A WATCH SCHEDULE

MAINTAIN WATCH-KEEPING duties. If you are aboard with others, split into shifts of sleeping and waking so someone is always on the lookout for a rescue ship or plane. The watch shifts also should examine equipment and pump up the buoyancy tubes after they deflate. Normal deflation occurs through the pressure valves; rapid loss of gas inside the tubes should be checked for possible tears that need mending.

If you are by yourself, watch for the rhythms of the sea. When are fish likely to visit the craft? What times might birds land? In addition to regularly attempting to gather food, constantly monitor the sky for weather changes and the solar still to ensure it is working properly.

WHAT TO DO AFTER ENTERING A LIFE RAFT

>>> Cut through the painter to set the raft adrift from the sinking ship. Then stand away from the rope and side of the raft to avoid getting entangled with the rigging.
>>> Stream the sea anchor.
>>> Close the raft canopy entrance and any other openings to retain internal heat.
>>> Maintain the craft with regular checks for leaks, water seeping into the bottom, and status of the solar collector.

STEPS TO PREPARE FOR LONG-TERM TRIP

>>> Secure all gear with cords. Loose gear likely will find its way overboard.
>>> Stay warm. A sail, tarp, or entrance flap provides some protection.
>>> During first 24 hours afloat, do not eat and take only a minimal amount of water. Ration food if necessary.
>>> Avoid sunburn, particularly on the tops of the feet. Be alert that ultraviolet radiation will be reflected from below, off the water.
>>> Keep all layers of clothing in anticipation of cool nights.
>>> Keep signaling devices where they can be immediately seized and used.

Life rafts sit high on the water and are easily tossed by ocean currents and wind.

SIGHTING LAND

LOOK FOR SIGNS in the water and air to signal nearby land.

In the water, look for the color to grow lighter near land as the waters become shallow. Look for waves refracted by the approach to land—they shift from parallel lines to bend in a V shape with the island in the center. On the island's lee side, the waves intersect and become turbulent.

In the air, look for peculiar cloud formations and birds such as gulls and petrels, which must stay within a few dozen miles of land. In general, the greater the number of birds, the closer the landfall.

Don't rely just on your eyes. Listen for the roar of surf breaking on a beach, as it often travels farther than the eye can see. Smell the air, especially during a fog or mist at night, for the scent of a mangrove swamp or burning wood. Listen for sea bird cries in the distance, but be aware that birds fly to hunt during the day and may not lead you toward land until dusk.

READ THE CLOUDS

>>> Look for fixed cumulus clouds in a clear sky. They may be formed by air cooling as it rises over land.
>>> If one cloud appears to be stationary but others are moving, the cloud could be over or slightly downwind from an island.
>>> Look for a woolly appearance to clouds fixed over islands.
>>> Clouds also hover over shoals and reefs.
>>> Look for a greenish or turquoise hue in the sky. It could be a reflection off an atoll's lagoon.

USE CURRENTS

TAKE ADVANTAGE of currents. Even though a survival craft has no keel and sits atop, not in, the water, you can use currents to help move toward rescue. You can propel a personal survival craft by paddling, but you need to conserve strength to survive. Paddle when you need to steer toward or away from something, or when you are preparing to make landfall through surf. Or use a paddle like a rudder, lashing it in place so you don't accidently drop it over the side.

If the current is with you, deploy the sea anchor unless you are traveling through coral and it might get snagged. Even if the winds are against you, a sea

anchor will pull a personal survival craft along if the currents are favorable. If you have no sea anchor, you can jury-rig one with a bucket, sail bags, oilskins, or anything that will provide drag. To get maximum effect of the sea anchor into a contrary wind, remove the craft's canopy and make as low a profile as possible to reduce wind resistance.

Ever-changing winds wreck havoc with sails, so beware sudden gusts with makeshift sails.

USING A SAIL

DO NOT SAIL unless you are near land since rafts lack keels and cannot be sailed into the wind. However, the weight of passengers will push the raft low enough in the water to allow tacking ten degrees off the wind. In order to take advantage of the wind, you'll need to create a sail. Use a tarp or other large cloth, or piece together whatever lightweight materials you have onboard. Drape over a T-shape mast made by two parts of an aluminum oar, lashed together.

Pad the bottom of the mast to avoid damaging the floor of the raft. A shoe's heel works well. Fully inflate the raft, sit high, and use an oar as a rudder. Hold the bottom edges of the sail; do not secure them, to avoid rips if the wind should gust. Tacking requires some practice. Try different angles and rudder positions to move into or across the wind. Going straight into the wind will require tacking along a zigzag route.

FOLLOWING SEABIRDS

>>> Frigate birds do not sleep on water. At dusk, they usually fly toward land.

>>> Shearwaters and petrels fly toward land at dusk and dawn.

>>> Terns. If you spot one, you know you are within 40 miles of land.

>>> Gulls. If you see three or more, you are within 50 miles of landfall or shallow coastal water. More gulls equals more likelihood of being near land.

>>> Black skimmers. Typical habitat lies within 25 miles of land.

TACKING

>>> Angle the sail to push the boat diagonally toward the wind.

>>> Adjust slightly, as necessary.

>>> Change course toward the wind.

>>> Relax your grip on the sail as the boat passes to the other side of the headwind, then reset it for the new course.

>>> Repeat steps above.

WATER

Imagine the torture: You're stuck in the middle of the ocean, the largest collection of water on Earth, and you cannot drink any of it. Don't succumb to temptation. Drinking seawater provides short-term relief but only aggravates thirst. / During the first 24 hours, don't drink any fresh water from the survival rations stored on a life raft. The body's reserves will be adequate, and most of the water drunk during this stage will be wasted as urine. After the first day, start by drinking a pint a day. Overzealous rationing in the early stages of survival at sea may speed the onset of health problems and lessen your ability to signal for help or perform other crucial tasks. / Find ways to augment your fresh stocks with rain, dew, or a solar still. And consider how undrinkable water can help you. Wet your clothes with seawater to cool your skin and reduce sweating. The Robertson family, adrift in the Pacific in 1972, used contaminated fresh water for enemas, which provided some relief from dehydration. / If you have little or no water, don't eat protein, such as fish or birds. The body requires more water to metabolize protein than it does other foods.

DRINKABLE WATER ON THE OPEN SEA

EVEN IF YOU HAVE a solar still, you'll also want to rinse any container you have and use it to collect rain. Look for dewy condensation, especially in the morning. Lick or mop it up with a rag.

Castaway Steve Callahan sucked the liquid out of the eyes and spinal columns of fish. To get the spinal fluid, hold the fish head down and cut through the spine just above the tail.

Then tilt the fish head-up and collect or suck out the watery fluid.

Dougal Robertson drank turtle blood to help him survive 38 days after his ship sank near the Galápagos Islands. Its salt concentration is about the same as human blood. "I made an incision in its throat. . . I tilted the cup and drained it. 'Good stuff,' I shouted. I felt I had just consumed the elixir of life," he wrote.

THE DANGER OF DRINKING SALTWATER

SEAWATER CONTAINS about 3.5 percent sodium chloride—table salt—in solution. That's almost four times the concentration of 0.9 percent salt in human tissue fluid. When you drink saltwater, your body tries to shed the excess salt through urination. But urine has a maximum concentration of 2.0 percent salt, so it leaves much behind. The body then tries to rid the remainder through further urination, resulting in a net water loss. In short, for every quart of seawater you drink, your body loses three-quarters of a quart of body water.

When you drink seawater, you feel your thirst quickly relieved. Then the thirst returns, much worse. Drinking more seawater severely raises the salt content of your body fluid, a condition known as hypernatremia. That leads, in succession, to apathy, delirium, and violence. Drinkers' lips, tongue, and mouth deteriorate as their bodies become dehydrated. Their exhaled breath sometimes takes on an offensive odor. Seawater drinkers who are not restrained may jump overboard. If they are held down, they may gradually lose consciousness. Their mouths will show signs of froth and their faces change color. Death comes from dehydration as the salt level rises in body fluids. Too much salt in the fluid surrounding body cells causes a loss of fluid within the cell walls, impairing their function. Scientists hypothesize that the madness associated with drinking seawater stems from the loss of fluid in brain cells.

USING SOLAR STILLS

>>> Inflate and fill still with seawater.

>>> Seawater drips onto a black cloth wick suspended inside the balloon.

>>> Seawater evaporates. Fresh water condenses on the inside of the balloon and collects in a reservoir. Salt, which does not evaporate, is left on the wick.

>>> Solar stills follow the greenhouse principle: Trapped sunlight raises temperature, turning liquid to vapor.

Drinking saltwater is the worst thing you can do. It will only speed dehydration and misery.

HAZARDS

Medical science drills its initiates with the adage, "Common diseases occur commonly." A similar rule applies on the water. If you look for common causes of death, look no further than drowning. It accounts for about 140,000 deaths every year. In many cases, cold water causes such a shock and drop in body heat that victims quickly lose the ability to tread water. Greek historian Herodotus noted this secondary cause of drowning after a sea battle: "Those who could not swim perished from that cause, others from cold." / Sun and wind, coupled with lack of fresh water, raise the risk of dehydration. Life craft failure spells almost certain death. Hazards in the water, from sharks to jellyfish to the toxins in many saltwater fish, underscore the dangers that lurk in a huge, hostile environment. / In addition to physical hazards, castaways face mental challenges. Steve Callahan found his mind under siege. For some, mental health shatters. Two survivors of the sinking of the *Essex* in 1821 sailed 4,500 miles in a 25-foot boat. When rescued, they expressed neither joy nor relief. They continued to clutch and gnaw at the bones of their deceased fellow crewmen.

PREPARE AND REPAIR YOUR LIFE RAFT

REPAIRING A TINY HOLE in an inflatable life raft may sound easy, but the sea complicates things. A rubber tube patch kit, such as you might use on a bicycle tire, works only when applied in a dry environment. If you must use a patch kit, partially deflate the tube, cut the patch an inch larger than the hole, and apply adhesive to the patch and tube surface. Let dry, apply a second coat, and press together when it becomes tacky. Wait 24 hours before fully inflating.

Raft-repair clamps are a better alternative, sealing any leak, even while wet. The clamps are paired oval disks of convex metal with rubber lips. Push the bottom clamp through the tear and align it with the fabric to cover the opening. Pair it with the upper disc, and squeeze them together with a bolt and wing nut.

how to

RIGHT A CAPSIZED LIFE RAFT

1 Position yourself in the middle of the raft edge that contains the inflation bottle.

2 Facing the wind, pull on the righting straps on the bottom of the raft to begin to turn it upright. You can increase the force by pulling yourself out of the water and crouching with your feet near the bottom edge. Stand next to the gas cylinder and continue pulling on the righting straps while leaning backward, using your body weight as leverage.

3 If the raft flips on top of you, swim out, from underneath, holding the righting straps.

4 If you need an extra breath, push up against the raft's floor to make an air pocket.

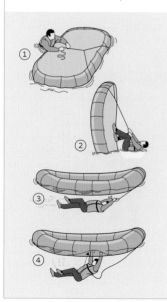

how to

SWIM OUT OF RIP CURRENTS

1 Stay calm and don't fight the current.

2 Swim parallel to shore until you exit the rip current, then swim to land.

3 If you cannot swim free, tread water until out of the current.

4 If still caught, signal for help from shore.

AVOID STINGING ANIMALS IN THE WAVES

>>> Stingrays. Live in shallow water in tropical and temperate zones. Shuffle feet to scatter them. Venomous spine near tail delivers severe or fatal injury.

>>> Stonefish. Live, camouflaged, in shallow water in Pacific, Indian oceans. The unwary step on their venomous dorsal spines.

>>> Other spiny fish. Beware of toadfish, zebrafish, and others with elaborate spines that inject toxin.

>>> Jellyfish. Tentacle stings inflict pain.

>>> Coral. Contact causes cuts, often accompanied by poison.

CHAPTER 8

ON THE WATER

267

SHARKS—AVOID THEM (OR FIGHT THEM OFF)

SHARKS ARE ATTRACTED by smells, such as body waste and blood; sounds, such as splashing and screaming; and light, such as bright reflections. In addition, be especially wary around groups of sea birds and dolphins, since not only are they drawn to the same food sources sharks seek, they are also food for larger sharks.

Keep an intense lookout for sharks from your life raft. If they are nearby, eliminate fecal matter, vomit, and food garbage by throwing it as far as you can. Urinate only in bursts, allowing each to dissipate before going again. If you fish, call a halt whenever sharks are near, and likewise do not clean fish in the water or toss fish waste overboard.

If you are in the water, don't move more than you have to if sharks are near. If you must swim, take strong strokes and do not flail about with irregular movements. Stay away from schools of fish.

From your life raft, counter an aggressive shark by jabbing at the shark's snout or gills with an oar, or by firing a rocket flare as a projectile.

EXPERT TIP In general, dangerous sharks have wide mouths and visible teeth, while relatively harmless ones have small mouths on the underside of their heads. However, any shark can inflict painful and often fatal injuries, either through bites or through abrasions from their rough skin.

U.S.ARMY

how to
FIGHT OFF A SHARK

1. If you face an aggressive shark while floating unprotected, slap the surface of the water with cupped hands to make a series of loud bangs, or shout underwater.

2. Kick the shark in the head or snout.

3. In a group of people, form a tight circle facing outward and kick or strike the shark with hard objects.

4. If the shark bites down, do not play dead. Hit its most sensitive areas: eyes and gills.

MAN OVERBOARD!

HYPOTHERMIA attacks an overboard victim immediately. Death from loss of body heat or drowning may occur within minutes unless the victim is rescued, dried, and made warm. Therefore, ship crews should become efficient at man-overboard drills, and occupants of life rafts should know the basics for recovering someone from the open ocean.

When someone goes overboard, the ship must be immediately halted. Yell "Man overboard!" to alert the crew. A ship traveling at 10 knots will have moved more than 300 feet away from the victim in just 20 seconds, so speed is of the essence.

If the victim is not found quickly after the alarm has been raised, notify the coast guard. Begin carrying out a search pattern in an expanding series of spiral square shapes, centered on the last place the victim was seen. Make a pan-pan radio call to alert other vessels and let them know of your intended search pattern.

WHAT TO DO IF
YOU FALL OVERBOARD

>>> Signal for help. Swimming in cold, rough seas—the most likely conditions in which someone goes overboard—could exhaust you and bring on cold shock.
>>> Keep the back of your head above the water to minimize heat loss.
>>> If wearing a life jacket, use the HELP position to stay warm. (See page 270.)
>>> If not wearing a life jacket, use the dead man's float. (See How To instructions for "Dead Man's Float" on page 259.)

essentials

SWIMMING WITH A LIFE PRESERVER

A life preserver that is correctly sized and adjusted can help save your life.

A LIFE JACKET can be your best friend in a survival situation—if you use it correctly.

ENSURE that the life jacket is correctly inflated and fitted before entering water.

CONSIDER SLIGHTLY deflating the jacket to allow for better arm movement in swimming strokes.

USE THE BACKSTROKE to save energy when swimming any great distance.

USE THE SIDESTROKE when tugging someone who is hurt or unconscious.

GROUPS have the strongest person lead the way, with the rest following in single file.

BREASTROKE to approach a boat or person in the water.

RESCUE AN OVERBOARD VICTIM

GOING OVERBOARD calls for immediate action. On a ship, alert crew to halt motion. Yell "Man overboard!" and give the victim's position. Drop a smoke flare and ring to mark the spot in daytime; use a flotation device with lights at night, and train a spotlight on the victim. Keep a lookout while the ship maneuvers for recovery—into the wind with propeller pointed away from the victim, who should be on the lee side. When the ship is alongside, the propeller should be halted. Get a rescue line to the victim and pull the victim to the deck. Avoid sending a rescuer into the water unless absolutely necessary.

In a life raft, throw a floatable object (life jackets are the logical choice, but an empty water jug will do) and extend a rope or pole to the victim. Try to avoid entering the water to help someone else, especially if the water is cold. If you have no choice, take a flotation device that will support two people.

HEAT-ESCAPE-LESSENING-POSITION (HELP)

>>> **For use with life jacket to retard loss of body heat while submerged.**
>>> **Clamp upper arms against sides.**
>>> **Cross lower arms over chest, cross ankles.**
>>> **Pull knees together and toward chest.**
>>> **If others are present, huddle to maximize body contact.**

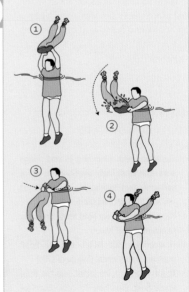

how to

MAKE A FLOATING DEVICE FROM PANTS WHILE TREADING WATER

1 Hold breath and remove pants, one leg at a time. Tie a knot at the bottom of each trouser leg, while continuously treading water.

2 Holding the waistband open, sling the pants from behind your head to slam the open waistband on the water before you. This forces air into the legs.

3 Hold waistband shut in front of you.

4 Let legs deploy under your armpits and behind you like water wings. When air seeps out of pants, repeat steps 2 through 4

FIRST AID

Cuts, sunburns, salt sores, cold injuries, and stings are the most common health hazards at sea. / Treat cuts with antibiotic, and do not drop blood near a life raft at sea. To remove an embedded fishhook, push it through until the barb clears the skin, then clip off the barb and reverse the metal out. Use cool compresses to treat burns. Cover affected areas to avoid further exposure. / Seawater ulcers are caused by softening of the skin and exposure to abrasive salts. They particularly attack victims who have lost body mass. Treat by keeping skin dry, brushing off loose salt crystals, and washing with fresh water. Nonpotable water is acceptable, as long as it does not contain salt. / Cold injuries should be treated as usual. (See First Aid for Hypothermia on page 224.) / Try to avoid marine stings by keeping limbs out of the water. Treat stings by soaking the affected area for 30 minutes in water that is hot but not enough to burn. This is believed to help break down sting-injected venom. Clean the affected area and remove any bits of stinger. If necessary, treat for shock.

CORRECTING VITAMIN AND PROTEIN DEFICIENCIES

SAILORS HAVE LONG KNOWN about diseases at sea linked to diet. British "limeys" got their name from the Royal Navy issuing lime juice to sailors to ward off scurvy, a disease caused by lack of vitamin C. Scurvy causes bleeding of the gums, loss of teeth, joint swelling, and interference with the ability of cuts and sores to heal.

Another common vitamin deficiency disease is beriberi, caused by a lack of vitamin B. Symptoms include loss of appetite, paralysis, and muscle cramps or twitching.

Taking vitamin capsules as a dietary supplement should prevent both diseases. You can also eat seaweed for a source of vitamins.

Protein deficiency, although not related to vitamins, results in loss of appetite, vomiting, an irritable mood, diarrhea, and loss of muscle mass. The cure is all around your raft: Catch and eat fish for their animal protein.

SIGNALING

Signals greatly increase the possiblity of rescue, and chances are they're already on your survival craft. Coast guard regulations require visual distress signals on all boats plying the oceans, coastal waters, Great Lakes, and major connecting waterways. The requirements are minimums; carrying extra signals is a wise precaution. / Use signaling devices first to alert rescuers that you are in trouble, then to help them pinpoint your location. Electronic devices such as VHF handheld radios and Emergency Position Indicating Radio Beacons (EPIRBs) are effective if their signals are strong and someone is listening. Signals sent by VHF radio—the emergency band is Channel 16—have an average range of 20 to 60 miles. EPIRBs send signals 200 to 300 miles on two frequencies monitored by military and civilian aircraft. Extend battery life by signaling for an hour or two, switching off for a while, and then rebroadcasting. / Flares are powerful signaling devices at night because of their bright, moving lights. / When rescuers are nearby, help them zero in on your survival craft with mirrors, smoke, streamers, kites, sea dye, or anything that attracts attention.

USE SIGNAL FLARES

SIGNAL FLARES and orange smoke can be used only once, so wait until a plane or ship is near before ignition.

Hold flares so as to avoid dropping sparks into your gear. To light, remove safety cap and strike igniter with cap's abrasive surface. A red flare burns for two minutes and can be seen up to five miles away. Aerial flares shoot 500 feet in the air. To activate, pull the flare's

chain outside the perimeter of the raft while holding the firing tube straight up. A variation adds a parachute. Aim parachute flares slightly into any wind to place the light overhead as it burns.

Orange smoke signals are ignited like flares. Wind, rain, and cold interfere with smoke's making a tall, bright column. In best conditions, smoke is visible more than five miles away in daylight.

SIGNAL FROM A BEACH

IF YOU ARE SAFE and secure on the beach, stay put and wait for rescue. Move only if you determine that rescue is not likely soon, that the site doesn't meet your survival needs, and that you know how to get where you want to go.

If you arrived on the beach in a survival craft, stay nearby. It will attract attention from sea and air. If you must leave, fashion a ground-to-air signal pointing out your direction of travel.

Survival craft carry a number of signaling devices, from an emergency locator beacon and signal mirrors to VHF radio and aerial flares. Choose a signal site close to your shelter in a clearing with 360-degree visibility. Flares and driftwood fires are useful in attracting attention once you hear the sound of a rescue team's engine. Your survival kit may also contain two Cyalume sticks and a strobe light for use at night. The Cyalume stick produces yellow light and will glow for up to eight hours; the other gives off a high-powered red glare, and will provide light for about 30 minutes. The strobe light flashes dozens of times per minute and will operate for hours, especially if switched on for short periods and then shut off.

Protect signaling equipment from dirt, water, wind, and beach sand.

DEPLOY DYE MARKERS

>>> Yellow-green fluorescent dye lasts 20 to 30 minutes in calm water, less in turbulence.
>>> Coloring makes surface surrounding survival craft contrast with seawater.
>>> Drop the dye powder into the ocean in daylight when a plane or ship approaches. Dye cannot be reused, so wait for the right time before releasing it.
>>> Dye will be visible up to ten miles away.
>>> Dye can cause burns if it comes in contact with skin. Avoid touching the powder.
>>> On land, place dye on snow for stark contrast.

When using flares, hold them out over the water to avoid dropping sparks in the boat.

When cave diving, adventure is the enemy. Adventure implies adrenaline, accompanied by a racing heart, and increased breath rate and oxygen consumption. Underwater, with limited gas supply, you want slow, steady respiration, relaxed movements, and plenty of time to exit through

the convoluted way you entered, often through zero-visibility silt, tight spots called restrictions, and dynamic currents. A most memorable dive—in a nightmarish sort of way—that taxed my skills of controlling my mind and body nearly proved fatal. I was solo diving in one of the remote underwater caves in the Bahamas known locally as "boiling holes," because they pump out water with enough force to break the surface 60 feet above. When the tide reverses, they suck water in, forming vortex-like whirlpools at the surface. Thus, timing a dive into these limestone mazes requires observation of the tidal cycle, winds, rains, and other factors that may affect the hydrodynamics and alter the six-hour cycle of these living caves.

National Geographic emerging explorer Kenneth Broad is an environmental anthropologist and underwater cave explorer who studies natural resource management.

With three tanks tethered to my sides, I entered one such hole at the end of the outgoing tide, where the flow was not as heavy, and the water clearest. Running my guideline, I slowly finned my way against the current through the tight, crust-filled entrance into a limestone bedding plane about 2 feet high and 50 feet wide, with walls a three-dimensional psychedelic montage of multicolored sponges, worms, and otherworldly creatures adapted to the twilight zone. Farther in, light dimmed until the cave became pitch-black, home to only the most bizarre of troglodytes.

There are several golden rules for cave diving: run a continuous guideline to the surface, carry at least three independent light and two independent breathing gas sources, and use a third of your gas supply for going in, and a third for coming out; save a third for emergencies. And, of course, keep mind and breathing under control. All was going smoothly until about 1,000 feet into the passageway—after being lured down a few false leads, I ran into a narrowing of the cave and a tight restriction. Having already dropped one of my three tanks along the way, I took off a second one to push ahead of me through the 20 or so gnarly feet, leading to what I could see was a big passageway indicated by a deep blue void past the walls. Gathering my composure and slowing my breath, I started to grind my way into the darkness, with tank in one hand ahead of me and reel of line unwinding in the other. The water flow was negligible and I figured I had a good hour until the cave started sucking water in from the open ocean. About halfway I felt the odd sensation of being pushed farther into the crack and was quickly enveloped by the particles of silt, sand, and organic matter that I had stirred up on the journey into the cave. The tide had switched earlier and gathered strength more quickly than I anticipated.

The realization that I was now driven into the narrows of this cave sent a jolt of electricity through me, a sensation as if a bright strobe light went off just inches from my face, triggering the rest of my body to breathe hard and jam my way forward toward wider space with irresponsible, uncoordinated urgency. After these initial reactionary spasms, quasi-sanity returned and I found my body wedged further into the Pliocene coffin. Worse yet, I found that the tank I was pushing ahead was now turned perpendicular and was jammed inextricably in front of me by the current. I was too far in to back out and had a metal cylinder blocking my way forward.

At this point, I went purposefully catatonic: enveloped in the blinding silt of my own struggle, and held firmly in place by the rock around me, I closed my eyes and concentrated for what seemed like eternity—but must have been no more than three minutes—on slowing my breathing and disconnecting my mind from my surroundings. Once under control, I began visualizing my way out of this mess, telling myself: "Use your hands and fins to feel around for even the smallest of crevices to try to spin around. Feel for a tie-off point to secure the guideline line to avoid a tangled mess reeling it out. Make yourself as small and thin as possible and then rotate; switch regulators and then leave the tank that is wedged behind you, already low on air, as a parting gift to the cave." I would have one tank to make it back out of the restriction and work my way against the flow to my staged air bottle, and would need to pull and kick my way to the exit against the increasingly heavy flow, leaving no air to spare should any obstacle occur. The happy ending I envisioned came true, with the warmth of the tropical sun shining down on me during my decompression stop. It is a feeling I can still conjure when the surprises of day-to-day life sneak up on me like the currents of the blue holes sometimes do.

Ever been stranded at home—maybe the car was in the shop, or you were laid up in bed? Or remember that 20-minute blackout last summer when you suddenly discovered your son had used the kitchen flashlight to play fireman? / Now magnify and extrapolate. Tiny incidents can deprive you momentarily of light, power, heat, telephones, comfort, or even access to the outside world. True emergencies could leave you without conveniences and amenities for days, even weeks. / That car did not break down on schedule; the blackout did not phone ahead. Neither will disasters, natural or man-made. So keeping your home a safe haven during a disaster requires one thing: preparing for it ahead of time. A few simple steps will make your home a haven and hospital, its own self-sufficient city. You don't have to spend a lot, and you don't have to give in to fear. You just need to think ahead. Knowing what could happen—and what to do when it does—could mean the difference between catastrophe and simple inconvenience.

IN THE HOME

WITHIN THIS CHAPTER

PREPARATION

The 16th-century Spanish writer Miguel de Cervantes said, "Forewarned, forearmed; to be prepared is half the victory." / Disaster can—and does—strike anywhere. Floods are the country's single most common natural disaster, and earthquakes threaten all but five states. Tornadoes, usually associated with the Midwest, have even ripped through downtown Atlanta. It may be impossible to anticipate and prepare for everything that could happen, but a simple risk assessment will help create a strategy that works for you and your family. / A tornado may keep you in the basement for a couple of hours—but its aftermath could leave you stranded for days. An earthquake may last less than a minute, but the city left behind could mean a Mad Max existence for weeks. Create an emergency kit to last at least three days, but consider one that spans two weeks. Design a communication plan with family members who may not be home when the event occurs. Above all, have everything you need at your fingertips. The advice and tips in this chapter, compiled primarily from the Department of Homeland Security, the Federal Emergency Management Agency, the American Red Cross, and local fire and emergency management officials, will help you conquer the unknown.

TYPES OF HOME DISASTERS

DISASTERS CAN BE natural or man-made. Floods, tornadoes, and other storms have long plagued humankind. Human disasters are all too common, with new substances and technologies. Chemical spills, accidents that release radiation into the air, and terrorism are more recent but just as threatening, and are likely to happen with little warning.

**DISASTERS THAT
REQUIRE SURVIVAL METHODS**

>>> **Natural disasters: "acts of God," usually weather-related.**
>>> **Chemical disasters: accidents or terrorism.**
>>> **Biological events: natural causes and terrorism.**
>>> **Nuclear incidents: plant accidents or terrorism.**

SURVIVING EVENTS THAT THREATEN YOUR HOME

If you're told to evacuate, get moving. If you are not told to evacuate, or somehow become trapped, follow these tips:

FLOODS: Head for an attic or upper story. If there's time, move valuables to higher floors, and fill bathtubs and sinks with water. Position sandbags to keep water away from your home.

HURRICANES: Nail the shutters down or cover windows with 1/2-inch-thick plywood (tape won't do the trick). Move to a room in the center of your home with few or no windows.

TORNADOES: Head to the basement. If you don't have one, huddle in a closet, bathroom, or center hallway on the lowest floor. In a high-rise, pick a hallway in the center of the building.

THUNDERSTORMS: Draw the blinds and shades to contain breaking glass, unplug appliances, and stay off the phone—the lines conduct electricity. Avoid bathing or running water for the same reason.

WINTER STORM: Camp near the fireplace. If you don't have one, go to the best insulated room. Close all doors to retain warmth.

EARTHQUAKES: No particular room will keep you safe. Shelter under a sturdy piece of furniture, or against an interior wall away from windows, bookcases, and tall furniture.

VOLCANOES: No particular room will keep you safe during a volcano, but be sure to close doors, windows, dampers, and vents to keep ash particles out.

WHEN NOT TO EVACUATE

THE RIVER IS barreling down, its banks spilling over, and there's just not enough time to escape. Or the air outside is acrid and stinging, too dangerous to venture into. Or you've heard on the radio that once you leave your neighborhood the roads are crisscrossed with power lines and covered in ice.

Sometimes it's just not possible to leave your home, even when you know a disaster is on the way.

If you're told to evacuate, don't waste a minute—go and go quickly. But if the word doesn't come, making the call to stay or go will be your first critical decision.

DECIDING WHETHER TO STAY OR TO GO

>>> First, listen. Turn on the television or radio and check the Internet for situation updates.
>>> Use your common sense and intuition. If debris is swirling in the air or you can actually see the tornado's funnel, it's probably best to stay put.
>>> Make a decision. Depending on alerts and weather conditions, you may want to seal yourself inside the house.

PACK YOUR HOME EMERGENCY KIT

THE EMERGENCY KIT. If you don't have one, get one.

The kit will be your single most important resource in an emergency. It should be stocked with enough food, water, first aid, and other items to let you make it on your own without gas, electricity, water, telephone, or other services for at least three days.

Create your kit in a portable container, like a covered trash can, camping backpack, or cooler. Keep it close at hand and show everyone in the house where it is. Rethink the contents at least once a year, replacing expired supplies and updating items to your family's changing needs and tastes.

EMERGENCY KIT INSIDER TIPS

>>> Avoid candles—they cause fires and should never be used for light or warmth.
>>> Do not pack your cell phone in the kit. Keep it with you at all times. Consider storing an extra cell phone battery in the kit.
>>> Keep at least one hard-wired phone in the house, in case cell networks are overloaded. Make sure your hard-wired phone does NOT rely on electricity.
>>> Put your entire disaster supplies kit in one or two easy-to-carry containers, such as a trash can, camping backpack, or cooler.
>>> If you want to be able to cook, consider purchasing a camping stove. Store it with your supplies, plus extra fuel for it. If you have a gas or charcoal grill, stock extra propane or charcoal.
>>> A fondue pot or chafing dish, plus fuel, may be useful for warming foods.

essentials

KIT CONTENTS

If you don't have an emergency kit, buy one or make your own. Your kit should include:

THREE-DAY supply of water (one gallon per person per day)

THREE-DAY supply of nonperishable food, can opener, and utensils

VITAMINS and other nutritional supplements

HAND-CRANK or battery-powered radio and flashlight; extra batteries

FIRST AID kit and manual

WHISTLE to signal for help

SANITATION and hygiene items

MATCHES and/or a fire starter

UNOPENED bottle of unscented liquid bleach for purifying water, if necessary

WRENCH or pliers to turn off utilities

SPECIAL NEEDS ITEMS such as prescription medications and eyeglasses

BATTERY-OPERATED cell phone charger and a copy of your manual

ITEMS for infants and pets

PHOTOCOPIES of IDs and essential prescriptions for all household members

CASH and coins

Avoid waiting until a storm is forecast to buy supplies. Maintain a consistent stock.

MAKE YOUR OWN EMERGENCY KIT

YOU ARE LIKELY to assemble a kit that is better suited to your family's needs just by gathering items at the hardware store, pharmacy, and supermarket. Even if you decide to use a prepackaged kit as a starting point, be sure to familiarize yourself with its contents before a disaster, and tailor it to your household's needs.

Prepackaged kits are widely available on the Internet and in some camping stores. But before you invest what is often a considerable sum in one of these, check out its contents.

EVALUATE A PREPACKAGED KIT

>>> Is the plastic sheeting at least 4mm thick?
>>> Are the items sturdy?
>>> Will the prewritten disaster plan work for your family?
>>> Are the food bars tasty?

EXPERT TIP Make a visual or written record of all of your household possessions. Record model and serial numbers. This list could help you prove the value of what you owned if those possessions are damaged or destroyed, and can assist you to claim deductions on taxes.

American Red Cross

SPECIAL ITEMS FOR WORK AND CAR

FOR WORK: Include as much as possible from the above list, but keep the pack portable. Include comfortable walking shoes in case you have to walk long distances. For the car: Include as much as possible from the above list, plus flares, jumper cables, a first aid kit, and cold-weather items like hats and gloves.

WATER

The human body is more than 50 percent water, and it loses a significant amount each day, even at rest. During an emergency you'll need to have—and possibly find—safe sources for replenishing it. / Figure on at least one gallon per person per day (this covers drinking and washing) and more for any children, nursing mothers or elderly people in your household. / Prepackaged, commercially bottled water is your best bet. It's been purified by the bottler and offers a reliable level of safety. Buy at least a three-day supply and store it in a cool, dark place. Mark the "use by" date on your calendar and replace it then with a new supply. / If you prefer to pack your own, consider buying food-grade water-storage containers from surplus or camping stores. If you're bent on using what's at hand, sanitize two-liter soft drink bottles with a mixture of unscented chlorine bleach and water (1 teaspoon per quart). Steer clear of containers that held milk or fruit juice—the proteins and sugars cling to these, offering bacteria a nice little petri dish. Avoid glass, as it breaks. And never use containers that have held gasoline, paint thinner or other toxic substances. / Fill the bottles with your local tap water as long as it's chlorinated. If not, add two drops of unscented chlorine bleach to each gallon of water before filling the bottles. Close the bottles with the original cap—making sure not to touch the inside with your fingers—and write the date it was filled on the outside using permanent marker. Store the water in a cool, dark place and replace it every six months.

EXPERT TIP To distill, fill a pot halfway with water. Tie a cup to the handle on the pot's lid so that the cup will hang right side up when the lid is upside down. Boil water for 20 minutes. The water that drips from the lid into the cup is distilled.

American Red Cross

essentials

GAUGING WATER NEEDS

Going thirsty is uncomfortable—and potentially dangerous. Incorporate these water basics into your home survival plan.

STORE at least one gallon of water per person per day. The average person will use half a gallon just for drinking.

CHILDREN, nursing mothers, the elderly, and sick people may need more.

EXTREME HEAT could double the group's water requirements.

A MEDICAL EMERGENCY also could require more water.

STORE at least a three-day supply of water, but consider storing enough for two weeks.

IF YOU DON'T have the room, store as much as possible.

IF SUPPLIES run low, never ration water. Drink what you need, when you need it. Then worry about finding more. You can tame your body's water needs by staying still and cool.

FINDING WATER INDOORS AND OUT

IF YOUR BOTTLED water runs low, you'll need to find alternative sources.

Start with the freezer's ice cubes. Liquids from your canned fruits and vegetables will also keep you hydrated.

Next scavenge what's trapped in the pipes. First, turn off the main water valve to block potentially contaminated water from flowing in from the outside. Open the faucet at the topmost level of the house, plug the basins at the lowest level, then turn on the tap and let air pressure work for you.

Then hit the water heater. Turn off the electricity or gas, open the drain, then shut the tank's intake valve. Plug basins, then turn on a hot-water faucet.

Filling bathtubs and sinks when a storm is on the way will also provide more water for flushing or cleaning, and, if needed, drinking. Don't forget to cut off potentially contaminated incoming water once everything is full.

Never drink water from radiators, waterbeds, swimming pools, hot tubs, or any part of the toilet. Water from pools and hot tubs is good for bathing and cleaning, but contains too many chemicals for drinking.

EVALUATE WATER AROUND YOUR HOME

WHEN YOU RUN out of inside water sources, look outside. Harvest rainwater in buckets, fill your bottles in streams, rivers or other moving bodies of water, or even find a pond, lake, or natural spring. Avoid water that smells, looks bad, or has stuff floating in it, though even the clearest outside source could harbor germs, bacteria, or viruses and should be treated before it's used, even for washing. If you can't purify, put off drinking the water as long as possible, but not so long that you become dehydrated. Never drink floodwater.

WATCHING YOUR WATER is tricky. Make sure everyone drinks at least one quart every day—and never ration water. Let people drink what they need and look for more when it's gone. Instead, try to trim needs by cutting activity, staying cool, and avoiding foods high in fat, protein, or salt—all thirst producers. Carbonated beverages won't keep you hydrated, and alcohol and caffeine will actually speed dehydration.

TREAT WATER FOR DRINKING

DRINK YOUR CLEAN, safe, bottled water first. Then move on to potentially suspicious sources or water gathered from outside—but always purify it if possible. Before treating water, let any suspended particles settle to the bottom, or strain it through layers of paper towel, a clean cloth, or a coffee filter. Then follow either the boiling or distillation methods below.

BOIL OR CHLORINATE WATER FOR DRINKING

>>> Boiling will kill most microorganisms.
>>> Once you bring water to a boil, keep the water at a rolling boil for one full minute.
>>> If you don't have the ability to heat the water, adding chlorine—think unscented bleach—can also achieve the desired effect of killing microoganisms. This makes the water safe for drinking, even though it will have a distinct taste and odor.
>>> Make sure the bleach contains at least 5.25 to 6.0 percent sodium hypochlorite (ditto for any commercial purification pills you buy).
>>> Add 1/8 teaspoon bleach to every gallon of water, stir, and let it stand for 30 minutes.
>>> If the water doesn't smell like bleach, add another 1/8 teaspoon and let it stand 15 more minutes.
>>> If you still can't smell the bleach, throw the water out and find a different source.

DISTILL WATER FOR DRINKING

>>> Distillation—collecting condensed water vapor—will remove even more microorganisms, as well as filtering heavy metals, salts, and chemicals.
>>> Affix a nonmeltable cup to the handle of a pot lid and collect water dripping off the lid as the pot boils.
>>> Distilling is the only way saltwater can be used. See Expert Tip on page 282.

FOOD

It's easy to imagine snacking on crackers to pass the time. But that is exactly the wrong thing to do. Instead, you'll need a well-planned supply of foods that simultaneously quell hunger, provide decent nutrition—and don't make you thirsty. / Long-lasting foods with lots of calories, carbohydrates, and nutrients should fill your emergency pantry. Stock enough for at least three days, but consider building a two-week supply. / Prepackaged emergency food and water kits are widely available on the Internet and at some camping stores. Most contain food bars offering an entire day's worth of nutrition. They're light, easy to store, and some claim a shelf life of up to five years. These kits may be excellent for grab-and-go bags kept at work or in your car—or even as a backup food supply in your home kit—but creating a cache of tasty, familiar foods that comfort as well as nourish is the best way to go. / Home-preserved foods will ensure a steady supply of family favorites. But the drawbacks—a relatively short shelf life and potential for contamination—should be considered. Home-preserved foods may not last as long as commercially prepared foods and may be more prone to food-borne illness, such as botulism. / Stock up on store-bought canned goods, such as soup, beans, fruit, vegetables, and tuna, which require no water, cooking, or refrigeration. Many are also packed in liquid, which can be drunk along with your water. Stick to low-sodium versions and avoid items high in fat and protein, which require more water for the body to metabolize. / Balance out the cans with dry goods like salt-free crackers and whole grain cereals. / If your family has special needs—an infant or grandparent—remember to stock items like premade formula (never powdered, which will require water) and easily digestible items like broth and fruit juices. / Most important, don't forget a manual can opener.

A BALANCED STOCKPILE of emergency foods will ensure your family's nutritional and emotional needs.

Women need 2,000 calories per day, and men need 2,400. Children need 1,000 to 1,800. Take only a third of your calories from fats, and include about four cups of fruit and vegetables per day. Carbohydrates supply energy. Fruit, crackers, cereals, and treats such as granola are great sources. Proper nutrition helps people weather stress, so pack vitamins.

Be sure to eat at least one well-balanced meal each day—it will give you strength for the unexpected. If food runs low, adjust your activity, not your diet. Healthy people can survive for a long time on half their usual calories, and for many days with no food at all. Children and pregnant women should eat a balanced diet each day.

essentials

WHAT TO STOCK

Canned or prepackaged fish, meats, soups. Canned fruits, vegetables, and legumes, especially those packed in water or natural juices. Consider "snack-size" or individual portions. You won't have to refrigerate unused portions. Many also have pull tops.

JUICE in foil-lined boxes or packets

MILK, either pasteurized in shelf-stable boxes, or evaporated in cans

PORTABLE, nutritious, long-lasting snacks packed with energy: granola bars, cereal or energy bars, trail mix, dried fruits and berries

DRY GOODS such as whole-grain cereals and salt-free crackers

LONG-LASTING items including peanut butter, jelly, and honey

COMFORT FOODS: candy, cookies, favorite treats and sweets (as long as they're not salty) instant coffee, tea bags (caffeine free is best)

AVOID THESE FOODS

>>> Salty foods; foods high in fat and/or protein. These will require you to drink more water.
>>> Freeze-dried or commercially dehydrated foods. These are compact and lightweight but often require a lot of water before they can be eaten.
>>> Food packaged in glass bottles and jars. They are heavy and may break. If stored improperly, they may also spoil sooner than items in nontransparent containers.
>>> Dried pasta, rice. These items will need water and cooking, which may be difficult.

EXPERT TIP In cold weather, a person requires more calories. Calories are best obtained by eating a balanced variety of foods containing carbohydrates, fats, and proteins. Most of the high-energy foods needed for hard physical work can be found in the starches and sugars of carbohydrates.

Girl Scouts.

PROPER STORAGE will ensure you can get the longest life out of your emergency rations and that they will be palatable when you need them. Keep all goods in a cool, dry place. Try to pick a storage area out of harm's way, for instance, on high shelves or an upper floor if you live in a flood zone.

Pack perishable foods, such as cookies and crackers, in airtight plastic bags, even when unopened. Stock extra self-seal bags. Store unopened packets of dried fruit, crackers, cereals, and other items liable to get stale or attract pests into screw-top jars or airtight canisters. The containers will preserve freshness after opening.

Before storing, check the packaging of items for holes or tears. Do not store anything with a torn package. Circle with a permanent marker the expiration or "use by" date on each product. For undated items, write your purchase date on the can. Keep older items at the front of the storage area, newer items toward the back.

Check your food supply every six months. Use any items that are close to the expiration or use-by dates. Replace with new items. Update your kit yearly to keep pace with the family's changing tastes and needs.

essentials

RECOGNIZING SPOILAGE

Look for the signs of food spoilage and contamination. Throw out:

SWOLLEN, dented, or corroded cans of food.

CANS that hiss or spurt when opened.

ANY ITEM with an unusual odor, color, or texture. If the food is unfamiliar and you're not sure of its condition, rely on instinct and also perform the edibility test (p. 89).

ANY FOODS—including canned goods—that have come in contact with floodwater.

ANY FOODS exposed to fire, even ones that seem undamaged. Heat, smoke, fumes, and chemicals used to extinguish fire can affect them. This includes food and water stored in refrigerators or freezers, whose seals may allow harmful gases inside.

ANY FOOD exposed to toxic chemicals. Foods packed in permeable containers like cardboard boxes and screw-top jars may be compromised. The same applies to fresh food such as fruits and vegetables, even those stored in the refrigerator. Canned goods may be used, but only if they are washed and immersed in a bleach solution (one teaspoon of bleach per quart of water).

ACIDITY AND SHELF LIFE

>>> In general, high-acid canned foods such as tomatoes, grapefruit, and pineapple can be stored on the shelf for 12 to 18 months.
>>> Low-acid canned foods such as meat, poultry, fish, and vegetables will keep two to five years—if the can remains in good condition and has been stored in a cool, clean, dry place.
>>> Inspect cans for signs of spoilage before opening and using.

REFRIGERATOR AND FREEZER RULES

WHEN THE POWER goes out—a likely event during a hurricane, tornado, flood, or winter storm—head to the fridge.

Since food there is likely to go bad once you open the door, make it the first batch you eat. Next, hit the freezer. A well-filled, well-sealed freezer should keep food safe for at least two days (a half-full freezer will last about 24 hours. Closely stacked items maximize the cold). To avoid keeping the freezer open for several minutes at a time, keep a "map" on hand that tells you what's in there and where to find it.

To extend the life span of your fridge and freezer items, use dry ice, if there's time to get it. Twenty-five pounds should keep the interior below freezing for three to four days. If you can't get dry ice, you can make your own ice in cold weather (never put the food itself outside, where it may spoil in the sun or be nosed by animals). Fill every bucket, carton, and can you've got with water, set them outside, then use the homemade ice to keep things cool. (This may not be an option if water is running low or if it's warm.)

Only after the fridge and freezer are empty should you move on to the canned and long-lasting items you've stored on the shelves.

EXPERT TIP Cans store indefinitely—wheat, vegetable oils, dried corn, baking powder, soybeans, instant coffee, tea, and cocoa, salt, noncarbonated soft drinks, white rice, bouillon products, dry pasta, powdered milk (in nitrogen-packed cans).

American Red Cross

COOKING WITHOUT GAS OR ELECTRICITY

MAKE SURE MOST of your items are safe to eat without cooking, but add a fondue pot or chafing dish to your stockpile (don't forget the cans of cooking fuel). If you have a fireplace, consider purchasing a cooking grill for it. Also keep a box of heavy-duty tinfoil on hand for warming food directly on the embers (some products are even designed specifically for this purpose). Remember: Never bring a camp stove or charcoal grill inside, where they can cause fire and toxic fumes.

WARMING CANNED ITEMS

>>> Canned items can be warmed right in the can, using the following steps.
>>> Remove the label, and disinfect the can with one part bleach and ten parts water.
>>> Open the can and warm it in a pot of simmering water.
>>> The water can be used again.

Work near windows to utilize natural light. Supplement with candles and hurricane lamps.

DATING YOUR FOOD

TRACKING THE DATES on your emergency food supply is an imperfect science. With the exception of baby formula and some baby food, no federal law requires manufacturers to date their products. When there is a date (more than 20 states require it), several different systems may be used.

Calendar dates—for instance, January 1, 2006—are mostly found on perishable items such as meat and poultry to tell you how long they will last. Cans, boxes, and other long-lived items are more likely to have codes. These indicate the date of packing and are used by manufacturers to track production.

But here's the catch: None of these is an expiration date. Sometimes cans will display clear calendar dates followed by the explanation "use by" or "sell by." These are freshness dates. After this date, the item may have lost some of its flavor or nutritional value. But in general it will remain safe to eat long after that date.

If a product does display a clearly marked "expiration date," pitch it once the date passes.

JULIAN DATES

A CAN'S CODED numbers sometimes follow a calendar formula, with MMDDYY or a more obtuse system that substitutes letters for the months, for instance, using A for "January." Yet another system uses consecutive or "Julian" numbers. In this four- or five-digit code the first number indicates the year of production and the following three numbers indicate the specific day of the year. For instance, 6001 means the item was packed in 2006 on the first day of the year, or January 1, 2006. The number 60012 may mean the item was packed on that day by the packing plant's second shift. But the only way to be sure is to call the manufacturer at the toll-free number offered on the can.

When temperatures start to dip outside, it may quickly become frigid inside, especially during a power outage. / Your first line of defense will be good old-fashioned bundling up. Trapped air acts as insulation, so layers are better than one heavy coat. Wool, silk, and polypropylene inner layers will hold more heat than cotton. Try to stay dry, and shed layers if you begin to sweat—evaporating perspiration can chill you. Don't be shy about wearing a hat in the house—nearly half your body heat escapes through the scalp. / Pick a single room in the house—preferably with a fireplace—and make it headquarters. Insulate the room against drafts with towels or rags under doors and blankets over opening such as hallways. Draw the blinds or cover the windows with blankets at night so heat does not escape. Close doors in other areas of the house. / Stay warm from the inside out by eating small, frequent meals and drinking warm beverages. Avoid alcohol and caffeine, which accelerate heat loss.

HEATING OPTIONS

WOOD-BURNING FIREPLACES are ideal (gas fireplaces may not work if electricity is required for ignition). Wood-burning stoves can effectively heat a small area. Remember that all fuel-burning heaters can cause fires and a buildup of deadly carbon monoxide, so ensure good ventilation. Ditto for kerosene heaters, which are so dangerous they are illegal in many places. Kerosene heaters must be refueled outdoors to avoid hazardous spillage, and must be used only with the specified fuel. Portable generators offer electricity in an emergency, but can quickly fill a room with carbon monoxide. Never—ever—operate a generator inside the house or in any closed space.

PORTABLE HEATER FUEL

>>> Always have a three-day supply of fuel on hand—but not too close at hand. All fuel should be stored away from the house in a locked or protected area.
>>> Never store flammables near fuel-burning appliances.

BUILD AN EFFICIENT FIRE

BUILDING A LOUSY fire will be more than an ego buster in an emergency.

Always have a three-day supply of wood, kindling, and newspaper. A fire starter or cigarette lighter works better than matches, which burn only a few seconds. Make sure your fireplace has a grate for stacking logs.

To build a fire like a Boy Scout, National Capital Area scouting executive Michael Donaghue says, place balled-up newspaper under the grate and pile kindling on top. Get the pile burning well, then lay two or three logs across the grate like railroad ties. Add two or three more on top, perpendicular to the bottom layer. This crisscross or "log cabin"-style fire will direct heat into the room instead of up the chimney.

A fire made of six or eight logs two to four inches in diameter should last about two hours and will sufficiently heat a medium-size room. Feed the fire to keep it going.

FIND FIREWOOD AND FUEL

>>> **If you run out of firewood and have to scavenge, avoid cutting branches from live trees. They will not burn.**

>>> **Burn scrap construction wood—paneling, two-by-fours—only if you know they have not been chemically treated.**

>>> **Never burn trash, cartons, or other items that may contain toxins and increase the risk of uncontrolled fires.**

CARBON MONOXIDE

CALLED THE "silent killer," carbon monoxide (CO) is the odorless, colorless, tasteless by-product of burning fuel. It kills an estimated 300 people in their homes each year, according to the U.S. Consumer Product Safety Commission, often because of faulty heaters.

Make sure your fireplace feeds to the outside and that the flue is open. Inspect chimneys and flues annually to ensure they are not cracked or leaking.

Portable generators should be used only outdoors, and should be placed away from vents that might suck exhaust inside. Use kerosene heaters only in well-ventilated spaces. Never use a charcoal grill, oven, range, or clothes dryer to heat your home.

Install battery-operated carbon monoxide alarms and test the units monthly. Be on the lookout for dizziness, nausea, headache, or irregular breathing.

EXPERT TIP Before buying a CO alarm, check to make sure it is listed with Underwriter's Laboratories (UL), standard 2034, or there is information on the package or owner's manual that says that the detector/alarm meets the requirements of the IAS 6-96 standard.

American Red Cross

SHELTER-IN-PLACE RULES

FOR ALL SHELTER-IN-PLACE emergencies—when you can't go outdoors—lock doors, close windows, air vents, and fireplace dampers, and turn off anything that brings outside ventilation into the house (i.e., air conditioning, forced air heat, exhaust fans, even clothes dryers.) Head for your sheltering room and seal with plastic sheeting.

Ten square feet of floor space per person will be enough to prevent carbon dioxide buildup for five hours (as long as no one's panting.) Keep the radio or television on for updates, and check the Internet if possible. Make sure you've got a hard-wired telephone in the room you select, since cell phone systems may be overwhelmed.

CHEMICAL AND HAZARDOUS MATERIALS INCIDENTS:

>>> Pick an interior room with as few windows as possible.
>>> Make sure the room is aboveground. Heavy chemicals can seep into basements, even when the windows are closed.
>>> Use duct tape that's at least .01 inch (10 mils) thick and precut plastic sheeting at least .004 inch (4 mils) thick to seal all cracks around doors, windows, and vents.
>>> Seal wall plugs, switch plates, and outlets.

NUCLEAR EMERGENCIES

>>> Put three things between you and radioactivity: time, distance, and thick shielding.
>>> Head to the basement, which offers shielding with thick walls and earth.
>>> If you don't have a basement but have a room made of concrete, go there.
>>> Avoid floors that are adjacent to flat roofs—radioactive particles from the fallout will collect there.
>>> Sit tight. Radioactivity loses most of its punch within two weeks.

BIOLOGICAL THREATS

>>> Purchase High Efficiency Particulate Air (HEPA) filters for your HVAC system. These contain randomly arranged fibers that trap almost 100 percent of particles, including many biological agents, (though they probably won't be much use against the tiny flu viruses of a pandemic).
>>> With these filters in your HVAC system, turn it on during a biohazard emergency. Remember that central air systems should offer good protection from biological contaminants.

SUPPLY KIT FOR SHELTER-IN-PLACE EMERGENCIES

>>> Plastic sheeting precut to fit room openings. Pieces should be at least six inches wider than each opening. The plastic should be at least .004 inch (4 mils) thick.
>>> Duct tape at least .01 inch (10 mils) thick
>>> Scissors
>>> Tone-alert radio
>>> Battery-powered or hand-cranked radio or television

SIGNALS

When disaster strikes, information is a two-way street: Authorities will be trying to reach you, but you've got to help them. / Governments and communities may use different methods, from low-tech approaches like sirens and loudspeakers mounted on poles and police cruisers outfitted with bullhorns, to sophisticated systems like automated telephone-alert networks that dial 2,000 households per minute with a message and instructions. Some communities issue a text message to cell phones, pagers, or other devices. The federal government is working on a similar technology for national emergencies. / The Emergency Alert System—a national public warning system perhaps best known for that piercing test tone over radios and televisions—sends information over major television and radio networks. (So don't forget your battery-powered or hand-cranked radio or television!) A more targeted technology is the NOAA weather radio, sometimes generically called a "tone-alert" radio. The National Oceanic and Atmospheric Administration broadcasts forecasts and warnings for dangerous weather, natural hazards like earthquakes, and incidents like chemical spills 24 hours a day from nearly 1,000 transmitters across the country. When one of these events threatens your area, the system sends a signal that activates your radio, which sounds an alarm, then broadcasts a message and instructions. / Find out in advance which methods your community uses. If it offers special services, such as text messaging, sign up for them. If they broadcast community specific information over a particular radio station, mark your dial. During a disaster, turn on your television or radio. And consider getting a tone-alert radio. It's a great resource if disaster strikes in the middle of the night.

SELECT A TONE-ALERT RADIO

>>> Choose a radio that is marked "public alert certified" by the Consumer Electronics Association.
>>> The certification ensures that the device will receive information about all emergencies, from severe weather to natural hazards and man-made disasters.
>>> Certified radios also issue specific alerts for specific geographic regions as well as information for dealing with state and national emergencies.
>>> Tone-alert radios are always on the watch, sounding a highly audible alarm even when in stand-by mode.

WHEN CALLING 911

>>> If you do need to call for help, speak clearly, and concisely. State your name, location and problem in one sentence.
>>> Listen for questions and answer them, making sure to speak slowly.
>>> When calling for medical help, provide information about the victim and anything else important, such as a tree blocking front door or your location in the house.

essentials

EMERGENCY CELL PHONE USE

Text messaging may be your best bet when wireless bandwidth is jammed.

JAMMED TOWERS may not be able to handle your voice call, but a text message—a much smaller data packet—has a good chance of squeezing through. If towers have been destroyed or are out of power, nothing will transmit. But, unlike a voice call, your text message will hang in the queue, waiting to be delivered even if power comes back for just an instant.

CTIA The Wireless Association recommends really getting to know your cell phone and its capabilities. Is it rigged for wireless Internet? Does it have a GPS chip? Have you activated these functions? Read your manual and call your service provider to find out.

PREPARE your phone, pager, or PDA with vital numbers; keep the phone fully charged and consider buying a battery-operated charger. For other safety tips, visit CTIA.org.

Keep camping gear handy, even in winter months, in case you need to camp at home.

FIRST AID

With any luck, first aid for a home-based survival situation may amount to little more than vigilance for and preventive care against signs of hypothermia, heatstroke, or dehydration. For more serious injuries that you can't treat yourself, you'll need to try to contact help. But having the right contents in your first aid kit and training such as CPR will help nonmedical people keep someone alive until help arrives. / Be especially watchful over infants and the elderly. For example, half of all cold-related deaths occur in people over 60, according to the National Oceanic and Atmospheric Administration, and about 20 percent occur in the home. / Good habits will also pay off. Store all food in covered containers and keep utensils clean—and remember to toss anything touched by floodwaters, including wooden or plastic cookware. Make sure to take out the trash at least once a day. / Hygiene is especially important. If the water's not working and you're not able to flush the toilet, you'll need to use some vessel with a tight lid (be creative—an empty plastic cat litter container might work, or one of those industrial tubs sold at hardware stores.) Line the container with a plastic bag each time someone uses it, if possible, and remove the waste right away. If you can't empty it after each use, make sure to sprinkle a little bleach inside and replace the cover. Make liberal use of towelettes, hand sanitizer, and, whenever possible, good old soap and water.

FOLLOW THIS RULE OF THUMB

WITH YOUR entire household living in a confined space, some general principles will help keep you well and healthy. Eat balanced meals, stay hydrated, and practice good hygiene. You can prevent at least some issues by keeping the environment and yourself clean and relatively germ-free.

CLOSE QUARTERS MAY breed emotional as well as physical issues, especially if the environment is stressful.

"Cabin fever" is the feeling of being trapped or stuck and it can make people irritable, depressed, restless, and lethargic. Depending on the family, says Dr. Paul Rosenblatt, a family social scientist at the University of Minnesota who has studied cabin fever, symptoms may begin after just minutes or may not show up at all.

To fight cabin fever, Dr. Rosenblatt says to open a window so you can smell and hear outside. Clean a closet, work on your photo album, start your tax returns, or finish some project you've been meaning to get to. If possible, phone people to make plans for getting together after the crisis. If all else fails, he says, put some space between you and the people making you crazy.

Then again, you may be so busy dealing with the crisis, you won't have time for cabin fever. Focus on the things you need to do to weather the disaster.

essentials

FIRST AID KIT

According to the American Red Cross, the minimum recommended contents for a family first aid kit are as follows:

ABSORBENT compress 5x9 dressing, adhesive bandages (assorted sizes), adhesive tape (cloth), one-inch antibiotic ointment packets, antiseptic wipes, aspirin (81 mg)—for heart attack symptoms

BLANKET to treat shock

CPR breathing barrier (with one-way valve)

INSTANT cold compress

GLOVES (large), disposable, nonlatex

HYDROCORTISONE ointment packets

SCISSORS for cutting tape, cloth, bandages, or other items

ROLLER BANDAGES in different lengths such as three and four inches

STERILE gauze pad (3x3, 4x4)

THERMOMETER, oral, nonmercury and non-glass, battery-operated type

TRIANGULAR bandage—sling or binder with splinting

TWEEZERS to remove splinters and ticks

FIRST AID instruction booklet

If you have power, watch for weather updates, but take breaks to avoid excessive worry.

how to

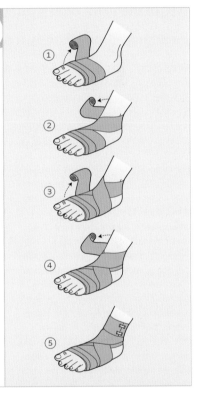

WRAP AN ANKLE

1. Start the ace bandage on the top of the ball of the injured foot. Wrap several times around the foot, working gradually toward the ankle. Make sure to apply equal, minimal tension to the bandage to support the ankle, but not cut off circulation.

2. Bring the bandage across the top of the instep and around the back of the ankle.

3. Cross the bandage back across the instep and wrap around the bottom of the foot.

4. Repeat steps two and three, overlapping each previous wrap by a slight offset.

5. Finish by wrapping bandage several times around the lower leg, just above the ankle, and secure with clips. Monitor toes for signs of decreased circulation: blueness, tingling, or cool to the touch.

EXPERT TIP In the case of an emergency, your first aid kit will enable you to act immediately. Your home medicine chest is not a substitute. If you have your supplies organized ahead of time, you'll save yourself both time and anxiety.

American Red Cross

HOW I SURVIVED: SNOWED IN by KEN GARRETT

n 2001, a winter storm driven by strong winds dumped 24 inches of snow and ice in the middle of the night on our rural community in the Virginia Piedmont. Broad Run is a small, rural town in north-western Virginia. Winters are typical of Virginia—we sometimes get snow, sometimes have to shovel, and

are rarely inconvenienced by more than a day or two of slippery roads. But on that night in 2001, we lay awake listening to the howling winds threatening to make the story of the three little pigs come true for our wooden house. Around two in the morning, the electric power failed for the final time. And it would remain off for seven days.

In our area, there are two power providers, which split customers right down the middle of our road. Some of our neighbors lost power for a week and others were out for just three days. We unluckily happened to be on the side that was out longer, but we could accept offers of help from our neighbors to whom we'd reached out over the years. It is so important to build relationships with your neighbors, no matter whether you rent or own, live in a detached home or high-rise.

In our neighborhood, if you have your own generator, you can do just fine as long as the fuel holds out or you

Photographer Kenneth Garrett photographs subjects worldwide for *National Geographic* and National Geographic books. He specializes in archaeology and paleontology.

can drive to get gas for it. Almost all of our neighbors own portable generators. However, these are expensive, and, depending on your electricity needs you're still going to have to chose: A fridge, freezer, and water pump are more than most generators can handle. Owning a generator also requires tolerance for the dangers of generators—intense heat and potentially lethal levels of carbon monoxide. If you decide to get one, plan ahead. Big storms in the past have caused generator shortages over hundreds of miles. When the storm arrives, it's too late.

Basic survival without electricity isn't that difficult for our family—we have no one on kidney dialysis and don't own expensive tropical fish—but water was a problem. Our water draws from a well and we use a septic system, so when we're without power, we're without water. After a day or two, we really wished we could flush the toilet, take a shower, and draw running water from the faucet to drink.

Normally, when we know a storm is coming, we run all of the bathtubs full of water to use for washing and flushing the toilet. Because the storm hadn't been predicted to be severe, we hadn't bothered to do so this time. We had a few gallons of water on hand, but nowhere near enough.

The worst part of the water issue, however, wasn't the liquid version, but the frozen kind. I'd inadvertently left a water hose in my home office on a frost-free fitting. The water that was left sitting in the hose when the power went out exploded. The office flooded, which required replacing everything—carpets and all. I have never made that mistake again: Now I turn off the water hose and drain it if there is the risk of a storm or if I'm going away for even a day or two in the winter.

Another major problem was the food in our refrigerator and freezers. When you live nearly a half-hour drive from a large grocery store, and probably an hour from the nearest 24-hour diner or restaurant, you tend to keep food on hand. We have a large refrigerator and two deep freezers for food storage. We hoped the power would return shortly, as it had several times in the past, so at first, we kept the refrigerator and freezer doors shut. In the past, even after two days, we'd found everything still frozen. The more full the freezers are, the colder the food stays. For example, if our largest freezer is chock-full, the food stays frozen for four days. This time, we weren't so lucky. As time wore on, we had to start salvaging what we could by taking food to neighbors with generators. But there just wasn't enough room in their freezers, so we had to throw away hundreds of dollars' worth of food.

As for heat, we'd designed the house so that we could potentially be fairly self-reliant, with large windows for natural daylight, a gas stove in the kitchen that we could light with a match, and a woodstove for heat. We have cell phones and a landline with corded phone to make phone calls.

However, with a mile and a quarter between us and the nearest paved road, we and some neighbors were trapped for a few days. It's times like these when a neighborhood really comes together. We had neighborhood storm parties at one another's houses, borrowed showers, shared our food, ate plenty of meals together, and played large card games by candlelight.

When the snow melted, we bought a 32-horsepower, four-wheel-drive tractor with a front end loader and a snow blade. I also made a resolution to research portable generators. Our household can survive everything except the loss of electricity.

Natural disasters such as hurricanes and tornadoes shake the foundations of our comfortable existence. According to Oxfam International, severe-weather events have increased fourfold in the last two decades, now totaling 500 events affecting 250 million people a year. / But deaths from such events are relatively minimal as the result of the cataclysm itself—rather, lives are lost due to secondary man-made problems such as inadequate shelter and water contamination. There is much you can do yourself to maximize your chances of surviving a catastrophe. First, learn what types of events are most likely to hit your area. Then familiarize yourself with your local emergency management system, including preparedness and response plans. Finally, take matters into your own hands by prepping your family, home, and car. / This chapter offers a primer on the most severe disasters that strike the United States: hurricanes, tornadoes, floods, forest fires, blizzards, thunderstorms, earthquakes, and volcanoes. All share the element of unpredictability and the potential for lethal strength. Combine the details offered here with the advice in Chapter 9, to create custom-tailored emergency plans.

STORMS & DISASTERS

WITHIN THIS CHAPTER

PREPARATION

It is essential to teach yourself and your family about the disasters that may strike your particular region. No region of the United States is completely hazard free. Lightning strikes indiscriminately. Floods deluge lowlands nationwide. Even earthquakes—often considered Pacific Coast occurrences—pose a moderate or greater risk to 40 states, according to the Federal Emergency Management Agency (FEMA). / So what's to learn? Beyond the basic categories of events, familiarize yourself with seasonal variations in risk, special equipment you may need for your area (such as sandbags for a flood zone), and local radio sources for emergency information. City websites, the American Red Cross, and FEMA are all good resources. Find out whether you need to bolt a bookcase to the wall (earthquakes) or gather plywood to protect windowpanes (hurricanes and tornadoes). Most important, research local evacuation routes and emergency shelters so you'll know your path if you get the call to clear out. (See page 304 for details on making a comprehensive disaster plan).

KNOW THE HAZARD THREATS IN YOUR REGION

HURRICANES RAVAGE all stretches of the East and Gulf coasts, and neighboring inland states may suffer heavy rains and flooding. Tornadoes have hit every state, and often touch down quite randomly, although Florida and the central U.S. "Tornado Alley" take the lion's share of twisters. Floods are a risk everywhere and forest fires threaten all heavily treed areas, especially the arid forests of the Rockies and West.

Blizzards can strike anywhere that receives even occasional snow, although the upper Midwest and Great Plains have them most often. Thunderstorms rage over the U.S. in all seasons, although less often in winter. Earthquakes pose a moderate or higher threat to most states. The highest threat is to regions west of the Rockies. Volcanoes are active in Alaska, Washington State, Oregon, California, and Hawaii.

ESTABLISH AN OUT-OF-AREA CONTACT PERSON

DESIGNATING A RELATIVE or close friend to be your family contact person is an important early step in your disaster plan. In the event of separation, your family can rely on this person to relay messages about one another's whereabouts and safety. Choose someone distant who won't be afflicted by the same event. Be sure each of your family members knows the person's full name, address, and phone number.

You may want to pick a contact person who also can be your host if you face an extended evacuation.

THE DIGITAL EMERGENCY ALERT SYSTEM

JUST A DECADE AGO, television and radio were the main sources of information during emergencies. When necessary, the local or federal government preempted shows by means of that familiar high-pitched tone, followed by warnings and evacuation notifications.

In this age of information overload, FEMA has worked to digitize the nation's Emergency Alert System. In 2006 FEMA announced the Digital Emergency Alert System in an effort to speed messages to first responders and the public. A collaboration with NOAA, public and private media outlets, and cell phone carriers, DEAS delivers real-time messages via satellite to cell phones, personal digital assistants (PDAs), computers, highway signs, television, and radio.

So if your power is on, you're plugged in—all the more reason to pack extra batteries for your radio and phone in your emergency supplies kit.

Depending on where you live, officials may also use sirens in times of danger, for instance when bringing swimmers in from the ocean as a lightning storm approaches. Such alerts are long, steady blasts—if you hear one,

it's time to tune in for news updates. And consider getting a tone-alert radio (details in Chapter 9) that will activate automatically to keep you informed at any time, day or night.

MAIL THESE TO YOUR EMERGENCY CONTACT PERSON

>>> Copies of vital documents: birth and marriage certificates, Social Security cards, passports, driver's licenses.
>>> Bank account and all insurance policy information for home, car, condominium, life, flood, fire, etc.
>>> All contact numbers for your immediate family, including work and cell phones.
>>> Updated photos of each family member (some people also send fingerprints).
>>> Descriptions of each person's physical characteristics, including blood type and any birthmarks or scars.
>>> Medical conditions and prescription information for each person.
>>> A list of family physicians, specialists, and day-care providers.
>>> List of household possessions and copies of receipts for the most expensive items.

CREATE A DISASTER PLAN

YOUR COMPREHENSIVE disaster plan actually began when you gathered information about your area's hazards and resources (see previous pages). Now, step two: With your family, write up a disaster plan specifying exactly what to do during different types of events. Assemble a disaster supplies kit (see Chapter 9), and then maintain and update your plan and kit regularly. Once you've done all of this, it's time to call a family meeting. Talk about the disasters that may strike your region. Together, agree upon an out-of-area contact person and a communications plan for getting in touch in case of separation. Several websites, including the Red Cross at www.redcross.org/contactcard, provide small cards on which you can write down essential phone numbers in case of emergency. Each family member should carry one. In addition, educate children how and when to call 911. Discuss and plan for the special needs of elderly or disabled family members.

During the adrenaline rush of a catastrophe such as fire, earthquake, volcanic eruption, or sudden flood, practiced escape routes are key. Identify and run drills to familiarize your family with paths out of your house or building, especially for earthquakes and fires. Draw and post a floor plan of your home with the routes marked. In addition, designate a local meeting place (such as a trusted neighbor's during a fire, or a local shelter during a storm) where separated family members can rendezvous. Write down all this information and store it in your disaster supplies kit.

essentials

WHAT TO TAKE IN AN EVACUATION

This will depend entirely on how much warning you receive before you need to leave. Always change into long pants, a long-sleeved shirt, and sturdy shoes. If you must leave:

YOUR DISASTER supplies kit, including medical supplies (glasses, contact lenses, dentures, prescription and over-the-counter medications) and first aid kit

RADIO, flashlight, separate batteries

BOTTLED WATER (one gallon per person per day if possible)

CELL PHONE with charger

A SPARE OUTFIT, bedding, and pillow for each family member

CAR KEYS and house keys

CASH and personal identification

PETS, in their travel carriers (don't forget their food)

IF YOU HAVE hours before evacuation, add:

NONPERISHABLE food items

SPECIAL ITEMS for infants (formula, diapers) or the elderly (walker)

MAP of the area

CONTAINERS for urine in case you get stuck in traffic

essentials

MUST-HAVE SKILLS TO DRILL

Older children and all adults
should know how to:

CALL 911 and family contact numbers

OPERATE a fire extinguisher

FIND two escape routes from every room in
the home. Don't forget to establish a meeting
point outside your home, close enough to
quickly assemble and verify everyone's safety.

FIND and open disaster supplies kit

HAVE current first aid and CPR training

KNOW WHERE utility shut-off valves are
for water, power, and gas

KNOW HOW to test and replace smoke
alarm batteries

EVACUATE YOUR PETS

ANIMALS ARE SPECIAL family members who often can sense danger—
and need comfort—before people do.
If you are a pet owner, be sure to pack
it food, water, and litter in your disaster supplies kit. Designate one family
member to find and comfort each pet
during a disaster (being clear to do this
only if it is safe). Evacuating with pets
can be tricky—shelters don't accept
most pets due to health codes—so
plan ahead to find a relative's home or
a pet-friendly hotel where the entire
family can stay together.

EVACUATE SAFELY

AUTHORITIES ORDER an evacuation
only when they think lives are in danger.
Speed is the key to a clean getaway. If
you do get the signal, spring into action
immediately. Urban areas urge residents to use mass transit, as it can be a
much speedier means of escape.

See Chapter 9 for what to take with
you. At this point you will be relieved
to have a planned destination point.
Hotels inevitably fill up quickly during
disasters. Call your safe-house contact
and let them know you're coming.
As a last resort, locate the nearest
emergency shelter (authorities will
announce these).

If you have time before evacuating,
plan your route. Check for road closures.
Decide how you will go. If taking
mass transit, buy passes in advance.
Otherwise, plan for your family to take
just one vehicle to avoid separation.
Choose one in good condition that can
remain stable in high winds (RVs are
not recommended). Keep that car's gas
tank filled.

EVACUATE BY CAR

>>> **On the road, use extreme caution: Severe
weather events tend to come in clusters,
so a hurricane may bring tornadoes, and
tornadoes may bring flash floods.**
>>> **Stay tuned to your car radio.**
>>> **Follow marked evacuation routes.**
>>> **Avoid shortcuts.**
>>> **Never drive into standing water if you can't
tell how deep it is.**
>>> **Stay alert for fallen trees, landslides,
broken water mains.**

STORMS & DISASTERS

CHAPTER 10

305

HURRICANES

Downpours, lightning, gales, tornadoes: Hurricanes bring them all under their swirling umbrella. These low-pressure tropical systems spiral into formation when warm air rising from the ocean collides with light, cooler winds higher up. / Ocean water must be at least 80°F and have some sort of disturbance at the surface. The vapor cools as it rises and is expelled outward at the top, creating a thick cirrus cloud layer, beneath which form deadly winds and thunderheads. At the center of is a column of calm, sinking air called the "eye." To be labeled a hurricane, the storm must carry sustained winds of at least 74 miles per hour. / Hurricanes give humans earlier warning than most natural disasters. Meteorologists spot them over the ocean before they head toward land, then broadcast a series of watches and warnings. But predicting a storm's path can be tricky: Cyclones can make surprising turns and have even been known to double back on themselves. / Landfall always weakens a hurricane rapidly, as its power source—warm ocean water—disappears. Thus coastal areas are the most vulnerable to damage. However, that doesn't mean they become harmless: Katrina, a category 5 storm over the water, had been downgraded to a 3 before it decimated the Gulf Coast.

Hurricane Isabel's eye, seen from the International Space Station on September 15, 2003.

WATCHES AND WARNINGS

KEEP INFORMED during hurricane season by tuning in to your preferred media outlet for National Weather Service updates. A "hurricane watch" for your area is an official announcement that hurricane conditions are possible within 36 hours. Now is the time to gather your disaster supplies kit, pack for a possible evacuation, fuel your car, and bring in outdoor toys and furniture. If your windows don't have storm shutters, gather plywood, nails, and tools in case you need to board up your windows in a flash.

A "hurricane warning," on the other hand, is a much more certain alert that sustained winds of minimum hurricane speed (74 miles per hour) or higher are expected in 24 hours or less. Pack quickly if you haven't already, close your storm shutters or board your windows, and get ready to mobilize in case of an evacuation. Hurricane warnings indicate potential property damage from either wind or storm surge, so they may stay in effect if the ocean water remains dangerously high even after the winds have slowed.

Tropical depressions and storms—often precursors to full-blown hurricanes—are also monitored by a watch and warning system (see Chapter 9 for details). If a tropical storm watch or warning is in effect for your area, stay tuned: It may soon be upgraded to a hurricane.

HURRICANE RATINGS

IN ADDITION TO naming them, scientists label hurricanes according to their wind speed in order to prepare for possible damage at landfall. Each category also indicates storm surge—a heightened wall of ocean water that travels directly underneath the cyclone, threatening coastlines.

THE SAFFIR-SIMPSON HURRICANE SCALE

>>> **Category One:** Winds 74 to 95 miles per hour. Storm surge generally four to five feet above normal.
>>> **Category Two:** Winds 96 to 110 miles per hour. Storm surge generally six to eight feet above normal.
>>> **Category Three:** Winds 111 to 130 miles per hour. Storm surge generally 9 to 12 feet above normal.
>>> **Category Four:** Winds 131 to 155 miles per hour. Storm surge generally 13 to 18 feet above normal.
>>> **Category Five:** Winds greater than 155 miles per hour. Storm surge generally greater than 18 feet above normal.

EXPERT TIP At the center of the hurricane is a calm area called the eye. The most severe part of the hurricane strikes immediately before and after the eye, so don't be deceived by a brief period of calm.

American Red Cross

WHAT TO EXPECT DURING A HURRICANE

IN MANY LANGUAGES, the term for a tropical cyclone translates into "big wind." "Hurricane" itself stems centuries back to the Maya creator god Hurakan, whose breath blew land into existence from the waters, and who later destroyed men with a great storm and flood.

Wind and flood: The profound fury of these forces is still the hallmark of hurricanes today, with rain, lightning, and occasional tornadoes punctuating the experience. Yet you can weather minor cyclones from your home (provided local authorities haven't given evacuation orders).

Don't waste a minute if a hurricane is headed your way. Spend the hours before landfall gathering supplies, staying tuned to the media, and following protocol through the watches and warnings phases (see previous page). No matter the storm category, you are in for a wild ride. Now is also the time to check on any neighbors—especially those living alone—who may be unable to batten down their own hatches. Help them prepare their house too, or invite them over to yours, being certain they bring essential items such as medicines with them.

IF YOU ARE HOME WHEN A HURRICANE HITS

>>> Get out your disaster supplies kit.
>>> Set refrigerator to maximum cool and keep the door closed.
>>> Fill all of your bathtubs and sinks with clean, cold water in case the water supply becomes tainted.
>>> Turn off utilities if told to do so; turn off propane tanks; unplug appliances.
>>> Close all your interior doors. Brace all exterior doors.
>>> Take shelter in an interior room, such as a closet or hallway. Stay away from windows, even if shuttered.

essentials

BRACING YOUR HOUSE FOR THE STORM

Reinforced homes sustain far less damage than others. Take these steps today to maximize your safety and minimize the poststorm bill:

CHECK the underside of your roof in your attic. It should be securely braced to the frame of the house. If necessary, add bracing or hurricane straps, which bind roof beams to the main frame. Some local governments require hurricane straps for all roofs.

CHECK your windows. Install shutters or gather plywood sheets to make your own.

CHECK your exterior doors. Most door bolts are not strong enough to withstand hurricane winds. Bolt-reinforcing kits, available at hardware stores, can provide the strength needed for a door to stay in place.

CHECK your garage door. Double-wide doors can easily collapse when high winds blow, allowing the wind to enter the home and blow out other doors and windows. You may need to retrofit yours with extra horizontal support beams and stronger hinges.

WAIT FOR ALL CLEAR

WHEN THE BIG WINDS have died, you will be anxious to return home. This is the time to tap some of your inner resources: calm and patience. Authorities will give you the "all clear" so you can return to your neighborhood as soon as possible. That could be hours or days, depending on the storm's severity.

If you weathered the storm from home, first check all people for injuries and administer first aid as necessary. Check Chapter 9 for instructions on surviving in the home for an extended time without power or water.

Whether you evacuated or not, your house now needs some attention. Follow the steps below, using extreme care to avoid injury.

AFTER THE STORM

>>> Stay tuned to the media for instructions and information once the storm has ended. Do not return home until officials say it is safe to do so.
>>> When you return, wear protective clothing and sturdy shoes.
>>> Inspect your home, looking for: structural damage, gas leaks, fire hazards.
>>> Examine any animals who stayed home, looking for injury and signs of shock.
>>> Clean up spills immediately.
>>> Watch for loose plaster and falling ceilings.
>>> Photograph and write down details of all damage.
>>> Use flashlights in the dark; do not use candles.
>>> If the natural gas is off, arrange for a professional to come and turn it back on.

IF STRANDED IN YOUR CAR

In an evacuation you may face lightning, tornadoes, and floods as well as violent rain and winds. If you find yourself stuck, follow this protocol to maximize your safety and minimize the poststorm bill:

MOVE car to the high ground if possible to avoid floods.

PARK out of falling range of tall trees.

TURN off engine, and turn on your hazard lights so that you can be seen by other motorists or potential rescuers.

TIE a brightly colored rag to your car antenna, if it is safe for you to momentarily get out of your car.

CALL 911. Give the dispatcher your name, location, and the weather conditions.

STAY in your car.

KEEP windows closed.

CHECK for injuries and administer first aid.

KEEP all people hydrated and fed.

AVOID metal objects in the car, which can conduct lightning.

STAY TUNED to your emergency radio.

IF YOU MUST use car radio, conserve your car battery by checking only occasionally.

REMAIN CALM. Help will come.

TORNADOES

The fastest winds on Earth are to be found only within the maelstrom of a tornado. Tornadoes occur when a low-lying layer of warm, moist air blows headlong into a higher cold front coming from the opposite direction. These unstable conditions can lead to a spinning effect, forming a column of viciously spiraling air that, at touchdown, sucks debris into its vortex. / Twisters most often form beneath a supercell thunderstorm—true tornadoes touch ground and cloud simultaneously. In addition to the flying debris that accounts for most tornado deaths, lightning and flash flooding can have fatal consequences. / The United States bears the brunt of global tornado violence each year, with an average of 1,000 events annually. The centrally located "Tornado Alley" states from Texas to South Dakota see most of these, but tornadoes have been recorded in every state. / Tornado prediction has improved immensely in recent years. Although funnels can form in seconds, the National Weather Service can keep you aware of when tornado conditions are likely. This section's survival advice is really quite simple: Find cover, the deeper the better.

You may hear the roar of a tornado long before you see it; take cover underground.

KNOW YOUR TWISTER FACTS

Sorting tornado fact from folklore can be a tricky business, yet accurate knowledge of the storms could save your life.

FOLKLORE: The land falls eerily silent just before a twister.

FACT: The storms more often cause a distant roar, like persistent thunder. Skies may appear a dark greenish color in tornado conditions. Large, pinging hailstones can also be a tornado precursor.

FOLKLORE: The extreme low pressure at a twister's center can cause a closed house to explode. You should crack open windows to prevent an explosion.

FACT: Doing this would actually invite the storm in, not protect your house.

FOLKLORE: Tornadoes are phenomena of the Midwestern and Great Plains states.

FACT: Any place can suffer a tornado, including wet areas such as lakes and rivers.

FOLKLORE: Tornadoes are always visible.

FACT: Many are hidden by the clouds of thunderstorms or hurricanes.

FOLKLORE: If caught on the road during a tornado, drive away from the storm at a right angle.

FACT: That may send you into the path of a sister twister. If the tornado is very close, abandon your car for the nearest shelter.

WATCHES AND WARNINGS

A "TORNADO WATCH" means that a tornado is possible in your area and local storm spotters have been alerted. Stay tuned to your preferred media outlet for updates. Watch for observable weather changes.

A "tornado warning," on the other hand, means a twister has been sighted and may be headed for your area. You may hear the warning from many sources, such as city sirens and the Digital Emergency Alert System. Get to safety immediately.

CLASSES OF TORNADO

IN 1971 meteorologists Theodore Fujita and Allen Pearson developed a scale for estimating twister wind speed based on the damage caused by each storm. Called the Fujita Scale, it was overhauled in 2007, with labels of EF1 to EF5, measuring least- to most-intense winds.

ADDITIONAL NATIONAL WEATHER SERVICE TORNADO CATEGORIES

>>> **Weak tornadoes (69%):** winds under 110 miles per hour, last an average of five to ten minutes, and account for about three percent of all tornado deaths.
>>> **Strong tornadoes (29%):** winds 110–205 miles per hour, may last 20 minutes or more, and account for 27 percent of all tornado deaths.
>>> **Violent tornadoes (2%):** winds exceeding 205 miles per hour, can last more than an hour, and account for 70 percent of all tornado deaths.

PREPARE A SAFE ROOM

DEEP, DEEP COVER is the secret to tornado survival. Basements make the ideal shelter, but many homes don't have one. Instead, you should pick a windowless, central room on the lowest floor of your home. This can be an interior closet, bathroom, or hallway.

You can also construct a fortified safe room, which can be sturdier than a closet for weathering high winds. FEMA brochure 320, "Taking Shelter from the Storm," provides detailed instructions about measuring and building your safe room. These rooms are well anchored to the floor, yet separate from any load-bearing walls, so they can stand independent of the rest of the house.

A few types of abode deserve special consideration. If you live in a high-rise, choose a center hallway on your floor in case you don't have time to get to the lobby. If you live in a mobile home, you will need to leave it for safety. Identify the closest sturdy building, and go there the minute a warning or siren sounds.

Although tornadoes themselves can last only seconds, tornado warnings may go on for hours. So keep your safe room to a place your family won't mind huddling in for a bit. It should be as clutter free as possible (and remember, no heavy objects on high shelves). Maintain a small disaster supplies kit and nonperishable food stash in it, if not all your emergency supplies. Make sure your whole family knows where to head.

essentials

PREPARE YOUR PROPERTY

Almost all tornado fatalities are caused by flying debris. Minimize your risk by ensuring that your house—and the objects in it—meet these standards.

STRENGTHEN your garage door.

KEEP TREES and shrubs trim; remove weak branches regularly.

REMOVE any debris or loose items in your yard.

CHECK that all of the walls of your home are bolted to the foundations, especially in rooms or dividing walls that have been added to the home after initial construction.

SECURE your roof to walls with bracing or hurricane straps.

INSTALL storm shutters on all windows.

STRAP your water heater and other large appliances to the wall.

PLACE BEDS and chairs away from glass panes such as windows, mirrors, pictures.

MOVE large or heavy items to low shelves.

BOLT large furniture to the wall.

STORE hazardous materials in a well ventilated area away from emergency and food supplies.

IF POSSIBLE, park your car in a garage.

how to

SURVIVE A TORNADO

1. Avoid driving or being outdoors when a watch or warning is in effect. If you are caught outside and see one approaching and there are no buildings nearby, pull over and leave your car immediately. It will only be a danger to you.

2. Find a ditch away from water sources, bridges, and overpasses, and lie in as flat a position as possible.

3. Cover your head and neck with your arms.

4. If water from a flash flood starts pouring into your ditch, get to higher ground as quickly as possible. If the only available higher ground is a tree, climb it. You cannot outswim or outrun a flash flood.

AFTER THE TORNADO

TORNADOES ARE unpredictable, often skipping one house while flattening its neighbors, or decimating a living room without touching the kitchen. Chances are good you will emerge from a tornado to find your walls still standing. When the fury has passed, listen to your preferred media outlet for an all-clear before leaving your shelter.

Wear protective clothing and sturdy shoes when you do return home. As you inspect your home for damage (see list), use extreme caution. If the power is out, carry a flashlight instead of candles. Clean up any spills as you go. Examine your pets for signs of injury and shock. Photograph

TORNADO DRILLS

TORNADOES TEND to be so quick that evacuations are rare, unless the storms hit as part of a large hurricane. If you live in a high-risk area, you'll need to not only prepare, but also make sure you can react quickly and efficiently. In addition to preparing the safe room in your home (see previous page), it is important to know the safe rooms for all buildings in which your family spends time, such as offices, church, libraries, athletic clubs, shopping malls, and school.

Next, practice specific tornado drills to increase the speed with which you can get to safety. If you have children, time your drills to make them fun. Practice what to do if you can't get to a safe room: drop underneath a heavy piece of furniture such as a table. Hold on to the table with one hand, while covering your neck and head with the other. This position will protect you best from flying objects.

and record details of all damage for insurance purposes. If you have neighbors who are elderly or live alone, volunteer to do the same for their homes.

CHECKING FOR DAMAGE

>>> Examine walls closely for structural damage.
>>> Check roof and foundation.
>>> Check water pipes for cracks.
>>> Check gas lines for leaks.
>>> Check wiring for fire hazards.
>>> Watch for loose plaster and falling ceilings.
>>> If the natural gas supply is off, arrange for a professional to turn it back on.

FLOOD

Flooding can occur on its own, or accompany many different types of natural disasters. Rivers overwhelmed by rain wash out waterfront property. Slow-moving hurricanes trigger flash floods and storm surges, both of which hurtle a wall of killer debris before them. Levees and dams burst in earthquakes or heavy storms, submerging entire neighborhoods or towns. / In fact, floods are among the deadliest and costliest natural disasters. They claim about 140 U.S. lives each year, primarily due to in-car drownings. Damages to roads and structures average $6 billion annually. Because of this, floods are the only hazard to be covered by federal insurance: FEMA's National Flood Insurance Program. / Flooding threatens all regions of the United States, high and low—even the smallest waterways are susceptible. Most floods in the West are triggered by snowmelt and rainstorms, while in the East, hurricanes and thunderstorms are the primary culprits. Regardless, when a deluge is rushing your way, you can be certain of a few things: The water will be contaminated. It will vanquish any car. And when it reaches your front door, it won't knock first.

Flooding often results from hurricanes, as experienced by residents of Baccaral, Mexico.

MAKE A FLOOD PLAN

BECAUSE FLOODS can hit anywhere, every family should make advance preparations for a deluge. See page 304 for how to draw up a general disaster and evacuation plan. Teach your family about survival techniques when stranded in water (details on following pages).

In your plan, include a paragraph about which household items should be moved to upper floors before a flood. These will include large appliances and valuable furniture. Store them in the highest place possible, away from windows, wrapped in burlap or blankets. If you have enough warning, you might also consider a storage unit out of harm's way.

Then make a sandbagging plan. Sandbag walls, which absorb incoming water, can be a life—and property—saver. Decide who will build your wall and where you will obtain supplies (even better, store these in your basement or garage at all times). A 1-foot-high, 20-foot-long wall of 100 sandbags will take two people about an hour to construct.

PREPARING YOUR HOME

>>> **If you live in a floodplain, reinforce your home now to keep your property as high and dry as possible.**
>>> **Use waterproofing compounds to seal the walls of your lowest floors, especially the basement, where most flooding occurs.**
>>> **Be sure your sewer drains have check valves, to keep floodwater from coming into your house through sinks and tubs.**
>>> **Raise your water heater, furnace, and electricity panel above floor level.**
>>> **Build physical barriers around your house such as levees and flood walls to keep waters at bay.**

Include instructions about minor flooding that won't lead to evacuation. In these instances, plan to sanitize bathtubs and sinks, then fill them with clean water in case the water supply is later contaminated. Finally, turn off all utilities (except natural gas) and secure outdoor items before heading to the highest level of your home.

WATCHES AND WARNINGS

FLOODS AND FLASH FLOODS are different beasts, so it is important to know the alert systems for both. A flood watch means flooding is possible in your area within the next day. Tune in to your preferred media outlet for National Weather Service updates, fuel your vehicle, and begin home preparations. A flood warning means flooding is happening or imminent; stay tuned and prep for a speedy evacuation.

In the event of a flash flood watch, which means that flash flooding is possible in your area within the next day, get ready to move to higher ground quickly. A flash flood can develop in just minutes, so a warning means that it is imminent or has already begun—move to higher ground on foot immediately.

More than half of deaths resulting from floods occur when people are trapped in vehicles.

DRIVING IN A FLOOD

IF YOU RECEIVE ORDERS to evacuate, go immediately. You probably won't need to drive far to higher ground, but every inch of water on the roads is an increased threat to your life.

Road travel during a flooding event calls for extreme caution. Most flood deaths occur while people are in their cars, which can be swept away by just two feet of water. Never drive onto a flooded road. In addition to the potential for causing drowning, water camouflages road damage and downed power lines, making accidents and electrocution common causes of flood deaths. Report downed powerlines.

Follow marked routes and respect all street barricades. If you face a flooded road, make a U-turn and retreat. If your car stalls or is suddenly surrounded by rising water, immediately abandon your vehicle. Hike to higher ground.

When you do reach safety in your car, park far away from all streams and gullies. After the flood have your car inspected for water damage. A mechanic should deem it safe before you use it regularly again.

On foot, remember that flooding is often a multimedia weather event—tornadoes, hurricane winds, and lightning may face you outside. You may need to measure the risk of each in severe weather. Familiarize yourself with the best strategies for facing each of these hazards so you can use a combination of them when choosing the safest place to stop.

CARS IN FLOODS

>>> Flooding is the number one weather killer in the United States.
>>> More than 50 percent of flood deaths occur inside vehicles.
>>> A mere six-inch flood can cause a car to hydroplane.
>>> A foot of water can flood a car.
>>> Two feet of water can wash away an SUV.

essentials

RETURNING HOME AFTER A FLOOD

Water-damaged homes require special caution when you reenter. Floods not only damage structures, they also leave behind a layer of filth that is highly hazardous.

ONLY return to inspect your home after local authorities give the OK.

WEAR sturdy shoes and clothing.

BEFORE entering, turn off outside gas lines.

OPEN all windows (there may be gas fumes).

HAVE an electrician examine all wiring.

HAVE a serviceman inspect and repair your septic tank, cesspool, pit, or leaching system.

HAVE an engineer or mechanic check for structural damage.

COVER broken windows or holes in the roof.

TOSS food touched by floodwater.

BOIL all drinking and cooking water for ten minutes until authorities clear your supply.

DISINFECT items that touched flood water.

DOCUMENT and photograph all damage.

IN A FLOODED BUILDING

IF YOU FIND YOURSELF trapped inside with rising waters, follow these steps to safer ground. Remember to call 911, but don't panic if all lines are busy. Authorities know your area is flooding and a rescue crew will be there soon.

FINDING SHELTER INSIDE

>>> Avoid touching floodwaters, which may be tainted by sewage or hazardous chemicals.
>>> Disconnect electric appliances only if you are dry, never if you or the floor are wet.
>>> Collect drinking water.
>>> Turn off gas and water.
>>> Grab warm clothing and first aid kit.
>>> Collect flashlights, signaling devices, emergency radio.
>>> Move to the highest point of your house.
>>> Wait for help.
>>> Do not try to swim to safety.

EXPERT TIP Floods usually result from heavy or prolonged rain, rapidly melting snow, or dam breakage. Flash floods can occur with little to no warning and are dangerous because of their swift currents and unpredictable nature.

Girl Scouts.

WILDFIRES

Fire is a natural way of cleansing a forest. Fires weed out underbrush, insect overgrowths, and microorganisms that harm flora. Ash returns vital nutrients to the soil. Although they clean by destruction, wildfires restore balance to the forest ecosystem. When they aren't overmanaged, that is. / Until recent decades, the United States squelched all wildfires as quickly as possible. Did this save lives initially? Yes. But it also led to forest overgrowth, which has in turn led to hotter and larger blazes—a primary reason wildfires have claimed headlines so often in recent years. / In 2004 alone, wildfires burned more than eight million acres across the country. These blazing infernos wreak far more havoc than their cousins of a century ago. Blackening large swaths of land, today's fires increase the risk of flooding, landslides, and debris flow. Smoke wafts far from the flames, polluting the air for miles around. / Today a program of controlled burns is attempting to return our woodlands to their pre–20th-century condition. The aim is to prevent cataclysmic fires that destroy everything in their wake.

After fires, forests can be salvage-logged for usable wood like this, near Burney, California.

EVACUATING IN A WILDFIRE

IF A WILDFIRE threatens your home, you will most likely have time to evacuate before it reaches you. Follow the guidelines in Chapter 9, with the additions below.

Leave a light on in every room to make your house more visible in the smoke. Lock valuables in your garage, then leave your front door unlocked in case firefighters need to gain swift entry. Check the FEMA and U.S. Forest Service websites for more details about protecting your home by keeping it "lean, clean, and green."

how to

MAKE A FIREBREAK

A trail cleared of any fuel can stop a blaze in its tracks. If you cannot leave your property when a wildfire approaches, constructing a firebreak is a good last resort for protection.

1 Gather as many able-bodied workers and strong tools as possible.

2 Identify a stretch of land between your house and the fire—preferably an area without overhanging trees, which can drop burning branches on the house side.

3 Mark a straight strip at least three feet wide.

4 Clear it of all vegetation—including roots—and any other flammable material.

5 Stay alert for approaching flames. Stop digging and escape if necessary.

On the road, drive carefully and follow premarked routes. If you become stranded in your car, you can survive a wildfire within its shelter. Don't try to escape the fire on foot.

SURVIVING A WILDFIRE IN A CAR

>>> **Roll up windows and close air vents.**
>>> **If you can drive, proceed slowly.**
>>> **Don't drive through heavy smoke.**
>>> **Park away from vegetation if you stop.**
>>> **Turn engine off, leave headlights on.**
>>> **Hit the floor and cover yourself with a blanket or jacket.**
>>> **Remain calm, even in increasing heat.**
>>> **Stay in the car until help comes or until the fire passes.**

FACING A FIRE ON FOOT

REMOVE YOUR PACK and synthetic fabrics, and abandon all camping fuel. Cover yourself with a dry cotton or wool blanket. Then determine your strategy.

You may be able to walk around a small fire. Otherwise, plan to go to ground: Get to the sparsest place possible for safety. Avoid gullies and canyons, which can feed flames. Quickly clear it of any brush. Lie facedown, cover your neck and face with clothing or dirt, and remain still and calm until the fire passes.

As a last resort, you can attempt to go through the fire. The idea is to move so quickly that the flames don't have time to ignite you.

BLIZZARDS

Snow, sleet, and freezing rain coat winter days with peril. When wind adds turmoil to a winter moisture system, blizzard conditions blow in. Technically, a blizzard refers to at least three hours of heavy snow and low visibility in minimum 35-mile-per-hour winds. / How do winter storms form? Three key components work together: cold, moisture, and what's known as lift. First, freezing temperatures are present, either in the cloud layer or near the ground. Second, water evaporating off lakes and oceans provides fuel for the system. Add a little lift from various forces that make moist air rise and voilà, heavy storm clouds threaten the skies. / A fourth factor—wind—is what transforms a storm into a blizzard. These are the most dangerous of all winter storms, capable of dumping many feet of snow in one spot and knocking out power for days. If accumulation is heavy, avalanches threaten. And if a quick thaw follows a spring blizzard, the snow-melt can cause serious flooding. / The best winter survival technique is to stay off the roads whenever the weather threatens. About 70 percent of winter-storm deaths are due to vehicular accidents. Another quarter involve people who die from hypothermia when stranded on foot or in a car. Other winter-storm killers include house fires from space heaters, carbon monoxide poisoning, and frostbite.

Remember when driving in snow: Even if your car has four-wheel-drive, others may not.

WATCHES AND WARNINGS

Winter precipitation can present multiple hazards, from freezing winds to icy roads.

A frost/freeze warning simply indicates that temperatures below 32°F are expected in your area. If precipitation is also forecast, the National Weather Service will issue a winter storm watch—expect freezing rain, sleet, or snow to hit your area. Check the media for more information, fill your car's gas tank, and prepare to hunker down.

If a storm is imminent or has begun, NWS will issue a winter storm warning. The granddaddy of these is the blizzard warning, which means your specific area is facing at least three hours of a violent snowstorm in sustained winds 35 miles per hour or greater.

VENTURING INTO THE STORM

DRESS IN WARM LAYERS and wear insulated boots, hat, and gloves. While still inside, warm your muscles by exercising and stretching for a few minutes. When you do begin shoveling, avoid overexertion.

Cover your mouth when outside to protect your lungs from subfreezing air. Talk as little as possible. As soon as your clothing becomes wet, change into dry layers.

If hypothermia presents, move the victim to a warm location, strip off wet clothing, and wrap in dry, warm fabrics. Warm the core of the body first—giving warm drinks—and seek medical help. If frostbite presents, life and limb are at stake. Get medical help immediately.

essentials

WEATHERING A BLIZZARD FROM HOME

If your cozy fireside evening stretches into days stranded inside, follow these steps until the melee passes. See Chapter 9 for emergency supplies to keep on hand.

STAY tuned to your preferred media outlet.

CONSERVE fuel by shutting off heat and doors to unused rooms.

WATCH fireplace and space heater use; both increase the risk of household fires.

IF USING kerosene heaters, keep fresh air circulating to minimize toxic fumes.

GATHER blankets and wrap up.

WEAR multiple layers of clothing.

WEAR hats and mittens, even inside.

USE flashlights, not candles, for light.

KEEP yourself well fed and hydrated.

KEEP a few faucets on a light drip of warm water to prevent freezing pipes.

IF STRANDED IN YOUR CAR

First, never drive in winter weather without a car stash of lock deicer, blankets, shovel, extra washer fluid, snacks, drink, and first aid kit. If you must wait out a storm in your vehicle, follow these steps:

PULL to the side of the road.

TURN on hazard lights and tie a colorful rag to the radio antenna.

SET lit flares in the most visible nearby spot.

REMAIN in your car.

DRINK fluids.

STAY warm by running the engine and heat for 10 minutes each hour.

KEEP a downwind window cracked and the exhaust pipe clear to prevent carbon monoxide fumes from filling the car.

HUDDLE with other passengers under blankets.

EXERCISE moderately to maintain warmth; do not overexert yourself.

SLEEP in shifts. One person should keep watch for rescue at all times.

CONSERVE battery power.

USE an interior light at night so rescue crews can see you.

ONCE the blizzard passes, if you are sure help won't find you, search for help on foot.

SIGNALING FOR RESCUE

IF YOU CAN'T TELEPHONE for help when stranded, you'll need to use old-fashioned distress signals. The standard U.S. distress signal is a repetition of any three long blasts—whistle blows, horn honks, headlight flashes. Make the three of equal length and repeat every few minutes. Use a whistle if you have one.

A message in the snow can be another excellent distress signal. Arrange branches or other objects on the ground to spell "SOS" or "HELP." If no materials are available, stomp the letters with your feet.

GET YOUR CAR OUT OF A SNOWDRIFT

1. Turn the steering wheel from side to side to release snow from the tires.

2. Rock your car by alternating between drive and reverse. Step on the gas when in drive. Avoid spinning the wheels, which may dig you in deeper.

3. Get out and use a shovel to clear more snow and debris.

4. For traction, sprinkle gravel or sand as close to the tires as possible.

5. With wheels pointed straight ahead, lightly step on the gas and ease forward. If helpers are pushing, have them on the sides toward the rear—never directly behind.

SIGNS OF HYPOTHERMIA

>>> Shivering
>>> Memory loss, incoherence
>>> Slurred speech
>>> Exhaustion
>>> Signs of frostbite
>>> Loss of feeling in extremities, including nose and earlobes
>>> Pale skin in extremities

BLIZZARD IN THE BACKCOUNTRY

AS A RULE, do not try to hike to safety—you are more likely to be found if you remain on the road with your car if you are on a paved road or if someone knows where you've gone. Stay with your car and if you are with others, huddle for warmth. Signal for help with a bright-colored object hung outside car and with an SOS signal (see previous pages). If you hear a plane approaching, use one of the car's mirrors to signal to it (see Chapter 2). Staying inside the car will keep as much heat as possible inside and will minimize the chance of suffering hypothermia.

EXPERT TIP If you are stranded, turn on the engine for brief periods to provide heat, leaving a window slightly open to avoid poisoning from fumes. Make sure the exhaust pipe is clear of snow. Do not remain in one position.

American Red Cross

LIGHTNING

Lightning strikes U.S. soil 30 million times a year at 100 million volts and temperatures up to 50,000°F. / Lightning shows itself as a luminous streak of electricity raging through the conduit between negatively charged particles in clouds and positively charged particles on the ground. A strike has a diameter of just one to two inches yet can shoot for miles through the skies. Its intense energy heats the surrounding air, causing a rapid expansion of gases that then boom in a thunderclap. / Lightning maintains the electrical balance between Earth and the atmosphere, a relationship scientists believe would disappear in minutes without thunderstorms. Ozone is a byproduct of this energy exchange, adding the precious protective gas to our atmosphere. Lightning also helps dissolve nitrogen in water, turning the necessary plant nutrient into a form that roots can absorb. / As beneficial as it is, such powerful energy is also extremely dangerous. Strikes are the second-worst weather killer in the United States, after floods. They claim about one hundred lives a year. We discuss other thunderstorm hazards such as tornadoes elsewhere in the chapter, so this section focuses on a key element of storm survival: How to avoid getting struck by lightning.

Avoid becoming a lightning rod, as with this high-rise in Panama City, Panama.

essentials

AVOIDING LIGHTNING OUTDOORS

Forget about staying dry. Just focus on dodging a strike.

BEST option: Get in your car, shut every possible crack, and avoid touching metal parts.

IF YOU must stay outside, find an open, low space on solid ground, avoiding standing water if possible.

MAKE yourself a small target by crouching on your toes, hands covering your ears, head between your knees.

TOUCH the ground as little as possible—it's conductive. Do not lie flat.

DON'T shelter under partially enclosed structures like sheds and carports.

STEER clear of all electrical fences and poles.

IF IN WOODS with no clearing, position yourself under the shortest trees you can find.

AVOID tall or isolated trees.

REMOVE any climbing ropes or electrical devices from your body.

SPACE yourself at least 15 feet from your companions.

how to

TREAT A LIGHTNING-STRIKE VICTIM

After lightning strikes a companion, you can safely touch him or her without being shocked yourself. Most victims who receive quick medical care survive, so call EMS or 911 immediately. Then check for:

1. Pulse. If none, administer CPR (see Appendix).

2. Respiration. If none, administer rescue breathing.

3. Burns at the bolt's entrance and exit sites. Treat as severe burns: Remove clothing only if it comes off easily, then apply a dry, sterile, nonadhesive dressing (no cotton). Avoid all liquids and creams.

4. Fractures and other trauma. Do not move victim if you suspect a spinal cord injury.

5. Signs of shock. If moving is OK, lay victim flat, feet elevated about a foot, and cover with a coat or blanket. Stay with victim until paramedics arrive.

EXPERT TIP The 30/30 Rule is the best general rule to follow to avoid lightning strikes. If, after seeing lightning, you can't count to 30 before hearing the thunder, go indoors. Stay indoors for 30 minutes after hearing the last clap of thunder.

American
Red Cross

EARTHQUAKES

On land and sea, the top layer of Earth's crust consists of many discrete tectonic plates. These drift very slowly over the planet's hot, liquefied interior. / When tectonic plates push or pull against each other, friction places stress at the edges where plates touch, called fault lines. The stresses build up incrementally over millions of years, with mounting pressure on the rocks holding these lines together. Eventually, immense pressure causes the fault to give way, in the violent rolling and shaking of a quake. / Sometimes two slide past one another along what's called a transform fault. When two plates converge, the colder, more solid one will subduct beneath the other, forming continental ridges. Sometimes plates diverge, stretching a low rift valley between them that will eventually fill with water and become a sea. / Although the planet experiences a half-million earthquakes a year, only about a hundred cause damage. Most earthquake fatalities stem from flying debris and structural failures, with fires and tsunamis following as secondary killers. By bracing your home and practicing earthquake drills, you can greatly increase your chance of survival.

Earthquakes can occur anywhere, as a result of geologic stresses building over years.

FORECAST: SHAKY GROUND

ALTHOUGH THERE IS NO WAY of accurately predicting a quake's date and time, researchers can pinpoint regions at risk for large temblors. In recent decades the U.S. Geological Survey has rolled out an earthquake warning system.

Often small tectonic shifts called foreshocks precede a big one, indicating that a fault is under stress. Scientists monitor foreshocks and alert the public to high-risk zones.

Another prediction tool is the calculation of quake intervals for a given region. Many faults shift on a semiregular schedule. Major quakes can also erupt from previously unknown faults, such as California's Northridge quake in 1994.

Some areas are quite prone to earthquakes. If you live near the Pacific Ring of Fire, you are at extremely high risk. Make earthquake preparedness your top disaster-plan priority. Most other U.S. regions carry a moderate risk, especially Mississippi Valley states such as Missouri that sit atop the New Madrid seismic zone, a fault system responsible for three severe quakes in 1811-12. Contact your local USGS office to learn the specific risk for your area.

EXPERT TIP If you are inside, immediately get away from windows. Get under something sturdy, such as a table, and hold onto it, or get inside a corner of a building. If you are outside, Head toward an open space, avoiding structures and soft-unstable soils.

American Red Cross

MAKE AN EARTHQUAKE DISASTER PLAN

WHEN CREATING your family disaster plan, be sure to include special provisions for temblors. Tour your house with your family and, in each room, identify the safest spot to drop, cover, and hold on. This should be a place under heavy furniture, in a load-bearing doorway, or against an inside wall away from any glass.

Although you won't evacuate before an earthquake, severely damaged structures may require you to leave afterward. Remind your family of your out-of-town contact person and meeting place. Teach your children that if a quake hits outside, the safest place to stay is on solid ground away from posts, trees, power lines, bridges, and highway overpasses.

Finally, stage regular earthquake drills. Quakes hit so suddenly that shock can paralyze you until it's too late to reach a doorway. Practice so that everyone's reflex is to drop, cover, and hold on.

essentials

BRACE YOUR HOME

In quake survival, there is no substitute for preparation—and no excuse for a hazard-filled home when the quake hits.

HAVE AN INSPECTOR check for structural problems (especially if a quake has hit since the last inspection).

FIX deep cracks in walls, ceilings, and foundations.

SECURE all shelves to the walls.

BOLT unstable or tall furniture such as bookcases to walls.

REINFORCE ceiling lights with bracings.

STAMP OUT fire risks by repairing any faulty wiring or gas leaks.

STRAP the water heater to the wall and, if not in a high-risk flood zone, bolt it to the floor.

KEEP the walls above beds and couches clear of heavy hangings.

MOVE heavy items to low shelves.

STORE breakables on low shelves in latched cabinets.

WHAT TO DO INSIDE

IF YOU ARE INSIDE when the trembling begins, it's time for those reflexes to kick in. Drop, take cover under the nearest safe place, and hold on. If your cover slides across the floor, slide with it. It is important to stay underneath it.

If you are in bed, stay there and cover your head with a pillow. Scoot to the farthest spot from windows and light fixtures. Hold on to the mattress.

It may be close to a minute before the ground quiets. The shaking often triggers automated systems such as sprinklers and smoke alarms: Regardless, stay where you are. Remain calm.

AVOID

>>> **Moving to a different location mid-quake**
>>> **Elevators**
>>> **Outside doors and walls**
>>> **Windows**
>>> **Wall hangings**
>>> **Ceiling lights**

EXPERT TIP Drop, cover, and hold on! Move only a few steps to a nearby safe place. Stay indoors until the shaking stops and you're sure it's safe to exit. Stay away from windows.

American Red Cross

WHAT TO DO OUTSIDE

ONLY IN BAD MOVIES do fissures swallow unsuspecting hikers. In fact, quaking ground very rarely kills people. So if the earth moves under your feet, resist the urge to run for cover as you would in a thunderstorm or hurricane.

Instead, move into the open, as far from any other objects as possible. Remain there until the shaking stops and debris has settled.

If you are in the mountains or near a cliff of any kind, watch for falling rocks and landslides. And if you are at the beach, run to higher ground or to a sturdy sheltered place several hundred yards away from the shoreline.

AVOID

>>> **All nearby structures**
>>> **Trees**
>>> **Streetlights**
>>> **Power lines**

AFTER A QUAKE

AFTERSHOCKS AND TSUNAMIS frequently compound the damage caused by an initial temblor. So proceed with extra care as you take stock and clean up.

The first priority after a quake is to examine all companions for injury and shock, applying first aid and calling EMS or 911 if necessary. Then put on protective clothing and boots. If it is safe to go outside, check on your neighbors.

Use the phone only in emergencies, as the lines will be overloaded. But do tune in to your preferred media outlet for information on road closures, tsunami warnings, and local fires. You will also learn information about the magnitude and epicenter of the quake.

Examine your home with extreme caution. As you open each cupboard, brace yourself to catch falling objects. Clean up spills such as paint and bleach first. If you smell gas or fumes, leave immediately and call for help.

Structural aspects of your home that will need professional inspection include the foundation, chimney, walls, and roof. In addition, check for leaks in any of your utilities, especially the gas lines and electrical lines. Water pipes are often damaged underground and should be inspected as well.

IF CAUGHT UNDER DEBRIS

>>> **Immediately protect your lungs by covering your mouth with a cloth.**
>>> **Check yourself for heavy bleeding and control it.**
>>> **Send a distress signal by tapping on a nearby object (pipes are excellent).**
>>> **If you have a whistle, blow it.**
>>> **Conserve your energy: don't shout until you hear rescuers very close by.**
>>> **Hold still; kicking may make the cave-in worse.**
>>> **Find a light source if possible (no matches).**

VOLCANOES

Created in Earth's outer core and rising through the mantle, magma pools beneath the crust in places called hot spots. When pressure pushes the magma through the crust, a volcanic eruption occurs. / Volcanoes are actually the result, rather than cause, of eruptions. Shield volcanoes such as Hawaii's Mauna Loa form when mafic lava gently oozes from a vent, creating layer upon layer of gently sloping igneous rock. These volcanoes tend to erupt gently and most often form under water. Cinder cones are small, relatively short-lived products of a more viscous lava—felsic—and form when magma erupts onto dry land. / Most of the world's famous volcanoes are composites, made from both mafic and felsic lava. These giants blast an array of deadly burning matter from their vents: lava, toxic gas, ash, and a molten debris soup known as pyroclastic flow. Each phenomenon can kill those caught in its path. / Luckily, volcanoes usually give ample warning before blowing their tops. Scientists monitor geothermal activity and issue warnings based on the likelihood of an eruption. If you live near active or dormant volcanoes—in Hawaii or anywhere in the Pacific Northwest—volcano preparedness should be a keystone of your disaster-planning process.

WATCHES AND WARNINGS

THE U.S. GEOLOGICAL SURVEY has developed a very specific alert system for geothermal hazards. Citizens who live within range of a volcanic region should take note of the best channels for receiving public messages about volcanic activity.

Hot gasses glow red above Kilauea, a volcano in Hawaii Volcanoes National Park, Hawaii.

PREPARING FOR AN ERUPTION

BECAUSE PEOPLE most often can leave the danger zone before a volcanic eruption, your disaster plan should focus on evacuation. Remind your family of contact numbers and out-of-town meeting places in case of separation during the vent. Review mudflow and landslide safety. Stock goggles and breathing masks in your disaster supplies kit.

If you live very close to an active or dormant volcano, your neighborhood may have "volcano evacuation route" signs posted at all times. Familiarize yourself with the signs and plan your route now. Schools in volcanic zones have drills and procedures in place for getting children to you safely. Make sure to understand the system.

In the unlikely event that you are stuck inside during an eruption, you will want to keep your indoor air breathable. Seal off your house as thoroughly as possible. Bring in all animals. Park your vehicles in a garage or barn. Then close all vents, windows, and doors, blocking cracks with thick blankets to keep outside air from coming in.

If you are outside during an eruption, seek shelter immediately.

U.S. GEOLOGICAL SURVEY VOLCANO STATUS

>>> **Normal:** Typical background activity of a volcano in a non-eruptive state. After a change from a higher level: Volcanic activity considered to have ceased, and volcano reverted to its normal, non-eruptive state.
>>> **Advisory:** Elevated unrest above known background activity. After a change from a higher level: Volcanic activity has decreased significantly but continues to be closely monitored for possible renewed increase.
>>> **Watch:** Heightened/escalating unrest with increased potential for eruptive activity (timeframe variable) or a minor eruption under way that poses limited hazards.
>>> **Warning:** Highly hazardous eruption under way or imminent.

EVACUATING DURING AN ERUPTION

If authorities issue an evacuation order, leave immediately, following the instructions earlier in this chapter. In addition:

TAKE a pair of goggles for each family member.

TAKE a disposable breathing mask for each family member.

FOLLOW recommended evacuation routes, which experts have prepared to lead you to safe ground.

RESIST the urge to pull over and watch. It may be tempting—fatally so.

STAY away from rivers and low-lying valleys, if possible.

AVOID areas downwind of the volcano, where the air will be hazardous.

AVOID zones marked "restricted," even if they appear safe to the eye.

SECONDARY HAZARDS

ERUPTIONS CAN TRIGGER an array of life-threatening events that don't involve lava. Foremost among these are mudflows called lahars—forceful streams of snowmelt mixed with ash and soil—that can travel up to 50 miles an hour and reach distances of 50 miles from the eruption site. Lahars are sometimes likened to quickly flowing concrete and can pose greater danger than lava itself.

In addition, heavy rainfall on fresh volcanic deposits can cause flash flooding. Watch for rising streams, remain on higher ground if possible, and avoid bridges. Other secondary hazards include earthquakes, tsunamis, landslides, rockfalls, acid rain, and ashfall.

Of these, ashfall can be the most pervasive, affecting areas hundreds of miles from the volcano. To protect yourself from these tiny, glassy shards, always wear long sleeves, pants, and a face mask or damp handkerchief. Cover your eyes with glasses or goggles, and keep vehicle engines off (unless evacuating).

Some cultures consider volcanoes sacred, as these are in East Java, Indonesia.

AFTER A VOLCANO

STAY TUNED to your preferred media outlet—radio, television, or Internet—for updates on the water supply, air quality, and road conditions. Remain in your shelter until authorities say it is safe to go outside. At this point, the largest threat to your health will likely be ash in the air, which can damage your respiratory system.

Ash can hang in the air for days, weeks and, in extreme cases, months. In 1815, ash and gasses from a volcanic eruption in Tambora, Indonesia—the largest in recorded history—partially blocked the sun's rays, causing a year of global cooling.

If you must go outside, be aware of the potential hazards.

AVOID

>>> Volcanic ashfall areas.
>>> Driving; cars stir up ash, which can clog engines.
>>> Inhaling air. Cover your mouth and nose with an N-95 disposable respirator, also known as an "air purifying respirator," available at hardware stores.
>>> Exposing your eyes to the air. Wear goggles.
>>> Wearing contact lenses, which make your corneas vulnerable to scratching. Wear eyeglasses instead.
>>> Exposing skin to airborne debris. Wear long-sleeved shirts and pants to avoid irritation from contact with ash.

essentials

RECOVERING FROM AN ERUPTION

Act quickly to prevent further damage to your house.

AVOID contact with any amount of ash if you have a respiratory ailment.

CLOSE windows, doors, and vents to help keep ash and gases from entering.

TURN off heating and air-conditioning units.

INSPECT walls and foundation for possible structural damage.

CLEAR roofs of ashfall.

USE extreme caution when working on a roof.

REPLACE disposable furnace filters or clean permanent furnace filters.

PURCHASE water if your drinking water has ash in it, until your supply can be tested.

HELP a neighbor—especially an elderly person—who may require special assistance.

EXPERT TIP If caught in a rockfall, roll into a ball to protect your head and neck. A tight ball will provide the best protection for your body. Your head and neck are more easily injured than other parts of your body.

American Red Cross

Mount Maharira is the highest mountain in Ranomafana National Park, Madagascar. Our destination, as field biologists on a biodiversity exploration expedition, is to climb the bare and remote mountain for the first time. Herpetologist John Cadle and I have convinced village elders to guide

us, despite their misgivings about it being "haunted" and designated off-limits by their ancestors. We walk briskly and single file through the savannah toward the southwestern boundaries of Ranomafana National Park. Our lead is Rakoto, the king himself. His village elders accompany us: Ramy, Talata Pierre, and Loret. I wear the tropical biologist's uniform—green army pants and green shirt with black fishing boots, and red Kelty pack. David Haring, the photographer, my brother Ted Chapple, and Richard Randriapiona complete the team.

Baaroom. Is it a cannon? *BOOM. BAAROOM.* The depth and breadth and loudness of the boom jolts my body and fear pushes out my breath.

The elders' response is instant. Rakoto and Ramy drop to their knees, their heads bowed down, moaning as if in pain. I drop too, out of instinct, forgetting the treachery of the roots.

"It's thunder. Just thunder," John says. John charges up the cliff and I follow

quickly before the elders can change their minds. Looking down, I carefully pull myself up over the rocks. I need to concentrate on the climb, and cannot see the summit; it's so steep I can't see anything but my feet. Suddenly I am there. The view is magnificent. I can see all the way to the Indian Ocean.

John stops and cocks his head toward a big gray boulder. We recognize the sound of a frog. We are so excited about exploring that we have forgotten the thunder only minutes before.

I wait patiently outside the boulder cave, looking out over the extraordinary views. On every side there are distant tree-covered mountains. We definitely are at the highest point in the region. In the middle of my spiritual awe, I notice the ominous black clouds to the east. They are coming our way fast. One second the sun is bright and then there's darkness, as if someone had turned off the lights. Why hadn't we been paying attention! Too late to find any shelter, I fight a rising sense of panic.

As John and Richard squeeze out of the granite crevice, the rain starts to fall. As I warn John of the storm and point to the east, he announces with pride he's found a frog. He opens his hands and there in his palms is a frog bigger than the Hope diamond.

And then the storm hits with fury. Rain comes down in torrential sheets with blinding force. I run for cover in a place with no cover. I cannot see anything. I crouch, pushing hard against a boulder, my arm over my face. The rain is so strong and the wind is pushing the sheets of rain against me. I shiver from the chill. My body hurts from the pelting of golf ball–size raindrops.

The lightning pierces the sky, brightening the darkened world. The thunder follows on its heels. Another bolt, thunder clashes. Sheets of rain. I remember my mother saying, "If lightning is followed immediately by thunder, the storm is on top of you." *BAROOM FLASH.* The thunderclap and lighting strike are simultaneous.

My mother's voice reverberates in my head: "Never stand in an open place in a thunderstorm because lightning strikes the tallest object." I think of Ben Franklin, I think of how we might die here. And there are no trees. We are the tallest things on this mountain. Lightning is striking this mountain. And lightning strikes whatever is sticking up toward it, and that is us.

I crouch in the rain. The lightning jolts the world into brightness. The bolts are so close I might touch them. The instant *BOOM* of the thunder reverberates throughout my body. Another strobe of lightning jags across the sky toward us. I am going to die here. I shiver and close my eyes. The wind increases and I think about our tents, but I can't open my eyes to see what is happening. My arms hurt from the pelting rain. I turn away from the wind and see Rakoto shivering, crouched under a rock. The fear of the ancestors shines through his eyes. Another lightning bolt pierces the sky. Will we die here?

And then the storm is over. It just stops. The darkness brightens, the sun shines, and joy melts over my body.

I'm not struck by lightning. I look around. John isn't struck by lightning. He still cradles the jewel-like frog in his hands. I look further: What a relief to see the rest of our party. However, the tents have not fared as well. All but one have blown away. Rakoto is shaking, but is still with us. Ramy and all the villager porters have fled to the safety of their village, Sahavondrona. That night we sleep together, wet in one salvaged tent, the tent that had been filled with heavy bags of rice. We are just happy to have survived. And the frog was indeed a new species.

APPENDIX

PACKING CHECKLISTS

THE AMERICAN RED CROSS
RECOMMENDS THE FOLLOWING IN A
STANDARD FIRST AID KIT:

○ Absorbent compress dressings, 5 x 9 inches
○ 25 assorted adhesive bandages
○ 10 yards of adhesive cloth tape
○ 5 packets of antibiotic ointment
○ 5 packets of antiseptic wipes
○ Aspirin
○ Space blanket
○ Breathing barrier, with one-way valve
○ Instant cold compress
○ 2 pair gloves, non-latex
○ 2 packets of hydrocortisone ointment
○ Scissors
○ 1 roller bandage (elastic band), 3 inches wide
○ 1 roller bandage (elastic band), 4 inches wide
○ 5 sterile gauze pads, 3 x 3 inches
○ 5 sterile gauze pads, 4 x 4 inches
○ Oral thermometer (No glass or mercury)
○ 2 triangular bandages
○ Tweezers
○ Instruction booklet for administering first aid

ITEMS TO PACK FOR TRAVELING INTO
THE WILDERNESS. YOU'LL NEED TO
MODIFY THIS LIST DEPENDING ON YOUR
PARTICULAR TRAVELING CONDITIONS,
SIZE OF GROUP AND SEASON AND
DURATION OF TRAVEL.

○ Knife (all-in-one tool)
○ Wire saw
○ Lighter/matches
○ Candle
○ Magnesium block and striker
○ Magnifying glass
○ Signaling mirror
○ Water purification system
○ 2 percent tincture of iodine
○ Water containers
○ Pots/containers for cooking
○ Tarp
○ Tent
○ Cord (100 feet)
○ Colored tape
○ Needle and thread
○ Pealess whistle
○ Flashlight
○ Compass and/or GPS

- ○ Spare batteries
- ○ Maps
- ○ High-energy foods (granola, hard candies, etc)
- ○ Powdered drink mixes, including one with caffeine
- ○ Padlocks—to secure gear, if necessary
- ○ Head lamp
- ○ Ace bandages
- ○ Antifungal foot cream
- ○ Duct tape
- ○ Sports drink powder for rehydrating (especially for combatting diarrhea)
- ○ Waist bag (front accessible)
- ○ Antibacterial liquid
- ○ Silica gel
- ○ Hand wipes
- ○ First aid kit (portable, from the list above)
- ○ Insurance documents, money belt
- ○ Book to read
- ○ Playing cards

ADDITIONAL ITEMS FOR TEMPERATE FORESTS:

- ○ Pepper spray (for use if bear attacks)
- ○ Fishhooks and line
- ○ Thin wire for snares
- ○ Solid containers for sealing food
- ○ Bear bell
- ○ Antivenum serum

ADDITIONAL ITEMS FOR RAIN FORESTS:

- ○ Over-the-counter treatment for diarrhea
- ○ Antihistamine treatment for allergic reactions
- ○ Epinephrine auto-injector pen; injection counters severe allergic reactions to stings and bites
- ○ Cream and shampoo to repel insects and treating head lice
- ○ Antivenum serum and elastic bandages for snakebite management
- ○ Lidocaine hydrochloride (relief for excruciating stings from conga ants, caterpillars, stingrays)
- ○ Sunscreen

- ○ Oral rehydration salts
- ○ Insect repellent
- ○ Mosquito netting
- ○ Hammock
- ○ Fishhooks and line

ADDITIONAL ITEMS FOR DESERT:

- ○ Extra water, easily carried
- ○ Small stove with fuel canister
- ○ Oral rehydration salts
- ○ Sunglasses
- ○ Lip balm
- ○ Sunscreen

ADDITIONAL ITEMS FOR MOUNTAINS:

- ○ Small stove with plenty of bottled fuel
- ○ Sunglasses
- ○ Avalanche transceiver
- ○ Crampons
- ○ Ice ax
- ○ Avalanche probe
- ○ Bear bell
- ○ Antivenum serum

ADDITIONAL ITEMS FOR COLD REGIONS:

- ○ Small stove with fuel canister
- ○ Sleeping pad
- ○ Sunscreen
- ○ Sunglasses
- ○ Cross country skis or snowshoes
- ○ Snow saw or shovel
- ○ Vitamins

ADDITIONAL ITEMS FOR TRAVEL ON WATER:

- ○ Fishhooks and line
- ○ Signal flares, whistle
- ○ VHF radio, EPIRB
- ○ 2 solar stills, containers to catch rain
- ○ Life raft repair kit

CPR

The following is from American Red Cross, First Aid/CPR/AED for Schools and the Community, Participant's Manual, 3rd Edition, 2006

When someone's heart stops beating, companions must immediately recognize the condition and take action. The victim's brain and other organs continue to live for a short while, until available oxygen runs out. Cardiopulmonary resuscitation (CPR) is designed to get oxygen into a victim's bloodstream with rescue breaths and chest compressions. The victim's heartbeat and breathing may spontaneously return after a while, or the procedure may keep the victim alive until proper medical care can be given.

CPR FOR AN ADULT:

① Put victim face up. Place two hands on center of chest. Heel of lower hand is on sternum (breastbone), and upper hand is on top of first hand. Keep fingers off chest by curling them upward.
② Kneel beside victim. Straighten arms and lock elbows. Shoulders should be directly over hands.
③ Push sternum straight down 1.5 to 2 inches in a smooth motion, using weight of your upper body.
④ After compressing, allow chest to return to normal height but do not remove hands.
⑤ Count 30 compressions, which should take about 18 seconds.
⑥ After 30 compressions, tilt the head back and lift the chin (called the "head tilt/chin-lift technique") to open the victim's airway. Give two rescue breaths, by pinching the victim's nose shut, taking a breath, making a seal over victim's entire mouth, and breathing in to make victim's chest rise.
⑦ Continue the cycle of 30 compressions and two rescue breaths until the victim shows obvious signs of life. After recovery, monitor victim closely.

CPR FOR A CHILD:

① Locate proper place for hands on sternum, as for adult.
② Use one or two hands. You may put one hand on chest and the other on child's head to keep airway open.
③ Compress chest about 1.5 inches using heel of dominant hand.
④ Give 30 compressions and 2 rescue breaths, as with adults.

CPR FOR AN INFANT:

① Place pads of two or three fingers about one finger width below nipple line.
② Use pads to compress chest 0.5 to 1 inch
③ Give 30 compressions and 2 rescue breaths, covering infant's nose and mouth with your mouth.

FIRST AID

If possible, call 911 for all emergencies.

I. ALLERGIC REACTION

SYMPTOMS Skin swells and turns red. Hives, itching. Weakness. Nausea/stomach cramps/vomiting. Difficulty breathing/obstructed airway. Low blood pressure/shock. POSSIBLE CONDITION Allergic reaction/anaphylactic shock (anaphylaxis). COURSE OF ACTION Check airway/move victim into most comfortable position for breathing. Keep victim calm. Administer antihistamine. For severe reactions, inject epinephrine with auto-injector.

II. BLEEDING—SURFACE

SYMPTOMS Bloody clothing. Blood spurting from wound. POSSIBLE CONDITION Torn or cut blood vessel. COURSE OF ACTION Cover open wound by pressing on a sterile dressing (e.g., gauze) and bandages to control bleeding and prevent infection. If wound requires continuous pressure, apply an elastic bandage. Place end of bandage against skin and roll it around wounded limb while gently stretching it. Start from end farthest from heart. When finished, tape or tie in place. Do not cut off circulation by wrapping too tightly. If blood soaks through, do not remove old dressing. Add more dressing and bandages. Do not completely close wound off from the air, except for certain chest and abdominal wounds.

III. BLEEDING—INTERNAL

SYMPTOMS Vomiting or coughing up blood. Bruised, swollen, tender, or hard flesh. Severe pain/inability to move injured body part. Weak, rapid pulse. Pale, bluish skin, or cool, moist skin. Excessive thirst. Confusion, drowsiness, unconsciousness. POSSIBLE CONDITION Injury to large blood vessel and deep muscle tissue, bleeding beneath skin. COURSE OF ACTION Apply ice to wounded area for 20 minutes at a time. Wrap in damp cloth or other barrier to prevent ice from prolonged contact with skin. Keep victim still and comfortable. Elevate injury unless doing so increases pain.

IV. BLISTERS

SYMPTOMS Painful, fluid-filled sac beneath skin. POSSIBLE CONDITION Skin irritation from friction or burn causing blister. COURSE OF ACTION If blister forms on skin unlikely to encounter abrasion, let blister disappear on its own. Never burst a blister caused by a burn. If blister forms in a place where it is likely to encounter abrasion and break: Wash the skin around blister. Puncture blister with sterilized needle (boil it for 10 minutes or heat it red in a flame, then remove carbon with gauze). Use fingers to expel fluid through puncture point. Cover with sterile gauze and bandage. Replace gauze when it gets wet from blister fluid.

V. BOILS

SYMPTOMS Red, tender spot on skin. Soft, pus-filled center forms amid tender area. POSSIBLE CONDITION

Skin abscess—deep, localized infection. COURSE OF ACTION Soak boils in warm water or apply heat packs to increase circulation and improve body's ability to fight infection. Do not attempt to drain boil until it forms a "head," or pustule. If large boil forms a pustule, lance it with a sterile needle or knife and drain pus. Cover with sterile gauze and bandage.

VI. BREATHING DIFFICULTIES
SYMPTOMS Slow or rapid breathing. Gasping. Clutching throat with one or two hands. Very deep or shallow breathing. Wheezing, gurgling. Dizziness. Unusually cool or moist skin. POSSIBLE CONDITION Asthma. Bronchitis. Hyperventilation, often caused by anxiety, head injury, or severe bleeding. Allergic reaction. Foreign object in airway. COURSE OF ACTION Switch person's position; lying on side with upper leg bent or sitting may improve breathing. To treat blocked airway (choking), give blows to the back; wrap your arms around victim's abdomen from behind, place fist just above navel, grab fist with other hand and make quick, upward thrusts into abdomen. If choking while alone, press your own abdomen into a firm object, or give yourself abdominal thrusts as you would for another choking victim. If victim is unconscious and not breathing, place victim on back, push down on forehead while pulling up on bony part of jaw to lift the chin. This "head-tilt, chin-lift technique" moves the tongue so air can reach the lungs. Check victim. If still not breathing, give two rescue breaths with each breath lasting one second. Pinch nose shut; take a breath and make a complete seal over victim's mouth; blow in to make chest rise. Check to see if breaths go in; check for pulse by feeling at side of windpipe. If breaths do not go in, clear airway. If victim has no pulse and is not breathing, begin CPR. If victim has a pulse but is not breathing, give 10 rescue breaths per minute until victim breathes on own.

VII. BROKEN BONES
SYMPTOMS Sudden, serious deformity. Bruising and swelling. Inability to move injured body part without great pain. Bits of bone sticking out of wound. Sensation of bones grating, or victim heard a "pop" or "snap" when injury occurred. Injured area is numb and cold. POSSIBLE CONDITION Bone fracture or dislocation. COURSE OF ACTION Rest injured area. Immobilize the injury as it was found; do not apply a splint unless the victim must move. Apply ice to injured area; keep a thin barrier between ice and skin. Elevate the injury unless doing so increases pain. If necessary, apply splint above and below fracture. Do not manipulate injured limb before splinting. Options include splinting the injured limb to another body part; making a soft splint or sling for injured arm, wrist or hand; and splinting a fracture with wood, metal, folded magazines, or anything else that is rigid and offers protection and support.

VIII. BURNS
SYMPTOMS Skin is red, dry, and swelling. In more severe cases, skin has blisters, appears wet or mottled, or skin turns brown or black. POSSIBLE CONDITION Thermal burns; radiation burns (sun's ultraviolet light). COURSE OF ACTION Cool burn with lots of cold, running water. Cover with sterile dressing and bandage. In severe cases, take steps to minimize shock. Do not let victim get too hot or cold. Do not apply ice except if the burn is small, and then for only 10 minutes. Do not attempt to clean or apply ointment directly on a severe burn.

IX. CUTS AND ABRASIONS
SYMPTOMS Removal of outer skin layers. Red rash caused by scraping. Bleeding from opening in skin caused by sharp object. POSSIBLE CONDITION Abrasion, laceration, puncture wound, or avulsion (tearing/removal of skin and soft tissue). COURSE OF ACTION Clean abrasions with soap and water to prevent infection. Care for open wounds with dressings and bandages (see Bleeding—Internal).

X. DEHYDRATION
SYMPTOMS Thirst. Dizziness. Dry mouth and nasal passages. Infrequent urination; urine is dark. Weakness/fatigue. Headache. Confusion, irritability, slurring of speech. POSSIBLE CONDITION Body has lost too much water to function properly (dehydration). COURSE OF ACTION Drink small amounts of water at frequent intervals. Keep clothes on; clothing barrier decreases water loss through sweating. Sugar or oral rehydration salts may be added to first water given to victim. Victim should refrain from physical activity while recovering. If victim must move, take frequent breaks for rest and water.

XI. DROWNING
SYMPTOMS Submerged victim does not breathe and/or has no pulse after being pulled from water. POSSIBLE CONDITION Water in lungs (drowning, partial drowning). COURSE OF ACTION Clear airway and follow guidelines under "Breathing Difficulties."Prepare to administer CPR.

XII. ELECTRICAL INJURIES
SYMPTOMS Thermal burns, usually one at entry point and one at exit point. Shock. Breathing difficulties or cessation; no pulse. POSSIBLE CONDITION Electrical burns. Electric shock. COURSE OF ACTION Do not approach victim until you are certain victim is no longer in contact with source of electricity. Cover burns with dry, sterile dressing and bandages. Treat for shock and give CPR as needed.

XIII. FROSTBITE
SYMPTOMS Lack of sensation in affected part of body. Skin appears waxy. Skin is cold and white, yellow, blue, or flushed. POSSIBLE CONDITION Freezing of body parts exposed to cold (frostbite). COURSE OF ACTION Remove clothing and jewelry from frostbitten area. Soak affected body part in warm water (no more than 105 degrees Fahrenheit) until color and warmth return. Apply dry, sterile dressings and bandages. Place gauze between frostbitten fingers or toes. Place frostbitten hands under armpits; place frostbitten feet against the skin of another person's belly. Do not rub frostbitten skin.

XIV. FUNGAL INFECTIONS
SYMPTOMS Skin, especially on feet and groin, is covered with irritating rash. Skin blisters, swells, itches, or scales. POSSIBLE CONDITION Opportunistic fungi growing on body. COURSE OF ACTION Keep skin clean and dry. Expose affected skin to sunlight. Treat with antifungal powders or ointments. Do not scratch affected area.

XV. HEAT-RELATED ILLNESSES
SYMPTOMS Cramps. Nausea. Dizziness, weakness. Skin that is pale, flushed, cool, moist, or ashen. Rapid, weak pulse. POSSIBLE CONDITION Heat cramps. Heat exhaustion. Heat stroke. COURSE OF ACTION For cramps, get victim to a cool place; give cool water to drink; massage and stretch affected muscles. For heat exhaustion, move victim to a cool place; loosen clothing; apply wet towels, fan victim's body; give cool water to drink. For heat stroke, follow steps for heat exhaustion; rest victim on side; do not let victim resume normal activities for rest of day.

XVI. HYPOTHERMIA
(COLD-RELATED ILLNESS)
SYMPTOMS Shivering. Numbness. Glassy stare. Unconsciousness. POSSIBLE CONDITION Entire body loses heat (hypothermia). COURSE OF ACTION Remove wet clothing; keep person dry. Gradually warm victim by adding blankets and dry clothing, and move to a warm, dry place. Place barrier between heat source and victim's skin. Give warm liquids, but none containing alcohol or caffeine. Do not immerse victim in warm water or otherwise warm too quickly, which could cause heart problems.

XVII. INSECT AND SCORPION STINGS; SPIDER BITES
SYMPTOMS Pain and redness in affected area. Allergic reaction. Excessive salivation (spider and scorpion poison). POSSIBLE CONDITION Bee or wasp sting. Scorpion sting. Spider bite COURSE OF ACTION For stings, scrape stinger out of skin with fingernail or credit card, or pluck out with tweezers. Wash with soap and water. Cover with dressing and keep it clean. Apply ice to reduce swelling. Check for anaphylactic shock. For scorpion or spider injury, wash the wound. Apply cold pack. If it is available, give antivenin.

XVIII. POISONING
SYMPTOMS Nausea, vomiting. Diarrhea. Sweating. Breathing difficulties. Chest or abdominal pain. Seizures. Headaches. Dizziness, weakness. Irregular pupil size. Eyes that burn or tear up. Burns on lips, tongue, skin. Abnormal skin color, especially ashen or pale. POSSIBLE CONDITION Poison ingested, inhaled, absorbed, or injected (spiders, scorpions, snakes, etc.). COURSE OF ACTION Remove victim from scene of poisoning. Check for life-threatening conditions and treat symptoms. If poison is from skin contact, flush skin with lots of water. Apply baking soda or calamine lotion to dry up sores from poison on skin. If poison was ingested, give water. If ingested poison was non-corrosive, induce vomiting to expel it from body, then

give water. If ingested poison was corrosive (acid or alkaline), do not induce vomiting. Give victim water and then a mild acid or alkaline to neutralize the poison.

XIX. RASHES
SYMPTOMS Weeping, scaling, inflamed skin. POSSIBLE CONDITION Skin rash caused by infection or dirt clogging pores. COURSE OF ACTION Treat rash like an open wound—keep in clean and cover it with dressing and bandage. If rash is moist, keep it dry. If rash is dry, keep it moist. Apply antiseptics, if available. Do not scratch rash.

XX. SEIZURES
SYMPTOMS Blank stare. Disorientation. Sudden, uncontrolled muscle movements (convulsions). POSSIBLE CONDITION Reaction to extreme heat. Diabetic reaction. Injury to the brain. COURSE OF ACTION Do not try to halt seizure or restrain victim. Do not put anything in victim's mouth. Protect victim's head with a cushion or folded clothing. If victim's mouth fills with blood, saliva, or vomit, roll victim onto side to let fluid drain out. After seizure, check for breathing and injuries caused by convulsions.

XXI. SHOCK
SYMPTOMS Irritability, restlessness. Altered state of consciousness. Nausea, vomiting. Excessive thirst. Rapid breathing and pulse. Skin that is cool, most, pale, ashen. POSSIBLE CONDITION Flow of blood is inadequate for body's major organs and tissues (shock). COURSE OF ACTION Have the victim lie flat and get comfortable. Elevate victim's legs about 12 inches. Keep the victim from getting too warm or cool. Monitor victim's breathing and pulse. Do not give food or water if immediate hospitalization is an option. If hospitalization is not an option, give victim warm liquids to drink.

XXII. SNAKEBITE
SYMPTOMS Pain around bite marks in skin. Allergic reaction. Strong pain and swelling around bite (pit vipers). Blurring of vision, loss of reflexes, slurring of speech, nausea, difficulty breathing (coral snakes). POSSIBLE CONDITION Venom injected into bloodstream by snakebite. COURSE OF ACTION For pit vipers—rattlesnake, copperhead, cottonmouth—wash the wound; keep the injured area still and lower than the heart. For coral snakes, treatment is same as for pit vipers, except apply an elastic band, starting farthest from the heart and rolling it around the wound. Keep the injured area still and lower than the heart. Keep victims calm. For all bites, do not apply ice, cut the wound, apply a tourniquet, or apply suction.

XXIII. SPRAINS
SYMPTOMS Swelling, bruising. Pain in affected area, especially ankle, knee, wrist, and fingers. Inability to use the injured body part normally. Weakness in affected body part. POSSIBLE CONDITION Tearing of ligament at joint (sprain). COURSE OF ACTION For mild sprains, rest and apply ice. For severe sprains, treat as for broken bones.

how to

TIE A HALF HITCH

Useful for tying to a horizontal beam

1 Pass the end of the rope around the beam to which it will be secured, then loop it around again without crossing itself.
2 Pull the end over and around the long end of the rope and push it through the loop you have just created.
3 Repeat the loop of the previous step, to create an identical half hitch below the first.
4 Pull tight.

TIE A BOWLINE

Useful for creating a loop that will not tighten, such as for pulling someone out of the water or anchoring something to a tree or post

1 Make a small loop (knot loop) in a rope.
2 With the working end of the rope, make another loop; thread the end through the knot loop.
3 Continue the working end around the back of the stationary end and back to the front.
4 Thread the working end through the middle of the knot loop, as shown.
5 Pull tight.

TIE A CLOVE HITCH

Useful for making a quick knot around a tree or post; secures items hanging between trees

1 Place a loop around object with working end of rope on top.
2 Run working end of rope around object a second time until it comes to where ropes cross.
3 Pass working end under the cross.
4 Tighten.

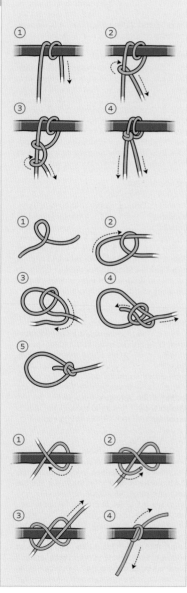

how to
USE SEMAPHORE SIGNALS

Semaphore messages are communicated by flags held at precise body positions as the sender faces the receiver. Each letter is formed by a combination of two flag positions, followed by a pause before proceeding to the next letter. Numbers are spelled out. Arm movements from one letter to the next are as compact as possible. Semaphore signals are visible over great distances.

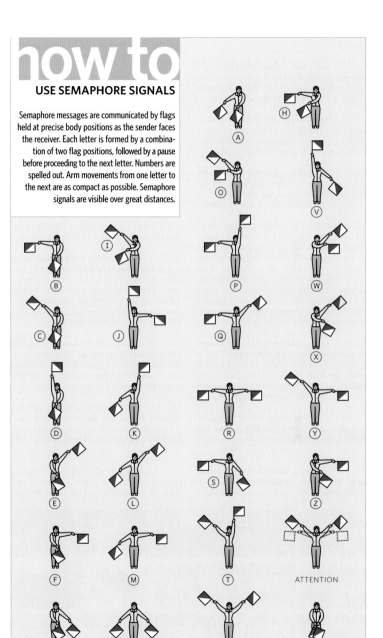

1 ACORNS **Hard, round, capped fruit** of the red and white oak tree. Remove cap and shell. Flesh inside is edible. White acorns have better flavor than red. Dry acorns. Eat plain or grind into flour to make coffee substitute.

2 BAMBOO **Giant, fast-growing grass.** Pith is edible, as are seeds. Split the outer shell of the cane and remove pith with knife. Cook like asparagus. Eat seeds raw. Good source of water. Shake a plant to listen for sloshing.

3 BARREL CACTUS **Desert plant with J-shaped barbs.** Good water source. Grows up to four feet tall. Has distinctively round, barrel shape. Get water from pulp. Do not mutilate the cactus unless it is a water emergency.

4 BEARBERRIES (KINNIKINNICK) **Evergreen shrub.** Has reddish bark, white flowers, and red fruits. Common at high latitudes. Berries and leaves are edible. Berries are best when cooked. Collect young leaves to make tea.

5 BIGNAY **Shrub or small tree.** Can be ten to 35 feet tall. Has long, pointy, shiny leaves. Flowers grow in clusters. Fruit is the width of a finger, fleshy, and dark red or black. Grows in tropics. Only the fruit is edible. Eat fruit raw. Poison concentrated in roots and other parts of tree.

6 BISTORT **Grow one to two feet tall. Has triangular, narrow leaves on a thin, straight stalk.** Grows in grassland and woods far into the north. Eat leaves in spring, roots in fall. Put leaves in salad. Soak roots to remove bitterness, then roast and eat. Dried, powdered root is antiseptic. Roots must be thoroughly cooked.

7 BLACK WALNUT **Fruit of black walnut tree. Look for hard, green globes with a thick husk on limbs with paired, serrated leaves.** Found in temperate forests. Crack open husk and shell, remove meat, and eat.

8 BLACKBERRIES **Dark, aggregate berries on thorny canes. Berries grow on fiercely sharp thorns on arching stems.** Canes grow in woods, scrub, and open ground in temperate climates. Fruit is popular with birds and other animals, so canes make good hunting sites.

9 BLUEBERRIES **Small, round blue, black or red fruit.** Grows on shrubs from ten inches to ten feet tall. Shrubs grow throughout temperate North, and on hills in Central America. Versatile food. High in vitamins.

10 BREADFRUIT **Fruit-bearing tree up to 50 feet tall.** Leaves more than two feet long. Fruits are large, with hard seed. Grows in tropics. Fruit pulp and seeds are edible. Eat fruit raw after removing skin, or slice, dry, and grind into flour. Cook seeds to make them edible.

11 BURDOCK **A biennial, flowered thistle. Stalks grow six feet tall. Velcro-like stick-tight heads.** Grows in northern temperate zones. Eat stalks, roots. Peel leaf stalks; eat raw or boiled. Eat roots baked or boiled. Do not eat leaves, which can be confused with poisonous rhubarb.

12 CATTAILS **Grasslike, water-loving plants.** Grows up to six feet tall. Produces distinctive brown heads. Stems, pollen, and young seed heads are edible. Gather young, tender shoots and eat raw or cooked. Boil young heads and eat like corn on the cob. Mix pollen with water to make dough for baking or frying. Use the fluff for tinder and leaves for weaving. Burn to repel insects.

13 CHICORY **Flowering plant on stems up to four feet tall. Thick, hairy leaves with sky blue flowers.** Grows like a weed throughout temperate Northern Hemisphere. All parts are edible. Eat the leaves raw or boil. Boil roots or roast and powder to make a coffee substitute.

14 CHOKECHERRY **Shrub that grows up to eight feet tall and bears dark fruit. Tiny, white flowers.** Grows in woods and swamps in temperate zone. Berries are edible, leaves and pits toxic. Do not confuse with buckthorn berries, which cluster along stems and cause vomiting.

15 CLOVER **Small plant with flowers** of white, cream, pale green, or pink. Leaves (in three lobes) and roots are edible boiled or raw. Roots are sweet. Smoke over a fire.

16 COCONUT PALM **Common palm tree.** Found throughout tropics, especially near coasts. Milk in the young nuts; nut meat. Dry coconut meat in full sun to preserve it. Drink the milk for vitamins and sugar. Boil nuts to render oil. Use husks for tinder, repel mosquitoes. At sea, floating coconuts are a good source of fresh water.

17 CRANBERRIES **Woody bush that bears red fruit.** Grows in cold parts of Northern Hemisphere, only in sunny, marshy ground. Collect red fruits. Eat raw, cooked, or dried. Juice is a treatment for urinary infections.

18 CROWBERRIES **Dwarf evergreen shrub.** Produces shiny, small black berries and needlelike leaves. Grows in arctic tundra. Berries are edible raw or dried. Dried fruits keep well. Berries remain on stems throughout winter.

19 DAISY **Ox-eye daisy is a bright perennial flower,** with yellow button inside a ring of white petals. Grows up to three feet tall in temperate zones throughout the world. Young stems and young leaves are edible. Flowers can be steeped to make tea to soothes coughs.

20 DANDELION **Low-growing weed.** Bright yellow flowers, hollow stems, jagged-edged leaves radiating from central stem. Grows throughout Northern Hemisphere. Every part is edible. Contains lots of vitamins A and C.

21 ELDERBERRIES **Shrub with dark blue-purple fruit.** Grows on multiple stems, up to 18 feet tall. Tiny white flowers. Found in open, wetland along lakes, and rivers. Flowers and fruits are edible; avoid small red fruits that may be toxic. Other parts of the shrub are poisonous.

22 FIREWEED **Flowering plant two to five feet high.** Has showy, large, pink flowers and lancelike leaves. Grows in cold regions, especially near seashores. Eat leaves, stems, and flowers raw, or cut into old stems and eat pith.

23 FISHTAIL PALM **Large tree.** Irregular, toothed leaves. Flowering shoot at tree top. Grows in tropics of south Asia. Flowering shoot—"palm cabbage"—and pith/juice are edible. Eat the palm cabbage raw or cooked.

24 GRAPES **A variety of vines bearing fruit in clusters.** Vines are straggly and produce coarsely toothed leaves. Wild grapes grow anywhere except high latitudes. Fruit and young leaves are edible raw or cooked

25 HAZELNUTS **Nut-bearing bush.** Large bushes or trees with oval or heart-shaped leaves. Nuts grow in bristly, leafy, or hairy husks. Found on temperate zones of American West Coast, in Europe, and East Asia. Eat raw or dried. Rich oil content makes them excellent for survival.

26 ICELAND MOSS **Stumpy moss.** Plant is a few inches high. Color ranges from gray to white or red. Grows only in the arctic. All parts edible. Boil to remove bitterness. Dried specimens last a long time without spoiling.

27 JUNIPER **Tree with tiny, scaly leaves.** Bears blue, berry-like cones ("berries") covered with a whitish wax. Recognize by crushing berries or sap to release the fragrant aroma of gin. Grows in temperate zones of Northern Hemisphere, plus mountains of Africa. Berries are edible; twigs can be made into tea. Eat raw berries.

28 LAMB'S QUARTERS **Annual, flowering weed.** Has dull green oval or spear-shaped leaves with mealy undersides and greenish flower spikes at the end of two- to four-foot stems. Distributed throughout temperate zones of Northern Hemisphere. Leaves and stems are edible.

29 LOTUS (WATER LILY) **Flowering water plant.** Leaves and flowers float on surface of still water. Leaves grow to four feet long. Flowers are yellow or pink. Fruit is flat and seedy. Yellow-flowered varieties grow in North American temperate zone. Pink variety grows in East Asia. All parts are edible. Pull up/dig up stems for baking or boiling.

30 MANIOC (CASSAVA) **Perennial shrub.** Grows three to nine feet tall. Has fingerlike leaves radiating from central, jointed stem. Found in all moist, tropical areas. Grind root into pulp. Cook for one hour to remove poison from the roots. Take remaining pulp and shape into cakes for baking. Manioc cakes and flour stay edible a long time if shielded from insects. Roots are lethal if eaten raw.

31 MAPLE **Common tree in scores of species.** Leaves have three distinctive lobes; fruits have two lobes and flutter as they fall. Grows throughout temperate forests. Eat young leaves and seeds. Cut a V-shaped notch in trunk and collect sap. Chew leaves or seeds; eat inner bark.

32 MARSH MARIGOLD **Flowering water plant.** Round, dark green leaves, five-petaled yellow flowers. Temperate zones to arctic; bogs, streams, and lakes. All parts are edible but must be cooked. Bring to a strong boil.

33 MOUNTAIN ASH **Small tree with orange or red fruits.** Clusters of white flowers three to five inches apart. Smooth, gray bark. Grows in woody and rocky places in temperate zones. Boil berries to reduce sharp taste.

34 MULBERRIES **Small to medium tree.** Berries look like large blackberries. Leaves are deeply lobed and serrated. Hardy tree grows in forests and fields of northern and southern temperate and tropical zones. Berries are heavily seeded but juicy. Eat berries raw, cooked, or dried.

35 NIPA PALM **Broad, short palm.** Trunk grows mostly underground. Leaves, shooting up from trunk, may be 20 feet tall. Dark brown seed heads. Grows in the mud of east Asian shorelines. Cut stalks and drink sugary juice. Seeds are hard but edible raw. Thatch roof with leaves.

36 PAPAW **Shrub or small tree with brownish-gray bark.** White, six-petaled, flowers. Fruits are two to six inches long—the largest indigenous to North America. Grows in temperate forests; northern variety is deciduous while southern is evergreen. Eat raw. Fruit is high in protein.

37 PINE **Common evergreen tree of various species.** Produces distinctive needles in clusters and sticky sap. Young cones, twig bark, and young needles are edible. Bake or boil cones. Chew bark. Steep needles to make tea. Use resin as glue and for emergency dental filling.

38 PORPHYRIA **Seaweed. A red algae with thin, satiny** fronds ranging from red to brown to purple. Grows in Atlantic and Pacific. Found from polar waters to tropical seas. Fronds are edible and tasty. Boil and mash. Do not eat if you lack water. Do not eat any if it has a bad odor.

39 PRICKLY PEAR **Low-growing cactus with jointed pads.** Flowers are yellow or red and produce red, egg-shaped fruit. Grows in arid climates of North and South America. Peel fruits and eat them raw or squeeze them for juice.

40 RASPBERRIES **Flowering, thorny canes.** Aggregate red berries flourish in summer. Grows in temperate zones from North America through Europe to western Asia. Berries are juicy and delicious. Eat raw in summer or cook into a syrup or jam. Canes have sharp thorns.

41 RATTAN PALM **Climbing plant that attaches to trees.** Stems may grow to 200 feet. Leaves are compound and flowers are white. Grows in tropical rainforests. Interiors of stem tips are full of starch. Some have gelatinous pulp around their seeds. Suck the pulp. Eat the palm heart.

42 REINDEER MOSS **Pale gray-green lichen** growing a few inches high. Found in much of North America. All parts edible. Soak it in water and wood ashes to make it soft and remove bitterness. Add the plant to food or milk. Strong bitter taste until treated.

43 ROCK TRIPE **Flat, gray-green to black lichen.** Grows over rocks, on boulders throughout North America. All parts considered edible. Scrape off rock. Wash it to remove grit, then soak to make it soft and remove the bitter taste. Test the plant for your reaction before eating.

44 ROSE HIPS (WILD ROSE) **Flowering brambles.** Resemble garden roses except thinner and less elegant. Flourishes in most temperate zones. Flowers drop petals and set red seedcases called "hips" or "haws" in summer. Hips contain edible, nutritious juice. Eat the flowers. Hips have the highest concentration of vitamin C of all fruit.

45 SAGO PALM **Small, spiny palm tree.** Has a thick outer rind like bamboo. Leaves are thin and palmlike. Grows only in tropical rain forests. Pith found in lower part of tree is rich in starch. Nuts and shoots are edible too.

46 SERVICEBERRIES **Shrub or small tree related to rose.** Has small oval leaves. Flowers are delicate, white, and last only a week. Tiny purple fruits ripen two to three months later. Grows in temperate regions of Northern Hemisphere. Fruits taste like blueberries. Eat berries raw.

47 SPATTERDOCK **Flowering water plant.** Leaves grow up to two feet long. Plants produce one-inch yellow flowers that grow into yellow-green fruits. Grows in water throughout North America. All parts are edible.

48 STERCULIA **Flowering, tall tree in many species.** May grow to 100 feet tall. Produces purple or red flowers. Resulting seedpods are segmented, red, and full of edible black seeds Grows in tropical forests. Nuts are flavorful. Eat raw or roasted. Nuts may taste like cocoa.

49 SUGARCANE **A tall grass with green or reddish stems.** Grows up to 15 feet tall. Flourishes in the tropics. Core of the stem is a source of sugary juice. Peel the stem. Chew the pith or squeeze out the juice. High-energy food.

50 SUMMER PURSLANE **A short, stubby annual herb.** Spreads along the ground. Thick, waxy leaves are shaped like canoe paddles, about one inch long. Flowers in summer with yellow or pink blooms. Grows throughout the world (except polar regions). All parts are edible.

51 SWEETSOP **Small tree with green, bumpy fruit.** Grows in rainforests. Flesh of the fruit is edible. Peel and eat raw. Ground seeds can be used to kill insects. Powder must be kept away from eyes, as it is a powerful irritant.

52 TARO **Cultivated and wild vegetable.** Plant has large tubers, long stalks, and arrow- or heart-shaped leaves. Thrives in tropics. Boil tuber and leaves. Must be cooked; raw flesh is toxic and will burn the mouth.

53 WALL PEPPER **Mossy, creeping sedum.** Flowering cover that creeps low to the ground. Grows in temperate zones. Succulent leaves. Add them to salad for a peppery taste. Leaves of plants with yellow flowers may be mildly toxic; fry them to remove toxins.

54 WILD FIG **Fruit-bearing tree.** Leaves are dark, shiny green. Fruit ranges from green to yellow-brown and has sticky juice. Grows in tropics and semitropics. Fruits are edible but may lack much taste. Eat raw or cooked.

55 WILD ONION **Flowering plant with large bulb.** Slender stems may grow a few feet high, topped with pink, white or purple leaves. Has a distinctive oniony odor. Grows wild throughout temperate regions; is cultivated throughout the world. Bulbs and young leaves are edible.Cook or eat raw. Some poisonous plants look like wild onion. Don't eat the plant if it lacks the correct odor. Creates a body odor that drives some insects away

56 WILD PLUM (SLOE) **Tall bush. Grows to 13 feet tall.** Has dark brown twigs, sharp thorns, white flowers, and small, bluish-black fruits. Grows in temperate zones of Northern Hemisphere. Fruits are tart but edible. Cook fruits down to jelly. Fruits attract birds.

57 WILD RICE **Tall grass.** Grain grows loosely in the head and turns dark when ripe. Grows in tropics and temperate fields. Roots and ore of stems in spring and early summer. Grain in fall. Peel stems and roots and eat raw. Parch the husks, break open, and eat the rice inside.

58 WILD STRAWBERRIES **Small, fruit-bearing plants.** Fruit looks like smaller version of cultivated strawberry. Grows in temperate woods and on mountains. Fruits are sweet and high in vitamin C.

59 WILLOW AND ARCTIC WILLOW **Common tree and shrub.** Grows near water and has distinctive, downward-drooping wands. Smaller versions grow in the Arctic. Found in temperate zones and high latitudes. Peel and eat the inner bark. Eat young leaves, which have lots of vitamins. Eat bark raw or boil it.

60 YAM **Climbing or creeping vine.** Leaves are heart-shaped or arrow-shaped. Root is a knotty tuber and may grow to weigh several pounds. Grows in the tropics. Tuber is edible when cooked. Must be boiled. May be harmful if not well-cooked.

Oceans and Major Lakes and Rivers

Only about one-quarter of Earth's surface is land. Major rivers and vast stretches of open ocean have challenged travelers—and survivors—for centuries.

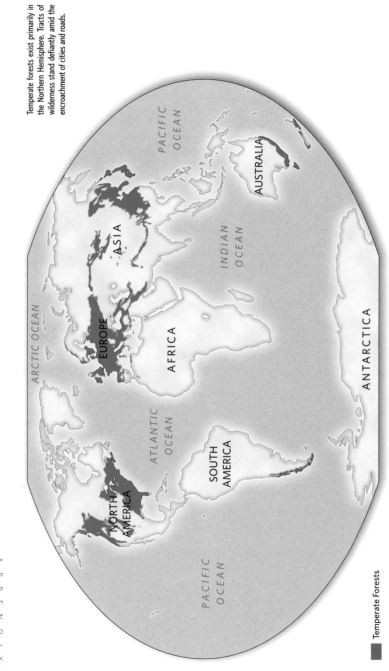

Temperate forests exist primarily in the Northern Hemisphere. Tracts of wilderness stand defiantly amid the encroachment of cities and roads.

ARCTIC OCEAN

PACIFIC OCEAN

ASIA

EUROPE

AFRICA

INDIAN OCEAN

AUSTRALIA

ATLANTIC OCEAN

NORTH AMERICA

SOUTH AMERICA

PACIFIC OCEAN

ANTARCTICA

Temperate Forests

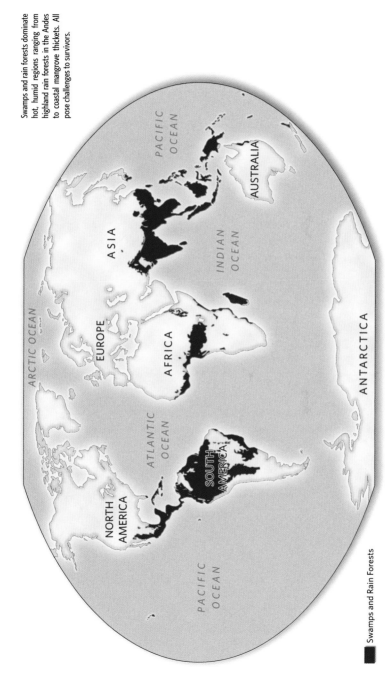

Swamps and rain forests dominate hot, humid regions ranging from highland rain forests in the Andes to coastal mangrove thickets. All pose challenges to survivors.

Swamps and Rain Forests

Movement of plates in the Earth's crust raises mountain ranges. The Andes of South America form the longest chain; the Himalaya of Asia are the highest.

ARCTIC OCEAN

EUROPE

ASIA

PACIFIC OCEAN

NORTH AMERICA

ATLANTIC OCEAN

AFRICA

INDIAN OCEAN

AUSTRALIA

PACIFIC OCEAN

SOUTH AMERICA

ANTARCTICA

High Mountains

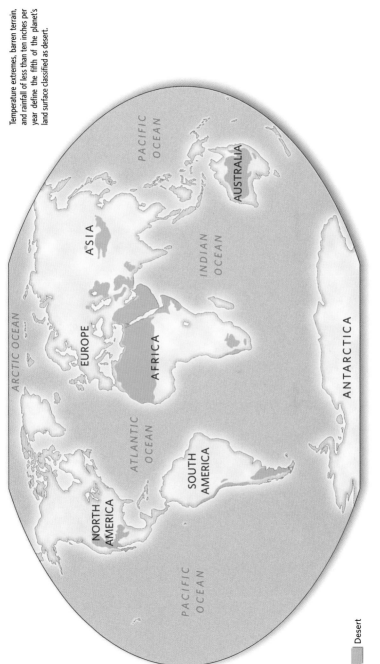

Temperature extremes, barren terrain, and rainfall of less than ten inches per year define the fifth of the planet's land surface classified as desert.

Desert

Short growing seasons, bookended by long periods of darkness and extreme cold, challenge polar survivors. Antarctica, a high desert, has no permanent settlers.

ARCTIC OCEAN

PACIFIC OCEAN

EUROPE

ASIA

AFRICA

INDIAN OCEAN

AUSTRALIA

ATLANTIC OCEAN

NORTH AMERICA

SOUTH AMERICA

PACIFIC OCEAN

ANTARCTICA

Poles and Subpolar Regions

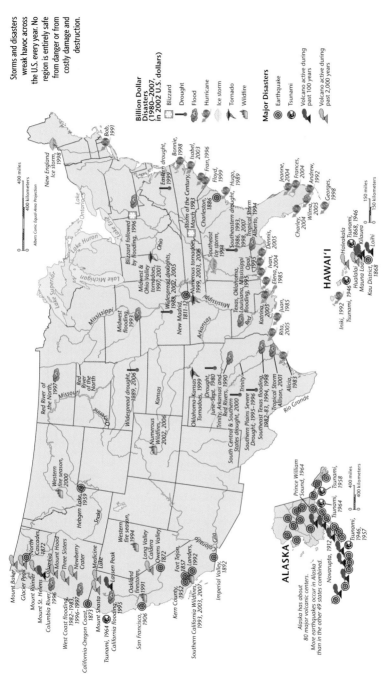

Storms and disasters wreak havoc across the U.S. every year. No region is entirely safe from danger or from costly damage and destruction.

Billion Dollar Disasters (1980–2007, in 2002 U.S. dollars)
- Blizzard
- Drought
- Flood
- Hurricane
- Ice storm
- Tornado
- Wildfire

Major Disasters
- Earthquake
- Tsunami
- Volcano active during past 100 years
- Volcano active during past 2,000 years

Albers Conic Equal-Area Projection

0 400 miles
0 400 kilometers

Lake Ontario
Lake Erie
Lake Huron
Lake Michigan
Lake Superior

New England Ice storm, 1998
Bob, 1991
Bonnie, 1998
Isabel, 2003
Eastern drought, 1999
Fran, 1996
Floyd, 1999
Hugo, 1989
Blizzard followed by flooding, 1996
Ohio
Midwest & Ohio Valley tornadoes, 1997, 2001
Storm of the Century, March 1993
Charleston, 1886
Southeast drought, 1986, 1993, 1998, 2000
Southeast Ice storm, 1994
Jeanne, 2004
Frances, 2004
Andrew, 1992
Georges, 1998
Charley, 2004
Wilma, 2005
Tropical Storm Alberto, 1994
Opal, 1995
Dennis, 2005
Ivan, 2004
Elena, 1985
Numerous tornadoes, 1999, 2003, 2006
New Madrid, 1811–12
Texas, Oklahoma, Louisiana, Mississippi flooding, 1995, 2007
Katrina, 2005
Juan, 1985
Rita, 2005
Tropical Storm Allison, 2001
Alicia, 1983

Mississippi
Arkansas
Red
Missouri
Red River of the North, 1997
Red River North
Midwest flooding, 1993
Widespread drought, 1989, 2006
Platte
Kansas
Numerous Wildfires, 2002, 2006
Oklahoma-Kansas Tornadoes, 1999
Drought, June–Sept. 1980
Trinity, Arkansas and Red Rivers, 1990
Trinity
South Central & Southern States drought, 2000
Southern Plains Severe Drought, 1995–1996
Southeast Texas flooding, 1982–83, 1994, 1998
Rio Grande
Colorado
Gila

Western fire season, 2000
Western fire season, 1994
Widespread drought, 1989, 2006
Snake
Hebgen Lake, 1959
North Cascades, 1872
Mount Baker
Glacier Peak
Mount Rainier
Mount St. Helens, 1996
Columbia River, 1996–1997
Mount Hood
Three Sisters
Newberry Crater
West Coast flooding, 1982–1983, 1996–1997
California-Oregon Coast, 1873
Medicine Lake
Mount Shasta
Lassen Peak
Long Valley Caldera, 1872
Owens Valley, 1872
Tsunami, 1964
California flooding
Oakland firestorm, 1991
San Francisco, 1906
Southern California Wildfires, 1993, 2003, 2007
Kern County, 1952
Fort Tejon, 1857
Landers, 1992
Imperial Valley, 1892

HAWAI'I
0 150 miles
0 150 kilometers
Haleakala
Tsunami, 1868, 1946
Hualalai
Mauna Loa
Kilauea
Loihi
Kau District, 1868
Iniki, 1992
Tsunami, 1946

ALASKA
0 400 miles
0 400 kilometers
Alaska has about 80 major volcanic centers. More earthquakes occur in Alaska than in the other 49 states combined.
Novarupta, 1912
Prince William Sound, 1964
Tsunami, 1964
Tsunami, 1938
Tsunami, 1964
Tsunami, 1946, 1957

INDEX

National Geographic Complete Survival Manual
Michael S. Sweeney

Published by the National Geographic Society
John M. Fahey, Jr., President and Chief Executive Officer
Gilbert M. Grosvenor, Chairman of the Board
Tim T. Kelly, President, Global Media Group
John Q. Griffin, President, Publishing
Nina D. Hoffman, Executive Vice President
President, Book Publishing Group

Prepared by the Book Division
Kevin Mulroy, Senior Vice President and Publisher
Leah Bendavid-Val, Director of Photography Publishing and Illustrations
Marianne R. Koszorus, Director of Design
Barbara Brownell Grogan, Executive Editor
Elizabeth Newhouse, Director of Travel Publishing
Carl Mehler, Director of Maps

Staff for This Book
Susan Straight, Editor
Mireya Mayor, Larry Stanier, Contributing Editors
Michele Kayal, Elizabeth Towner, Contributing Writers
Sam Serebin, Art Director
Erin Benit, Illustrations Editor
Tiffin Thompson, Researcher
Nicholas P. Rosenbach, Map Researcher and Editor
Michael McNey and Mapping Specialists, Map Production
Ric Wain, Production Project Manager
Marshall Kiker, Illustrations Specialist
Linda Johansson, Design Assistant
Connie D. Binder, Indexer
Jennifer A. Thornton, Managing Editor
R. Gary Colbert, Production Director

Manufacturing and Quality Management
Christopher A. Liedel, Chief Financial Officer
Phillip L. Schlosser, Vice President
Chris Brown, Technical Director
Nicole Elliott, Manager
Monika D. Lynde, Manager
Rachel Faulise, Manager

Founded in 1888, the National Geographic Society is one of the largest nonprofit scientific and educational organizations in the world. It reaches more than 285 million people worldwide each month through its official journal, *National Geographic,* and its four other magazines; the National Geographic Channel; television documentaries; radio programs; films; books; videos and DVDs; maps; and interactive media. National Geographic has funded more than 8,000 scientific research projects and supports an education program combating geographic illiteracy.

For more information, please call
1-800-NGS LINE
(647-5463) or write to the following address:

National Geographic Society
1145 17th Street N.W.
Washington, D.C. 20036-4688 U.S.A.

Visit us online at
www.nationalgeographic.com/books

For information about special discounts for bulk purchases, please contact National Geographic Books Special Sales: ngspecsales@ngs.org

For rights or permissions inquiries, please contact National Geographic Books Subsidiary Rights: ngbookrights@ngs.org

Library of Congress Cataloging-in-Publication Data available upon request.

ISBN 978-1-4262-0429-6 (regular)
ISBN 978-1-4262-0430-2 (deluxe)
ISBN 978-1-4262-0389-3 (trade)
Printed in China
11/TS/03

MAPS

Olympic N.P.

North Cascades N.P.

Wash.

Mt. Rainier N.P.

Glacier N.P.

Montana

Theodore Roosevelt N.P.

N. Dak.

Oregon

S. Dak.

Crater Lake N.P.

Idaho

Yellowstone N.P.

Redwood N.P.

Grand Teton N.P.

Wind Cave N.P.

Badlands N.P.

Lassen Volcanic N.P.

Wyoming

Neb.

Nevada

Utah

Rocky Mountain N.P.

Yosemite N.P.

Great Basin N.P.

Colorado

California

Arches N.P.

Black Canyon of the Gunnison N.P.

Kings Canyon N.P.

Capitol Reef N.P.

Bryce Canyon N.P.

Canyonlands N.P.

Great Sand Dunes N.P. & Pres.

Sequoia N.P.

Zion N.P.

Death Valley N.P.

Grand Canyon N.P.

Mesa Verde N.P.

Channel Islands N.P.

Joshua Tree N.P.

Petrified Forest N.P.

Arizona

New Mexico

UNITED STATES
MEXICO

Saguaro N.P.

Carlsbad Caverns N.P.

Guadalupe Mts. N.P.

Texas

Kobuk Valley N.P.

Gates of the Arctic N.P. & Preserve

Big Bend N.P.

Alaska

Denali N.P. & Pres.

Wrangell-St. Elias N.P. & Preserve

Lake Clark N.P & Pres.

Katmai N.P. & Pres.

Kenai Fjords N.P.

Glacier Bay N.P. & Pres.

| 0 | miles | 400 |
| 0 | kilometers | 600 |

Virgin Islands N.P.

American Samoa N.P.

Selected National Parks
by Primary Terrain or
Temperate Zone

■ Temperate Forests
■ Swamps and Rain Forests
■ High Mountains
■ Desert
■ Poles and Subpolar Regions
■ Oceans, Major Lakes
  & Major Rivers

■ Other National Parks

Voyageurs N.P.
Isle Royale N.P.
Acadia N.P.
Me.
CANADA
U.S.
Vt.
N.H.
Minn.
Wis.
Mich.
N.Y.
Mass. ● BOSTON
R.I.
Conn.
NEW YORK
N.J.
● PHILADELPHIA
Pa.
Cuyahoga N.P.
Ohio
Iowa
Ill.
Ind.
Md.
Del.
● WASHINGTON
W. Va.
Shenandoah N.P.
Va.
Kan.
Mo.
Ky.
Mammoth Cave N.P.
N.C.
Ok.
Ark.
Tenn.
Great Smoky Mts. N.P.
S.C.
Congaree N.P.
Hot Springs N.P.
Miss.
Ala.
Ga.
La.
Florida
Biscayne N.P.
Everglades N.P.
Dry Tortugas N.P.
Hawai'i
Haleakala N.P.
Hawai'i Volcanoes N.P.

miles 0 400
kilometers 0 600

miles 0 200
kilometers 0 300

Water meets stone at Acadia National Park, which is scattered over Maine islands and a bit of the state's mainland. The largest portion of the park lies within Mount Desert Island, a rugged, lake-dimpled rock shaped like a lobster claw. The ocean water is cold all year long, reaching no higher than 50 to 55°F in summer, which makes hypothermia a risk for anyone taking an extended swim. Strong storm waves in spring and fall also raise dangers, knocking waders off their feet and carrying them away from shore. Watch your step along the beaches—algae make shoreline rocks and ledges slippery. You'll need to take a boat to get to Isle du Haut and Baker Island. Boat schedules are available at the park visitor center. Wear a personal flotation device on the often-choppy open water. Overnight backpacking is not allowed in the park. If you're lost and hungry, look for the blueberries that grow throughout the park as well as mussels that thrive in the shallow coastal waters. Blueberries ripen from mid-July through August. Picking and eating them is permitted in the park, but park boundaries are irregular, with much of Mount Desert privately owned.

At Cuyahoga Valley National Park, the climate is typical of northern Ohio: four distinct seasons, ranging from hot, humid summers to cold, snowy winters. Visitors should prepare for unpredictable weather by dressing in layers they can add or take off. Graded hiking and biking paths are popular, but backcountry trails and terrain can be rugged.

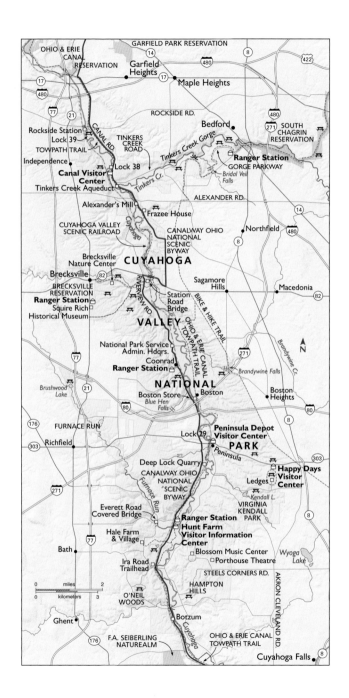

Shenandoah National Park is 105 miles long, north to south, but narrow. If you get lost, double back, sit tight on a ridgeline, or head toward the bisecting Skyline Drive highway. Use foliage and branches to make a debris hut for shelter. Water is plentiful, but beware of slippery rocks near falls.

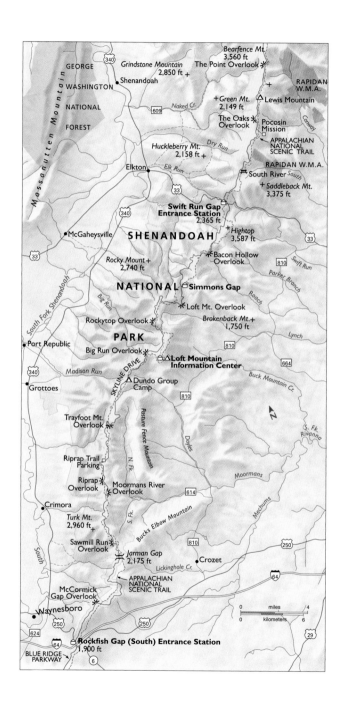

Congaree preserves the largest bit of old-growth, floodplain forest in North America. Canoes provide the best access. The park provides canoes, paddles, and life jackets; visitors should bring their own food and water, insect repellent, change of clothes, and shoes for use in water (not flip-flops). Beware of snakes and alligators.

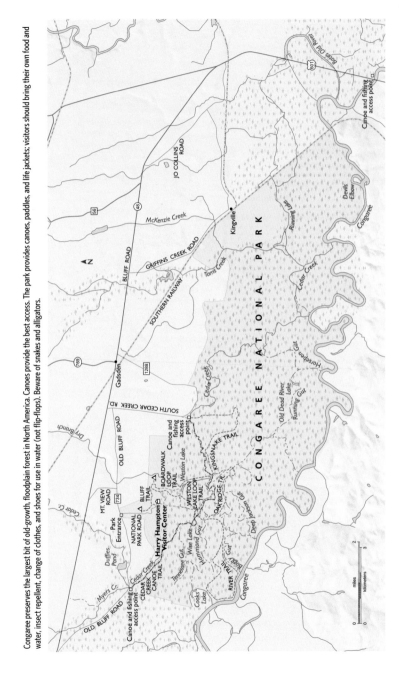

Unique in the United States, the National Park of American Samoa contains five kinds of rain forest: lowland, montane, coast, ridge, and cloud, scattered over three islands in this American territory. Aside from the beaches and scenic roadways, the park has little flat terrain. The coastline and jungle-covered mountains make Samoa, which means "sacred earth," a land of spectacular scenery. Pack proper hiking shoes for the rugged, rocky, wet terrain. Make sure to clean and thoroughly dry your feet each night. Rainfall averages up to 200 inches a year, so prepare to get wet.

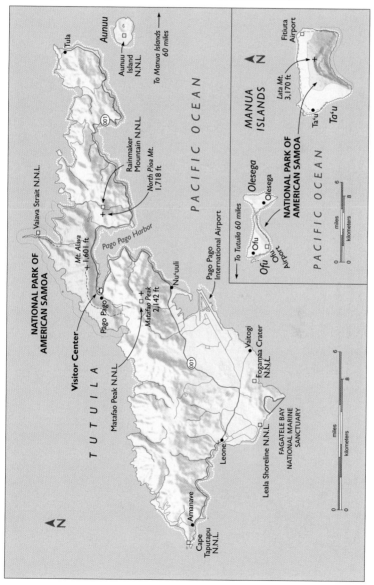

Everglades National Park gives visitors a taste of a subtropical ecosystem in the continental States—from mangrove swamps, to exotic bird and animal life, to curtains of sawgrass and walls of lush vegetation that impede travel. The best time to visit is during the dry season, December to April. Hot, humid summer days may encourage heat-related illnesses. You'll need to apply mosquito repellent year round. The park has many safe and scenic trails. However, do not swim, and keep an eye out for alligators, snakes, and other potentially dangerous animals. Gators are unlikely to threaten you unless you threaten them first.

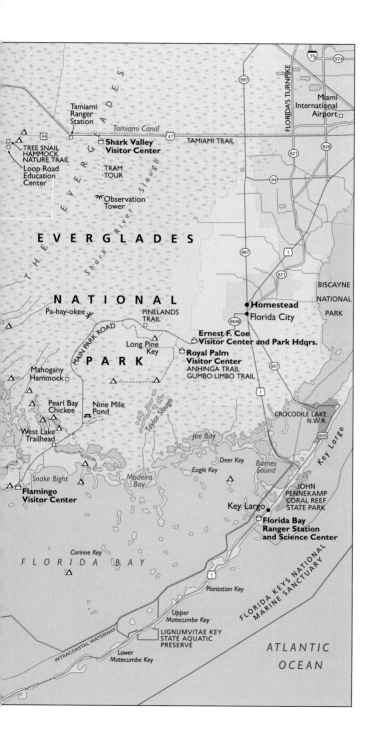

75
924
997
FLORIDA'S TURNPIKE
Miami International Airport
Tamiami Ranger Station
Tamiami Canal
94
TREE SNAIL HAMMOCK NATURE TRAIL
Loop Road Education Center
Shark Valley Visitor Center
TAMIAMI TRAIL
41
TRAM TOUR
821
826
94
Observation Tower

E V E R G L A D E S

The EVERGLADES

Shark River Slough

997

N A T I O N A L

Pa-hay-okee
PINELANDS TRAIL
Homestead
Florida City

BISCAYNE

NATIONAL

PARK

MAIN PARK ROAD
Long Pine Key
Ernest F. Coe Visitor Center and Park Hdqrs.
9936

P A R K
Royal Palm Visitor Center
ANHINGA TRAIL
GUMBO LIMBO TRAIL
997

Mahogany Hammock
1

Pearl Bay Chickee
Nine Mile Pond
Taylor Slough
CROCODILE LAKE N.W.R.
905
Key Largo

West Lake Trailhead
Joe Bay

Snake Bight
Madeira Bay
Deer Key
Eagle Key
Barnes Sound

Flamingo Visitor Center
JOHN PENNEKAMP CORAL REEF STATE PARK

Key Largo
Florida Bay Ranger Station and Science Center

Corinne Key

F L O R I D A   B A Y

1
FLORIDA KEYS NATIONAL MARINE SANCTUARY

Plantation Key

INTRACOASTAL WATERWAY
Upper Matecumbe Key
LIGNUMVITAE KEY STATE AQUATIC PRESERVE
Lower Matecumbe Key

ATLANTIC OCEAN

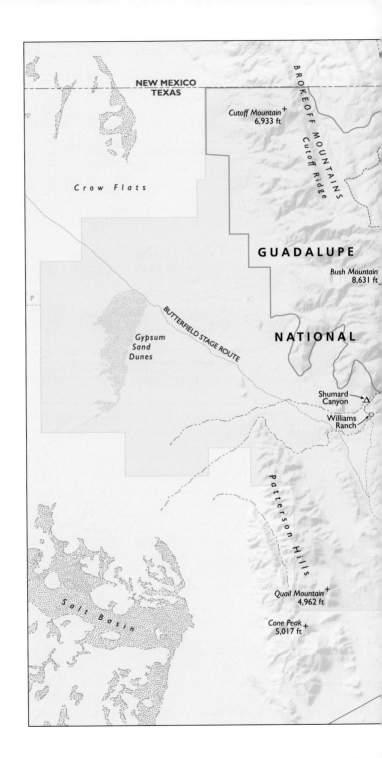

NEW MEXICO
TEXAS

Cutoff Mountain⁺
6,933 ft

B R O K E O F F   M O U N T A I N S
Cutoff Ridge

Crow Flats

GUADALUPE

Bush Mountain
8,631 ft

Gypsum
Sand
Dunes

BUTTERFIELD STAGE ROUTE

NATIONAL

Shumard
Canyon

Williams
Ranch

Patterson Hills

Quail Mountain⁺
4,962 ft

Cone Peak⁺
5,017 ft

Salt Basin

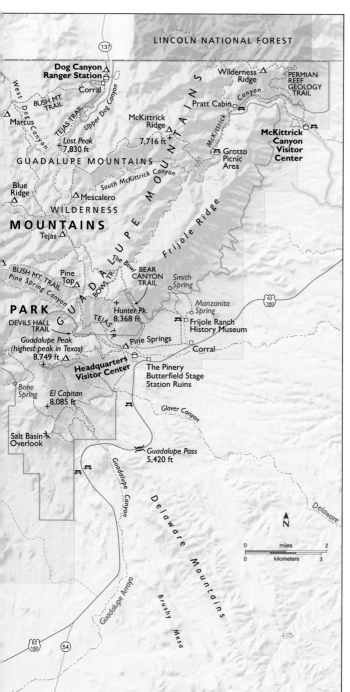

The park combines impressive mountains and desert. Although springs flow at the mountains' base, carry plenty of potable water. Take a map and a compass or GPS, as the park is managed as a wilderness and has few signs to mark trails. Wear sturdy boots, and seal them against sand if you plan to walk among the western dunes. Watch out for rattlesnakes, which are common. Mescalero Apaches, the park's former residents, took their name from their primary food source—mescal, the heart of the agave plant, which still grows in abundance. Avoid collecting plant food except in an emergency.

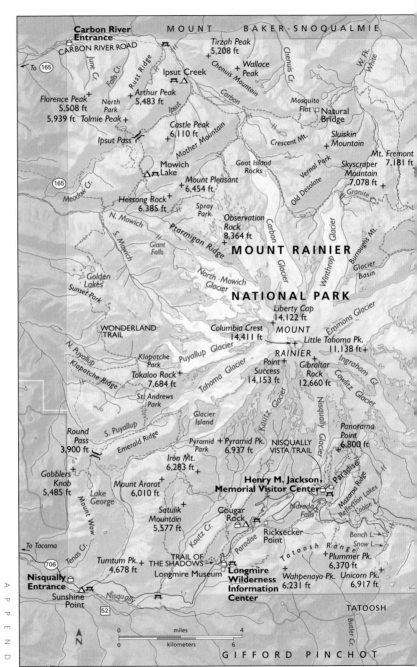

MOUNT BAKER-SNOQUALMIE

Carbon River Entrance
CARBON RIVER ROAD

To (165)

June Cr.
Falls Cr.
Rust Ridge

Ipsut Creek

Tirzah Peak
5,208 ft

Chenuis Cr.

Wallace Peak

Chenuis Mountain

Carbon

W. Fk. White

Florence Peak
5,508 ft
5,939 ft Tolmie Peak

North Park

Arthur Peak
5,483 ft

Ipsut

Castle Peak
6,110 ft

Mosquito Flat

Natural Bridge

Crescent Mt.

Sluiskin Mountain

Mt. Fremont
7,181 ft

Ipsut Pass

Mather Mountain

Mowich Lake

Mount Pleasant
6,454 ft

Goat Island Rocks

Vernal Park

Old Desolate

Skyscraper Mountain
7,078 ft

Granite

(165)

Meadow Cr.

Hessong Rock
6,385 ft

Spray Park

Observation Rock
8,364 ft

Carbon

Carbon Glacier

Winthrop Glacier

Glacier Mt.

Burroughs Mt.

Glacier Basin

N. Mowich

Ptarmigan Ridge

North Mowich Glacier

MOUNT RAINIER

S. Mowich

Giant Falls

Golden Lakes

Sunset Park

WONDERLAND TRAIL

NATIONAL PARK

Liberty Cap
14,122 ft

Columbia Crest
14,411 ft

MOUNT

Emmons Glacier

Little Tahoma Pk.
11,138 ft

N. Puyallup

Klapatche Park

Puyallup Glacier

Klapatche Ridge

Tokaloo Rock
7,684 ft

St. Andrews Park

RAINIER

Point Success
14,153 ft

Gibraltar Rock
12,660 ft

Ingraham Gl.

Cowlitz Glacier

Tahoma Glacier

Glacier Island

S. Puyallup

Emerald Ridge

Kautz Glacier

Nisqually Glacier

Round Pass
3,900 ft

Pyramid Park

Pyramid Pk.
6,937 ft

NISQUALLY VISTA TRAIL

Panorama Point
6,800 ft

Gobblers Knob
5,485 ft

Lake George

Iron Mt.
6,283 ft

Mount Ararat
6,010 ft

Henry M. Jackson Memorial Visitor Center

Narada Falls

Paradise

Mazama Ridge

Reflection Lakes

Louise L.

Mount Wow

Satulik Mountain
5,577 ft

Cougar Rock

Kautz Cr.

Ricksecker Point

Bench L.

Snow L.

To Tacoma

Tenas Cr.

(706)

Tumtum Pk.
4,678 ft

TRAIL OF THE SHADOWS

Longmire Museum

Paradise

Tatoosh Range

Plummer Pk.
6,370 ft

Nisqually Entrance

Sunshine Point

Nisqually

(52)

Longmire Wilderness Information Center

Wahpenayo Pk.
6,231 ft

Unicorn Pk.
6,917 ft

TATOOSH

Butler Cr.

N

0 miles 4

0 kilometers 6

GIFFORD PINCHOT

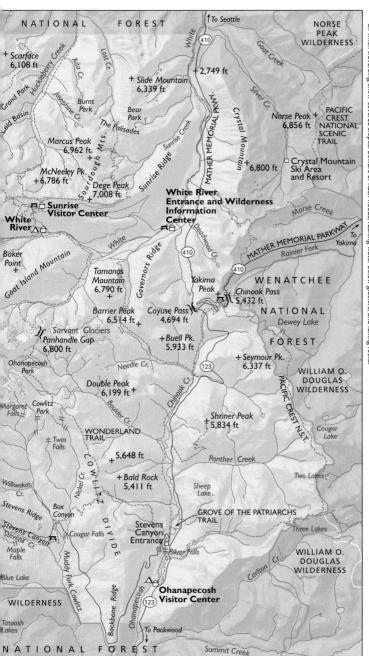

NATIONAL FOREST

↑ To Seattle

410

+ Scarface
6,108 ft

Huckleberry Creek

Ada Cr.

Lost Cr.

White

Goat Creek

NORSE
PEAK
WILDERNESS

Grand Park

Josephine Cr.

Old Basin

Burnt
Park

Bear
Park

The Palisades

+ Slide Mountain
6,339 ft

+ 2,749 ft

Silver Cr.

Marcus Peak
6,962 ft
+

Sunrise Creek

MATHER MEMORIAL PKWY.

Crystal Mountain

Norse Peak +
6,856 ft

PACIFIC
CREST
NATIONAL
SCENIC
TRAIL

McNeeley Pk.
+ 6,786 ft

Sourdough Mts.

Dege Peak
7,008 ft +

Sunrise Ridge

+ 6,800 ft

□ Crystal Mountain
Ski Area
and Resort

⌂ **Sunrise
Visitor Center**

**White River
Entrance and Wilderness
Information
Center**

Morse Creek

**White
River** △⌂

White

Governors Ridge

Deadwood Cr.

410

MATHER MEMORIAL PARKWAY →
Rainier Fork

To
Yakima

Baker
Point
+

Goat Island Mountain

Tamanos
Mountain
6,790 ft +

410

Yakima
Peak

Chinook Pass
5,432 ft

WENATCHEE

Barrier Peak
6,514 ft +

Cayuse Pass
4,694 ft

NATIONAL

Dewey Lake

Sarvant Glaciers
Panhandle Gap
6,800 ft

+ Buell Pk.
5,933 ft

FOREST

*Ohanapecosh
Park*

Needle Cr.

+ Seymour Pk.
6,337 ft

WILLIAM O.
DOUGLAS
WILDERNESS

Double Peak
6,199 ft +

Chinook Cr.

Boulder Cr.

*Margaret
Falls*

Cowlitz
Park

Shriner Peak
+ 5,834 ft

*Cougar
Lake*

‡ Twin
Falls

**WONDERLAND
TRAIL**

Panther Creek

PACIFIC CREST N.S.T.

*Williwakas
Cr.*

+ 5,648 ft

Two Lakes

Stevens Ridge

Nickel Cr.

Box
Canyon

+ Bald Rock
5,411 ft

Sheep
Lake

Stevens Canyon

**GROVE OF THE PATRIARCHS
TRAIL**

Three Lakes

*Stevens
Canyon*

Cougar Falls

**Stevens
Canyon
Entrance**

Silver Falls

Carlton Cr.

WILLIAM O.
DOUGLAS
WILDERNESS

*Maple
Falls*

Muddy Fork Cowlitz

C O W L I T Z   D I V I D E

Blue Lake

WILDERNESS

Backbone Ridge

△

**Ohanapecosh
Visitor Center**

123

*Tatoosh
Lakes*

Ohanapecosh

NATIONAL FOREST

↓ To Packwood

Summit Creek

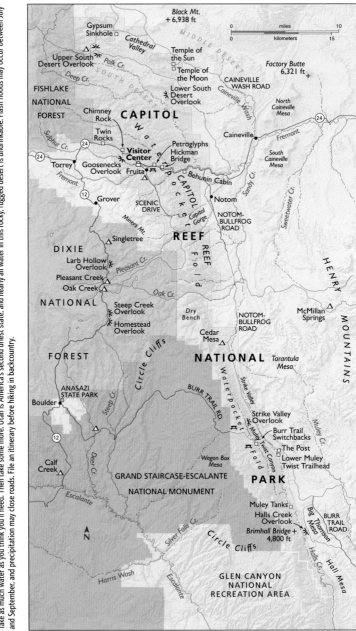

Take as much water as you think you'll need. Then take some more. Utah is America's second driest state, and nearly all water in this rocky, rugged desert is undrinkable. Flash floods may occur between July and September, and precipitation may close roads. File an itinerary before hiking in backcountry.

Stay on trails at Petrified Forest National Park to avoid damaging the delicate desert floor and getting cut by the sharp edges of petrified logs. No water is available outside developed areas, so carry what you need with you. Avoid contact with wildlife, which may carry hantavirus and the microbes that cause rabies and bubonic plague.

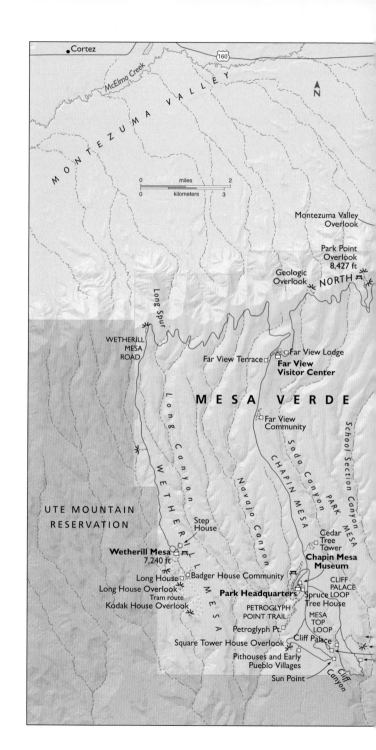

.Cortez

McElmo Creek

160

M O N T E Z U M A   V A L L E Y

N

miles   0 —— 2
kilometers 0 —— 3

Montezuma Valley
Overlook

Park Point
Overlook
8,427 ft

Geologic
Overlook

NORTH

WETHERILL
MESA
ROAD

Long Spur

Far View Terrace

Far View Lodge

Far View
Visitor Center

M E S A   V E R D E

Far View
Community

Long Canyon

Navajo Canyon

Soda Canyon

CHAPIN MESA

PARK MESA

School Section Canyon

W E T H E R I L L

UTE MOUNTAIN
RESERVATION

Step
House

Wetherill Mesa
7,240 ft

Long House

Long House Overlook
Tram route
Kodak House Overlook

Badger House Community

M E S A

Park Headquarters

PETROGLYPH
POINT TRAIL

Petroglyph Pt.

Square Tower House Overlook

Pithouses and Early
Pueblo Villages

Sun Point

Cedar
Tree
Tower

Chapin Mesa
Museum

CLIFF
PALACE

Spruce LOOP
Tree House

MESA
TOP
LOOP

Cliff Palace

Cliff Canyon

Visitors to the ancient, abandoned cliff dwellings at Mesa Verde National Park should make sure they're physically prepared for the strenuous climbing. The park's more challenging attractions are not for people with heart conditions, fear of heights, or close quarters. Parents should keep a close watch on children along trails and canyon rims.

The six million-acre park surrounding and including Mount McKinley, North America's highest mountain, is a backcountry hiker's paradise. Backpackers should protect their supplies against grizzly bears. Moose are common and should not be approached. Avalanches are a threat on McKinley in summer.

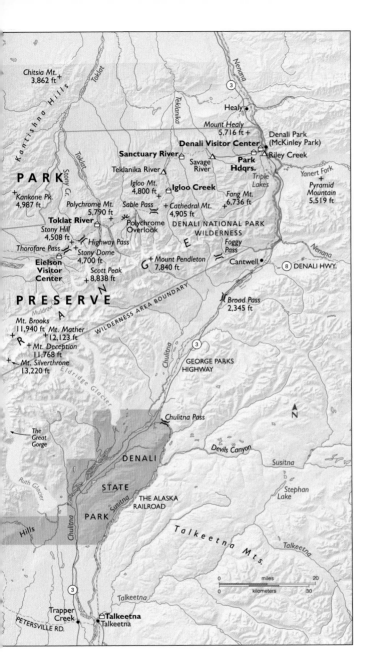

Chitsia Mt.
3,862 ft

Kantishna Hills

Toklat

Teklanika

Nenana

3

Healy

Mount Healy
5,716 ft

Denali Park
(McKinley Park)

Denali Visitor Center

Riley Creek

Sanctuary River

Savage
River

**Park
Hdqrs.**

Teklanika River

Triple
Lakes

P A R K

Stony Cr.

Toklat

Yanert Fork

Kankone Pk.
4,987 ft

Igloo Mt.
4,800 ft

Igloo Creek

Pyramid
Mountain
5,519 ft

Polychrome Mt.
5,790 ft

Sable Pass

Cathedral Mt.
4,905 ft

Fang Mt.
6,736 ft

Toklat River

Polychrome
Overlook

DENALI NATIONAL PARK
WILDERNESS

Stony Hill
4,508 ft

Highway Pass

Foggy
Pass

Nenana

Thorofare Pass

Stony Dome
4,700 ft

Mount Pendleton
7,840 ft

Cantwell

8 **DENALI HWY.**

**Eielson
Visitor
Center**

Scott Peak
8,838 ft

P R E S E R V E

Muldrow

WILDERNESS AREA BOUNDARY

Broad Pass
2,345 ft

Mt. Brooks
11,940 ft

Mt. Mather
12,123 ft

Mt. Deception
11,768 ft

Chulitna

3

Mt. Silverthrone
13,220 ft

Eldridge Glacier

GEORGE PARKS
HIGHWAY

Chulitna Pass

N

The
Great
Gorge

Devils Canyon

Susitna

DENALI

Ruth Glacier

STATE

Susitna

THE ALASKA
RAILROAD

Stephan
Lake

PARK

Chulitna

Hills

Talkeetna Mts.

Talkeetna

miles   20
kilometers   30

3

Talkeetna

Trapper
Creek

Talkeetna

PETERSVILLE RD.

Talkeetna

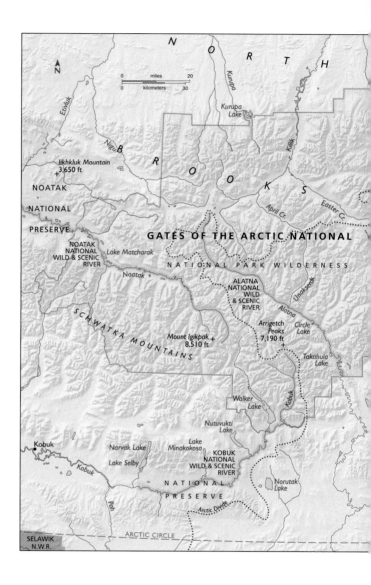

Rugged and remote, Gates of the Arctic lies entirely above the Arctic Circle and is best reached by plane. Weather is unpredictable, and snow may fall in any month. Prepare for clouds of mosquitoes and gnats in June and July; carry repellent, a head net, and insect-proof shelter. Beware of glaciers and grizzlies.

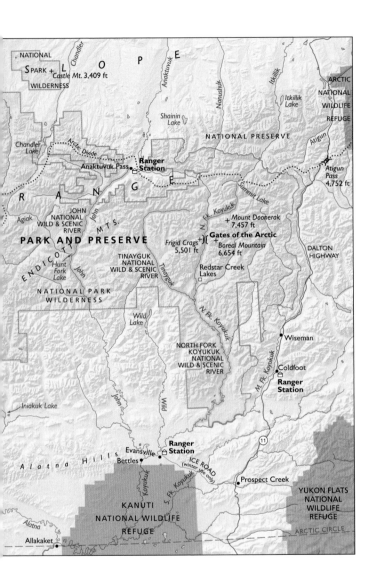

NATIONAL
SPARK + Castle Mt. 3,409 ft
WILDERNESS

Chandler

Anaktuvuk

Nanushuk

Itkillik

S L O P E

ARCTIC
NATIONAL
WILDLIFE
REFUGE

Itkillik
Lake

Shainin
Lake

NATIONAL PRESERVE

Chandler
Lake

Arctic Divide

Atigun

Ranger
Station
Anaktuvuk Pass

Atigun
Pass
4,752 ft

R A N G E

Summit Lake

Agiak

JOHN
NATIONAL
WILD & SCENIC
RIVER

N. Fk. Koyukuk

+ Mount Doonerak
7,457 ft

PARK AND PRESERVE

John

M T S.

Frigid Crags)(+ Gates of the Arctic
5,501 ft + Boreal Mountain
6,654 ft

DALTON
HIGHWAY

E N D I C O T T

Hunt
Fork
Lake

TINAYGUK
NATIONAL
WILD & SCENIC
RIVER

Tinayguk

Redstar Creek
Lakes

John

NATIONAL PARK
WILDERNESS

Wild
Lake

N. Fk. Koyukuk

NORTH FORK
KOYUKUK
NATIONAL
WILD & SCENIC
RIVER

Wiseman

M. Fk. Koyukuk

Coldfoot

Ranger
Station

Iniakuk Lake

John

Pilw

A l a t n a   H i l l s

Ranger
Station

Evansville
Bettles

Koyukuk

S. Fk. Koyukuk

ICE ROAD
(winter use only)

11

Prospect Creek

YUKON FLATS
NATIONAL
WILDLIFE
REFUGE

Alatna

KANUTI
NATIONAL WILDLIFE
REFUGE

Allakaket

ARCTIC CIRCLE

Glacier Bay, shaped and reshaped by rivers of ice, is well named. Hikers are physically tested by rugged terrain. Stay off glaciers unless you're experienced or have a guide, and don't get too close to icebergs or calving glaciers in a kayak or boat. Carry insect repellent and avoid the bears.

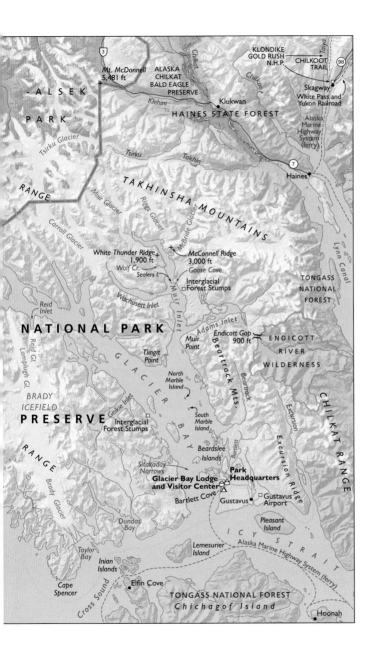

Mt. McDonnell
5,481 ft

3

ALASKA
CHILKAT
BALD EAGLE
PRESERVE

KLONDIKE
GOLD RUSH
N.H.P.

CHILKOOT
TRAIL

98

Klukwan

Chilkat

Chilkoot

Skagway
White Pass and
Yukon Railroad

ALSEK

PARK

Klehini

Tsirku Glacier

Tsirku

HAINES STATE FOREST

Takhin

Alaska
Marine
Highway
System
(ferry)

RANGE

TAKHINSHA MOUNTAINS

7

Haines

Muir Glacier

Riggs Glacier

McBride Glacier

Carroll Glacier

Lynn Canal

White Thunder Ridge
1,900 ft

Wolf Cr.

Sealers I.

McConnell Ridge
3,000 ft

Goose Cove

Interglacial
Forest Stumps

TONGASS
NATIONAL
FOREST

Reid
Inlet

Wachusett Inlet

Adams Inlet

NATIONAL PARK

Muir Inlet

Muir
Point

Endicott Gap
900 ft

ENDICOTT

Reid Gl.
Lamplugh Gl.

GLACIER

Tlingit
Point

Beartrack Mts.

RIVER

WILDERNESS

BRADY
ICEFIELD

North
Marble
Island

BAY

Beartrack

CHILKAT RANGE

PRESERVE

Geikie Inlet

Interglacial
Forest Stumps

South
Marble
Island

Excursion Ridge

Excursion

RANGE

Brady Glacier

Sitakaday
Narrows

Beardslee
Islands

Glacier Bay Lodge
and Visitor Center

Park
Headquarters

Bartlett Cove

Gustavus

Gustavus
Airport

Dundas
Bay

Pleasant
Island

ICY

STRAIT

Taylor
Bay

Lemesurier
Island

Alaska Marine Highway System (ferry)

Inian
Islands

Cape
Spencer

Elfin Cove

Cross Sound

TONGASS NATIONAL FOREST
Chichagof Island

Hoonah

Gulf of Alaska

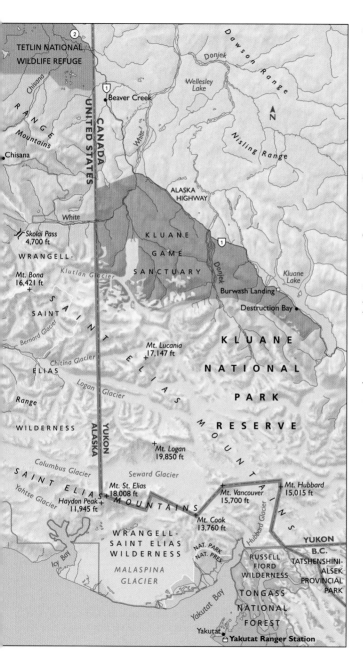

Wrangell-St. Elias is not only huge—six times the size of Yellowstone—it's also run as wilderness. Backpackers and rafters must be skilled and self-sufficient or hire expert guides. Leave itinerary details behind. Seek safe sites for river crossings. The best visiting time is summer, but prepare for clouds of mosquitoes.

TETLIN NATIONAL
WILDLIFE REFUGE

Chisana

Dawson Range

Donjek

Wellesley
Lake

Nisling Range

N

Beaver Creek

UNITED STATES

CANADA

White

ALASKA
HIGHWAY

White

Skolai Pass
4,700 ft

WRANGELL-

KLUANE

GAME

SANCTUARY

Klutlan Glacier

Mt. Bona
16,421 ft

Donjek

Kluane
Lake

Burwash Landing

SAINT

Bernard Glacier

Destruction Bay

KLUANE

Chitina Glacier

Mt. Lucania
17,147 ft

ELIAS

Logan Glacier

NATIONAL

Range

WILDERNESS

YUKON
ALASKA

PARK

RESERVE

Columbus Glacier

Seward Glacier

Mt. Logan
19,850 ft

MOUNTAINS

SAINT ELIAS

Yahtse Glacier

Mt. St. Elias
18,008 ft

Haydon Peak
11,945 ft

MOUNTAINS

Mt. Vancouver
15,700 ft

Mt. Hubbard
15,015 ft

Icy Bay

WRANGELL-
SAINT ELIAS
WILDERNESS

MALASPINA
GLACIER

Mt. Cook
13,760 ft

NAT. PARK
NAT. PRES.

Hubbard Glacier

YUKON
B.C.

RUSSELL
FIORD
WILDERNESS

TATSHENSHINI-
ALSEK
PROVINCIAL
PARK

Yakutat Bay

TONGASS

NATIONAL

FOREST

Yakutat

Yakutat Ranger Station

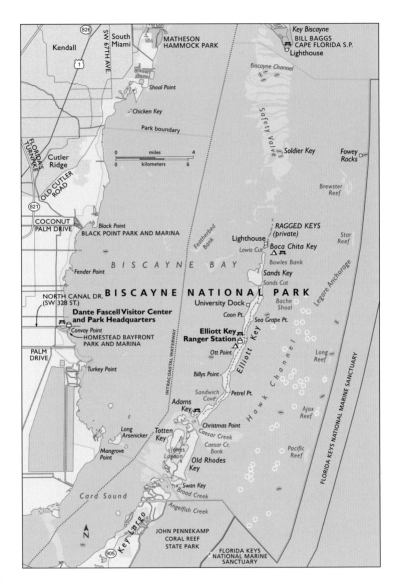

Ninety-five percent of the park is water, best seen from a glass-bottomed boat in the bay or a canoe along the mangrove shoreline. The best visiting time is December through April. Summer has calmest waters, along with mosquitoes and storms. Don't touch coral; it is easily damaged and can inflict painful cuts.

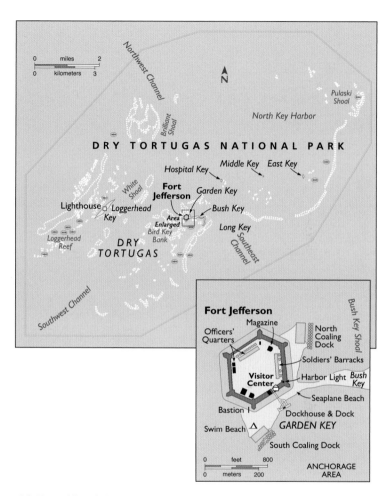

Only 85 acres of this park of 100 square miles is above water. Small islands and coral reefs stretch seven miles into the Gulf of Mexico west of the Florida Keys. The most prominent landmark is Fort Jefferson, a 50-foot-high stone hexagon intended to protect gulf shipping. It dominates the 16-acre Garden Key. The park is accessible only by boat and floatplane. Private boats must anchor offshore; there are no public slips or moorings. Visitors to this subtropical park must bring all of their own supplies, including fuel, food, and water. The park has no fresh water for campers, and no water to operate showers for those who swim in the warm surf to rinse off. The shallow waters teem with fish and several varieties of turtles, which pirates once hunted for their meat and eggs. Offshore waters also are home to the occasional yellow stingray and barracuda. Although not aggressive, barracuda are territorial and should not be approached by swimmers or snorkelers. Consider taking a 200-meter swim from Garden Key to the "desert island" of Bush Key, if it's open, but beware of sharp coral. April and May offer the best weather for visitors. Hurricane season usually lasts from June to November, and winter seas are rough.

ATLANTIC OCEAN

miles 2
kilometers 3

N

Whistling Cay

Congo Cay

Lovango Cay

Cinnamon Bay

NORTH SHORE RD.

Peter Bay

Grass Cay

Windward Passage

Hawksnest Point

Trunk Bay

20

Mingo Cay

Durloe Cays

Hawksnest Bay

Thatch Cay

Middle Passage

Hawksnest Bay

Hawksnest Bay

Trunk Bay

Catherineberg

Sugar Mill (ruins)

Caneel Bay

Caneel Bay

10

Biosphere Reserve Center

Caneel Bay

20

SAINT THOMAS

32

Caneel Hill 719 ft

CENTERLINE ROAD

38

Visitor Center

GIFT HILL RD.

Red Hook

VEHICLE FERRY

Cruz Bay

10

Steven Cay

Cruz Bay

104

Redhook Bay

PILLSBURY SOUND

32

Gift Hill 827 ft

St. James Bay

Great St. James Island

Rendezvous Bay

To Charlotte Amalie

Great Cruz Bay

Bovocoap Point

Dittlif Point

Little St. James Island

Dog Island

CARIBBEAN SEA

The more-than-7,000-acre park lies mainly on St. John Island but includes portions of neighboring St. Thomas. Its terrain ranges from mangrove swamps to high-elevation forests, to desert-like lands, acacia scrub and white sand beaches. The climate is pleasant in every season, with high temperatures typically in the 80s the 90s. Pack sunscreen and sunglasses to protect against burns and bright sunlight reflecting off the water. The park is open year-round, but peak times for visitors extend from December to April. Hurricanes have occasionally pummeled the Virgin Islands in summer and early autumn, with the most recent blowing through in 1996. There's no overnight backpacking. The Cinnamon Bay park campground is open year-round. It limits stays to 14 days from December to mid-May, and 21 days at other times. The park is one of the most breathtaking in the National Park system. Its vistas are spectacular in its lush heights and amid the vegetation that ring the island's bays, especially when framed by palm trees, bougainvillea, and oleander. When the weather is clear, the water near the shore appears turquoise and dark blue, spectacularly set off by white sands. More than 20 miles of trails wind through the dense vegetation and past the ruins of the slave-run sugar industry of St. John. If you climb for a better view, be careful of the moderately strenuous trails and the slopes.

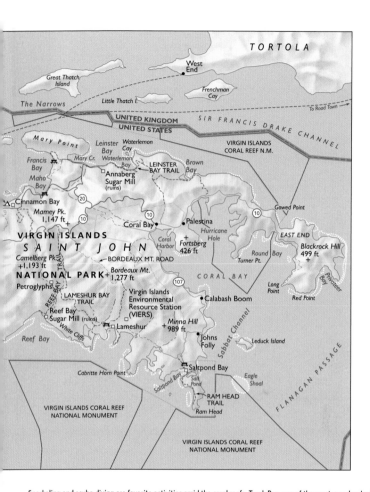

Snorkeling and scuba diving are favorite activities amid the coral reefs. Trunk Bay, one of the most popular destinations, has a snorkeling trail in the shallow water. Buoys mark the triangular trail; snorkelers can see the floor of the bay 10 to 20 feet below them in the clear water. Do not go barefoot in creeks and surf, and do not touch the delicate, complex, and beautiful coral that forms the reefs ringing the island. You may pick up rocks among the coral reefs, but return them where you found them. "Leave no trace" is an important tenet of the park's ecosystem. On shore, avoid the island's toxic manchineel trees, which are common to the Caribbean and Central America. They have a superficial resemblance to apple trees, grow up to 50 feet high, and have shiny leaves, gray bark, and spikes of small flowers that produce a greenish, apple-like fruit. They are extremely poisonous, as evidenced by the moniker that Christopher Columbus gave them, "death apples." Manchineels commonly grow near the shore, acting as windbreaks that help keep beaches stable. Trees in the park typically are identified by warning signs. Rain running off manchineel may produce a milky substance that raises blisters on skin. Smoke from burning manchineel wood may cause blindness, and eating the fruit may cause death.

NOTES